ECONOMIC SYSTEMS IN HISTORICAL PERSPECTIVE

George J. Viksnins

KENDALL/HUNT PUBLISHING COMPANY
4050 Westmark Drive   Dubuque, Iowa 52002

TO

MARA

CONTENTS

PREFACE

Will capitalism survive? Is socialism really dead? I have made an effort to be truthful, but not neutral in my view of economic systems. As a result, what emerges is a text that contains somewhat one-sided arguments — a book that can be described as both polemical and idiosyncratic. In an age when textbooks are often packaged like Pablum, designed to offend no one, this volume may not prove very popular.

Yet, I don't think that I shall be the only teacher using it as a text to teach comparative economic systems. My main reason for writing it is the fact that I find the three or four leading texts in this field rather unsatisfactory. Without naming names, one is too much like an encyclopedia, including references to at least a hundred economists, and a score of theoretical/political schools. A more recent book provides detailed discussions of quite a large number of countries, which may be very difficult for the average student to think about and sort through. Another is too simple by far, while the two or three others are competent, but somewhat boring. In my opinion, there is a very strong tendency in this field to overemphasize Marxist theory and Eastern European/Soviet details, without saying much about the rest of the world, which leaves out many very interesting issues for comparative analysis. I have set out to do a book that also deals with North-South issues explicitly in addition to the more traditional East-West comparison. Of course, many teachers will probably want to supplement this text with some additional readings in those more customary areas, such as spending more time on Marx, but they would now have the opportunity to emphasize other issues of considerable interest, particularly developments in dynamic Pacific Asia. I have written this book after nearly thirty years of full-time teaching at Georgetown, with my professional specialization being primarily Asian economic development. However, I have also taught a comparative economic systems during the summer for about 20 times, under the auspices of Georgetown's Institute for Comparative Political and Economic Systems (ICPES), which is now in its 28th year, as well as during the regular school year recently. The ICPES program brings approximately one hundred student leaders from all over the United States and now the rest of the world as well for a very intensive six weeks of academic courses, internships, site briefings, and lectures. The backgrounds of these students are really varied — ranging from economics majors in schools ranked above Georgetown to over-achievers from places that I haven't even heard mentioned before the student had applied to the program. It is for this reason that I have included a brief review of standard Keynesian macroeconomics, as well as a bird's eye view of the history of economic thought in the beginning chapters. (Therefore, quite a few teachers teaching a thoroughly prepared and more uniform group of students can de-emphasize the first few chapters — make them optional assigned reading — perhaps, simply begin with Chapter 5).

This text will differ from the standard comparative economic systems book in a number of ways. First, I consider myself an "unrepentant capitalist-roader" — a "right-wing economist," having great admiration for Hayek, Schumpeter, Friedman, and the so-called "voodoo economics" school. There aren't very many of us, I fear, and adoptions may suffer as a result. Still, it is quite possible that some fair-minded teachers, who disagree with my views almost completely, will still use this book to expose their students to a different viewpoint, perhaps in order to get a few of them mad, excited, interested, and disturbed. I myself have often deliberately used rather left-wing texts and readings over the years, in order to motivate some serious discussion, with heat often generating some light as well. Nevertheless, I strongly believe that economic freedoms and political democracy usually tend to go together — a centrally planned economy, with government ownership of the means of production, has always in practice also meant a single-party government. On the whole, the economic performance of market-oriented economies has been quite superior to that of centrally-planned countries. Indeed, having been born in Latvia, now once again an independent country and having spent my childhood in Europe right before, during, and after the Second World War, I bring a very personal strong bias in favor of individual freedom and the market economy to my discussion of these matters. We left Latvia in a great hurry in 1944, since my family was on the list of those to be "repressed" in the Stalin era. I have also lived in Thailand for a couple of years, and watched closely what went on in Cambodia and Vietnam after their "liberation." At times, perhaps I go a little overboard — the purple prose should perhaps be toned down — and I did do a bit of that before publication.

As already noted, a second conscious differentiation of the product involves considerably greater emphasis on North-South issues — two chapters on competing explanations of underdevelopment, a contrast of China and Japan, and a chapter on "the capitalist-roaders of Asia." Again, many teachers will probably wish to spend somewhat more time on the recent history of the Soviet Union, and will elect to assign chapters in other texts, articles that they themselves have written, or other selections.

Despite the fact that I have confessed to a pro-market bias in this introduction, I find that many of my conservative students tend to be seriously lacking in compassion — while most liberals seem to lack common sense — and I hope that yet a third aspect of product differentiation becomes evident to my readers. Some of my right-wing posturing may actually be deliberate. Perhaps, I could be described as "a closet moderate." I would happily endure some increase in my income taxes, if I could be sure that poor children got to drink some milk or eat some vegetables as a result. As the world socialist system disintegrates, and China as well as Vietnam experiment with the market, there is a temptation simply to declare a victory for the market — and to cancel the course. However, Marxism has played a tremendously important historical role, and socialist solutions are by no means dead. It may also be argued that real-world political decisions have been greatly affected by the very existence of the other alternative — the U.S. and the Japanese may be more conscious of egalitarian concerns because of the challenge posed by socialist arrangements, for example. At the same time, socialist challenges to the legitimacy of capitalist-oriented governments are certainly softened by the mistakes (horrors, may I say that?) witnessed in the U.S.S.R. during the Stalinist era, in the P.R.C. during the Great Leap Forward and the Cultural Revolution, and at Tiananmen Square, as well as in Cambodia under Pol Pot. To be fair about it, the examples of Chile and South Africa also suggest that market-oriented regimes do not invariably promote democracy and human rights.

There are many people to thank for their assistance in this effort. The writing got started during a very pleasant year at the University of California at Irvine — thanks to Max Fry, Charlie Lave, and Jack Johnston, among others. A number of colleagues have read bits and pieces of the draft, including Adhip Chaudhuri, "Sam" Crane, Stuart Brown, and a handful of others, whom I don't want to embarrass unnecessarily. Word processing was handled most cheerfully and efficiently by Pia Maschio, John Schorn, Sabrina Spahr, and Jeanne Murphy, as well as a number of student assistants (Shirley Kan, Michiko Wada, Natasha Braginsky, and Trinh Doan) in the Georgetown economics department office. Any theoretical errors are entirely my fault, but typos can certainly be blamed on them as well. Last, but not least, let me thank several classes of students at Georgetown, both during the summer and also the regular year, who used this volume in draft form, and helped to improve the final product — in particular, let me acknowledge the contributions of Alex Nyikos and Rafic Naja.

All in all, I have tried to write an unconventional text — a book that will make you, the professor, refute some of my arguments and contentions, and also force our students to think, to argue among themselves, and to learn. If there are things in here that you find outrageous, please let me know — I'll change them or respond to your criticism, if I feel that I cannot. I am certainly willing to be convinced that I've made a mistake or overstated the case, but I hope that I've given you an alternative to the "Lite Comparative Economics" of some other texts. ■

George J. Viksnins

CHAPTER ONE

INTRODUCTION

*E*conomics is most simply defined as the study of choice. A somewhat more formal definition of economics is "the science that studies the allocation of *scarce resources* to satisfy the *unlimited wants* of mankind." The focus in the second definition is upon the fact of relative scarcity. Some fifty years ago, shortly after the second World War, it was fashionable to talk about futuristic utopias, when goods and services would be so cheap and readily available, that economizing behavior would no longer be necessary. By the end of the 20th century, the average family would have its own space ship, electric power would be "too cheap to meter," and the economics profession would disappear (or become a humble, useful trade, sort of like dentists, said Keynes). Most of the citizens of Western Europe and North America, with a focus on the United States particularly, a bit later, were said to be members of an "affluent society," with their needs and wants pretty much satisfied. In a popular book by that name, as John Kenneth Galbraith argued in 1959, most Americans were becoming so satiated, that thousands of Madison Avenue hucksters had to be hired by the business sector to engage in "want creation." The popular image of the United States in the early 1960s was one of ever growing opulence and optimism about the future despite a widening conflict among generations, brought on in part by the war in Vietnam. In the mid-1990s, the need to economize now is much more evident to the average American or European. The requirement of economic efficiency is today much more obvious to all other people as well — as it has been in poorer countries right along. Clearly, no society on this planet has ever been able to afford to satisfy completely the various wants of all of its members, and the central purpose of economics is to analyze the allocation of resources in order to improve such satisfaction of unlimited wants. A favorite phrase of conservative economists is the saying: "there ain't no free lunch." Ungrammatical though it may be, it illustrates the point that every economic decision has an *opportunity cost* — what you could have earned in the next best use of your time or other resource. To think as economists do, you must be aware of the study of choice, the rational consideration of alternatives.

As you probably learned in your introductory economics course, we seek to analyze and understand three basic questions: "What?" "How?" and "For Whom?" The first question asks a society: What is to be produced?" Should production facilities and human labor be used to make guns or butter, private cars or airplanes, surgical operations or football games? How many Bibles and how many pornographic movies should be produced in 1997? The "How" question raises the "choice of technique" issue — an economy can produce a hotel, for example, by using a wide variety of labor and capital combinations, locate it on a tiny square block of land in Manhattan or several acres of ground in Las Vegas. Animals can be allowed to graze over huge areas of land in California or Wyoming without much labor input, or fed a diet of beer, bread, or grain — literally be given a daily massage by their owners to improve the texture of the beef — as it is done in Kobe, Japan. In most societies, the third question "For Whom?" is this productive activity taking place?, is already largely answered by their chosen solutions to the first two questions. To put it somewhat more formally, production decisions (What? and How?) strongly influence the distribution of purchasing power (For Whom?). If a society has determined that it will produce tennis lessons, aided by a ball machine and a VCR, this strongly implies employment and income for tennis instructors, payments to the owners of patents for the two machines, and others contributing resources to the increased output of tennis lessons. If that society decides to shift resources to piano lessons instead, those individuals associated with playing and making pianos are likely to gain a greater share of claims to total output. Even Lenin, in the early days of the Soviet conversion to communism in Russia, is said to have said: "He who does not work shall not eat." This basic idea — that contributions to production determine the distribution of income — appears to hold true in most societies, though this linkage is the strongest in market oriented economies.

Four Central Issues: Resource Allocation

Economics (and economists) is/are generally conveniently divided into two categories: "Micro" and "macro." The micro economist usually wrestles with two central issues — resource allocation and income distribution. For the sake of convenience, this is often presented as the "efficiency vs. equity" trade off. The first goal (of at least four) of any economic system is that of an "efficient allocation of resources." Theoretically, reference is usually made to reaching a "Pareto optimal solution" — formally defined as a situation existing when any rearrangement of resource inputs would produce a reduction of the value of total output. Or, a bit more simply, no one can be made "better off," without making someone else "worse off," or poorer. Operationally, therefore, the "best" resource allocation would probably mean maximizing the level of Gross National Product, or GNP.

As we develop this introductory chapter a bit further, let us go off on a bit of a tangent and talk about the "uses and abuses of GNP." Clearly, increases in GNP do not necessarily correspond perfectly to greater happiness or improvements in the average standard of living for a particular country, because of both measurement problems and distribution questions. Increases in total output do not necessarily mean a higher level of consumption for everyone. Greater spending for military hardware, more IRS forms and regulatory reports, and higher fees charged by lawyers will all serve to raise GNP, while probably reducing total utility in the society. Nevertheless, GNP per capita figures appear to be highly correlated to other socioeconomic indicators, such as life expectancy, literacy, caloric intake, and so on.

As you will no doubt recall, Gross National Product is the "sum total of final goods and services produced by a nation, valued in current market prices, during some period of time, usually one year." GNP consists of expenditures on consumption of goods and services (C), business investment for plant and equipment, including new housing and additions to inventories (all called I), government purchases of goods and services (G), plus net exports of goods and services (X - M). Thus, GNP (as well as GDP):

$$Y = C + I + G + X - M = C + S + T$$

The left-hand side of the equation, C + I + G + X - M, represents the "creation of income," while C + S + T is called the "disposition of income." Note the GNP and national income generally tend to be used quite interchangeably — the difference between them consists of depreciation and sales taxes, a relatively constant amount (or a predictably increasing amount, to be a bit more precise). GNP minus factor income earned abroad is called Gross Domestic Product — for most countries, the difference between GNP and GDP is not very large (though purists might disagree with this). Another way of measuring aggregate activity is to derive GNP by using the "value added" approach on a sector by sector basis.

It may be easiest to understand exactly what GNP measures by considering what is excluded from it. First, by using the "value added" methodology, intermediate goods and services are excluded from the total. For example, a law firm retained exclusively by General Motors would not get counted, since the cost of its services would be included in the final good, new cars, which would be a part of C, if sold to a consumer, or a part of I, if sold to a taxicab company or added to a dealer's inventory, or G, if sold to a governmental entity, or X, if shipped to Canada. In all four instances, the $14,995 "sticker price" for a new Olds would have subtracted from it all of GM's purchases from domestic business firms, in this case, the fees of the law firm. Another example might be a loaf of bread, costing $1.29 — if Safeway or Giant bought it from the bakery for $1.10, then 19 cents goes to "value added" for "wholesale and retail trade." If the wheat in it cost 50 cents, chalk up that as "value added" for agriculture, another 43 cents as "value added" for manufacturing (the flour mill and the bakery), with the remainder going probably to transportation, perhaps a little bit to banking and finance, energy, and a few other sectors. Thus, each final sales price is divided among the various sectors contributing to the total value or price of that product, and intermediate goods and services are excluded from GNP.

A second exclusion covers illegal activities, such as the drug trade, prostitution, smuggling, and the like. In a number of less developed countries (LDCs), GNP per capita would be much higher, if the dealings of the "underground economy" could be measured and counted. Certainly this is also true of the U.S. and the ex-socialist world, but more about that later. Of course, such activity does influence GNP in the second and the third (and further) rounds of consumption and perhaps investment or government purchases. If a heroin dealer sells $100,000 worth of that deadly substance, that initial sale does not get counted in GNP or national income, but the dealer's purchase of a Cadillac (but not a Mercedes) counts the same as any other Caddy, as does his new condo in Miami or Honolulu. A third exclusion is very similar — gifts and transfers are not counted in GNP. If a rich uncle leaves you a million or you hit the California lottery for ten million dollars, neither amount effects the 1997 GNP of the U.S., but your increased purchases of both consumption and investment goods (for example, a newly built house) certainly do. Increased government transfers, such as welfare or social security payments, also do not increase GNP directly.

A fourth exclusion covers trading in existing wealth, including land and most financial transactions. If you buy a house in Georgetown for $200,00 and resell it for $2 million ten years later, GNP does not change as a result of a capital gain — except for the real estate agent's commission, which does get counted in both cases (when you buy and when you sell). If you buy common stock in XYZ Netsurfer at $2 and sell it at $40, once again, your capital gain is not counted in GNP — except for the broker's commission and your higher level of C, when you organize a champagne brunch the following Sunday for all economics majors. Selling a piece of land or a rare painting for many times its purchase price will, again, add to the "value added" of the broker or the art gallery and probably be reflected in a higher C for both you (and your agent), but would not be counted in GNP directly.

Finally, a fifth exclusion pertains to non-market activity of most kinds. Most "do-it-yourself" work does not get included, nor does income earned through barter. If you are well versed in plumbing, and fix your neighbor's toilet in exchange for his changing the oil in your car or mowing your lawn, those transactions do not enter the nation's GNP. If you hire a housekeeper for $1000 a month, GNP goes up by that amount but, if you marry him and he stays home to take care of the kids and the house, GNP will fall by the amount of his former salary. Finally, if you grow tomatoes, cucumbers, and lettuce in your back yard, GNP will only be affected when you pay cash for seeds or plants, fertilizers, and pesticides, but your loving labor in thinning, weeding, and talking to the plants will count for nought as far as GNP accounts are concerned.

There are some exceptions to this rule of not counting non-market activities — government statisticians calculating their country's GNP figures are supposed to include "food and fuel produced and consumed on the farm." An urban dweller collecting firewood in the park and growing tomatoes in a whiskey barrel doesn't count in GNP, but a genuine farmer doing both of the above is, at least theoretically, counted. "Food and fuel produced and consumed on the farm" is known as an *imputed* value in the United Nations standard national income framework, as is the "rental value of owner-occupied housing." A major problem arises, however, in assigning prices to such subsistence-level economic activity, particularly for the purpose of making international comparisons. In most less developed countries, or LDCs, the "farm-gate" prices for agricultural products are very low, and rentals for huts in the middle of the jungle will be hard to estimate. A simple anecdotal example of this issue may prove to be edifying. If I want a chicken-and-rice dinner some summer evening, I climb into my gas-guzzling Ford Taurus SHO and cruise over to the "Social Safeway" on Wisconsin Avenue near Georgetown. I wheel an industrial size shopping cart down the aisle, Muzak playing in the background, air conditioning humming away — GNP is going up! — until I find the right section of the central aisle, featuring a pre-cooked, pre-chewed TV dinner of my favorite brand. Returning to the check-out counter, I hear the scanner beep the prices of my purchases, amounting to $3.89, say, from somewhere under the register — $2.69 for the pre-chewed dinner, fifty cents for the cucumber and seventy for the tomato. (GNP is going up rapidly, as the electronic scanner totes up the total and figures out my change!) I get back home and my dear wife energizes an entire wall representing our oven, microwave, toaster, blender, TV receiver and VCR all in one combination. (GNP is going up!) I open a bottle of 1991 California Riesling (quite expensive these days), and GNP has probably risen by $10-20 when we are finally done with dinner.

Compare and contrast all this income-generating activity with a Meo hill tribe family somewhere in the mountains above Chiang Rai in northern Thailand. The husband went out into the back yard, and killed a chicken (local market price probably less than 40 cents) and scooped up a few handfuls of rice (again, local market price of a few pennies). The wife threw a few pieces of wood on the smoldering embers and rinsed out the pot. At most, their dinner added a dollar or so to Thailand's GNP, suggesting that my utility for a similar dinner was many times higher than that of my fellow diner in Chaing Rai.

Other examples of vast price differences for the same goods and services can also be mentioned. An elementary school teacher in the Philippines earns about $100 per month, while in the U.S., it is at least ten times that amount. A gallon of gasoline currently costs about 35 cents in Saudi Arabia and more than $4 in Japan. A taxi ride of one mile in Mexico is a tiny fraction of its Washington cost, as will be most other services, since most wage rates are much lower in "Third World" countries. The problem of systematically greatly under-valuing services and partially-traded goods in the context of LDCs has led to a good deal of serious research on this topic. The most comprehensive adjustments have been made by the so called "International Comparisons of Purchasing Power" project, jointly organized by the United Nations and the World Bank. That methodology uses the "binary comparisons" approach — if we want to compare the GNP per capita of two countries, say Zambia and Thailand, the standard methodology would be to take the GNP per capita figures in the national currencies, and divide by the current U.S. dollar exchange rate (actually, a three-year average rate) for the *kwacha* (Zambian money) and the *baht* (Thai money), respectively. The use of US dollars for the official calculation tends to understate the per head GNP's of countries such as Zambia and Thailand considerably, because few international investors want to hold kwachas or bahts for portfolio purposes, while there is a brisk demand for U.S. dollars.

The "binary comparisons" methodology would not in theory use the U.S. dollar exchange rate at all — but try to compare the goods and services produced in the two countries directly. Zambian output in kwachas is already known — the analyst would then go to Thailand and recalculate its GNP by using kwacha prices prevailing in Zambia for rice, chickens, cab rides, school teacher's salaries, and so on. That would give us one ratio — let us say that Thailand's GNP per capita is 4.0 times as high as Zambia's by using kwacha prices for all output. Then the procedure would be repeated by pricing all

Zambian GNP components in baht prices prevailing in Thailand. That would give us a second ratio of GNPs per capita, say, Thailand might be ahead by 3.6 — and we could then average the ratios and say pretty convincingly, with some margin of error, that the standard of living in Thailand is about 3.8 times higher than in Zambia. Repricing both Thailand's and Zambia's GNP is, of course, also possible using U.S. dollar prices. At times, the statistical difficulties require a lot of ingenuity — there are for example, many varieties of fish and tropical fruits (the wonderfully tasting but horribly smelling *durian*, for example) available in Thailand, but not known in the U.S. Nevertheless, we can infer some comparable prices for similar very expensive food products ("top-of-the-line" pears or melons, say) and come up with reasonable guesses. On average, it had been established in the past that this repricing procedure increases LDC national income per head by a factor of about 2.0 to 2.5 (today 3.5 to 4.5) if we make this adjustment. (This is often called the "Rule of Four-Ninths" — take the official figure from the World Bank, and divide by 4/9.) Today, it is closer to a "Rule of One-fourth." Thus, China's GNP per capita is probably closer to $2,300 and India's may be near $1200, if we make this adjustment to the official World Bank data given in Table 1-1. Table 1-1 shows the ten largest countries in the world (from the standpoint of population) and shows that in today's world there are enormous differences in living standards, ranging from an income per head of about $25,000 in the U.S. to $220 in Bangladesh and $310 in India in 1993.

A special problem has always been presented by the centrally planned economies (CPEs), such as the now defunct USSR and mainland China. Their statistical reporting of economic aggregates did not adhere to the U.N. System of national-income-and-product accounts. Instead of GNP, the communist governments computed a Net Material Product aggregate, which excluded services, and involved also some double counting of industrial and agricultural production. The use of exchange rates to convert ruble figures into U.S. dollars, for example, also presented enormous difficulties, since the ruble was not a convertible currency. What was/is a ruble worth? It is (June '96) now more than 5000 to $1, and has been falling rapidly. However, if you were a tourist in Moscow ten years ago, officially it would have been about $1.50 — still, if you were a rather bold tourist and were willing to do a bit of black market trading, a ruble could cost you as little as 10 cents or even less in 1986. If you were a West European businessman interested in marketing Soviet products of particular interest to the planning authorities (and/or provide a little kickback), the effective price of a ruble often was much lower still. In the past two years, partly due to the break-up of the Comecon system and economic mismanagement, there has been tremendous inflation in Russia, and the GNP figures have been very difficult to calculate.

As the foregoing has tried to illustrate, economists and statisticians have been wrestling, at the World Bank and elsewhere, with these problems of measurement — primarily, the under-pricing of output in subsistence-type economies and the lack of a meaningful foreign exchange rate in most CPEs. Recognizing the difficulties of precise measurement, Table 1-1 presents the latest World Bank estimates for 1978 and 1993 GNP per capita data for ten of the world's most populous countries, covering nearly three quarters of mankind. Since mainland China was not a member of the World Bank in

Table 1-1: GNP per capita, Ten Largest Countries,
Ranked by Population, 1978-1993

Country	Mid 1990 Population (millions)	GNP per capita 1978 (US$)	Annual Growth (1980-93)	GNP per capita 1993 (US$)	Life Expectancy 1992
China	1162.2	n.a.	7.6	490	69
India	883.6	180	3.1	310	61
US	257.8	9,590	1.7	24,740	76
Indonesia	187.2	360	4.2	740	63
Brazil	156.5	1,580	0.3	2930	67
Russian Federation	148.7	n.a.	-1.0	2340	71
Japan	124.5	7,280	4.1	31,490	80
Pakistan	122.8	230	3.1	430	62
Bangladesh	115.2	90	2.1	220	56
Nigeria	105.3	560	-0.1	300	51

Source: World Bank, *World Development Report*, 1994.

1978, we do not have a number for it for that year, but a reasonable guess would be $220-$240. (When the P.R.C. joined, initial World Bank estimates listed it at a considerably higher level, but they have been revised downward significantly.) Historically, per capita GNP for the Soviet Union was estimated at 25-50% of the U.S. level, but — as the Comecon fell apart — those numbers decreased greatly. The World Bank first estimated a per capita GNP of $1780 for 1990, when the USSR still existed, but we now have standard estimates for Russia (and fairly similar numbers for other republics) at around $2300 for 1993.

What stands out quite clearly from the data in Table 1-1 is the fact that the standard of living in the United States and Japan is vastly higher than in the remaining eight countries. Is the main explanatory factor for this the availability of resources, geography, the quality of the labor force, or is it something else? To be sure, the United States is a resource-rich country, but Japan certainly is not. Resource endowment and the quality of the labor force are about the same in the U.S. and the former USSR, with the Soviets slightly ahead in resources, but somewhat behind in human capital (as implied by the lower life expectancy, listed at 71 by the World Bank, but much lower by other sources).

Why is the U.S., with about the same resource endowment as Brazil, about eight times as productive? In particular, why is Japan fifty to sixty times ahead of other large Asian countries in national income per head? To be sure, Japan has a highly educated and homogenous labor force, but that favorable factor would seem to be largely offset by its lack of raw materials and a relatively small amount of arable land. It is certainly true that in the poorest Asian LDCs, the labor force is often malnourished, living near the edge of subsistence; many are illiterate and suffer from various diseases (note some of the shockingly low life expectancy rates in Table 1-1). China, in contrast to India and Bangladesh, has made great progress in providing for the basic human needs of its population in health and education. Still, China's richest provinces lag far behind Japan and, for that matter, Taiwan, Hong Kong, and Singapore, and a number of other Asian nations discussed in Chapter 13.

The main explanation for these enormous differences, in my opinion, lies in the economic system adopted by the various countries. From the point of view of efficiency in resource allocation, "capitalism" is clearly superior. It is tempting to give you, the students, a bold face definition of capitalism for you to memorize. Nevertheless, I will avoid the temptation, and talk about why I am doing so a little bit. "Capitalism" is characterized by:

1. private ownership of the major means of production, land and capital;

2. clear-cut property rights, defined and enforced by an independent judiciary system;

3. organized markets (and supporting institutions, e.g., accounting firms, bankruptcy law, deeds) for competitive trading of commodity contracts and financial instruments; and

4. a central decision-making role for the individual entrepreneur.[1]

While the above provides a useful general characterization of a market type economy (MTE), it avoids giving a pat, concise definition of capitalism. Capitalism is an evolutionary system, and a definition fitting England in the 18th century would hardly suffice to describe Japan or Hong Kong today. The kind of capitalistic system that is studied in most micro-economics courses describes households as maximizing utility, business firms as maximizing profits, market for both goods and factors of production as purely competitive (with monopolies and oligopolies an exception), and government nowhere to be seen. The textbook model leads to wonderful general equilibrium results in the long run — factors of production leave unprofitable industries, inefficient firms shut down, the marginal utility of the last widget bought equals the marginal cost of the last one produced, workers are paid the value of their marginal productivity, and the representative firm breaks even in the long run. The representative firm pays for labor,

---

[1] Footnote on following page.

land, capital, and entrepreneurship exactly as much as they are worth (their "opportunity cost"), and produces at the lowest point on its average total cost curve. Though no real world economy has ever come very close to the "Pareto optimal" allocation of resources, we can conclude that MTEs, such as the U.S. and Japan, are probably a good deal closer to it than the other countries covered in Table 1.

Four Central Issues: Income Distribution

The main argument of the proponents of "socialism," and most admirers of the centrally planned economies (CPEs), is the greater emphasis on equity or, which is certainly not the same thing, equality in the distribution of income. "Socialism," on the whole, is also difficult to define simply; real world CPEs are as different from the elegant models of decentralized socialism supervised by a knowledgeable and benevolent Planning Board as MTEs are from the purely competitive paradigm of the micro textbooks.[2] "Socialism" is characterized by:

1. hierarchical planning of resource allocation by the state;

2. prohibition of the private ownership of the major means of production, especially land, and a virtual elimination of property income for individuals;

3. bureaucratic control of most prices and wages (with full employment of labor being the norm);

4. state supervision and/or control over foreign trade, travel and even contacts with foreigners.

Again, while not giving a neat definition of socialism, the above characteristics summarize reasonably and concisely the most important features of economic organization that were found in most CPEs. Considerable differences can be noted among CPEs

---

[1] The entrepreneur is defined by Joseph Schumpeter as that individual, often of humble or "unexceptional birth," who performs the act of "innovation." An innovation can be defined as "a new product, a new mode of production, a new market, or source of supply." The entrepreneur destroys existing production functions, which entails considerable personal risk. He is driven by the profit motive — indeed, by something more: "...the will and the drive to found a private kingdom." Cf. Joseph A. Schumpeter, *The Theory of Economic Development*, translated by Redvers Opie (Cambridge, Mass.: Harvard University Press, 1934). This volume was originally published in German in 1911. See also Joseph A. Schumpeter, *Capitalism, Socialism, and Democracy* (Harper & Row, 1946). More on all this will be said in Chapter 5.

[2] Probably the best known theoretical model of socialism is the so-called Lange-Taylor model. Cf., Oscar Lange and Fred M. Taylor, *On the Theory of Socialism* (University of Minnesota Press, 1938). A more recent attempt to describe an ideally functioning socialist system is Branko Horvat, *The Political Economy of Socialism* (M.E. Sharpe, 1982).

as well — Hungary's 1987 "goulash communism" was quite different from rigid discipline and central decision-making of China in the 1950s. Among the countries in Table 1-1, the U.S. and Japan are MTEs. China and Russia were CPEs, but are moving away from that and the others are somewhere in between these two categories.

The issue of income distribution has been one of the most widely discussed and debated fields in the economic literature in recent years, in particular in that much maligned sub-specialty of the discipline known as "development economics" or "economics of the LDCs." Statistics concerning the distribution of *national income* are usually divided into wages, rent, interest, and profit. While there is some evidence that the share of wages in the national income of most MTEs has remained remarkably constant over time, despite institutional changes, at about three-fourths of the total, and that after-tax corporate profits fluctuate only between 2–5% of national income (a surprise to many young critics of exploitative "capitalism") we cannot pursue this point much further in a book devoted to a comparison of CPEs and MTEs, since the CPEs do not report national income on that basis (state enterprises can extract rents and earn profits, possibly charge interest, but that is viewed as "going to the people," is it not?). Therefore, we need to discuss the distribution of *personal income*, usually consisting of all reported and taxable money income going to individuals or households.

How should a society distribute the fruits of its productive efforts to its members? Most people would use terms like "fairness" or "equity" in framing an answer. Some may even be tempted to use "equality" in answering — particularly if they are juniors in college, who can vote but usually have little or no income. It is extremely unlikely that any of us would really insist that "equity" means complete "equality." If we think of a primitive society of a few dozen families working common fields and hunting as a group, even then we might grant that "fairness" requires a larger share for larger households, and a bigger reward to the hardest-working farmer and the most knowledgeable and successful hunter among us. Going slightly beyond that simple society, we would probably be willing to grant a higher wage to people in unpleasant or dangerous jobs, in order to induce someone to take them, or to those in professions requiring years of unpaid preparation (doctors, lawyers, professors, and architects), in order to reward them for the opportunity cost of those years. We might have some misgivings about paying a lot more money, in the name of fairness, to those physically more gifted (NBA centers and NFL linebackers), but would probably see that it makes sense to do so — in order to produce contests attractive to customers. Similarly, few of us would pay to watch chess matches or bridge tournaments limited to players of only average intelligence (say, I.Q. of 100 plus or minus 10 points), which a totally egalitarian approach to life might lead us to advocate. Most people would also probably agree that an experienced master of his craft (a full professor?) should receive quite a bit more than a journeyman (an associate professor?) or an apprentice (a fresh assistant professor?) — lest the most competent of them go to another university or leave teaching altogether. However, in these last few examples, we are raising a few fuzzy issues — most people would argue that income differentials due to political or monopoly power (the full professor married to the dean's sister), as well as family position or inherited fortune, do not necessarily make sense either economically or ethically. How far one is willing to go in narrowing income differentials by using the government's tax and transfer system is a matter of personal opinion and public choice. Some conservatives take the position that "taxation is theft," while liberals point out that rich people's dogs eat filet mignon, while the children of the poor do not get enough milk.

On the issue of government redistribution, many of my conservative friends seem to be totally lacking in compassion, while most liberals are sadly devoid of common sense. Clearly, punitive tax rates on personal incomes will reduce productive effort and/or reported income, but I think that it is fundamentally quite fair that I pay somewhat more taxes proportionately than the struggling assistant professor. On the other hand, a handsome subsidy to people not working will call forth a larger supply — and free public education and/or a good-sized tax rebate for tuition (as in the 1996 campaign) leads to the poor taxpayers of Watts paying for the schooling of the sons and daughters of the well-to-do families of Newport Beach.

In any case, that's probably enough of philosophical musing about valid and not-so-valid reasons for differences in family income — let us examine some facts. Figure 1 is a representation of the well known Lorenz Curve — we plot the cumulative distribution of personal income received (usually before taxes) on the vertical axis against the number of recipients on the horizontal. An absolute equal distribution of income would produce a 45° line — at point A, the first 20% of income recipients would receive exactly 20% of total personal income; at point B, the first 40% of income would go to the same percentage of recipients, and so on. The actual distribution of total personal income, however, is a curve below the 45° line — as shown by point C, the lowest 40% of all income recipients receive a far-less-than proportional share of total income, in this case, only 15%, while the top 20% of the income distribution in practice often receive as much as 50%. This comparison, of the top 20% to the bottom 40%, is a rather easily calculated measure of a country's income distribution — these so-called inequality ratios are shown in the second column of Table 1-2. On this basis, Brazil, Peru, and Kenya have the "worst" distributions of personal income in the world—for example, in Brazil, the top 20% of households get fully two thirds of total personal income. The share going to the lower income groups is very small — the bottom 40% of the population very seldom reaches even 20% of total income in most so called less developed countries (LDCs). Clearly, there are serious problems of measurement here as well — barter activities and subsistence-level food production are not easily measured by the "household personal income" concept.

A more generally used measure of income distribution is the "Gini coefficient," found by dividing the shaded area in Figure 1 by the area of the triangle below the 45° line. Conceptually, the Gini coefficient would approach zero, if the Lorenz curve were very close to the 45° line, but a coefficient of 1.0 would signify total inequality, with the one highest income household getting it *all*.

In the real world, Gini coefficients range from around 0.2 for a few relatively homogeneous and formerly socialist countries in Eastern Europe (Czechoslovakia, Hungary) to as high as 0.6 in a handful of LDCs. Among the countries shown in Table

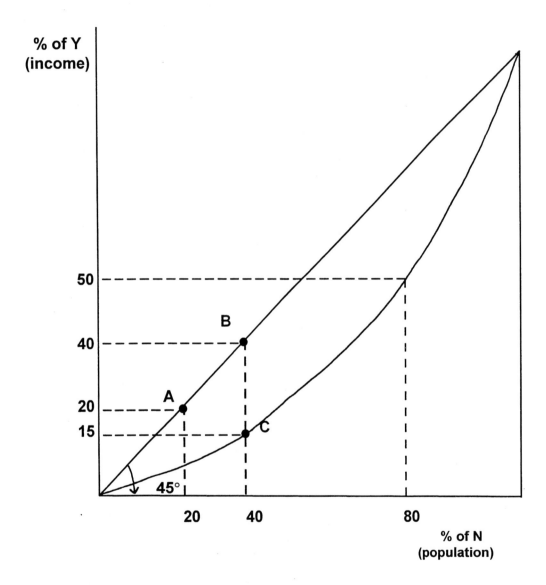

Figure 1.
A Hypothetical Lorenz curve

Table 1-2: Two Measures of Income Distribution, Selected Countries, Various Years

I. MDC's

Country	Gini Coefficient	Top 20% to Lowest 40%
France	.354	2.41
Germany	.329*	2.14
Japan	.282	1.71
Sweden	.279	1.74
Hong Kong	.400	2.90
United Kingdom	.393	3.03
Canada	.354	2.43
United States	.369	2.67
Australia	.374	2.72

*West Germany in 1988.

II. LDC's

Country	Gini Coefficient	Top 20% to Lowest 40%
Peru	.443	3.64
Thailand	.426	3.27
Mexico	.493	6.65
Brazil	.610	9.64
Malaysia	.473	4.16
Philippines	.377	2.87
Tanzania	.572	7.74
Colombia	.474	4.98
Ghana	.358	2.40
India	.311	1.94
Sri Lanka	.294	1.70
Korea	.331	2.14

Source: for Gini coefficients, Malcolm Gillis, *et.al.,* 1996, *The Economics of Development* (New York: W.W. Norton, 1996), p. 73, inequality ratios calculated from data in that table. For the three socialist countries included in that table, the Gini coefficients range from a low of 0.227 for Hungary to 0.229 for Poland and 0.252 for Bulgaria.

1-2, Brazil is the highest, with a Gini of 0.610, with Peru, Mexico, and Tanzania nearly in the same range. It is well established that the distribution of income in LDCs is considerably more unequal than in the more developed countries (MDCs), with no MDCs or industrialized countries above 0.5. While there are enormous problems of measurement, the distribution of income in the Soviet Union was really not much more equal than in the U.S., with a Gini coefficient of approximately 0.3 being reported. This is a bit surprising. Many millionaires in America live by clipping coupons on tax exempt state and local bonds, and bank presidents get salaries twenty or thirty times those of a beginning teller, not to mention stock options and other benefits. In the Soviet Union, on the other hand, property income was virtually abolished, and its wage and salary levels were such that no one could become a millionaire (legally). Yet, high level party functionaries, "progressive" artists and authors, athletes and entertainers are able to enjoy standards of living vastly better than those of the average Soviet citizen. Members of the managerial elite (called the "nomenklatura") lived in special guarded estates (just like the rich of Miami and Laguna Beach), had a car and driver provided by their ministry, vacationed at special "dachas" (vacation residences) on the Black or Baltic Sea, shopped in special stores (where there are never any lines), and had privileged access to health care and education for their children. While this has been changing recently, the basic structure is still in place in Russia. To be fair about it, many American, Japanese and European business executives also have company provided "perks" (business conferences in Aspen and tickets to the Redskins games, lavish expense accounts and golf club memberships), which lead to great difficulties in measuring income inequalities. Still, the communist regimes, which seized political power on the basis of a promise to eliminate inequality and continue to promise "full communism," were in practice not significantly different from many MTEs on this score. Furthermore, while most people in the bottom 20% of the income distribution in the U.S. usually do not have to worry about their next meal, those in the bottom 20% in the former Soviet Union are certainly concerned about the basics of food, clothing, and shelter today. Still, it is very true that the poorest citizens in both countries have to watch with envy at the bus stop in the cold rain, as a member of the elite whizzes by in a cozy limousine.

Now back to the main thread of our story in this section — what happens to income distribution over time? Do we know anything about the level of per capita GNP and the behavior of the Gini coefficient? Few topics in economics have produced as much heated debate and as little agreement as this one. For most industrial countries, or "more developed countries," MDCs, over the past century or so, the data (and problems of measurement are great) seem to support the so called "inverted-U hypothesis,"

---

[3] Simon Kuznets, *Economic Growth and Structure: Selected Essays* (W.W. Norton & C ompany, 1965) as well as his *Postwar Economic Growth: Four Lectures* (Harvard University Press, 1964). For a considerably more complicated view of the American "income revolution," see Martin Bronfenbrenner, *Income Distribution Theory* (Aldine-Atherton, 1971), especially Ch. 3. A more recent overview of this topic will be found in Arne Bigsten, *Income Distribution and Development: Theory, Evidence, and Policy* (Heinemann, 1985).

associated with the research of Russian-born Nobel laureate, and erstwhile Harvard professor, the late Simon Kuznets.[3] As the name of the hypothesis suggests, as income increases over time, the value of the Gini coefficient for a country first rises, remains stable for a while, and then falls. Or, to put it a bit more crudely, in the early stages of growth, "the rich get richer," but eventually the benefits of progress begin to "trickle down" to the middle class and even to the bottom 20% of the distribution. While apparently that awful term "trickle down" has never actually been used by any respected development economist, even in the early days of the subject, it may be useful to engage in a bit of armchair theorizing about *why* income and wealth did in fact "trickle down" — became more widely distributed in the MDCs — and *whether* such trends are likely to be taking place in the LDCs in the next century.

Considering the past century in the U.S., for example, the so-called "robber barons" amassed vast personal fortunes around the turn of the century, while the life of the average "working man" was, to use a well-worn phrase, "nasty, brutish and short." Inequality probably rose rather significantly over the 1870–1920 period, but improved substantially in the subsequent fifty years — 1920–1970 (the Gini coefficient probably has not changed significantly since then and indeed may have gone up once again, however). The first reason that can be mentioned to explain the fall in the Gini coefficient during the middle years of the twentieth century is the rise in wage rates. In part due to slower population growth and the development of strong labor unions (on the supply side) and the need for more skilled labor in manufacturing, construction, and other sectors (the demand side), real wage increases pushed most families into the "middle class," and permitted a great deal of upward mobility for the sons and (a bit later) daughters of the "working class."

A second reason for this phenomenon can be mentioned in almost the same breath — mandatory education and the spread of literacy, which greatly contributed to improved labor productivity. (In passing, one is tempted to speculate that one reason why U.S. distributional improvements seem to have stopped in the past couple of decades may be due to falling educational attainments and a disastrous high school "drop out" rate.) A third factor, again closely related, would be the extension of voting power to more people, both legally and in practice (I have in mind the elimination of poll taxes and other impediments to minority group participation in the political process) — even eighteen year olds being allowed to vote. This immediately brings to mind a closely-related explanation of greater equality in income distribution — the role of government.

For most Western democracies, the activism of the government tends to be the most obvious explanation of greater equality and the lowered incidence of poverty, though evidence suggests that the reduction in poverty in the period after World War II has more to do with overall growth than special government programs. Government involvement has meant progressive income taxes and steep levies against inheritances (though both have been successfully avoided in practice, and the estate tax was effectively lowered in the 1980s), taxes on land and other property (usually proportional to value), and higher taxes on luxury consumption goods (though "excise taxes" in the U.S. are a very minor revenue source). Government anti-trust laws and legislation aimed at protecting the consumer may also have had some impact in promoting greater equality. Perhaps more importantly, the system of government transfers — welfare, unemployment compensation, social security, and special subsidies to certain kinds of expenditures (food, rent, medical care, and education) — has provided a "safety net" for the lowest income groups in most societies. It has been reported that the "dole" in a number of Western European MTEs is so generous that most young people do not have to work — and spend most of their time in the coffee shops or their local pubs discussing the short comings of American capitalism and the depredations of multinational corporations (the dread MNCs). While it is widely believed that government transfer programs in the U.S. have been the main reason for a fall in the incidence of poverty — from about 30% of the population in the early 1950s to around 10% today — a strong argument can be made that most of this reduction has been due to economic growth, and not to special public sector programs. Still, on a net basis, the government's tax and transfer system has undoubtedly contributed to a lowering of the Gini coefficient in the U.S. and most other industrial countries.

Yet another reason, not very obvious and difficult to measure, concerns the role of the financial system. In most MTEs, especially Japan and the United States, the growth of financial assets per capita has been enormous, a good deal faster than GNP growth. Generally speaking, many more people today own "a piece of American business," either directly or indirectly, than sixty or seventy years ago. Around the turn of the century, Standard Oil was the creature of John D. Rockefeller—today Exxon is owned by millions upon millions of share holders. In addition, many more people have "a piece of the pump" indirectly, through insurance policies and/or pension plans. The number of Americans owning stock is said to be around 40 million — while it is true that many own an "insignificant number" of shares, it is also true that it is not possible to identify a single majority owner for most of the "Fortune 500" of the largest U.S. corporations. Indeed, in most cases, it will not be possible to identify a single individual, or even a family, with as much as ten percent of the outstanding stock of a major corporation. Even individuals not owning stock directly, but just having a checking and a savings account in a bank or other depository institution, will have some equity stake in the "means of production" — by virtue of their deposits with a "financial intermediary," they are participating in the overall financing of economic activity and business ownership in this country.

In general, there does not appear to exist a genuine "trade off" between efficiency (in resource allocation) and equity (in the distribution of income), as is sometimes argued. Most industrialized MTEs have experienced falling Gini coefficients along with rising GNPs per capita during the middle years of the 20th century — and the Gini coefficients of the CPEs appear to be only slightly lower than those of the U.K., Canada, the U.S., and Australia. Whether the experience of the MDCs can be repeated by most LDCs is a most difficult question — there exists some evidence that the "inverted U hypothesis" does apply to LDCs, but other investigators have argued that economic growth has only a "trickle-up effect." Some market oriented LDCs, such as Taiwan and Korea, have certainly experienced a significant lowering of inequality, partly due to economic growth and partly to conscious policy efforts, while Brazil and Mexico had shown some growth, but without any such change taking place. Whether the structural factors mentioned above will be applicable to most LDCs in the future can probably only be addressed on a case-by-case basis.

Four Central Issues: Price Stability

In normative terms, an economic system should seek a Pareto-optimal allocation of resources consistent with an equitable distribution of income, which we have termed the "micro-economic trade off," though the term "trade off" may be misleading. Still, I do mean to suggest strongly that MTEs are far ahead of the CPEs on a net basis in this area. The "macro economic trade off" may be another matter, for most CPEs have managed to compile a superior record of price stability as well as very low official unemployment rates. Whether this macro "success" is more important than the "failure" to increase productivity and efficiency at the micro level is a matter of personal judgment — would you be happy with gasoline prices at 40 cents per gallon, even if you couldn't get any quite often, or with a zero unemployment rate, if you had to sweep floors in a Tashkent factory for the rest of your life?

Let us talk a bit about price stability as a goal. Should the overall annual inflation rate average to zero? Some economists would argue that a modest overall inflation rate, of about 2 to 3 percent per year, has certain benefits. For example, it may be the inevitable consequence of quality change in most industrial products; that it helps to re-allocate labor and other resources from stagnant to growing sectors of the economy; or that it is an inevitable consequence of measurement problems (it is even known in the press that the CPI has an upward bias). Others might argue that a mild deflationary bias, price decreases averaging 2 to 3 percent per year, would enable businesses to pass on productivity improvements to the average consumer. Still, on average, prevailing opinion among professional economists probably would support zero price change as optimal, as least disruptive and controversial.

Let's briefly consider the benefits and costs of a moderate inflation rate — say, 6-10% above the world rate of price increase for a hypothetical country. As mentioned above, this could assist in the re-allocation of resources to the more dynamic sectors of the economy — wages would be rising most rapidly, for example, in those occupations with the most severe labor shortages. it would be a signal to substitute surplus commodities, with falling prices, for those in shortest supply, where such substitution is feasible. Those goods with the highest price increases should call forth the greatest supply increases as well, if such goods can be produced locally. In addition to this re-allocation function, there may also exist favorable redistribution consequences. While this may be a bit of a fairy tale, it is possible to argue that the early stages of a moderate inflationary episode involve a transfer of purchasing power (and political influence) from lenders (old and decrepit landowners and bond-holders) to borrowers (handsome dynamic entrepreneurs?). In the latter part of the 19th century in Japan, for example, power was thusly transferred from the existing feudal landowning nobility and their retinues (*the daimyo and the samurai)* to the emerging capitalist entrepreneurs and skilled technicians.[4]

Another redistributional aspect that has received more attention in the development economics literature is the concept of "forced saving." While there are various ways of analyzing this, it is sufficient for our purposes to point out that "inflation is a tax on cash." The government, often called the "public sector" (though its long-run interest in genuine representation of the general public as opposed to powerful pressure groups seems questionable), earns real resources by issuing additional money — with a transfer taking place *from* the holders of existing money and near-money balances *to* the government. Whether the government prints a bill with a face value of $1000 or $1, the cost of production is about the same — well under one dollar (about three cents today). The difference between the face value of money and its production cost is called "seigniorage." The ultimate transfer is from the holders of existing dollar balances — if their $100 in cash or in the bank now has a purchasing power of only $50, they have been forced to save $50 in real terms, hence the concept of "forced saving." Theoretically, the government might invest the proceeds of seigniorage in development finance — indeed, the early literature on this topic strongly suggested that this would be the case. To recapitulate briefly, the reallocation of resources and redistribution of income under mild inflation might be beneficial on both efficiency and equity grounds.

However, in rather short order, the costs of inflation are likely to outweigh such potential benefits. First, seigniorage revenues in theory might be invested in productive development projects, but there exist politically powerful pressure groups in the real world — which will wish the government to subsidize sensitive consumption categories instead. In a world of 50% inflation, can food prices be allowed to rise by that amount? Can rents? Would government workers not demand at least a 50% salary increase? What about urban transportation and other utility bills? As the late Harry Johnson argued, ...the proceeds of such an inflation tax are likely to be wasted on subsidizing certain categories of politically sensitive consumption rather than being productively invested in development.

Second, business and individuals are forced "to waste real resources" in order to forecast and adjust to inflation, rather than seeking to improve long-term efficiency and reduce production costs. (If this involves hiring additional economists to forecast the future, the waste to some of us may seem especially gruesome!) Third, the balance of payments consequences are usually unfortunate. The necessary official devaluation of the local currency will be bitterly resisted by importers and consumers of imported goods, while market interest rates will probably lag behind inflationary expectations.

---

[4] The *daimyo* were the feudal nobility, ruled by a hereditary *shogun* (you may have read the book by James Clavell, or—more likely—seen the TV series by that title) and the *samurai* were a professional warrior class. For more economics and less sword-play, see G.C. Allen, *A Short Economic History of Modern Japan, 1867–1937* (George Allen & Unwin, 1962). These matters are taken up at greater length in Chapters 11 and 12.

Therefore, fourth, investment demand is likely to exceed the supply of saving by a large margin — resulting in the destruction of competitive financial markets and the emergence of a system of "financial repression." In a typical LDC, the central bank will usually lack the monetary policy tools (and/or the "credibility") to bring the inflation rate under control, and this year's mild inflation rate of 6-10% may well rise to 15-20% next year. Since that would normally require an interest rate on government bonds and bank deposits in the range of 19-24%, it is likely that politicians will seek to limit permissible interest rates to, say, 12% per year, resulting in a regime of financial repression — most simply defined as the persistence of negative real rates of interest. Thus, the costs of relatively moderate inflation are likely to exceed its benefits in rather short order.

To cite Harry Johnson again, for a fine summary:

> ...*inflationary fiscal and monetary policies have a variety of deleterious effects on economic development and efficiency. The most serious are, first, the distortions in the economy caused by the effort to protect certain segments of the population from the effects of inflation, for example by holding down the domestic price of food or of urban transport to shield the industrial worker, or by holding down interest rates to channel real income to manufacturing firms; and second, the disturbance of the normal processes of investment decision by extreme uncertainty about the short-term rate of inflation to be expected. These effects of inflation are harmful both to economic development in general and the possibility of basing development on industrial exporting in particular. It must be recognized, however, that the reason for endemic inflation in a less developed country is almost invariably political inability to agree either on the taxation required to finance the development program or, more generally, on the division of the national income among the claimants to it. Inflationary financing represents the only available way of bridging the deep political divisions.*[5]

There are a number of ways that a CPE can pursue the goal of price stability that are generally not feasible for an MTE government. Government enterprises can be prohibited to increase prices, period. The balance of payments need not be a problem, if all foreign contacts are controlled by the state. Black market dealings in foreign exchange do need to be severely punished, but stringent controls over imports will probably work in the short run. If there is no financial market, and only a single bank, interest rates do not matter very much. Inflationary expectations will not be allowed to develop, if shortages are met by the use of quotas and queuing (the 2Q principle — "queuing" is a British term meaning "waiting in line"). Freezing all prices over long periods of time will tend to lower efficiency in resource allocation and probably worsen the distribution of income as well. If wheat and rice must be delivered to the government regardless of cost and market price, producers will try to grow other crops or seek to make other adjustments (cheating

---

[5] Harry G. Johnson, *Economic Policies Toward Less Developed Countries*, (The Brookings Institution, 1967), pp. 75–76. See also Arnold C. Harberger (ed.), *World Economic Growth* (Institute for Contemporary Studies, 1984), especially Ch. 15.

on weight and quality) and buyers will find wasteful uses for such subsidized goods (feeding bread to livestock). Producers will concentrate on products not subject to price controls and farm workers will tend to engage even more in industrial and commercial side-line activities (wood carvings and tulips instead of bread and potatoes).

While officially-measured inflation in most CPEs had been much lower than in MTEs, which had been a major propaganda point for the regimes of the former category, there has existed a lot of repressed inflation, as shown by the 2Q principle and by the piling up of bank deposits. The cost of standing in line to buy inferior goods became so onerous that people gave up participating in the official economy, and simply allowed their deposits to rise, in the vague hope that conditions will eventually change for the better. In the last few years as prices were freed, there has been a general "flight from the ruble," to "gold and goods," as shown by the rapid depreciation of the exchange rate from about 100 rubles in 1991 to more than 5000 to the U.S. dollar in mid-1996.

Four Central Issues: Full Employment

A second major macro-economic indicator that usually shows the superiority of CPEs is the full employment of labor (and, by implication, of other factors of production). During the past twenty years, the official unemployment race in the U.S. rose briefly above 10% of the labor force only in 1982 — while it remains around that level in a number of Western European countries. It is currently nearing 3% in Japan and is a bit above 5% in the U.S., but it is certainly true that historically the central planners had succeeded in eliminating unemployment — to be without a job would lead to your being branded a "parasite." It is rather difficult to begin discussing this thorny issue. Soviet disinformation would have us believe that there are long "bread lines" of the unemployed in the U.S. and in Western Europe, waiting for the next meal to be given to them (grudgingly) by a charitable organization. According to Marxist historians, involuntary unemployment, caused by the impending collapse of "mature financial-monopoly capitalism," is growing ever more serious, and minority group members will be particularly hard hit. It is certainly true that the unemployment rate (and the drop out rate from school) among black teenagers is a national disgrace. However, the overall unemployment rate in most LDCs and in Western European countries is much worse than here in the U.S. Over the last fifteen years, we have created a lot of new jobs, whereas Western Europe has not. The U.S. unemployment rate is only around 5 percent and unemployment benefits are relatively generous, and other transfer programs are available as well. Perhaps the system is not heading toward inevitable destruction.

Clearly, full employment is an important national goal — as recognized by the passage of the Employment Act of 1946 (establishing the Council of Economic Advisers — implicitly to provide advice to the President about how to reach that goal) and the Humphrey-Hawkins Act somewhat more recently. Other things being equal, we would be better off, if the nation's labor force were fully employed and our GNP level were equal to "potential GNP." There are, however, at least two areas of some controversy — first, how to measure full employment and, second, what are the chief causes of unemployment? Theoretically, a good definition of "full employment" would be a situation, where the number of people looking for work is exactly equal to the number of vacancies, with also perhaps some seasonal unemployment being allowable. Twenty years ago, the "full-employment unemployment rate" was generally held to be about 4% of the labor force — and potential GNP was defined as the value of output that could be produced if unemployment was at that level (the student will recall "Okun's Law" — each 1% reduction in unemployment is associated with a 2%-3% rise in real GNP). Today economists are less sure about both the full employment number and Okun's Law.

With regard to causality, two major approaches can be contrasted. The first of these, associated with the so-called Keynesian approach, assumes that unemployment is a *macroeconomic* problem, primarily caused by inadequate aggregate demand. Implicitly, unemployment is viewed as being involuntary—those without work are all willing, able and qualified to take jobs, but there are just too few positions for them to fill. This is the "conventional wisdom" of the 1950s and the 1960s, summarized by the so called Phillips Curve (shown in Figure 2). Plotting the inflation rate (for change in the price level) on the vertical and the unemployment rate on the horizontal axis, we show the traditional "trade off" between prices and output/employment. If the economy was at point Z, with virtually no inflation and an "unacceptably" high unemployment rate of 6% — we could move back to E, the "full employment" rate of 4% — by accepting additional price increases of 1-1.5%. Conversely, at W, employment is "over-full" and the inflation rate an "unacceptably" high 4%. At Z, government policies to stimulate the economy were needed — higher spending, lower taxes, and a more rapid expansion of the money supply. At W, these policies should be thrown into reverse — lower government expenditures, raise taxes and put the brakes on money growth. Ah, yes. Those were happy days for the economics profession —Republicans were happier at Z than at W, but we all knew how to move the economy toward E (which is approximately where it was more often than not.) We will return to a more thorough discussion of the Phillips Curve in Chapter 4.

An alternative approach to explaining what causes unemployment is to focus on its microeconomic determinants. The so-called "Natural Rate of Unemployment," associated with Milton Friedman, suggests that government macroeconomic policies are essentially useless for trying to lower the unemployment rate. It seems possible to argue that much of today's unemployment is voluntary — in the U.S., some people who are out of work do not find it desirable to accept jobs that are offered to them. Alternatively, while there is no shortage of jobs in the aggregate, employers are not willing to hire the unemployed, because of minimum wage laws, social security contributions, insurance and other regulations, and so on. While this point of view is usually represented in the textbooks as a vertical long-run Phillips Curve, with upward-ratcheting short-run curves, I do not think that such graphics effectively present the argument, and will avoid presenting such a graph. The main point is clear, however — macroeconomic attempts to manipulate aggregate demand will not affect the unemployment rate very much. As Milton Friedman says, monetary policy cannot be used to "peg" the jobless rate.

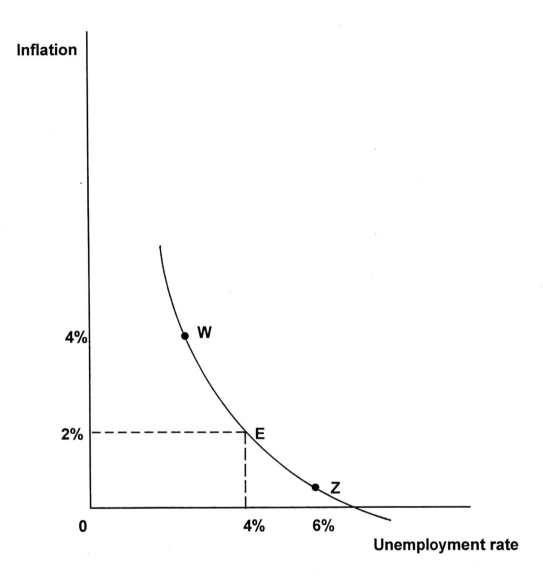

Figure 2.
The Phillips Curve

Summary

These four central issues: resource allocation vs. income distribution, and price stability vs. full employment, are usually presented as two trade-offs. It is probably true that a single-minded commitment to any one of the four will produce less-than-optimal consequences in the other areas. Let us consider briefly a full employment strategy — any worker without a job would always be employed by the government, as a matter of right.

It would not be difficult to put such a policy into practice — leaf raking and washing off of subway graffiti are always employment-generating possibilities. However, what about the other three goals? If all the jobless were put to work thusly, and paid well — would that not challenge our notions of income distribution equity? Or price stability? If they could contribute more in the private sector, would not such a program greatly lower resource allocation efficiency? Alternatively, we could legislate a system of zero price change, making it a federal crime to change wages or prices. Would that be fair? Just? Efficient? If the price of corn would be frozen in the U.S., but rising in Canada, what should we do? If steak disappeared from the shelves, who would handle that shortage? If we froze the wages of economics professors, what about their consulting income? If we froze that too, what about the income of their wives and children, if they only taught Tuesdays and Thursdays, and could stay at home all other days?

Efficiency in resource allocation, equity in the distribution of income, reasonable price stability and nearly full employment of labor are four central goals of any economic system. Most MTEs succeed better on the microeconomic goals of efficiency and equity than on the macroeconomic goals of avoidance of inflation and unemployment, where the CPEs appeared historically to show better results. Macroeconomic stability, however, seems to imply a great loss in microeconomic efficiency, without much gain on equity grounds. On the whole, in the past, a good many people crossed from the East to the West in Germany, and there are no cases of people swimming away from Hong Kong to reach mainland China, so that the net effect seems rather obvious, at least up to now — the economic accomplishments of the capitalistic order, combined with the political freedoms available in most MTEs, have produced a positive vote of confidence in favor of capitalism.

Three Organizing Principles

Following Robert Heilbroner, it is possible to answer the "What, How, and For Whom?" questions in three rather general ways. These three are tradition or custom, command or coercion, and market or profit. Let us conclude this introductory chapter with a brief discussion of each.

Historically, and probably for most of mankind even today, tradition, custom, and perhaps simple inertia determine their daily economic activity. Guidance about what is to be grown in the fields, how you milk a cow or slaughter a pig, and when this is to be done is handed down by the previous generation — "for whom?" does not need to be asked either: some for the rulers, and the rest for the family. In most customary or traditional societies, the household tends to be self sufficient, and the produced surplus above subsistence needs of the family is small. A number of examples of such societies can be mentioned — feudalism in Europe was based upon traditional patron-client relationships. Under the manorial system, serfs were tied to their land, and supplied labor to the lord of the manor in exchange for civil protection from robbery and other crime. As capitalism developed in western Europe, such labor obligations to the manor could be "repurchased" or "commuted" by cash payments, which was often done. According to Heilbroner, in ancient Egypt, sons were expected to follow in their father's occupational footsteps, as a matter of legal and moral right. Similarly, the caste system of India made sure that there would be enough sweepers and warriors by making these occupations hereditary. The basic control system of a traditional society is a normative one — "you should," "you really ought to," "it is expected that..."

A second broad organizing principle is that of a command/coercive economy. In ancient Egypt, tradition in occupational choice was one control mechanism, but command ranked as close second. What shall we produce? Well, how about a couple of pyramids? In both the USSR until 1991 and mainland China today, resource allocation was primarily decided by the political power of the central planning authorities. Certainly, the people in the prison camps worked because of coercion, and many others outside the camps also performed their duties reasonably well, because the thought of prison camps was then often present. Clearly, the forces of tradition and government command also influence economic activity in capitalist societies — all American taxpayers are painfully aware of April 15 — but we are much less concerned about coercive sanctions in our daily lives.

Finally, a third method of organizing economic activity is that of the market economy. What is to be produced? Those goods and services which yield the highest profit — goods and services produced at a loss will be discontinued. How is it to be done? Combining factors of production — land, labor, capital and entrepreneurship — into the "least cost combination," — will be the long run optimum. For whom? For the owners of the production factors — without our necessarily knowing who they are, those people with the highest marginal contribution to the production process will also receive the largest distributional claims on the output that is produced.

As we shall discuss in the next chapter, the market economy is quite a revolutionary idea. It challenges the traditional strictures of the customary society — when someone says "it's always been done this way" or "you really ought to," the capitalist asks whether it makes sense to do so today. The commands of government can also be questioned and resisted — all the government needs to do is to establish the "rules of the game," but beyond that, individual decision making, fast and flexible, will produce a superior social order, to which we now turn. ■

SUGGESTED READINGS

Bronfenbrenner, Martin, *Income Distribution Theory* (Aldine-Atherton, 1971).

Friedman, Milton, *Bright Promises, Dismal Performance: An Economist's Protest* (Harcourt Brace Jovanovich, 1983).

Harberger, Arnold C. (ed.), *World Economic Growth* (Institute for Contemporary Studies, 1984).

Heilbroner, Robert L., *The Worldly Philosophers* (Simon & Schuster, 1980).

Hoover, Kevin D., *The New Classical Macroeconomics* (Elgar, 1992).

Kindleberger, Charles P., *World Economic Primacy, 1500-1990* (Oxford University Press, 1996).

Kuznets, Simon, *Population, Capital, and Growth* (W.W. Norton, 1973).

Lesourne, Jacques, *The Economics of Order and Disorder* (Oxford University Press, 1992).

Maddison, Angus, *Dynamic Forces in Capitalist Development* (Oxford University Press, 1991).

Okun, Arthur M., *Prices and Quantities: A Macroeconomic Analysis* (The Brookings Institution, 1981).

Rostow, W.W., *The World Economy: History and Prospect* (University of Texas Press, 1978).

Sen, Amartya, *Resources, Values and Development* (Basil Blackwell, 1984).

Wallace, Iain, *The Global Economic System* (Unwin Hyman, 1990).

Weintraub, Sidney, *Our Stagflation Malaise* (Quorum Books, 1981).

Wolf, Charles, Jr., *Markets or Governments: Choosing Between Imperfect Alternatives* (MIT Press, 1988).

CHAPTER TWO

ADAM SMITH AND
COMPETITIVE CAPITALISM

*F*eudalism in Western Europe was an economic and political system closely tied to land. In the political realm, it generally consisted of small local communities, governed by personal loyalties and obligations, tradition and custom. Most economic activity involved subsistence agriculture and handicrafts. As agriculture became more productive, and horses replaced oxen as draft animals, larger markets could develop and the transportation system improved. In the sixteenth century, the influx of "windfalls" from the opening New World frontier began to challenge the existing sociopolitical order, as rapid inflation in a number of countries weakened previous claims on output and income. In Marxist terminology, the "thesis" of the land-based feudal system, tied to personal loyalties and traditional modes of production, was challenged by an "antithesis," the market. The market was an institution emphasizing mobility, impersonal calculation of profit and loss, and a new rationality beyond the powers of secular and religious authorities. The "synthesis" of the two contending forces eventually produced a system we today call "capitalism," but its full development required the establishment of a number of significant pre-conditions. We now turn briefly to these necessary changes in sociopolitical conditions, which pre-dated the emergence of the free market economy. To anticipate further discussion of this point, think about whether these pre-conditions have been met successfully in the typical "Third World" country today — and what the prospects are for their development in the near future.

Pre-Conditions to Capitalism

Somewhat paradoxically, the emergence of capitalism in Western Europe was closely tied to the development of a strong nation-state. In the interim period, as feudalism was coming to an end, this was a bit of a paradox, because greater concentration of power in a single central government initially placed some obstacles in the path of the full development of a free-market economy. Still, the economic benefits of a nation-state quickly began to outweigh the costs of centralized political power. We can develop a number of related arguments in this connection. First, the nation-state led to the development of a sense of national unity and the use of a common language, as a bewildering variety of local dialects and minor languages eventually coalesced into standard English, French, and German. Second, the development of a national monetary unit, a generally accepted currency, was another major accomplishment of the centralized nation-state — the use of standardized money greatly reduced the transaction costs of impersonal market dealings. Imagine some Arab traders from Byzantium landing on a Baltic coast in the 11th Century, and meeting a Latvian or an Estonian maid in the mists of a December morning — they want to buy a chicken and some apples, and have a bag of silver coins for that purpose — how did they communicate? Establish a price and an exchange rate? Archeological discoveries of early "dirlam hoards" in the Baltic region and even in Russia provide clear evidence that they did so, but it must have been indeed difficult.

Another easily-overlooked contribution of the centralized nation-state is the establishment of a standardized system of weights and measures, defining precisely what a "bushel" and a "peck" meant. This was as important as defining the gold content of a pound sterling in order to facilitate impersonal and standardized market exchange. We could spend a lot more time on the very important role of the government in defining and protecting property rights, and establishing "law-and-order" procedures for the enforcement of commercial contracts. An organized system of land tenure — including formal surveys and legal titles — is a most important precondition for long-term productivity improvements and investment in agriculture. Protection against piracy and other violent challenges against property rights constitute another key function of the nation-state — which also subsidized foreign adventures and the development of a system of colonies, about which more will be said later.

In addition to the development of a strong nation-state, a second major pre-condition to the emergence of capitalism was the establishment of a philosophical justification for market-oriented economic activity — in the main, this was provided by the Protestant Ethic or the Reformation. In medieval Europe, and in many rural societies even today, mercenary and profit-seeking activity was regarded with great suspicion, even disdain. St. Thomas Aquinas, writing in the 13th Century, devoted considerable attention to the concept of a "just price." The priestly "Scholastics," who followed Aquinas, wrestled mightily with the moral questions raised by the changing economic order, but are today generally either ignored or dismissed as apologists for feudalism and the immense wealth held by the Catholic Church itself. E. K. Hunt aptly refers to religious sanctions against greed and selfishness as the "Christian paternalist ethic":

> ...It was the lust for wealth that the Christian paternalist ethic consistently condemned. Thus, the doctrine of the just price was intended as a curb on such acquisitive and socially disruptive behavior. Then as now, accumulation of material wealth was a passport to greater power and upward social mobility. This social mobility was eventually to prove totally destructive to the medieval system because it put an end to the status relationships that were the backbone of medieval society.[1]

---

[1] E. K. Hunt, *Property and Prophets*, Fifth Ed. (Harper and Row, 1986), p. 9.

The Protestant Reformation challenged the authority of the Catholic Church not only on matters of doctrine, but its social teachings as well. Whereas before there was one individual in a predominant hierarchy in charge of determining what a just price should be, and what constitutes usury (an excessively high interest rate on loans), there now might be several people in a city (a Catholic priest, a Lutheran minister, and a Calvinist pastor) each claiming to interpret correctly the teachings of the Bible.

While neither Calvin nor Luther can be viewed as endorsing earthly riches and supporting profit-maximizing activities, with the passage of time, Protestant doctrines came to be interpreted as a philosophical justification for the emerging new market system and the accumulation of wealth. Max Weber's famous book, *The Protestant Ethic and the Spirit of Capitalism* discussed this linkage at great length. To a considerable extent, the relationship of worldly success to the concept of "pre-destination" is at the heart of such reasoning — if God has already decided that Mr. Jones is to be one of the "elect," one of those "saved," surely Mr. Jones' success on this earth is but a sign of his prospective eternal glory. Mr. Jones is encouraged to behave appropriately to his "elect" status — to consume modestly, to support the church (of course), and to build his fortune for the glory of God, with His full support, so to speak. For the early capitalists: "Accumulate! accumulate! accumulate! that is Moses and the prophets!" Other familiar maxims come to mind: "Early to bed and early to rise, makes a man healthy, wealthy, and wise . . ." as well as "A penny saved is a penny earned." Eventually, this extensive popularization of such platitudes led to the development of a school of thought known as "Social Darwinism" — marrying Charles Darwin's biological theory of "natural selection" with the concept of pre-destination. Quite a neat theory emerges — the rich deserve to be rich not only because they are superior group of the human race, taller and smarter than the rest of us, but perhaps also because they have been especially blessed by the Lord himself. (If my students have ever wondered whether any sociopolitical ideas are too far right-wing for me, this *may* be one . . .) Nevertheless, it is very important to recognize that the Protestant Reformation, with its emphasis upon the individual and "faith," provided a much more suitable ethical system for wealth accumulation and profit maximization than the paternalistic ethic which preceeded it. It is also important to think about the differences in the world view of the Judeo-Christian civilization, broadly speaking, and that of other religions, but more on that later.

A third precondition to the emergence of capitalism and urbanization is the agricultural revolution, which took place in Europe over the several centuries before Adam Smith wrote *The Wealth of Nations* (1776). The development of knowledge about irrigation techniques and crop rotation increased agricultural productivity sufficiently to permit the development of cities to house manufacturing establishments and year-round markets and to support ever larger groups of artisans, mechanics and traders. In sharp contrast to many LDC's today, where capital cities are sometimes carved out in the middle of the jungle (e.g., Brasilia) or rely principally upon imported consumption goods (e.g., Jakarta, Lagos), European cities of the 16th and 17th Centuries developed in a "balanced, symbiotic relationship" to the surrounding countryside. Incomes of the rural people had to be sufficient to buy what was being produced in the cities, while the urban labor force was being provided food and raw materials by the agriculturalists. The growth of cities was constrained by both demand and supply conditions in the surrounding countryside — the prosperity of each was inescapably tied to the well-being of the other.

A fourth, and final, pre-condition to the emergence of capitalism was the totality of scientific and technological progress taking place over the several centuries before Adam Smith. Probably the most important of all is the "idea of progress," the strange and novel suggestion that people's understanding of the physical universe would inevitably improve, that laws of chemistry and physics were waiting to be discovered and tested, and that science was mightier than human institutions (and perhaps stronger than transcendental beliefs as well). A revolution in communications and transportation was taking place, facilitating and producing "windfall gains" from the frontier, in the form of precious metals as well as new products. The printing press was especially important in facilitating the development of a market economy. In a barter-only system, the search and information costs associated with each transaction are very high — each potential seller must not only find a willing buyer, but also a buyer willing to sell something of use to the first party. It is very instructive to take a look at the newspapers of a couple of hundred years ago in this connection. Most of the space in a Philadelphia paper of 1790, for example, was devoted to the sailing and arrival of ships and other commercial information — reducing search and information costs, and facilitating the emergence of a money economy.

Mercantilism

. While we cannot compress the two-volume work on *Mercantilism* by Gustav Heckscher into a few pages, let us recall again the somewhat paradoxical role of the nation-state. Many of the benefits of standardization and legalization associated with the development of a strong central government were absolutely essential pre-conditions to the emergence of the free-enterprise economy, but strict governmental controls over economic activity associated with the early days of centralized political power provided initially powerful barriers to the development of capitalism. For example, the early version of mercantilism, called "bullionism," simply completely prohibited the shipment of precious metals across national boundaries, regardless of the benefits of trade and potential profits. As E. K. Hunt points out:

> . . . *Spain, the country into which most of the gold from the Americas flowed, applied bullionist restrictions over the longest period and imposed the most severe penalty for the export of gold and silver: death. Yet the needs of trade were so pressing and such large profits could be made by importing foreign commodities that even in Spain merchant-capitalists succeeded in bribing corrupt officials or smuggling large quantities of bullion out of the country.*[2]

---

[2] *Ibid.*, p. 23.

After the early bullionist period, most emerging national governments concerned themselves with the maintenance of a *favorable balance of trade,* an excess of exports over imports, in order to bolster domestic employment, to build up local industries, but — above all — to amass gold and silver reserves to finance military adventures and political expansion ("specie"—the old term for precious metals — was viewed by mercantilist writers as the "sinews of war.")

A series of governmental policies designed to assure a favorable balance of trade was employed by mercantilistic regimes. The one most familiar to students of early American history is the "colonial system," which treated the overseas colonies of the "mother country" as specialized producers of raw materials and a market for industrial products. In that connection, you may vaguely recall some unpleasantness about tea in Boston. Those who have seen the movie, *Ghandi,* will remember that he led a march of Indians down to the ocean as an act of civil disobedience — to make . . .salt! That did not sit well with the British colonial authorities, who threw him in jail for this bit of industrial entrepreneurship.

In addition to the system of exploiting economic relations with the colonial areas, mercantilistic governments followed a number of other policies to foster a favorable trade balance. High tariffs and outright bans on imported luxury goods were often employed; tax advantages and even export subsidies were sometimes used. Joint-stock trading companies (such as the East India Company and the Hudson Bay Company) were given geographical monopolies, in order to avoid the unsightly prospect of British traders competing with one another. In some cases, governments sought to control individual consumption by using the so-called "sumptuary laws"—legislation designed to prohibit "unseemly expenditures." For example, silk, velvet, and gold, could only be enjoyed by the nobility — thus, newly rich merchants or prosperous farmers were prohibited from wearing and using such items. Going off on a tangent for a moment, in the modern world, the guiding principles of such sumptuary laws seem to re-emerge from time to time. For example, at the time of the Arab embargo of oil shipments to the United States, and the worldwide oil shortage of the early 1970's, a number of countries found it more expedient to force drivers to use their cars every other day, or to prohibit Sunday travel, than to allow gas prices to rise to market clearing levels. A long list of rationing and conservation proposals was furiously debated in this country, since a rise in gasoline prices was curiously viewed as only "hurting the poor." Mercantilist passions are with us still — and "liberals" are quite willing to dictate your personal consumption patterns, rather than allowing the market system to work.

Adam Smith is generally regarded as the Father of Modern Economics. He wrote *The Wealth of Nations* as a reaction, as a polemic, against the worst excesses of the mercantilistic system of governance. In many respects, his most famous book remains (to me) the best introductory text for the rather-disorganized field known as development economics, or the Economics of the Less Developed Countries.

The full title of Smith's volume is instructive, I believe: *An Inquiry into the Nature and Causes of the Wealth of Nations* (1776). The nature of a nation's wealth did not consist of gold and silver in the central government's treasury, said Smith, but its productive capacity. Its productive capacity could be expanded by capital investments and improvements in the labor force. Smith stressed especially the importance of labor specialization — his example of the "pin factory" is usually cited: ten men working together, each contributing a specialized function to the overall process, were able to produce thousands of pins per day. On the other hand, a single individual working by himself probably could not produce even ten or twenty. If specialization could produce such enormous increases in productivity in a particular industry or a single country, there is no reason why this principle would not apply internationally as well, reasoned Smith. In his own words:

> *"...We trust with perfect security that the freedom of trade, without any attention of government, will always supply us with the wine which we have occasion for; and we may trust with equal security that it will always supply us with all the gold and silver which we can afford to purchase or to employ, either in circulating our commodities, or in other uses."* [3]

The argument that gold and silver constitute the "sinews of war" is rather silly, argued Smith, since "...fleets and armies are maintained, not with gold and silver, but with consumable goods."[4]

In a further elaboration of this idea, Adam Smith developed the *Theory of Absolute Advantage,* which says that countries should specialize in the production and exporting of those products for which they are the lowest-cost producers. Another oft-cited example from *The Wealth of Nations* concerns Portuguese wine. Yes, said Smith, it would be possible to grow grapes in hot-houses in Scotland, at great expense, to ferment the juice and produce a beverage distantly related to wine — but would it not be much more efficient to produce more cloth in the mills of Scotland and trade it for Portugal's wine? This idea was further developed by David Ricardo as the *Theory of Comparative Advantage,* which says that trade is likely to benefit a country even if it does not produce anything more efficiently than all of its trading partners. A country can be the highest cost producer in both cloth and wine — and it will still benefit by concentrating on one of the goods, the one with the lowest relative cost of production. As long as relative prices are sufficiently different in the two countries before trade, and transportation costs not prohibitively high, an opening of exchange will benefit both through specialization. The beginning of economics as a science (or a field of study) is closely linked to these classical arguments in favor of free trade — if you think a bit more about it, both Smith and Ricardo are also asserting implicitly that the well-being of England is determined primarily by the welfare of individual consumers (and that the interests of the state or the business community are of a secondary importance).

---

[3] Adam Smith, *An Inquiry into the Nature and Causes of the Wealth of Nations* (Everyman's Library, 1910), ed. by Ernest Rhys, p. 381.
[4] *Ibid.,* b. 383.

A third argument against mercantilism made by Adam Smith is his overall critique of monopoly power. Smith's view of businessmen as individuals was a rather realistic and skeptical one — in a famous and oft-quoted passage, he noted that " . . . people of the same trade seldom meet together, even for merriment and diversion, but the conversation ends in a conspiracy against the public, or in some contrivance to raise prices." Monopoly power becomes particularly pernicious, argued Smith, if it is supported by the police power of the state. Indeed, it is possible to interpret Smith's position on this point even more strongly — a faithful follower of Adam Smith would probably say that monopolies can only exist if they receive a governmental sanction, for otherwise competition would quickly destroy them. Smith felt that the corporation, just being invented as the joint-stock company at this time, could never compete with the flexible and aggressive individual proprietor, guided by his self interest. Thus, the corporation could be entrusted only with repetitive and boring tasks, such as running turnpikes and river barges. Smith would certainly have disliked giant geographic monopolists, such as the East India Company. The charging of "artificial prices," well above the cost of production, would only be possible because of regulations, mainly governmental — such as statutes of apprenticeship. On the whole, however, Smith believed that the self-interest of the individual entrepreneur would challenge such restrictions, and that competition would win in the long run.

Finally, Smith objected to mercantilistic restrictions on foreign trade using an idea elaborated by David Hume a bit earlier — the so-called "price-specie-flow mechanism." The P.S.F.M. says that a favorable balance of trade leading to an inflow of gold and a subsequent expansion of the money stock in the mercantilistic country would tend to be self-reversing. To focus on this a bit more slowly, the mercantilists wanted an excess of exports over imports (X >M). In turn, such a favorable balance of trade would lead to an inflow of precious metals — Au, Ag would be rising (Au, Ag are the chemical symbols for gold and silver, dimly remembered from my disastrous career as a freshman chemistry major) would be going up in the mercantilistic nation. This increase in gold holdings, in turn, will increase that country's money supply — usually by a multiplied amount, since gold usually would serve as legal banking system reserves. An expansion in the money supply would generally tend to be inflationary — the so-called "Quantity Theory of Money" asserts that the price level is directly and proportionately dependent upon the stock of money (about which more later in this chapter). The rise in prices would now make imports much more attractive, and decrease the relative competitiveness of exports. Thus, the larger the favorable trade balance, said David Hume and Adam Smith, the more surely it would lead to monetary expansion and inflation in that country — leading to its inevitable reversal. Policies designed to assure a favorable trade balance at all costs were inefficient both theoretically (the concept of absolute advantage) and practically (the specie-flow theory). In connection with this latter concept, there is a very strong suggestion that the larger the favorable trade balance, the more quickly it would be reversed. (This tendency *should* also hold in the long run in today's world — a favorable balance of trade should expand demand and lead to upward price pressure.

However, Japan and West Germany have managed to have both low inflation and trade surpluses for quite a few years.)[5]

The "Invisible Hand"

In addition to providing theoretical and practical arguments against the mercantilistic policies and practices, *The Wealth of Nations* also began to present a general world-view of competitive capitalism, which placed a great deal of faith on the curative powers of a free-market economy. Adam Smith began the science of economics, which seeks to explain the allocation of resources and the distribution of income. He and his followers assume complete rationality in decision-making by business firms and individuals. Business firms will leave unprofitable industries, attracted by greater profit opportunities in other sectors of the economy. Rational consumers will shop around for the best possible buy. In the long run, labor and capital will be employed efficiently — and the role of the government was to be relatively minor. Smith sought to describe the workings of a free-market economy in the absence of mercantilistic regulations — in a sense, to prove that the rational pursuit of enlightened self-interest will lead to "the greatest good for the greatest number."

Smith's view of business activity and profit maximization by individual firms was quite benign on balance. While he did not use the term *caveat emptor* to describe the functioning of free markets, a brief discussion of this concept may be instructive. The literal translation of *caveat emptor* is "let the buyer beware," interpreted in the world of the 1990's as the idea that consumers should be extremely cautious and wary, since they are likely to be tricked or cheated by business firms. Therefore, they need legal or special protection of some sort — a Consumers' Product Safety Corporation sponsored by the government or a special local TV or radio station service looking after consumer's interests, at a minimum. The 1776 interpretation of this concept by Adam Smith was vastly different — businessmen could not exploit their customers, simply because alert customers would themselves search for the highest quality product at the lowest price. Prices can be kept above what Smith calls the "natural price" only by governmental intervention. This point is aptly summarized by the following paragraph from *The Wealth of Nations:*

> . . . *Consumption is the sole end and purpose of all production; and the interest of the producer ought to be attended to, only so far as it may be necessary for promoting that of the consumer. The maxim is so perfectly self-evident, that it would be absurd to attempt to prove it. But in the mercantile system, the interest of the consumer is almost constantly sacrificed to that of the producer; and it seems to*

---

[5] Why is this so? An interesting discussion could be developed here — certainly a key point is that money growth is no longer automatically linked to gold inflows or foreign exchange reserves. Governments are also able to discourage imports and encourage exports in a number of ways.

consider production, and not consumption, as the ultimate end and object of all in-dustry and commerce.[6]

While Adam Smith had not yet understood the concept of *marginal utility*, which was explicitly elaborated only about a hundred years later, the basic idea of demand adjusting to supply and vice versa are easily learned from a careful reading of *The Wealth of Nations*. While Smith did not use diagrams, a brief review of elementary microeconomics is in order.

In Figure 3, the initial equilibrium of supply and demand is at a price of $2.95 and a quantity of mousetraps of 1000 per week. An increase in the wages of labor, a higher interest rate, or a higher rent for the land on which mousetrap factories are situated (or a tax rise) reduces supply from S_0 to S_1. The leftward shift in the supply curve reduces the quantity bought from 1000 units per week to only 800, while the price rises from $2.95 to $3.50. Those consumers deciding not to buy mousetraps at the new higher price are those for whom the marginal utility of one additional mousetrap is the lowest. As you learned in the beginning economics course, another way of explaining the reduction in quantity demanded is by referring to *income and substitution effects*. As the market adjusts from the old equilibrium at E to the new equilibrium at E^1, those consumers deciding not to buy mousetraps at the higher price of $3.50 are both those with low incomes as well as those who would rather buy something else, in assessing the marginal utility of a dollar of their spending. Indeed, they may be "the poor," but they may also be rich people owning two or three mousetraps — and deciding, very rationally, that one more mousetrap would have been nice to have at $2.95, but not at $3.50. The rise in the market price forces the marginal consumers out of the bidding. Some may leave the market because they cannot afford the product, but most are probably buying something else due to the substitution effect.

Conversely, competition among sellers also contributes to an efficient long-run equilibrium. To paraphrase Adam Smith, when we go to a butcher, a baker or a brewer, it is not necessary to appeal to their benevolence, to assure them of your political loyalty, or to bring up old school and family ties. Very simply, it is in their self-interest under capitalism to provide you with the best products at the lowest price. The "invisible hand" is very simply the process of competition — buyers are bidding against each other to pay the *highest* price for a particularly choice cut of meat, while the butchers are each trying to undercut the other by offering it at the *lowest* possible cost. In an often-quoted passage, Adam Smith says that each seller

> *. . . endeavours as much as he can both to employ his capital in the support of do-mestic industry, and so to direct that industry that its produce may be of the greatest value; every individual necessarily labours to render the annual revenue of the society as great as he can. He generally, indeed, neither intends to promote*

---

[6] Adam Smith, *An Inquiry into the Nature and Causes of the Wealth of Nations*, (The Modern Library, 1985), p. 338.

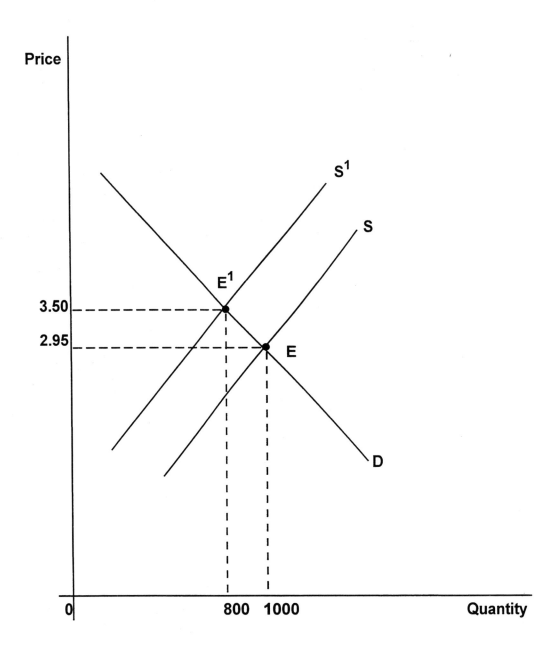

Figure 3.

*the public interest, nor knows how much he is promoting it....(He) intends only his
own security; and by directing that industry in such a manner as its produce may
be of the greatest value, he intends only his own gain, and he is in this, as in
many other cases, led by an invisible hand to promote an end which was no part
of his intention. Nor is it always the worse for the society that it was no part of it.
But pursuing his own interest he frequently promotes that of the society more ef-
fectually than when he really intends to promote it. I have never known much
good done by those who affected to trade for the public good." [7]*

In Figure 4, equilibrium is again given by the intersection of D_0 and S_0 at a mousetrap
price of $2.95 and a quantity exchanged of 1000 mousetraps per week initially. Now
suppose that the price of cat-food falls, and there is a downward shift in the demand for
mousetraps to D_1. The price per unit declines to $2.50 and only 900 mousetraps can
be sold at a "reasonable return" then. As the market adjusts from E to E^1, it is the
marginal producer who gets forced out — his production cost per unit is, say $2.75. At
E, he was still in the mousetrap-making business, earning a modest profit of 20 cents
per trap, but At E^1, he is losing a quarter per unit, and will start looking around for a
new field of business. Again, while the marginal producer may be "poor" and operating
a "small" business, that is not necessarily the case.

Smith explained this principle very clearly. The "natural price" of any commodity
would be determined by wages, rent, interest and profit accruing to the factors of
production used to make the mousetrap. If the market price rose above this long-run
production cost, new firms would be attracted to the industry and existing ones would
be trying to expand their scale of output. On the other hand, industries where the
representative firm was not earning enough to meet the full costs of production — where
the market price was temporarily below the natural price — would just be shrinking in
size. To quote Smith again:

"*...The quantity of any commodity brought to market naturally suits itself to the
effectual demand. It is in the interest of all those who employ their land, labour,
or stock, in bringing any commodity to market, that the quantity never should exceed the effectual demand; and it is the interest of all other people that it never
fall short of that demand." [8]*

Most classical microeconomics, later explained more formally and mathematically
by Alfred Marshall at the end of the 19th century, can be found in Adam Smith's
path-breaking book. The philosophy of individualism and rationality are the corner-
stones of Smith's analysis. Thus, the benevolent nature of free-market competition was
clearly recognized by Smith, who also provided convincing arguments for limiting the
role of government in order to give the "invisible hand" a better opportunity to guide the
affairs of mankind. As noted above, in his day Smith felt that corporations or "joint-stock
companies" were only suited to routine and riskless tasks, such as banking, insurance,

---

[7] *Ibid.*, p. 225.
[8] *Ibid.*, p. 58

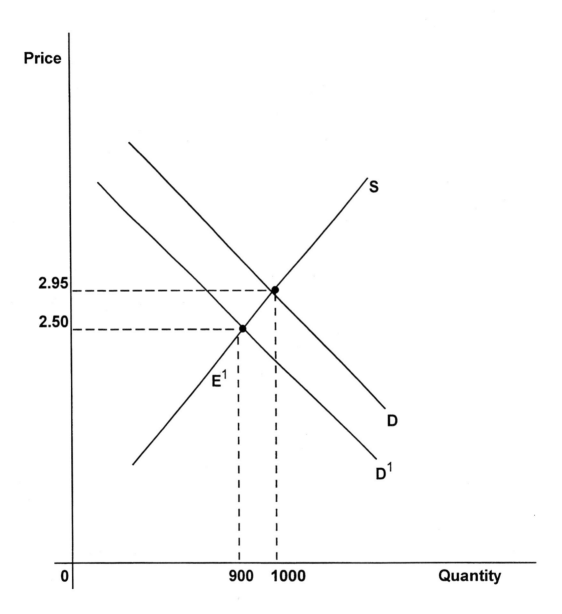

Figure 4.

and public utilities, but could not compete with the individual entrepreneur in other fields of business activity. As far as the government is concerned, Smith would certainly approve of national defense and law-and-order expenditures, and "defending the dignity of the magistrate or the sovereign." Smith would possibly sanction also outlays for education and public utilities, such as roads and ports, but seek to employ a "benefits-received" principle in paying for most other projects. For example, as Smith pointed out:

> . . . The expense of institutions for education and religious instruction, is likewise, no doubt, beneficial to the whole society, and may therefore, without injustice, be defrayed by the general contribution of the whole society. This expense, however, might perhaps with equal propriety, and even with some advantage, be defrayed altogether by those who receive the immediate benefit of such education and instruction, or by the voluntary contribution of those who think they have occasion for either one or the other.[9]

Smith is often viewed by contemporary economists as a rather naive defender of free market economics — indeed, as an apologist (the modern word might be "spin doctor") for capitalism. On a closer reading of Smith, he seems to approve of the growth of trade and commerce — the rationalism of the market challenging feudal pretensions and social stratification. Yet, he clearly recognizes at least two major problems — "alienation" and an unequal distribution of income. The worker, according to Smith, becomes "as stupid and ignorant as it is possible for a human creature to become." Not only is he unable to carry on a rational conversation, or have any "generous, noble, or tender sentiments," but he also becomes corrupted in his physical health as well (Al Bundy?). He is "incapable of exerting his strength with vigor and perseverence, in any other employment than that to which he has become bred." He does become ever more specialized in his particular task, but at the "expense of his intellectual, social, and martial virtues." Secondly, in any society the poor provide both for themselves and "the enormous luxury of their Superiors." The rich can indulge themselves in "every sort of ignoble and sordid sensuality" (I did think of Orange County when I read that), in many cases by simply receiving rent and interest. Also, all of the "indolent and frivolous retainers upon a Court" (White House staff?) are fed, clothed and housed by the labor of those paying taxes. In a society of 100,000 families, we will find the richest 100 living very well indeed — who don't labor at all, but "either by violence, or by the orderly oppression of Law," make more than the next 10,000 families in it. And yet, Smith concludes all that on a positive note — the market system grows so rapidly and produces so much, that there is enough "to gratify the slothful and oppressive profusion of the great," and to supply abundantly the wants of artisans and peasants.[10]

---

[9] *Ibid.*, p. 483. A thorough-going Smithian would be horrified, one would think, by our system of heavily-subsidized and government-guaranteed loans to college students, for example.

[10] Further detailed discussion of all that can be found in Peter Minowitz, *Profits, Priests, and Princes: Adam Smith's Emancipation of Economics from Politics and Religion* (Stanford University Press, 1993). See also Patricia H. Werhane, *Adam Smith and His Legacy for Modern Capitalism* (Oxford University Press, 1991), and Jerry Z. Muller, *Adam Smith in His Time and Ours: Designing a Decent Society* (Free Press, 1993).

Classical Macroeconomics

In this section, we will construct a "straw-man" for the sole purpose of demolishing it. The five ideas of so-called "classical macroeconomics" will seem simplistic even to most beginning students. Certainly a full professor of economics at Cambridge or Yale would never have endorsed them in the form in which they will be presented, but we can also see that they had some relevance to the 19th century, when the overall level of national income was considerably lower. It might also be noted that most classical economists were mainly interested in microeconomics — assuming that markets would work. If that was the case, special problems of macroeconomic stability should not arise. Or, if they did, they would be self-correcting. The so-called "classical economics" is represented by the thinking of Alfred Marshall (1842-1924), who published his influential *Principles of Economics* in 1890 — continuing the explorations of Adam Smith, David Ricardo, and John Stuart Mill. In the twentieth century, Marshall's student and his successor at Cambridge, Arthur C. Pigou (1877-1959), is often mentioned along with Irving Fisher (1867-1947) of Yale University as representing classical (or sometimes, neo-classical) macroeconomics. Since most classical economists were interested primarily in problems of value and distribution (in essence, microeconomics), and assumed that macroeconomic issues (full employment and price stability) would resolve themselves more or less automatically, it seems a bit unfair to fault them for not developing a fully-specified macroeconomic framework. Further, let us mention a second introductory comment, to which we shall return, which is that economic theory tends to follow changes in the economic behavior of the "real world" with a fairly substantial lag. In other words, Marshall was probably writing about the "real world" of the 1860's and 1870's, while Pigou and Fisher were describing reality around the turn of the century, or even earlier. (As we shall see in Chapter 5, Marx was probably greatly influenced by the economic reality of the 1820's and 1830's, writing in the 1860's.)

Say's Law

With these warnings firmly in mind, let us now turn to an exposition of five key macroeconomic precepts of "classical macroeconomics," which suggests that the economy tends to equilibrium at full employment. The first of these is Say's Law, named after a French contemporary of David Ricardo's, Jean-Baptiste Say, which says very simply: "Supply creates its own demand." Somewhat more exactly, the basic insight of Say's Law is to say that increases in output should produce an increase in household income sufficient to buy an equivalent value to whatever is being produced. In terms of a simple example, if one additional pair of shoes costing $79.95 is produced, that means that wages, rent, interest, and profit exactly equal to $79.95 are being ultimately paid to various households — sufficient value to buy an equivalent of the increase in output. This suggests that there should never exist a general "glut" of commodities produced but not bought. Still, quite obviously, the recipients of additional income or purchasing power are not required to turn right around and consume all of the additional income that they may receive — they are, of course, perfectly free to save, or withhold from the circular flow of consumption spending, a significant part of their income that is received. Under ordinary circumstances, they are unlikely to hold onto cash received — literally, to stash it away under the matress (or bury it in the back-yard), but this conceivably could happen. If the money is deposited in a financial institution or used to buy open-market securities, it is quite likely to return to the circular flow of spending.

Loanable Funds

Thus, a second classical idea concerns the use of savings — this is the so-called "loanable funds" theory of interest, an idea challenged by Keynes and the Keynesians, as we shall see later. The demand for loanable funds, I, is identical with the Keynesian concept of the "marginal efficiency of capital." As can be seen in Figure 5, a high interest rate in the market for loanable funds will mean a low demand for borrowing by investors, while a low interest rate would elicit a high demand for such borrowing. The level of investment spending therefore, will be inversely related to the market rate of interest — at an interest rate of 24%, F_0 of investment projects would be undertaken, while at 12%, it might come to F_1, and, finally, at 8%, the total could be F_2 in seemingly profitable investments. On the other side of the market, savings, the classicists argued, would be directly or positively related to the market rate of interest. Hypothetically, at an interest rate of 24%, a total of F_3 would be saved, while a 12% interest rate might elicit total savings of F_4.

As suggested by Figure 5, saving and investment would be at an equilibrium level of F_2 with a market interest rate of 8%. It might even be suggested that 8% is the "natural" rate of interest — that rate of interest at which society's "time-preference" for present consumption is just exactly equal to the "marginal productivity" of capital. This theory is closely associated with the writings of noted Austrian economist Eugen von Bohm-Bawerk in the 1870's.

If the market interest rate temporarily rises above the natural interest rate — say at 24%, as shown in Figure 5, the level of saving, (at F_3), would greatly exceed desired investment (of only F_0). In the classical world, savers would rush to buy bonds, which would bid up bond prices and lower their interest rates. Thus, in a recession, saving would initially exceed investment, but interest rates would thereby be reduced, due to the inflow of excess savings into the bond market, leading the economy back to equilibrium. In the world of our graphic example, a market interest rate below 8% would generate an excess of investment demand above available savings, causing a short-lived inflationary boom. As business firms sought to borrow more, to issue new bonds in excess of F_2, bond prices would fall and interest rates would go back up to "natural" levels. Thus, classical economists would tend to view recessions in economic activity as being associated with temporary and self-reversing "over-saving" or, on the other hand, temporary inflationary booms with "over-investment" — both moving back toward equilibrium as the interest rate moved back toward its natural level.

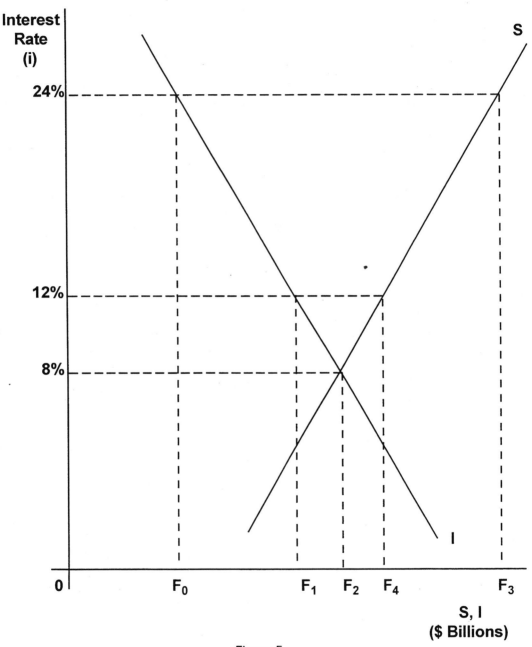

Figure 5.

Marginal Productivity

A third classical notion in macroeconomics concerns the relationship between wage rates and the level of employment. The classicists all viewed unemployment as essentially "voluntary" and, therefore, temporary — as the result of workers being unwilling to accept the prevailing wage rate, which was to be equal to the marginal revenue productivity of labor. Let us consider that idea. Imagine a winter day in London around the turn of the century. As you and your good friend Billings sat in a cozy warm carriage in snowy London in 1897, and drove past a dark factory with a long line of unemployed workers snaking around the corner, you might have been tempted to say: "I say, Billings, look at those poor blokes! They're shivering from the cold air — couldn't the government do something?" Billings, with his handsome income from a small rubber estate in Penang, would probably have replied: "Good heavens, old chap, what maudlin sentimentality! Didn't you pay attention in Professor Marshall's lecture on wage rates? A worker's marginal productivity will equal his wage rate — or else he's out of work, don't you see?" So you said: "Oh, yes, in a few months, we'll pass this way again, and those unsightly lines of the unemployed will have disappeared." "Yes, yes, you've got it, old chap," says Billings. "It's all for the best." You and Billings could then concentrate on an enjoyable lunch-time game of whist or cribbage, without any undue pangs of guilt. One might even hear some chap mutter "Laissez faire!" at the next table...

That little anecdote is a bit of a caricature, suggesting that all classical economists had a cruel disdain for the plight of the unemployed, which obviously was not the case. Furthermore, there certainly is a grain of truth in the *marginal productivity theory*. As you learned in beginning micro-economics, in many production processes, capital and labor are substitutable for each other — and at lower wages, more workers would be used instead of labor-saving machinery (or, at least, the temptation to adopt such machinery would be smaller). Certainly, from the viewpoint of the individual firm, or even an entire industry, a lower relative cost for labor would tend to increase employment. How quickly unemployment would be eliminated is another question — it may well be that the next time that you and Billings took that fancy carriage through a working-class neighborhood, six months later, with the same men lining up for work that there might be unpleasantness of some sort.

You have probably heard that economics is often called "the dismal science". To a considerable extent, that term (coined by Carlyle) appears to be associated with an early version of the marginal productivity theory, known as the "Iron Law of Wages." Writing around 1800, roughly a contemporary of David Ricardo (who held similar views), an English clergyman named Thomas Robert Malthus wrote a very pessimistic little tract, *An Essay on the Principle of Population,* which argued that, in the long run, population tends to increase geometrically (1, 2, 4, 8, 16, 32, and so on). At the time of his writing, the population of America had doubled in the space of twenty-five years, as an example. On the other hand, food production, limited by land quality and availability, could only increase arithmetically, argued Parson Malthus. Thus, there would be an inevitable tendency for output per capita to shrink — historically, explosive human population growth had been held down mainly by "positive checks" (all negative, in fact, such as wars, famine, and disease). Workers' wages would tend to fluctuate around the subsistence level is the central message of the Iron Law of Wages. If wages temporarily rose above the minimum necessary to provide for food, clothing, shelter, and raise enough workers to replace the labor force, the working poor will produce more children — and in 12-to-15 years, wages will have to fall below subsistence to eliminate the surplus workers. A grim theory, indeed, — with a heartless message for policy, the idea that "the relief of the poor defeats its own purpose." For Mr. Malthus himself and those of his social status, the possibility of "preventitive checks" was mentioned — such as chastity and late marriage. To conclude — avoid temptation and wait until you can support a family, for the upper classes, and not much hope for any improvement for the lower.

While later writing repudiated the Iron Law of Wages, as many workers in America and Western Europe earned wages well above subsistence and joined a rapidly growing middle class, the basic approach of the "classical school" to the problem of unemployment was microeconomic in nature. Unemployment was viewed as temporary, usually associated with business cycles, and would be eliminated by market forces, assisted by individual effort. Even after World War II and the Keynesian Revolution, most people still felt that jobless persons should do something about their plight themselves — search harder, accept a lower wage or an unpleasant job temporarily, seek more education and improve skills, and so on. It is only very recently that unemployment has become viewed as nearly exclusively a macroeconomic problem, to be solved by public sector job creation programs and/or stimulative government policies.

Another aspect of market-oriented adjustment to a less than full employment situation in classical economics involves the stabilizing effect of falling prices in a recession. As the general level of prices decreases, the purchasing power of money balances rises. This tendency of existing cash holdings to be worth more and more in a recession is known as the *Pigou Effect*. Clearly, if you have $1000 in cash or in the bank and the price index is at 100, your purchasing power will be double its original level, if all prices fall to 50% of their previous level. Falling prices are generally also associated with lower interest rates, so that the price of bonds (and their overall purchasing power) will rise as well. (A quick example — a bond issued last year, when interest rates were 10%, sold for $1000 and paid $100 per year. If interest rates this year are 5%, new bonds paying $50 annually are now being sold for $1000. What's your old bond worth? Well, that depends on when it matures, but surely a good deal more than $1000.) However, without getting into long and involved analysis of bonds, whether it matters if they are government vs. private and the relevance of other financial assets, the basic insight of the Pigou Effect is the argument that the value of real balances, M_s/P (the money supply divided by the price level) rises in recessions. The real wealth of existing wealth-holders rises, and eventually that should translate itself into a higher level of consumption spending, serving to push the whole economy back toward a full-employment equilibrium.

The Gold Standard

A fourth argument that could be used to support the self-adjusting and stabilizing system of classical macroeconomics concerns the operation of the classical gold standard. With a few lapses, mainly associated with wars, all major currencies were then freely convertible into gold and, therefore, each other. This system of currency convertibility and relative price stability lasted from the 1790's to the 1930's, roughly a century and a half. We have already mentioned briefly its central idea — the specie-flow theory of David Hume and Adam Smith. A country with a balance of trade surplus would tend to experience inflation, as gold flowed in and the money supply expanded, while a deficit in international trade would rather quickly lead to a domestic contraction and falling prices in that country.

Until 1931, the price of gold was constant at $20.67 per ounce and the gold content of both the British pound and the American dollar was fixed. Any suggestion that this could be altered in any way would immediately brand you as a "dangerous Bolshevik." As a result of treating the rules of the international gold standard as a given, as something almost pre-ordained, the exchange rates of most major countries remained fixed. For example, during this era the pound sterling was equal to $4.87, give or take a few pennies either way. This stability of exchange rates was readily assured by the operation of impersonal market forces, by the working of the system of so-called "gold points," which were the upper and lower limits of exhange rates during the gold standard era. If we assume that it costs five cents to ship a British pound's worth of gold from New York to London, what would be the most that you would ever pay for 1000 pounds sterling in a New York bank? Let's say that you walked into J.P. Morgan & Co. in 1902 and they wanted to charge you $5000 — would you pay that? Of course not — you could always go down the street to the mint, and exchange your dollars for gold. How much would your 1000 pounds cost you that way? Obviously no more than $4920 — $4.87 for the gold in a pound sterling plus five cents for the shipping, for a maximum price for pounds in New York of $4.92. (Yes, that would include insurance and everything — it was more than a nickel in the early days of the gold standard and a bit less than that later, due to lower transport costs and better communications.)

When would the Amercian dollar move toward $4.92, the *upper gold shipping point?* Imagine a graph with supply and demand in equilibrium at $4.87 (the so-called "mint par"). What might make a pound sterling more expensive? Or, to use another way of saying it, what would cause a depreciation of the U.S. dollar? Clearly, either a rightward shift in the demand for pounds, or a leftward shift in the supply schedule of pounds — or a little bit of both? What might cause such shifts? Let's get back to the answer after the next paragraph. Now imagine you're a British tobacco importer in 1906, needing to pay $10,000 to a North Carolina shipper. What is the lowest dollar amount that you would accept for a pound sterling in buying these dollars? The *lower gold shipping point* would be $4.82 — because you could always buy $4.87 for a British pound in gold and ship it for a nickel. Thus, the absolute limits on exchange rate movements were set up by these gold points — the dollar could never be lower than $4.92, or more expensive than $4.82 to one pound.

The answer to the question we posed just a moment ago now becomes obvious, doesn't it? If the exchange rate is moving toward $4.92, there is an *excess demand* for pounds sterling, due to inflation in the U.S., all other things being equal. The supply of pounds would be reduced, since the U.S. exports to Great Britain would have decreased. In the reverse situation, an *excess supply* of pounds would push the rate toward $4.82, the lowest amount an alert British trader would accept for his domestic money, which would be due to inflation in the prices of English goods. A U.S. balance of trade deficit with the U.K. (due to U.S. inflation) would move the exchange rate toward $4.92. This, in itself, would have a corrective impact, the slightly higher dollar price for pounds making imports from the U.K. more expensive and causing U.S. exports to look more attractive to the U.K.

One final idea needs to be introduced here — the concept of "the rules of the game." Before World War I, the London money market was the hub of the international financial system, and the Bank of England unquestionably the most important financial institution in the world. If the U.K. was experiencing inflation and the pound was beginning to weaken (move below $4.87 relative to the American dollar, say, to $4.84, who in London would feel most threatened? If British importers were tempted to turn their pounds into gold, from where would this gold ultimately have to come? Initially, the importers might get the gold from their commercial bankers "in the City," but where would the "city banks" turn to replenish their reserves? Yes, of course, the Bank of England would be very worried about a falling pound — and would be thinking about taking some restrictive measures at this time, i.e., well before the exchange rate fell to its theoretical minimum. The "rules of the game" idea refers to the policy to increase in the "Bank Rate" (the discount rate charged by the Bank of England) that would take place almost automatically, if the pound sterling was falling — and short-term funds flowing out of London. Conversely, if short-term capital was coming in, and the pound appreciating, there would be a tendency for the central bank's interest rate to be lowered. Still, the burden of adjustment would primarily fall upon the central bank of the deficit country. The main target of classical monetary policy was the exchange rate, and the only tool was the central bank's lending rate.

While the United States did not have a central banking institution before World War I (the Federal Reserve System was established in 1914), our largest commercial banks also generally participated in the "rules of the game" system, raising their interest rates when the dollar's purchasing power in international trade was falling. An appreciation of the dollar would conversely signal that interest rates could be lowered — nevertheless, as noted, the burden of making adjustments was primarily upon countries experiencing balance of payments deficits and a resulting weakening of their currencies. Thus, inflation in any given country would lead to a shrinkage in its exports and an expansion in imports; the trade balance deficit would cause a fall in its exchange rate; and, the decline in the exchange rate would require its central bank to increase the discount rate. This would lead to a general rise in other interest rates ("tight money"), a decline in investment, a decrease — or a slower rate of increase — in national income and employment. In short, the "discipline" of the currency depreciation under the gold standard would quickly reverse the inflationary policies followed by any government.

The benefits of the gold standard, essentially lasting until 1931, though limping rather badly after World War I, were considerable. Fixed exchange rates greatly facilitated foreign trade and investment. Earlier in this chapter, I mentioned your friend Billings, with whom you were lunching at the club; we had said that his uncle had left him a small estate in Penang, which paid him 500 pounds per year. Think about the mind-boggling implications of such a statement today! Do you know of any real investments that could be described in terms of a fixed annual income? I do not, except perhaps for a portfolio consisting entirely of bonds or CD's. To say that an estate in Penang yields an annual net income of 500 pounds is to say volumes about the stability of prices, costs, exchange rates, and output in those bygone days! Another benefit of the classical gold standard was its ability to discipline inflationary monetary and fiscal policies of participating governments through the "rules of the game" system explained above. On balance, this resulted in low and stable interest rates — prior to World War II, the all-time high in the New York Federal Reserve Bank's discount rate was 7%, a ridiculously high rate used to deal with the inflationary "panic" of 1920-21 (and which was never exceeded until the double-digit inflation of the 1970s). These low interest rates enabled past generations, those of our great-grandparents and even before, to finance investments in bridges, tunnels, and other public utilities that we are still using today. Foreign trade and investment were greatly facilitated, though at the considerable cost of putting domestic economic goals a distant second to the objective of international currency stability.

The Quantity Theory

The fifth, and final, macroeconomic theory of the classical economists is the idea that the price level is directly and proportionally related to the supply of money. In its most rigid form, the Quantity Theory of Money says $\Delta P/P = \Delta M_s/M_s$, where P is the general price level and M_s is the quantity of money (usually defined as currency in circulation plus demand deposits, or transaction accounts). The strong version is associated with the ideas of Irving Fisher of Yale, whose book *The Purchasing Power of Money* (1911) elaborated the argument outlined in this section. Most other economists would use a somewhat weaker statement, $P = f(M_s)$, which says that the price level is primarily a function of the supply of money. It is indeed hard to believe that the inflation rate will exactly equal the rate of growth of the quantity of money.

The Quantity Theory of Money is generally derived from Irving Fisher's Equation of Exchange, $M_sV_t = PT$. In this equation, M_s is the money supply, as defined above, T is the number of transactions per time period (say, one year), and P is the average price of each transaction. V_t is the transactions-velocity of money, always found as a residual, found by taking the dollar value of all transactions in the economy during a given year and dividing that total by the supply of money. Based on data concerning debits to checking accounts, for example, which would include many payments not included in

GNP (payments for intermediate goods and services, transfer payments and financial transactions, in the main), the transactions-velocity of money is more than 50 times per year. A more useful definition of velocity from an operational point of view is the income-velocity of money, as derived from $M_s V_y = PQ = Y$, where Y is simply GNP. M_s is the supply of money, as before, while Q is "real GNP" — currently produced output of final goods and services. The income-velocity of money can be derived simply by dividing GNP in current prices (about \$7.5 trillion or \$7500 billion in the U.S. in 1996) by the money supply (around \$1100 billion), to get a number a bit below 7 times per year.

Using the MV = PQ version, we can finish up our discussion of classical macroeconomics — of the "straw man," which we have constructed for the sake of focusing on Keynesian criticisms of classical views. It is strongly implied by all of the aforementioned arguments that Q, or real GNP, will tend to remain constant at full-employment in any given year. This first assumption is basically due to Say's Law, the idea that supply creates its own demand, and that aggregate demand and aggregate supply will tend to be equal to each other. The second assumption covers a constant velocity of money; given normal circumstances, the number of times that a dollar "turns over" in a given year will be primarily determined by habit and custom. If people are paid once a week, velocity will approximately equal 52; if once a month, V will equal 12 and so on. Such methods of payment and spending patterns change rather slowly if at all. Thirdly, the derivation of the Quantity Theory approach assumes that the price level is essentially a *dependent* variable — that most firms are "price takers." Under conditions of pure competition, you will undoubtedly recall, the firm faces a horizontal demand curve. That means that the individual firm can only adjust its output to prevailing supply-and-demand conditions, but cannot influence the market price by its actions. If all three of these conditions are met, with both Q and V basically constant and P a dependent variable, the Quantity Theory of Money will hold true — the price level will depend upon changes in the supply of money.

Summary

Though classical macroeconomics may have limited validity for industrialized countries today, it taught that free-market forces would lead to a stable equilibrium at the full-employment level. First, Say's Law argued that the market for goods and services would produce an equilibrium of supply and demand, since increases in output would also imply higher incomes for consumers. Second, the "loanable funds" theory strongly suggested that the bond market would contribute to such equilibrating tendencies — temporary over-saving would cause interest rates to fall, and investment to rise, until equilibrium of S = I at the "natural rate of interest" was obtained. Third, unemployment would be cured by a fall in the relative price of labor, causing firms to substitute labor for capital (and perhaps land). Fourth, a country experiencing unemployment and a recession would also inevitably be subject to falling prices which would lead to an appreciation in "real balances." Fifthly, and finally, the country undergoing a temporary recession would become more competitive, exporting more, gaining a favorable balance of trade. This would lead to higher gold reserves, which would cause an expansion in its money supply.

This whole story, which seems a bit implausible in 1997, and was subject to valid criticism much earlier, was a rather reasonable one for the world as it existed in the 19th century. Most consumers were then governed by Say's Law, since increases in income were generally used to support higher levels of consumption. It was only later in the twentieth century, as the average family's income rose comfortably above subsistence in most Western capitalist countries, that one would have to consider the possibility of significant fluctuations in the consumption-income relationship. A working-man's family in the mid-19th century would quickly spend all of a day's or a week's wages on the necessities of life, i.e., food, shelter and clothing, with little left over. It is only much later that the average family would earn enough so that it would have the luxury of deciding whether to consume now or at some time in the future. As long as discretionary saving did not account for a significant part of national income, Say's Law seems perfectly valid — increased output would generate higher incomes, leading to a greater demand for consumption goods.

As we shall see, there are logical flaws in the "loanable funds" theory of interest rate determination. However, elaborating a bit further the point developed in the previous paragraph, in the 19th century saving tended to equal investment — relatively few people accumulated significant savings in the form of financial assets. Whenever new financial assets were issued, mostly in the form of corporate stocks and bonds, their creation was then usually associated with real investment in plant and equipment. The modern financial system of millions of savers entrusting their funds to thousands of financial institutions had not yet developed. Today financial institutions often invest these funds in uses far removed from productive investment in the local economy — lending in the foreign inter-bank market, buying bonds of various governments and state enterprises, trading in mortgages and consumer credit derivatives, and so on. A hundred years ago, it is fairly safe to assert, most lending was done by commercial banks and other financial institutions for "productive" purposes in the local market.

Thirdly, the marginal productivity theory of wage determination does not appear as far-fetched in the historical context of a hundred years ago as it does today (or certainly did even in the 1930's). As mentioned briefly earlier, the possibility of substituting capital for labor generally exists in rather simple industrial processes as well as in agriculture. Furthermore, a hundred years ago the labor union movement in the United States was virtually non-existent and rather weak in Europe, and wages could fall in a recession. Indeed, you will recall that Samuel Gompers set up the American Federation of Labor (AFL) in 1886, but that a number of court cases in the U.S. even around the turn of the 20th century held that labor unions were conspiracies in restraint of trade (the Clayton Act in 1914 specifically exempted labor unions from anti-trust laws). Large and powerful labor unions covering entire industries, engaging in collective bargaining with the legal encouragement of government (the Wagner Act of 1935), were not developed until the 1930's with the formation of the Congress of Industrial Organizations (CIO). When the classical economists were writing about wage determination a hundred years ago, labor markets were rather competitive and a lower money wage would have created more jobs, all other things being equal.

The fourth theoretical argument, as you will recall, pointed out the stabilizing properties of the price-specie flow mechanism, the tendency of the economy to regain equilibrium due to the influence of the foreign trade sector. Assume that the U.S. is experiencing inflation and that the U.K. is not. The dollar's purchasing power would fall below $4.87 for a pound sterling in the exchange market (let's say, it now costs $4.90 per pound) — the U.S. export sector would tend to contract while British export sector jobs would expand. Actually, in reality exchange rates would seldom change much. In the fifty years or so before World War I, very small changes in the "Bank Rate" in London were usually sufficient to keep both inflations and recessions in check throughout the gold standard world. If the inflation in the U.S. persisted, interest rates here would rise, while the rates in the U.K. would fall, in line with the "rules of the game." Government interference in foreign trade and payments was minimal back then, and relatively small changes in foreign exchange rates and interest rate levels were sufficient to push participating economies in the direction of full employment equilibrium with stable prices.

Finally, the Quantity Theory of Money also generally works quite reliably in the long run. While Irving Fisher's argument that a 10% increase in the money supply will result in a 10% rise in prices would be accepted by few economists today, it refers to a much simpler and poorer economy and a more rudimentary financial system. Classical economists viewed money primarily as a medium of exchange, used for transactions purposes — an increase in the money supply would tend to lead to an increase in spending for goods and services. John Maynard Keynes, writing in 1936, recognized that money also serves as a store of value — dividing the total demand for money into transactions, precautionary and speculative motives. Under certain conditions, such as at the time of his writing, in a deep recession with falling prices, any given increase in the money supply would probably not lead to any increase in prices at all. It would have been difficult to increase the money stock back then, since few people were interested in borrowing. Indeed, if the Federal Reserve had been able to stop the contraction of money supply in 1931, the economic history of the U.S. would have taken a far different course; it is not too far out to suggest that World War II might have never happened. ■

SUGGESTED READINGS

Backhouse, Roger, *A History of Modern Economic Analysis* (Basil Blackwell, 1985).

De Cecco, Marcello, *The International Gold Standard: Money and Empire* (Frances Pinter, 1984).

Eichengreen, Barry J., *Golden Fetters: The Gold Standard and the Great Depression, 1919–1939* (Oxford University Press, 1992).

Heilbroner, Robert L., *The Making of Economic Society,* Seventh Ed. (Prentice-Hall, 1985).

Heilbroner, Robert L., (ed.), *The Essential Adam Smith* (W.W.Norton,1986).

Hunt, E.K., *History of Economic Thought: A Critical Perspective* (Harper Collins, 1992).

Minowitz, Peter, *Profits, Priests, and Princes: Adam Smith's Emancipation of Economics from Politics and Religion* (Stanford University Press, 1993).

Muller, Jerry L., *Adam Smith in His Time and Ours* (Free Press, 1993).

Reisman, D.A., *Adam Smith's Sociological Economics* (Croom Helm,1976).

Rima, Ingrid H., *Development of Economic Analysis,* Fourth Ed. (Richard D. Irwin, 1986).

Rockwell, Llewellyn H., Jr. (ed.), *The Gold Standard: An Austrian Perspective* (Lexington Books, 1985).

Shelton, Judy, *Money Meltdown* (The Free Press, 1994).

Sowell, Thomas, *Classical Economics Reconsidered* (Princeton University Press, 1974).

Werhane, Patricia, *Adam Smith and His Legacy for Modern Capitalism* (Oxford University Press, 1991).

Wood, John Cunningham, *Adam Smith: Critical Assessments* (Croom Helm,1983).

CHAPTER THREE

THE KEYNESIAN REVOLUTION

*T*his chapter begins with a brief overview of Keynes' criticisms of classical macroeconomics, equally briefly reviews the basic algebra of some simple Keynesian models,
and summarizes the standard macroeconomic system presented in most beginning
economics courses. I find it useful to provide a bit of a distinction between the "economics
of Keynes" and "Keynesian economics," and will say a few words about that in the
concluding section. When President Nixon said in 1971 that "we are all Keynesians now,"
I decided that I was one no longer — John Maynard himself probably would not want to
be included in that company. Politicians eagerly seized upon Keynesian economics as a
way of assuring re-election, as reflected by Nixon's remark.

In the previous chapter, we mentioned Irving Fisher of Yale, whose 1911 book, *The
Purchasing Power of Money* provides a useful summary of classical thinking about
macroeconomic issues, dealing primarily with monetary theory. It is interesting to note
the significance of the ordering of words in the title of John Maynard Keynes' most
important book, *The General Theory of Employment, Interest, and Money* (1936),
where money comes in as a distant third in the title. First and most important, as far as
Keynes is concerned, economists should provide a general theory of what forces
determine the level of employment, the first word in his title. The answer to that question,
as we all learned in the Principles course, is that the total aggregate demand, $Y = C + I
+ G + X - M$, is most important, where Y is GNP or national income, C is personal
consumption spending for goods and services, I is investment (increases in business
plant and equipment, new residential construction and changes in business inventories),
G is government purchases of goods and services (both federal and local government,
but not including transfer payments), plus X for exports and minus M for imports of
goods and services. Theoretical niceties concerning interest rates and money are very
much of a secondary order of importance, both in Keynes' title and in his theory.

As far as his critique of classical macroeconomics is concerned, let us begin with one
of Keynes' most famous quotations: "in the long run, we are all dead." That remark is
an apt general summary of his overall assessment of classical economics concerning
their view of the inevitable tendency of an economy to a return to a full-employment
equilibrium with stable prices. While eventually the arguments outlined in the previous

chapter may prove to be valid, in a strict theoretical sense, these tendencies could be given a powerful assist by deliberate government policies, argued Keynes, which could and should be used to stabilize aggregate demand. More specifically, "in the long run, we are all dead" might also be thought of as a basic criticism of the so-called Pigou Effect, briefly defined in the previous chapter. That effect was that falling prices in a recession would increase the purchasing power of existing money balances, M_s/P would rise as the price level fell (another name for the Pigou Effect is the "real-balance effect"). While theoretically it may well be true that real balances appreciate in a recession as prices fall, there are at least two significant practical questions that remain unanswered: first, is the real-balance effect potentially sufficient in its magnitude to counter the reduction in aggregate demand due to an increase in unemployment and, second, how quickly will the newly-rich holders of money balances actually start to increase their consumption spending? As the experience of the decade of the 1930's suggests, it is very possible that cumulative deflationary expectations can neutralize the Pigou Effect entirely for at least several years — if real estate and commodity prices fall by 20% in one year, may it not be likely that they will fall even more the next? Even if you had the cash or deposits in a sound bank, would it not be prudent to wait a bit before buying? Thus, the practical significance of the real-balance effect is today seriously questioned by most economists, particularly in a situation of deflation affecting almost all countries and all markets simultaneously.

Secondly, Keynes was particularly scornful of the "loanable funds theory of interest." While the classical school viewed interest as a *real* phenomenon — a reward for abstinence on the part of consumers, which was also equal to the marginal productivity of capital — Keynes considered the existence of interest as primarily a *monetary* concept, a payment necessary to overcome the liquidity-preference of wealth-holders. In the world of Keynes and the Keynesians, saving does not depend upon the interest rate at all, but is primarily a function of income. As shown by Figure 6, there exists a whole family of savings functions, with S_0 corresponding to some low level national income (Y_0), which would equal investment at an interest rate of i_0, while S_1 at a higher income level would be in equilibrium with investment only if the interest rate were forced down to i_1. Finally, it is possible that income at some hypothetical level of GNP, Y_2 would be so high, leading to S_2, — so that no positive real interest rate would lead to a savings-investment equilibrium. There could be no equilibrium between saving and investment, unless the economy was back to a much lower level of intended savings once again (unless the investment schedule could be shifted rightward ?). In any case, the loanable funds approach is not of much use, since it misrepresented savings behavior by a single schedule, and we might as well start all over again, said Keynes.

Thirdly, the classical treatment of wage determination was criticized by Keynes on both practical and theoretical grounds. As a practical matter, in the 20th century, in England and the U.S., money wages were "sticky" in a downward direction — few union leaders in the troubled and militant 1930's would have dared to go to their membership with the suggestion that a cut in hourly wages might be desirable to keep up overall employment in the industry. After all, this was the era of pitched battles in union

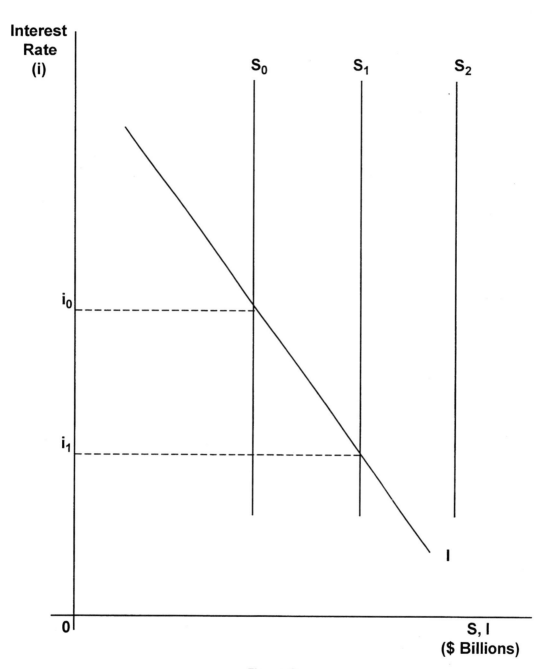

Figure 6.

organizing, with armed strikers on one side and "strike-breakers" on the other. Further-more, theoretically, the impact of a reduction in overall wage rates is probably indeter-minate. As Ingrid Rima has summarized it:

> *"... Involuntary unemployment, according to Keynes' analysis, results if there ex-ists what Keynes termed insufficient aggregate demand. It is not possible to stimulate aggregate demand by forcing workers to accept across-the-board wage cuts. Such cuts impair worker spending and are, in that sense, self-defeating (i.e., they further reduce aggregate demand). Moreover, in a competitive economy, wage cuts engender price cuts. With a falling price level, the real wage effect of cutting money wages is aborted. Thus Keynes argued the necessity of finding an alternative to wage cutting for stimulating aggregate demand."* [1]

That alternative, quite clearly, should be increased government spending — or possibly lower taxes or an increase in the supply of money, but, as we shall see, the overall impact of the latter two alternative policies is likely to be both weaker and less certain than that of a government expenditure boost.

With respect to the price-specie-flow mechanism and the "rules of the game" approach to monetary policy, it should be noted that Keynes had a philosophical aversion to the gold standard, shared today by many, if not most, economists. He called gold "the barbarous relic" — believing that modern economic systems should consist of more sophisticated institutional arrangements. Indeed, if we think about it logically, it does seem a rather silly waste of resources to base a monetary standard on gold. Imagine explaining that system to a Martian. You would have to patiently tell it that our monetary standard was based upon extracting tons of rock from beneath the earth in one part of the planet, such as South Africa, sifting through these tons for a few flakes of the yellow metal in order to collect it and melt it down into bars, which are then shipped —at great risk and expense — across a vast ocean, in order to be buried under the ground once again, in Fort Knox or in the vaults of the Bank of England. Silly, isn't it? In the view of John Maynard Keynes, allowing the foreign trade position of a country to dictate all domestic monetary policies is rather foolish — it is definitely a case of having "the tail wag the dog." To use Keynes' own words in this connection:

> *"... Under the influence of this faulty theory the City of London gradually devised the most dangerous technique for the maintenance of equilibrium which can pos-sibly be imagined, namely, the technique of bank rate coupled with a rigid parity of the foreign exchanges. For this meant that the objective of maintaining a do-mestic rate of interest consistent with full employment was wholly ruled out. Since, in practice, it is impossible to neglect the balance of payments, a means of controlling it was evolved which, instead of protecting the domestic rate of in-terest, sacrificed it to the operation of blind forces. Recently, practical bankers in London have learnt much, and one can almost hope that in Great Britain*

---

[1] Ingrid H. Rima, *Development of Economic Analysis*, Fourth Ed., (Irwin, 1986), p. 421.

*London have learnt much, and one can almost hope that in Great Britain the tech-
nique of bank rate will never be used again to protect the foreign balance in conditions in which it is likely to cause unemployment at home."* [2]

In this regard, Keynes strongly criticized the *laissez-faire* system of the classicists,
and in passing he mentioned mercantilistic writers quite favorably. For Keynes, the
national interest of maintaining full employment was considerably more important than
reliance upon a self-stabilizing system of international trade and payments. Devaluing a
national currency, if need be, would have been much more acceptable to him than a
lengthy period of adjustment to a trade deficit, requiring high interest rates and
considerable unemployment, particularly if many other countries were also trying to
follow this "orthodox" route of dealing with a balance of trade problem by tightening
credit at the same time.

Finally, as we noted in the previous chapter, the most powerful single classical
macroeconomic theory was the Quantity Theory of Money, derived from the Equation of
Exchange, $MV = PQ$. In order for us to say that $P = f(M_s)$ — that the price level essentially
depends upon the supply of money — as noted in the previous chapter, three important
assumptions must hold. First, the level of Q, or real output, must be fixed — basically,
this would be due to Say's Law and the loanable funds theory ($C + S = C + I$ near or at
full employment). Second, the velocity of circulation, V, must also remain unchanged —
as Irving Fisher put it, velocity would be determined by "habit and custom." If money is
considered to be almost totally as a medium of exchange, its annual turnover would be
primarily determined by the frequency of wage and salary payments — about 12 times
per year, if such payments were made monthly, 26 times per year for payments every
two weeks, and so on. Such institutional arrangements would change very slowly over
time, if at all, and V was assumed to remain constant. Thirdly, the price level, P, was to
be viewed as a dependent variable — basically, the pure competition assumption. If all
producers were "price-takers," facing a horizontal demand curve, there could not be any
movements in prices dictated by supply conditions or market power. If these three
conditions all hold true, it is possible to say, as Irving Fisher argued, that an increase of
X percent in the quantity of money will also cause the same X percent increase in the
general level of prices.

In this regard, Keynes came up with another famous line almost as famous as "in
the long run we are all ..." — "there's many a slip 'twixt the cup and the lip."

*"... If, however, we are tempted to assert that money is the drink which stimu-
lates the system to activity, we must remind ourselves that there may be several
slips between the cup and the lip. For whilst an increase in the quantity of money
may be expected, cet. par., to reduce the rate of interest, this will not happen if
the liquidity-preferences of the public are increasing more than the quantity of
money; and whilst a decline in the rate of interest may be expected, cet. par., to
increase the volume of investment, this will not happen if the schedule of the marginal efficiency of capital is falling more rapidly than the rate of interest; and
whilst an increase in the volume of investment may be expected, cet. par., to in-*

marginal efficiency of capital is falling more rapidly than the rate of interest; and whilst an increase in the volume of investment may be expected, cet. par., to increase employment, this may not happen if the propensity to consume is falling off. Finally, if employment increases, prices will rise in a degree partly governed by the shapes of the physical supply functions, and partly by the liability of the wage-unit to rise in terms of money. And when output has increased and prices have risen, the effect of this on liquidity-preference will be to increase the quantity of money necessary to maintain a given rate of interest." [3]

The above paragraph from Keynes himself may appear to be a bit mysterious at first reading. It is, however, a fine summary of his theoretical apparatus — and I would suggest that you return for a re-reading of it after finishing this chapter. (I realize that this chapter is a bit of a rehash of basic macroeconomic theory, and seems a little out of place in a comparative economic systems text, which traditionally contain chapters on Sweden and Yugoslavia. However, I find that many of us appreciate a bit of repetition of material that we ought to have learned before — and that a more thorough understanding of the Keynesian system gives us an insight of how most economists think the U.S. economy presently works.)

Keynesian Algebra: The Basics

While Keynes himself was not ever tempted to summarize *The General Theory* in a couple of equations, many Keynesian economists have done just that. We will discuss three versions of the basic Keynesian model in this section, each just a bit more complicated. The simplest model consists of just three equations — it ignores the special role of government, by simply splitting government spending (G) between consumption (C) and investment (I), and includes tax collections in saving (S) implicitly. Thus, in Model I, in its most general form,

(1) $C = a + bY$

(2) $I = I_0$

(3) $Y = C + I = C + S$

The first equation, the consumption function, has a constant vertical-intercept, a, interpreted as that amount of consumption which would take place even if GNP, or Y, were equal to zero. The slope of the line, b, is called the *marginal propensity to consume* (MPC). In Model I, the MPC plus the marginal propensity to save, MPS, equals one. Thus, the MPS equals (1-b). Investment spending, I, is assumed to be given at I_0 (investment outlays were approved and voted upon by last year's board of directors). Substituting in equation (3), we replace C by (a + bY), and I by I_0, to get from Y = C + I, to:

---

[3]   *Ibid.*,p. 173. *Cet. par.* refers to "ceteris paribus," a phrase meaning "everything else remaining the same."

$$Y = (a + bY) + I_0, \text{ or } Y - bY = a + I_0, \quad (I)$$
$$\text{or } Y = \frac{1}{1-b}(a+I_0)$$

The term outside the parentheses, $1/(1-b)$, will be recognized by one and all as the simple Keynesian multiplier. If, as mentioned above, MPC + MPS = 1, then the multiplier, k, can be defined as:

$$K=\frac{1}{1-MPC'} \text{, or } K=\frac{1}{MPS}$$

Using the latter formula, we can simply say that the multiplier is the reciprocal of the marginal propensity to save. In Model I, the moment that you know the value of either k (the multiplier), or the MPC, or the MPS, you can immediately infer the values of the other two. For example, if the MPC (called b in Equation (I)), is 0.80, the MPS must be 0.20 — and k, the multiplier, equals $1/(1-b)$ or $1/(1-.8)$ or $1/.2$ or 5.0 To use an arithmetic example, assume a = \$700 billion, b = 0.8, and I_0 = \$300 billion. Then, using the summary formula,

$$Y = 1/1 - b(a + I_0),$$

we get

$$Y = 1/.8(700 + 300) = 5(1000) = 5000$$

This level of GNP (or Y) at \$5 trillion would then give us the following table:

Y	C	S	I	C + I
5000	4700	300	300	5000

Note that here the basic equilibrium condition is both S = I, and Y = C + I. The last, column C + I can be regarded as the "creation of income," whereas C + S (the sum of the second and the third column) is the "disposition of income." If we consider the line just printed as the equilibrium for January 1997, and the board of directors of a corporation just voted to increase investment outlays in February by \$20 billion, keeping in mind that b, the marginal propensity to consume, is equal invariably to 0.8 (80 cents out of each dollar newly received will be spend on consumption), we get the following:

Month	Y	C	S	I	C + I
Jan.	5000	4700	300	300	5000
Feb.	5000	4700	300	<u>320</u>	5020
Mar.	5020	4716	304	320	5036
Apr.	5036	4728.8	307.2	320	5048.8
May	5048.8	4739.04	309.76	320	5059.04
	etc.				

Since we know that K, the multiplier, equals $\Delta Y/\Delta I_0$ (the change in GNP divided by the change in autonomous investment, is equal to 5.0 (K = 1/1-MPC = 1/1b = 1/1-.8 = 1/.2

= 5), the final equilibrium (about a year later) will be $100 billion higher than the initial level (the rise in investment of $20 multiplied by five):

	$\underline{Y}$	$\underline{C}$	$\underline{S}$	$\underline{I}$	$\underline{C + I}$
New Equil.	5100	4780	320	320	5100

Thus, the first use of Model I is to illustrate the concept of the simple Keynesian multiplier. To look at a couple of examples, if the MPC = .5, then the MPS = .5, and the multiplier (K) equals 2. If the MPS = 0.1, then the MPC = (fill in the blank mentally) and the multiplier equals ten.

As a slight tangent, it is widely known that the marginal propensity to consume for poor households and individuals is very high. It is quite logical that a person making $10,000 a year would spend 98% for consumption and save perhaps 2%, while an individual earning $100,000 would have, say, an MPC of 0.7 and save $30,000. Logically, this idea can also be applied to countries having different per capita income levels — thus India and China, currently only around $300 to $500 per capita per year, might have an MPC = .95 or even more, might they not? That would imply an MPS of .05, and a multiplier of (fill in the blank). A multiplier as high as 20, or even more, should make it very easy to increase per capita income, shouldn't it? Each investment of a billion rupees or yuan will lead to an increase in aggregate demand of 20 times as much, right? Yes, algebraically, that is certainly correct — yet, is the algebra relevant? Would additional government spending in both of those countries truly result in a sustainable increase in the real standard of living for the average person? Probably not, the increase in aggregate demand, or GNP, would mostly simply lead to higher prices. Even though the multiplier may be very high in poor countries, stimulating aggregate demand (the essence of Keynesian algebra) is vastly less important than considering aggregate supply conditions. Thus, a high multiplier is not necessarily a "good thing."

The second concept that we can discuss briefly in the highly abstract and simplified world of Model I is the so-called "Paradox of Thrift." Going back to the original equilibrium, we have:

$\underline{Y}$	$\underline{C}$	$\underline{S}$	I	$\underline{C + I}$
5000	4700	300	300	5000

If that represents equilibrium in January, but then in February households decide to increase their saving by $100 billion, which simply means that, therefore, consumption must fall by an equivalent amount. Note also continuing declines in March and April:

	$\underline{Y}$	$\underline{C}$	$\underline{S}$	I	$\underline{C + I}$
Feb.	5000	4600	400	300	4900
Mar.	4900	4520	380	300	4820
April	4820	4456	364	300	4756

How long will the contraction continue? What we have basically done here is to shift the consumption function downward by \$100 billion — in the original model, it had been $C = 700 + .8Y$; as people decided to save more, the intercept (a) was reduced, so we now have $C^1 = 600 + .8Y$. Using the formula,

$$Y = 1/1\text{-}b(a + I_0),$$

we plug in $b = 0.8$, $I_0 = 300$ (as before), but a new lower a, to get:

$$Y = 1/1\text{-}.8(600 + 300) = 4500.$$

National income (or GNP) will fall until $Y = 4500$, when $S = I = 300$ once again; unless I changes, Y will fall due to a rise in S. Why is this called "The Paradox of Thrift?" Basically, it brings out the fact that saving in the Keynesian context is always considered a negative act — an increase in aggregate saving means a reduction in consumption (a downward parallel shift in the consumption function), which produces a multiplied reduction in national income, or GNP. This can also be neatly demonstrated graphically, as in Figure 7. The investment function in Model I: is simply a horizontal line at $I_0 = \$300$, while the savings function is the mirror image of the consumption function — if $C = a + bY$, then $S = \text{-}a + (1\text{-}b)Y$. In this case initially $S = \text{-}700 + .2Y$, with $S = I$ at $Y = \$5000$ billion. An increase in savings to $S^1 = \text{-}600 + .2Y$ leads to reduction of Y to \$4500 billion, as we have just seen algebraically. This inverse relationship between saving and income should seem paradoxical to most people, since any family is pretty sure to have a higher income next year as the result of foregoing consumption spending and doing some saving this year. In the Keynesian system, in its standard textbook formulation, the financial markets are completely ignored. An increase in investment does increase saving, through the multiplier process, $S = f(Y) = f(I)$. But the reverse does not hold true, investment is not a function of savings. This may seem quite paradoxical to many of us in a broader sense, since countries such as Japan and West Germany with high savings rates have been able to finance significant capital formation and rapid rates of growth, while the U.S. has had a much lower savings/income ratio. This, of course, is one of the major arguments raised by the "supply-siders," discussed in the next chapter.

Model II is just slightly more complicated — it brings in the government sector in a crude way, and makes consumption a function of disposable income (GNP minus taxes). For the sake of simplicity, let us assume "lump-sum taxes" — every citizen of voting age simply gets a bill on June 1 for his or her share of the annual taxes to be collected, to be paid within a month. In general, we have:

(1) $C = a + b(Y \text{-} T)$

(2) $T = T_0$

(3) $I = I_0$

(4) $G = G_0$

(5) $Y = C + I + G = C + S + T$

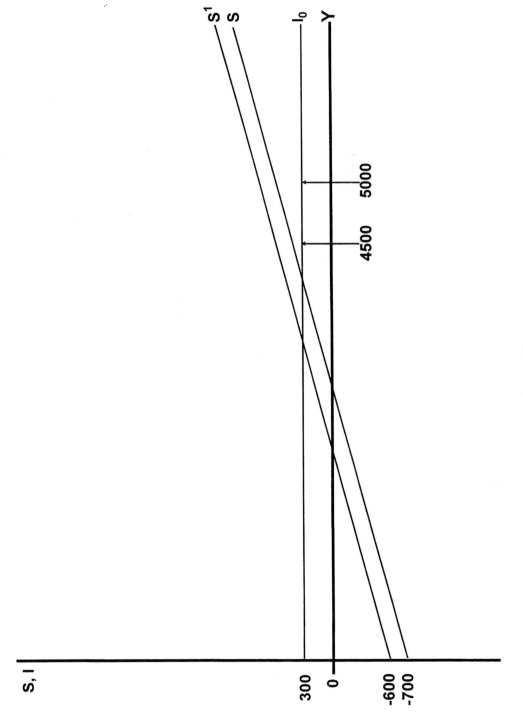

Figure 7.

where G stands for government purchases of goods and services (assumed to be controlled by the Appropriations Committee, which does not necessarily talk to Ways and Means) and T stands for taxes (set by Ways and Means). By substituting into equation (5) and rearranging terms, we get:

$$Y = \frac{1}{1-b} (a+I_0+G_0-bT_0) \quad (11)$$

If G is greater than T, the government runs a deficit, adding to the floating supply of government bonds. In the first model, S = I was the equilibrium condition; here it is S + T = I + G. If G is greater than T, S must be greater than I by the same amount. For the sake of understanding this simply, let's say that all investment must be financed by the sale of corporate bonds. If investment is $100 billion and G - T = -$20 billion, savers will buy $120 billion in bonds. On the other hand, if the government budget shows a surplus, T - G = +$20 billion, and investment is still at $100 billion, savers will buy $80 billion in corporate bonds, and the government will pay back (retire) $20 billion of the floating supply of public debt held by both consumers and investors (business firms). Thus, in the Keynesian system, financial markets do not matter; it is assumed that corporations and governments can always borrow as much as they need. To make this more vivid, I say that the government debt is like a "soundless accordion." In the world of Keynesian algebra, it can expand and contract as needed. (In the real world, there's sometimes a nasty noise in bond markets!) But, here, if either I or G go up, income will rise by a multiplied amount in order to restore the I + G = S + T equilibrium.

Let us plug a few numbers into Model II, and play with it a bit.

(1) C = 500 + 0.75(Y-T)

(2) T = 200

(3) I = 300

(4) G = 200

(5) Y = C + I + G = C + S + T

[handwritten: $MPC + MPS = 1$]

By substituting the general formula given for Model II earlier, we got:

$$Y = \frac{1}{1-b} (a+I_0+G_0-bT_0) \quad (II)$$

Substituting the values given above, we get

$$Y = \frac{1}{1-.75} (500+300+200-.75(200))$$

$$Y = 4(850) = 3400$$

Note that the MPC here is 3/4 and therefore the MPS must be 1/4, but the multiplier is 4. As the formula implies, any change in autonomous consumption (a), business investment (I_0), or government spending (G_0) will produce a four-fold change in GNP(Y), due to the size of the multiplier. Let us again assume that the economy is in equilibrium in January:

Y	T	C	S	I	G	C + I + G
Jan. 3400	200	2900	300	300	200	3400

Assume that the Appropriations Committee votes an increase of $40 billion in government spending; the situation in February:

Y	T	C	S	I	G	C + I + G
Feb. 3400	200	2900	300	300	<u>240</u>	3440

The last column, C + I + G, represents "income creation" in February in excess of the "disposition of income" (on C + S + T). Thus, in March, income rises and C and S expand (note that taxes do not go up, since we have assumed "lump-sum" tax payments in this model). Using b = MPC = 0.75 (or 3/4):

Y	T	C	S	I	G	C + I + G
March 3440	200	2930	310	300	240	3470

Income creation in March leads to further expansion in April, but we're also ready to give the final figures achieved at equilibrium about a year or so later (using the multiplier).

Y	T	C	S	I	G	C + I + G
April	3470	200	2952.5	317.5	300	240	3492.5
Year later (new equil.)	3560	200	3020	340	300	240	3560

As if by magic, at the new equilibrium, Y = C + I + G once again and I + G = 540, as does S + T = 540. The government budget was initially in balance at $T_0 = G_0 = 200$, but it now shows a deficit of 40, which is financed by S - I = 40, so we need not worry. (The accordion expanded...)

Model II is generally introduced separately in order to discuss two important Keynesian concepts: the "tax multiplier" and the "Balanced Budget Theorem." Going back to the general formula for Model II we had:

$$Y = \underline{1} \, (a_0 + I_0 + G_0 - bT_0) \quad \text{(II)}$$

Note that any change in lump-sum taxes (T_0) would first have to be multiplied by -b. Thus, the tax multiplier (K_T) for Model II is always negative and one less than the government spending multiplier.

$$K_T = \frac{-MPC}{1 - MPC} = \frac{-b}{1-b} = \frac{-MPC}{MPS} \text{ or } -b(K_G),$$

Let's check for another set of numbers before we return to our case! Therefore, if b = 0.8, we now can infer three things: MPS = 0.2, the regular multiplier is 5.0, and the tax multiplier is -4.0). If the MPC = 0.75, as in our arithmetic example we are currently using, the tax multiplier is -3.0. More generally, the tax multiplier equals the government spending multiplier times minus MPC (or b). Thus, a tax decrease of $40 billion, voted in February by the Ways and Means Committee would produce the following:

Month	Y	T	C	S	I	G	C + I + G
Jan	3400	200	2900	300	300	200	3400
Feb.	3400	160	2930	310	300	200	3430
March	3430	160	2952.5	317.5	300	200	3452.5
April	3452.5	160	2969.5	323.6	300	200	3469.4
About a year later	3520	160	3020	340	300	200	3520

At the new equilibrium level, about a year later, S + T once again equals I + G — the government budget deficit of $40 billion is financed by saving being $340 billion, of which $300 billion is used to buy corporate bonds to finance investment and the remainder is used to buy additional bonds issued by the government.

As noted above, in Model II the tax multiplier is always one less than the government spending multiplier and has the reverse sign. Let us do a couple of examples to be more sure. For example, assume an MPC (or b) = 0.9 — since the regular government multiplier (K) is 1/1-b = 10, then the tax multiplier, -b/1-b = .9/.1 = -9.0. Shall we do one more? (I can hear some saying "spare us," but others just catching on.) Assume MPS = 1/3; if that's given, what do you know? Regular multiplier is 3.0, from K = 1/MPS; the MPC is 2/3, from MPC + MPS = 1; the tax multiplier is -2.0, from -MPC/1-MPC = -2/3/1/3. OK? (Yes, let's stop).

The "Balanced Budget Theorem," applicable strictly only to Model II, states that "a simultaneous and equal increase in both government spending and taxes will cause an equivalent increase in GNP." Consider our numerical example, where the MPC is 0.75. An increase of $100 billion in both government spending (G_0) and total taxes (T_0) will not leave Y unchanged at the equilibrium level of $3400 billion. The regular multiplier, 1/1-b is four (+ 4.0) — so an increase of G_0 by $100 billion would push Y up by $400 billion. An increase in T_0 would be subject to the tax multiplier (-b/1-b here, while more generally, $K_T = -b(K_G)$, where K_T is the tax multiplier and KG is the multiplier applicable to government spending). Plugging the MPC = 0.75 into that formula, we get -.75/1 - .75 = - 3.0. Thus, a tax increase of $100 billion would produce a GNP decrease of $300 billion. Adding plus $400 and minus $300 billion gives us a net of plus $100 billion, exactly what the Balanced Budget Theorem states — that increasing both sides of the government budget has a multiplier of one.

If GNP is at $3400 billion, as in our arithmetic example, and we calculate that $3700 billion in aggregate demand is equivalent to "full employment," we have three ways of getting there, following Keynesian policies. First, we could increase government spending by $75 billion — it has a multiplier of four, so that's the simplest way (also politically most attractive, since we could target such spending to projects near and dear to the hearts of media moguls, and convince voters of our altruism). Second, we could cut taxes by $100 billion, since the tax multiplier is -3.0. (That would be mildly popular with the voters, but consumers would probably buy Big Macs, ice cream cones, and football tickets, not health foods, Perrier water, or scholarly studies of poverty, which we may want to control!) Third, of course, we could use the insight of the Balanced Budget Theorem, and increase both spending and taxes by $300 billion, if people are averse to increasing the public debt (The Balanced Budget Amendment, if eventually passed, would make deficit spending nearly impossible.)

The basic framework of the Keynesian model is by now thoroughly understood. We can bring it a bit closer to reality by making a couple of modifications in Model III, but it is clear that aggregate demand, $C + I + G$, accounts for most changes in economic activity — and that changes in aggregate demand can most easily be controlled by manipulating G. In its general form, Model III is given by:

(1) $C = a + b(Y - T)$

(2) $T = T_0 + tY$

(3) $I = I_0 + eY$

(4) $G = G_0$

(5) $Y = C + I + G = C + S + T$

Substituting into the aggregate demand equation, we have:

$$Y = (a + b(Y - (T_0 + tY))) + (I_0 + eY) + G_0$$

Removing all the parentheses, we get:

$$Y = a + bY - bT_0 - btY + I_0 + I_0 + eY + G_0$$

Rearranging all Y terms to the left-hand side of the equation, we obtain:

$$Y - bY + btY - eY = a + I_0 + G_0 - bT_0 \text{, or}$$

$$Y(1 - b + bt - e) = a + I_0 + G_0 - bT_0$$

Dividing both sides by the expression in the parenthesis gives us:

$$Y = 1/1 - b + bt - e(a + I_0 + G_0 - bT_0) \quad \text{(III)}$$

which is the general solution to Model III. The two changes that we have made are quite simple — we've made taxes endogenous in equation (2). T_0 can be called autonomous taxes (just as "a" is called autonomous consumption), while "t" can be called the marginal propensity to pay taxes — or, more simply, the marginal tax rate. In equation (3), investment is also sub-divided into an autonomous element, I_0, and an induced one, where "e" is the marginal propensity to invest. The term outside the parenthesis in the general solution to Model III can be called the "super-multiplier;" as you can see from the formula, any change in a, I_0, or G_0 will be multiplied by this term to determine the change in Y. Let us now consider a numerical example of Model III (although we could keep on going, this will be the last piece of algebra).

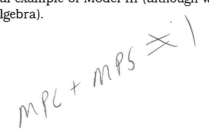

(1) $C = 400 + .7(Y - T)$

(2) $T = -100 + .1Y$

(3) $I = 130 + .12Y$

(4) $G = 500$

(5) $Y = C + I + G = C + S + T$

The intercept of the tax function, T_0, is usually negative, reflecting the fact that at very low levels of GNP(Y), government transfers (unemployment benefits, welfare, social security, and so on) would be larger than revenue collections. We have arbitrarily chosen a low marginal tax rate of 10%; in more complex models, various non-linear tax functions would be used to reflect progressivity of the tax system. Investment is also here a linear function of GNP, with the marginal propensity to invest (similar to accelerator-type models discussed in macroeconomics courses) assumed to be equal to 12%. Substituting in the general solution for Model III, we get:

$$Y = 1/1 - .7 + (.7)(.1) - .12(400 + 130 + 500 - .7(-100))$$

$$Y = 4(1100) = 4400$$

Substituting this value of GNP into the various equations (start with taxes), we get:

Y	T	C	S	I	G	C + I + G
4400	340	3242	818	658	500	4400

A change in government spending of $100 billion would be multiplied by the "super-multiplier" to find the new equilibrium:

$$K_G^* = 1/1 - b + bt - e = 1/1 - .7 + .7(.1) - .12 = 4$$

Thus, the new equilibrium level of GNP would be $4800, with the following results:

Y	T	C	S	I	G	C + I + G
4800	380	3494	926	706	600	4800

Note here that initially, at Y = $4400 billion, the deficit was $160 billion — an increase in government spending of $100 billion would have led us to expect an increase in the deficit to $260 billion. However, due to the higher tax collections at the new, higher level of GNP, the deficit increased only to $220 billion.

Let us next consider the impact of changing taxes. A tax cut of $100 billion, going back to the original equilibrium GNP of $4400 billion, might have been expected to increase the deficit from $160 billion to $260 billion — however, the tax multiplier here is -2.8 ($K_T = -b(K_G) = .7(4.0) = -2.8$), which yields:

Y	T	C	S	I	G	C + I + G
4680	268	3488.4	923.6	691.6	500	4680

Thus the deficit only increases from $160 billion to $232 billion, with $28 billion in additional revenues due to the expansion of Y of $280 billion — and a marginal tax rate of 10%. To a limited extent, this Keynesian argument that an expanding economy will restore some of the revenue loss of a decrease in taxes was behind the Democratic tax reduction of the 1960's and the Reagan "Tax Revolution" of the 1980's, about which we'll say more in the next chapter.

The simple arithmetic of the Balanced Budget Theorem no longer holds in the world of Model III. The government spending multiplier in our numerical example is equal to 4.0, while the tax multiplier turns out to be minus 2.8. Here, an increase of both sides of the government budget by $100 billion would produce a GNP increase of $120 billion — but we could have easily changed the numbers to make the "balanced budget multiplier" less than one. (For example, b = .8, t = .2, and e = .06, would yield a government spending multiplier of 3.3 and a tax multiplier of 2.64.)

The General Theory of Keynes

While the simple algebraic models of Keynesian economics that we have just discussed dominated the teaching of elementary macroeconomics for several decades, slightly more advanced treatments did allow some room for the role of money and interest rates in the Keynesian world. The algebra that we have reviewed is at the heart of the system, however. Any target level of nominal GNP (or Y) can be reached directly by manipulating G. The use of tax policy is secondary — it usually produces a much smaller multiplier, and cannot be targeted as specifically as spending.

Figure 8 is a simplification of Keynes' demand for money function. Keynes discussed four motives for holding money (1) the transactions demand (income-motive) for money, generally assumed to be proportional to the spending unit's income and "the normal length of the interval between its receipt and its disbursement," (2) the business motive, "to bridge the interval between the time of incurring business costs and that of the receipt of the sale-proceeds," (3) the precautionary motive, for "contingencies requiring sudden expenditure" (losing at poker, or paying a traffic fine come to mind), or for making "advantageous purchases" (at the time of Keynes' writing, remember that Visa or American Express did not yet exist), and (4) the speculative motive, cash held for the express purpose of making investments in the financial markets, in bonds and stocks.[4]

---

[4] *Ibid.*, p. 195–196.

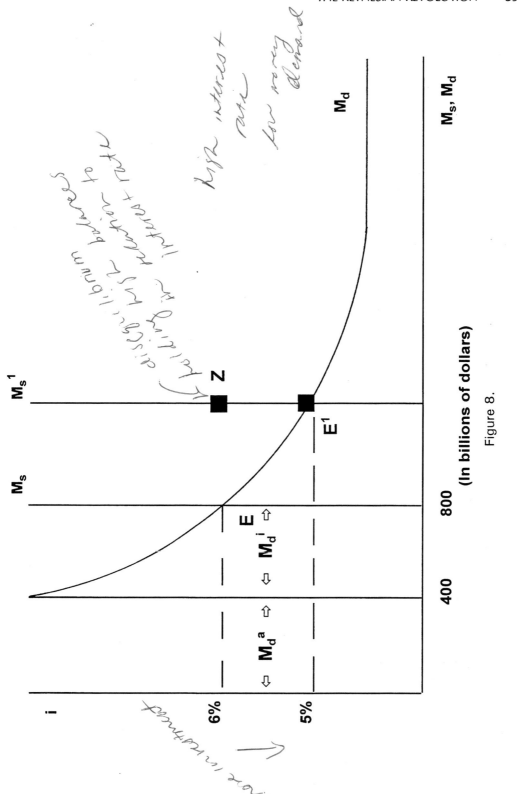

Figure 8.

The first three motives are fairly easy to understand; they are generally called the demand for money for "active balances," assumed to be proportional to GNP in the aggregate. Thus, $M^a{}_d = f(Y)$ in Figure 8 is drawn as a straight vertical line. As can be seen in the graph, the demand for speculative balances — another term for these is "idle balances" — is inversely related to the interest rate, $M^i{}_d = f(i)$, where i is the interest rate on long-term bonds. Note that when i is high, the distance between total money demand and $M^a{}_d$ is small, indicating a low quantity of idle balances demanded. In Fig. 8, at a 6% interest rate, the demand for active balances appears to be $400 billion and the demand for idle balances about the same. Thus, if the total supply of money is $800 billion, the graph says that people would be willing to hold that amount at a 6% interest rate — mentally dividing it roughly in half between "active" and "idle" balances.

The concept of idle or speculative balances needs a bit more explanation — it is unlikely that most students reading this are actively playing the bond market, or even know personally people who do so regularly. Yet, a thorough understanding of this requires an insight into the bond market (it's really not very hard — many of my former students from Money and Banking in the mid-1960's are today making six-figure incomes as Wall Street brokers and dealers). Government and corporate bonds are generally issued in denominations of $1000, and carry a fixed annual interest payment, say, $60 per year. Let's assume that we are talking about very long-term bonds, maturing 25 or 30 years in the future, so that the fact that you'll get $1000 for the bond at some future maturity date doesn't affect present supply-and-demand forces very much.

This relationship of market interest rates and "old" bond prices is an inverse one — for very long-term bonds, nearly perfectly so. A bond issued for $1000 yesterday, having a 6% coupon, would perhaps be worth only a little more than $500 tomorrow, if market rates climb to 12%. That bond would be trading at a "discount" in the secondary market, a very "deep discount," in this example. In other words, just to understand this clearly, tomorrow the government or corporations would be issuing new bonds of the same maturity, with a "face value" of $1000 also, but paying $120 per year for a good long time. What would be the market price any rational investor is willing to pay for your old $60 per annum bond?   *129. of 1000*

Conversely, however, what if market interest rates fell to 3%? New bonds would now offer only $30 per year for a $1000 investment; your old bond is now "twice as good as the new ones." Would the rational investor pay nearly $2000 for it? Would it be trading at a "premium" of well above its original face value? Of course? Yes. This discussion is necessary for a complete understanding of Keynes' speculative-motive. Under normal historical conditions, bond interest rates have seldom risen above 12% (1982 was very unusual). Thus, at "high" rates, the bond market is "bullish" — nearly everyone expects rates to fall, and bond prices to rise. (A "bull," cleverly used by Merrill Lynch in its advertising, bets on rising prices. A "bear" expects prices to fall.) If interest rates are high, people want to hold little cash (or short-term financial instruments) and be fully "invested" in long-term securities such as bonds or mortgages.

bond value det. by interest fluctuations

At low interest rates, such as 3% or even lower, the market becomes progressively "bearish." If the interest rate falls to very low levels, as it did during the Great Depression in the 1930's, the demand for money becomes infinitely elastic — a condition known as "the liquidity trap." In the horizontal segment of the M_d curve in Fig. 8 and monetary policy is powerless — if the central bank doubled the money supply, it could not force interest rates down below a certain floor. I have deliberately not specified what that floor might be — but rates below 1.5-2% as a long-term yield are so unusual (1936-37?), that most people would rather hold cash than to risk a capital loss of an equivalent amount by buying bonds.

The main channel for money to influence economic activity in the standard Keynesian system is through the bond market. In a liquidity trap, of course, the central bank is powerless — "money does not matter." Under more normal conditions, at point E in Fig. 8, an increase in the supply of money, from M_S to M^1_S, will have the economy in a disequilibrium situation, shown by point Z. There, people are holding excessively large money balances in relation to the rate of interest at 6%. The *only* option in this highly restrictive theoretical world is for people to start buying long-term bonds, forcing the rate of interest down to i_1, where they are once again happy with the distribution of their wealth. In turn, this reduction in the interest rate from 6% to 5% will lead to higher investment, as shown in Figure 9, a rise from $500 billion to $550 billion, say. This is implicit in the investment demand diagram — investment is a function of its profitability, defined as the spread between the "marginal efficiency of capital" (r, more simply thought of as the expected rate of return from real capital goods) and the market interest rate (i). In order for the economy to be in equilibrium, the rates of return from both real and financial assets must be the same, after accounting for risk and transactions costs. This idea is at the heart of Keynesian business cycle theory — in 1976, for example, interest rates on financial assets were very low in comparison to the rates of return expected from real assets, especially as inflation heated up in 1979-80. Thus, since r > i, I rose as did GNP (or Y). On the other hand, explaining the 1980-82 recession, as the unemployment rate in the U.S. rose above 10% and when the prime rate hit a record 21.5%, the rate of return on paper assets soared well above the expected returns on houses and shopping malls, and a relatively brief but sharp recession set in.

Let us point out what has been omitted — people's expectations regarding commodity prices are assumed to remain neutral. While the liquidity trap, with very low interest rates prevalent in the bond market, seems to imply deflationary expectations, this idea is not explicitly addressed in *The General Theory*, and is ignored by the followers of Keynes. More recently, the so-called "rational expectations school" has raised this issue, but only in a highly formalistic and rather useless manner. Second, the quantity and quality of labor and capital are viewed as given — as the economy moves from one equilibrium position to the next, it is assumed that the aggregate supply curve does not shift. Third and fourth, the distribution of income and the degree of competition are assumed not to get in the way of aggregate demand shifts — though, in the real world, the size of the multiplier probably depends crucially on whether government spending programs affect the very poor, the middle class, or the very rich. Fifth, and finally,

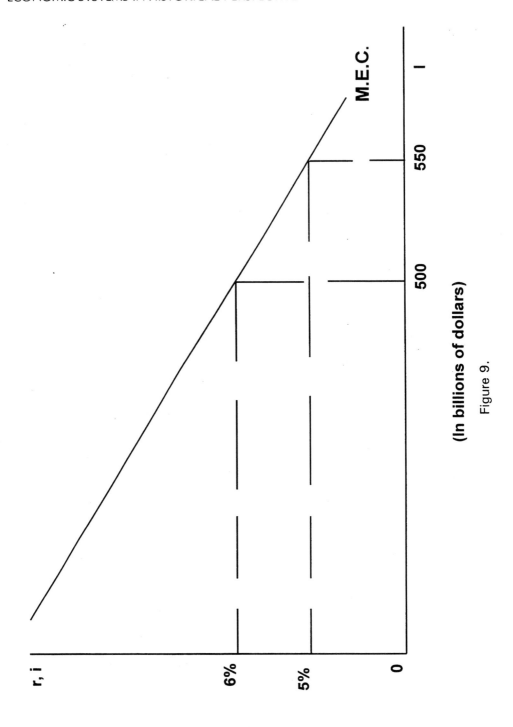

Figure 9.

consumer tastes and technology are treated as constants, though income-leisure choices are probably very important determinants of the shape of the aggregate supply curve.

Almost as an afterthought, let us conclude this section by saying a few words about Figure 10, a Keynesian aggregate supply curve. Plotting prices on the vertical, and real output (Q) on the horizontal axis, Keynesian analysis is usually most relevant only under conditions of very low aggregate demand, such as the region between points A and B in Figure 10. Here fiscal stimulation of the economy through higher G (or lower T) will produce gains in output and employment without causing prices to rise. Most of the time, however, the post-World War II U.S. economy has found itself in the region between B and C, where a higher aggregate demand (a shift from AD" to AD'") meant both gains in output and employment as well as somewhat more inflation. Beyond point C, we are in the purely classical world of the Quantity Theory of Money, where an increase in aggregate demand produces no further gains in output and employment, but only leads to inflation. Whether the AS curve itself is fixed and stable is, of course, the topic of the next chapter.

The Economics of Keynes and Keynesian Economics

Although an entire book has already been written on the differences between what Keynes himself said and what has been argued by his followers, let us conclude this chapter by considering briefly a popular interpretation of Keynesianism.[5] One of the leading American followers of Keynes was Alvin H. Hansen, Littauer Professor of Political Economy at Harvard, a very important populizer of Keynes' work. His 1938 book, *Full Recovery or Stagnation?*, carried the basic outline of the so-called "secular stagnation hypothesis," which he continued to support until at least the early 1960's. His paperback volume, *A Guide to Keynes,* elaborating the IS-LM framework discussed above, was like the Bible to a generation of graduate students taking up economics in the post World-War II period.

While we are oversimplifying somewhat, Hansen argued that there is an inevitable tendency for personal saving to rise, both relatively and absolutely, in a mature capitalist economy. For a linear consumption function, C = a + bY, such as we have used in this chapter, and is found in most elementary texts, the marginal propensity to consume (b) is constant, of course, but it can easily be seen that the average propensity to consume (C/Y) falls as Y rises. It may well be, suggested Hansen and other Keynesians, that the linear representation of the consumption function is incorrect, and that non-linear consumption functions are needed to show that the MPC also tends to fall as income rises in wealthy societies. Moreover, in addition to rising personal savings, Hansen noted the nearly automatic nature of business saving, through depreciation allowances and retained earnings of corporations. In his words:

---

[5] See Axel Leijonhufvud, *On Keynesian Economics and the Economics of Keynes* (New York: Oxford University Press, 1968).

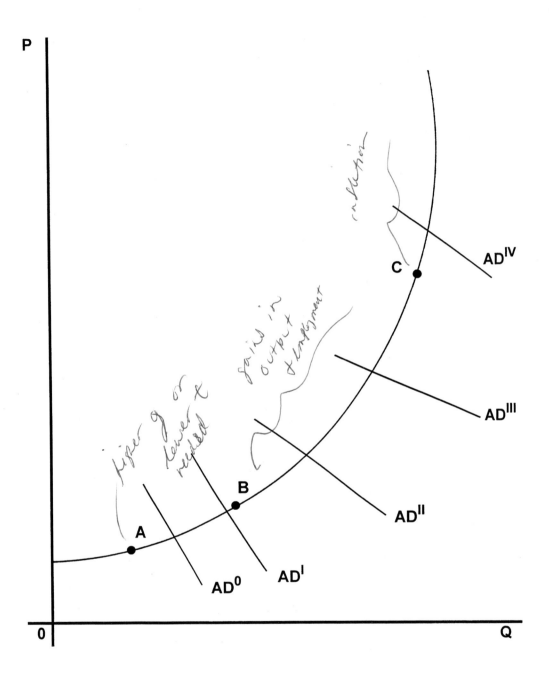

Figure 10.

"... The philosophy of stabilization was nourished in the traditional outlook of the nineteenth-century epoch of expansion. It feared the boom even more than the depression. But now, owing to deep-seated causes inherent in the essential character of a non-expanding economy, secular stagnation stalks across the stage, or at least shows its face. If there is no surging investment boom to be checked, great fluctuations in deficit financing must be avoided, lest any rapid reduction should aggravate and intensify the underlying tendency toward investment stagnation."[6]

Hansen cited a number of major factors, and implied a few others, in support of his "secular stagnation" or "economic maturity" thesis. First, there was a decided slowdown in the rate of population growth; in the late 1920's and the 1930's American population growth was slowing substantially in comparison with the turn of the century. Second, the "widening" of investment due to the opening up of the West and the integration of the frontier into the national economy was also slowing — roads, railroads, and lines of communication were all in place, and the need for new investments was much smaller. Third, Hansen felt that there would be a "dearth of great new industries" — after all, the automobile and electricity had already been invented, so what else was there?

Under these conditions, with a chronic excess of saving over investment, monetary policy becomes powerless — as the generation of graduate students of the 1950's and the 1960's were taught by professors mastering the new Keynesian message, "money does not matter." The "animal spirits" of businessmen are very bearish, to use Keynes' phrase (perhaps "mousish" or "rabbitish" would be a better adjective), the money market is in the "liquidity trap". Interest rates cannot be forced any lower and at lower rates, investment would not respond. Also, the value of the multiplier is probably falling.

With a secular diagnosis of oversaving, the only answer lies in permanent deficits in the government budget — what Hansen called "compensatory fiscal policy." According to him, this was also the message of Lord Keynes:

"... Keynes' proposals are designed to offer a substitute for a completely planned socialistic or communistic economy. His solutions are, as we have seen: (1) the rigid maintenance of the rate of interest below the marginal efficiency of capital until full employment is reached, (2) the forced redistribution of income through taxation designed to increase the propensity to consume, and (3) socially controlled investment."[7]

Such Keynesian orthodoxy was increasingly embraced by most "modern" economists in the 1950's or 1960's, whose role as advisors to both government and private organizations could be expanded nicely, and by politicians and bureaucrats, whose decisions concerning "socially-desirable" investments could lead to votes and empire-building, respectively. As a general rule, this created a good deal of pressure to expand

[6] Alvin Harvey Hansen, *Full Recovery or Stagnation?* (New York: W.W. Norton & Company, Inc., 1938), pp. 301-302.
[7] *Ibid.*, p. 29.

public sector activities across the board, providing a general theory for doing so. While, in theory, Keynes' analysis is compatible with a cyclically balanced budget — surplus years of inflationary pressure cancelling deficit years of inadequate aggregate demand — in practice, government deficits were politically much more attractive than surpluses. Leading mainstream economists such as Hansen, were always ready to provide theoretical justifications for an expanding public sector (and a growing public debt):

> *"... As productivity has increased in all modern nations, one of the areas of diversified consumption that has been developed is that of free services of different kinds supplied by the community as a whole. An ever-increasing part of our standard of living consists of community consumption as distinguished from private consumption. An increasing part of the productive resources of advanced industrial nations is devoted to the production of community services. This is the explanation of ever-growing governmental budgets. If we followed the advice of so-called 'sound finance' and sharply curtailed government-service outlays, the propensity to consume for the community as a whole (public and private) would decline, and aggregate demand would fall. No modern country could have achieved its varied and rich standard of living without this historical expansion in the area of social and public services."[8]*

To be against the expansion of all magnanimous and beneficial public sector services, particularly if they served to maintain an ever-shrinking "marginal propensity to consume," branded one as a "know-nothing," a primitive "moss-back" creature of decidedly "anti-modern" views. If your academic colleagues did not provide sufficiently rigorous censure of your old-fashioned views, progressive media organs would ensure that they would be held up for suitable ridicule. Still, through about forty years of Keynesian orthodoxy, critical ideas and skeptical opinions managed to survive — and today seem to display a good deal more energy and imagination in explaining "the way the world works" than the conventional wisdom of Keynesian economics. Still, a careful reading of *The General Theory* reveals much more insight that has been discarded than the basic ideas, which have made their way to elementary text-books in greatly over-simplified form. ■

SUGGESTED READINGS

Bleaney, Michael, *The Rise and Fall of Keynesian Economics: An Investigation of Its Contribution to Capitalist Development* (Macmillan, 1985).

Colander, David C. and Harry Landreth (eds.), *The Coming of Keynesianism to America* (E. Elgar, 1996).

Eichner, Alfred S., *Toward a New Economics: Essays in Post-Keynesian and Institutionalist Theory* (M.E. Sharpe, Inc., 1985).

Hansen, Alvin H., *Economic Policy and Full Employment* (McGraw-Hill, 1947).

---

[8] Alvin H. Hansen, *Economic Policy and Full Employment* (New York: McGraw-Hill Book Company, Inc., 1947), p. 45.

Hutlon, Will, *The Revolution That Never Was: An Assessment of Keynesian Economics* (Longman, 1986).

Kindleberger, Charles P., *Manias, Panics, and Crashes* (Basic Books, 1978).

Klein, Lawrence R., *The Keynesian Revolution*, Second Ed., (Macmillan, 1966).

Krugman, Paul, *Peddling Prosperity: Economic Sense and Nonsense in the Age of Diminished Expectations* (W.W. Norton, 1994).

Lawson, Tony, and Hashem Pesaran (eds.), *Keynes' Economics: Methodological Issues (Croom Helm, 1985)*.

Leijonhufvud, Axel, *On Keynesian Economics and the Economics of Keynes* (Oxford University Press, 1968).

O'Donnell, R.M. (ed.), *Keynes as Philosopher-Economist* (St. Martin's, 1991).

Shaw, G.K. (ed.), *The Keynesian Heritage*, 2 vols. (E. Elgar, 1988).

Temin, Peter, *Did Monetary Forces Cause the Great Depression?* (W.W. Norton, 1976).

Weintraub, Sidney, *Keynes, Keynesians, and Monetarists* (University of Pennsylvania Press, 1978).

Wells, Paul (ed.), *Post-Keynesian Economic Theory* (Kluwer, 1995).

CHAPTER FOUR

MACROECONOMICS IN DISARRAY: WHERE ARE WE TODAY?

*A*s noted in the previous chapter, Keynesian analysis is essentially focused upon aggregate demand, $Y = C + I + G + X - M$ (with the foreign trade sector, $X - M$, usually left out entirely, particularly in American textbook presentations in the 1950's, when U.S. imports amounted to only 2-3% of GNP.) Generally speaking, standard Keynesian views could probably be summarized by saying "demand will create its own supply" — thus, a complete refutation or reversal of Say's Law of classical macroeconomics. (You will recall, I hope, that Say's Law was just the reverse — "supply creates its own demand.")

It was a lot of fun to do economics in the early 1960's, when I began graduate work and teaching. It was relatively easy to understand the standard aggregate demand system in macroeconomics and to figure out the MR = MC rule of profit maximization in microeconomics. In the latter field, oligopolies and labor unions were a bit of a problem for the analysis of pure competition, but we could always hope that they could be made to go away. In macro, however, the Keynesian system was greatly strengthened by the introduction of the "Phillips Curve" — which assumed and analyzed a stable "trade-off" between inflation and unemployment. Initially developed for about a hundred years of data for the U.K. by British economist A.W. Phillips to analyze wage inflation, it argued that upward pressure on wages was inversely related to the unemployment rate, implying that trade unions were less timid in their wage demands when the labor market was very tight, i.e., the unemployment rate quite low.

Applying this idea to the United States was relatively easy in the 1946-69 period, a time span of about 20 years. As can be seen in Figure 11, most years in that period of time would be up quite near E — the mid-point of the unemployment-inflation trade-off of only about 2% in price increases and 4% in unemployment, the "old" full-employment rate. Back then, it was fun to do economics in the early 1960s — one week you could be working for a conservative think-tank, lamenting the long-run dangers of a 5% inflation rate at a position such as point B, and arguing passionately that we should be willing to accept a 1% increase in the jobless rate for a gain of 3% less inflation. Conversely, at point A, the same person could conceivably be found at Brookings, writing about the

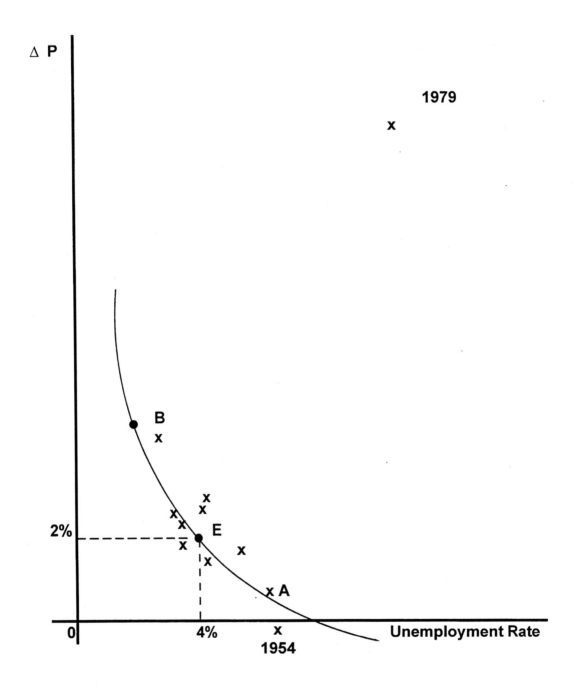

Figure 11.
Phillips Curve, 1946–69

tragic loss of potential output at a 5.8% unemployment rate (unacceptably high), in a year when the Consumer Price Index actually fell slightly (e.g., 1954). Surely all reasonable people would be willing to "buy" a 4% unemployment rate, even if it meant an additional price increase of less than 2% per year.

In the 1970's, a lot began to go wrong with the Phillips Curve "trade-off." The so-called "Misery Index," derived by adding the inflation rate and the unemployment percentage, which had remained in the single-digit range during the 1950's and the 1960's, rose significantly in the early 1970's. Jimmy Carter's "spin doctors" devised this measure in his victorious campaign of 1976, to beat Gerry Ford, only to have the Misery Index lead to truly miserable results (for him) in the 1980 election. In the late 1970's and early 1980's, the Phillips' Curve appeared to have lost all relevance — the U.S. economy was experiencing "stagflation," high unemployment combined with unacceptably high inflation rates. In 1979-80, for example, the inflation rate reached nearly 20% for a couple of months, on an annualized basis, while the unemployment rate hit a double-digit level by itself a few years later. Interest rates rose ominously, to an all-time high of 21.5% for the prime rate, and 14% for the Federal Reserve's discount rate (the rate charged by our central bank to commercial banks for short term loans — as mentioned in Chapter 2, the previous historical high had been 7%, set in 1921). Plotting inflation and unemployment for the late 1970's and the early 1980's on Figure 11 would show a cluster of points off in the upper right-hand corner of the graph, suggesting that the Phillips Curve "trade-off" had lost all relevance. What had happened in the 1970's? We shall briefly discuss eight possible explanations of "stagflation" in this introductory section. They are presented in a listing of ascending importance, at least in my opinion, starting with the relatively weakest and ending with what I consider the most significant. However, a number of these hypotheses are inter-related, and the exact ordering is probably not all that important.

The first hypothesis is in last place only due to its vagueness. In addition to devising the Misery Index, Jimmy Carter also spoke a good deal about the nation's "malaise," a term which we can use to include everything not explicitly taken up under the other seven headings. One would certainly mention here several deeply disturbing sociological trends, such as the changing role and nature of the family, widespread drug abuse, and an alarmingly high drop-out rate from high schools (or even before) among teenagers. The disappointing performance of the educational establishment, caught up in a game of generating credentials rather than teaching and nurturing the young, would need to be mentioned, but could be the subject of many bitter books. The role of the media in shortening the national attention span might be suitably analyzed under this heading, as could pressure-group politics. The weakening of the "Protestant work ethic" should be mentioned as well as the divisive debate over Vietnam. But, let us leave these very general sociological and political musings for others to pursue, and talk about other hypotheses more comfortable for an economist.

A second rather appealing hypothesis is the "market power" argument. Here one could speculate about the growing influence of powerful "labor union bosses," if one is an anti-union conservative, or the greed of grasping multi-national corporations and conglomerates, if one is an anti-business liberal. In general, this is an appealing explanation, since it is always nice to have a specific "scape-goat," against whom we could take some direct action — "turn the anti-trust laws against the unions!" or "outlaw all mergers!" could serve as the rallying cry, and we could *do* something, act in a simple and satisfying way to fix things. However, without denying that union shortsightedness as well as inept and greedy management have greatly harmed American competitiveness in several significant industries, there is relatively little support for the market power hypothesis in terms of statistical data. In the past ten-to-fifteen years, many U.S. industries became less concentrated, in part because of rising imports, and a number of labor market studies show non-union wage rates rising faster than those of union members. Moreover, labor union membership as a percentage of the number of people employed has been declining steadily and one of the most powerful labor unions in the country has actually accepted a "roll-back" in wage rates (the UAW in the mid-1980s). Thus, our search for explanations continues.

The next hypothesis involves the role of resources, especially oil and gas. One version of this hypothesis is that the world as a whole is running out of energy resources — and stagflation is explained as a leftward shift of the aggregate supply curve, resulting in both lower output and higher prices. Another alternative is a version of the market power explanation, with particular emphasis on OPEC. A few years ago, the rhetorical question: "What happened to the Phillips Curve in the 1970's?" would have been answered by most people first and foremost mentioning "oil," "OPEC," or "the energy crunch." Again, a tempting explanation, giving us a specific target to attack, but one which does not carry as much weight as is commonly believed. While the price of oil was raised enormously in 1973-74 and again in 1979-80, the overall impact on the CPI of energy generally, and imported oil specifically, is not sufficient to explain more than a very small part of the overall inflation of the 1970's. Only 1.3 percent of the 17.2 percent rise in the CPI was due to energy in the 1973-74 period. In 1979-80, consumer prices rose by a somewhat larger 26.8% — but only with about five percent (or less than one-fifth of the total) due to energy cost increases. Yet in combination with other factors still to be discussed, the price rises engineered by OPEC certainly served to contribute to an atmosphere of shortages and constraints, to a national mood of malaise and uncertainty.

A fourth hypothesis that can be mentioned involves the term "international" generally, perhaps "Japan and Germany" in particular. To make this hypothesis sufficiently general to include a number of potentially significant components, let us say that the international economic situation changed in a number of significant ways in the decade of the 1970's, facilitating the international transmission of inflationary pressures and contributing to a rise in U.S. unemployment. It is certainly true that U.S. manufacturing firms dominated world markets in the 1950's and the 1960's — indeed, many companies were not generally very much interested in developing and improving a capacity to export, having a huge domestic market as their first priority. U.S. imports were less than 5% of GNP for most the post World-War-II period, and U.S. policy-makers seldom took foreign repercussions into account at all. The dollar was the only convertible currency at the beginning of this period, with virtually all central banks holding their foreign exchange reserves exclusively in the form of dollars. The dollar became the international standard for private dealings as well, even if American firms were not necessarily involved — for example, Europeans and Japanese buying oil in the Middle East would write their contracts in dollars. After all, back then, the "dollar was as good as gold" — the U.S. Treasury stood ready to sell gold at $35 an ounce to all official institutions wanting to buy it (but, because the U.S. government had *said* they would, few actually came to buy). This promise, after all, was the center-piece of the so-called "Bretton Woods System."

By the mid-1960's American hegemony over the world economy was slowly being eroded. The Europeans had set up their common market (EEC) and the Japanese had rebuilt their war-ravaged country with amazing rapidity. Some other Asian, Latin American, and East European countries were beginning to emerge as exporters of manufactured goods as well. Most countries in Latin America lessened their economic dependence on the U.S., both as a result of deliberate policies and market forces. As the stock of dollars held by foreigners began to exceed the Treasury's gold stock, in part due to the dollars generated by U.S. military spending in Vietnam and elsewhere, some official holders of dollars (e.g., France) began to question whether it was in fact as "good as gold." During the 1960's the U.S. was running a balance of trade deficit, while Germany and Japan had substantial surpluses — as long as that imbalance persisted, it became evident that something had to give. While the end of the Bretton Woods System has been analyzed at considerable length elsewhere, the dollar was twice devalued by Nixon (first by raising the official gold price by 10% to $38.50 in 1971 and then to $42.22, a couple of years later, but finally closing the Treasury's gold window entirely). By the end of the decade of the 1970s, gold was more than $800 per ounce, and the purchasing power of the U.S. dollar relative to the German D-mark and the Japanese yen had been cut in half. The international monetary system has been characterized by considerable instability since 1973. Most industrial countries have switched to "floating rates," but most less developed countries (LDC's) attempted to keep their currencies at a fixed rate, by "pegging" to the U.S. dollar or a basket of major currencies. However, as inflation accelerated in the U.S., and the dollar declined during the 1970s, there was a lot of pressure on other countries to follow inflationary policies — and a general lessening of the credibility of all monetary authorities. The price of gold seems to be a good indicator of such overall credibility — by the end of the 1970s, it had soared to nearly $900. Its current price, at around $400, seems to suggest that more than half of such trust, in fact, has been restored.

A fifth hypothesis, which could also be the subject of a book-length treatment in itself, involves the steady decline in U.S. productivity. Productivity is usually defined as output per hour of labor input — real GNP growth assuming a constant level of employment. In the 1950's, productivity in the American economy improved by about 3% per year. In the 1960's, the rate of productivity growth slowed to about 2% per year — but, in the 1970's, the average rate was only 1%, and very close to zero by the end of the decade. It is a rather puzzling, and also very complex, phenomenon that we cannot even begin to analyze carefully here. What is pretty clear is that rising productivity lowers labor costs per unit of output, and contributes to keeping prices low — under competitive conditions, productivity increases will actually cause prices to fall. While some attempts have been made to link the productivity slowdown to the decline of the "work ethic" and the general malaise discussed earlier, that is probably a bit simplistic, and certainly difficult to measure. It is likely that a more thorough explanation has to involve an examination of trends in investment, saving and employment, but considerations of brevity will not alow a detailed discussion.

As a general observation, economic policies in the United States have not been very conducive to productive investment and savings in the 1950-1980 period (since 1980, that has changed somewhat, but more on that later). Inflation and a steeply progressive tax system increasingly discouraged industrial investment in productive plant and equipment, on balance, while favoring residential real estate and other tax shelters (did someone say "Whitewater?"). While tax rates remained unchanged in the 1970's, with the top individual income tax rate at 70%, inflated incomes pushed even average-income families into higher marginal brackets, often making the tax consequences of investment decisions more important than their economic rationality. During the decade of the 1970's, the marginal tax rate faced by the average American family doubled. Saving was doubly penalized by the regulation Q maximum rate ceiling (at a little over 5%), while such interest income was generally taxed at the household's top marginal rate. On the other hand, most consumer borrowing was subsidized by the tax system, fueling a speculative boom in residential real estate, while the stock market remained very lack-luster throughout the decade of the 1970's. Coupled with this slowdown in personal savings and productive investment, the past decade also experienced a significant change in employment patterns. More jobs were being created in the service industries (and in government, finance and real estate), where productivity growth was likely to be low, since capital-labor ratios are generally relatively constant. Computers may open some doors for productivity gains in education and health, and government as well but, these are not showing up in statistical analysis as of yet. Still, as mentioned earlier, the slow-down in productivity growth is a puzzling and complex issue, for which a complete explanation will have to be sought elsewhere.

"Government policy errors" is the sixth hypothesis in our explanation of the stagflation of the 1970's. Each reader is cordially invited to make up her own list of at least 34 such errors, but we can limit this discussion to a mere handful. Monetary policy comes to mind first — the growth of M1, the money supply conventionally defined (consisting of currency plus checking accounts), accelerated in the 1970s. In the decade of the 1950's, the money stock expanded by 22 percent, in the 1960's by 53 percent, but in the 1970's, by 91 percent. Second, LBJ's fiscal policy tried to combine "guns and butter" (Nam and the Great Society) at no cost to the voter. The legacy of this piece of governmental irresponsibility greatly affected budgets in the 1970s, as overly generous entitlement programs presented their bills for payment. To keep the length of this reasonable, let us mention just very briefly governmental generosity to pension recipients (who may not be able to do much else, but who do vote quite regularly), looser enforcement of eligibility for government transfer recipients, special provisions for the handicapped, health and safety requirements, minimum wage laws, expensive government retraining efforts, and — let's be done with it for now — energy regulations. We could spend a good deal of time also on Nixon's various "phases" of wage and price controls in the early 1970's, and Carter's guidelines to be administered by a special council (COWPS). While greatly increasing the costs of doing business an contributing to the government deficit, each of these various programs was designed to "do good," of course, but in the aggregate these policies greatly retarded American competitiveness in world markets and created a real budgetary monster.

The next-to-last explanation concerns the changes in labor force structure from the 1950s to the 1970s. It is interesting to contrast 1955 and 1975 on this score — in 1955, the head of the family was "Joe", the steelworker in Pittsburgh, while twenty years later the twice-divorced "Bruce," the hair-stylist in Laguna Beach, probably was a more typical member of the labor force. Also, in the mid-1950s, there were much fewer secondary workers in the labor force than there are now. The employed as well as the unemployed generally were "heads of household" — so that the unemployed were fathers lining up early in the foggy morning in Pittsburgh or Cleveland to answer a "Help Wanted" sign. In 1955, the wives of unemployed husbands were calling their friends to see if they knew of some opening somewhere. Back then, the personal stigma of being without work was enormous, and government transfer programs, especially unemployment benefits, were also much less generous than today. The unemployed in 1975 may have included someone drawing a private pension, but perhaps not yet Social Security — actually retired, but getting unemployment compensation for the maximum allowable period. At the other end of the spectrum, he or she may have been a 10th grade dropout, who worked for a while at a fast-food outlet, but found playing basketball and hanging out more more attractive, since the unemployment check can be augmented with an occasional $20 from grandmother. The unemployed may also include the spouse of a doctor or a lawyer, whose tax bracket and vacation preferences, make a year-round job irrational for his or her intellectual spouse (who is also really into tennis, self-discovery, painting, acting, or writing). While we would wish that all of these people could find meaningful and rewarding jobs, to be unemployed in 1975 was and is in 1997 is a far different experience from being out of work in 1957. It is certainly true that classified pages of most major newspapers have thousands of "Help Wanted" listings every Sunday, including entry-level jobs for unskilled workers. Thus, it is hard to believe that most of the joblessness and homelessness in the 1990s was due to inappropriate macroeconomic policies.

Another aspect of the labor force structure hypothesis involves the geographic and occupational mismatch of people and jobs. The so-called "Snow Belt" (or the "Rust Belt") of the northeast and the Great Lakes states has a surplus of workers —certainly our farming communities have also suffered, recently. On the other hand, job opportunities in the "Sun Belt" have been expanding rapidly. Clearly, it is very difficult to match the skills of an unemployed automobile-assembly worker in Detroit ("Joe") to a job as a hair-stylist in Newport Beach or Orlando ("Bruce"). For a while, there was a clear-cut shortage of engineers — during the late 1970s, there was a surplus — and now we appear to be facing a shortage again. Currently, there appears to exist a surplus of eager young

Table 4–1: Selected Statistics on Employment and Unemployment
1955, 1975, & 1985 (in thousands)

	1955	1975	1985	1995
(1) Civ. Labor Force	65,023	93,775	115,461	132,304
(2) Total employment	62,170	85,846	107,150	124,900
Males	42,621	51,857	59,891	67,377
as % of (2)	68.6	60.4	55.9	53.9
16 – 19	2,095	3,839	3,328	3,292
as % of (2)	3.4	4.5	3.1	2.6
Females	19,551	33,989	47,259	57,523
as % of (2)	31.4	39.6	44.1	46.0
16 – 19	1,547	3,263	3,105	3,127
as % of (2)	2.5	3.8	2.9	2.5
(3) Unemployment	2,852	7,929	8,312	7,404
Males	1,854	4,442	4,521	3,983
as % of (3)	65.0	56.0	54.4	53.8
16 – 19	274	966	806	744
as % of (3)	9.6	12.2	9.7	10.0
Females	998	3,486	3,791	3,421
as % of (3)	35.0	44.0	45.6	46.2
16 – 19	176	802	661	602
as % of (3)	6.2	10.1	8.0	8.1
Long term (27 weeks & over)	336	1,203	1,280	1,278
as % of (3)	11.8	15.2	15.4	
Married men, spouse present	2.6%	5.1%	4.3%	3.3%

academicians in the social sciences and the humanities — but this may change again in the next 5-10 years.

Table 4.1 provides some useful statistical detail on what we have just been discussing. Males represented nearly 70% of the employed as well as 65% of the unemployed in 1955. Working teenagers constituted a little less than 6% of the people holding down jobs, but more than 15% of the unemployed. The unemployment rate among married men living in households with the spouse present was only 2.6%, and among "experienced workers" (to be a bit less sexist) about 4.8% — both numbers probably reflecting only people only temporarily between jobs. Only a little more than one in ten jobless people had been out of work for 27 weeks or longer.

Twenty years later, in 1975, labor force participation rates for women had increased very significantly, and nearly 40% of those employed were females. As Table 4.1 shows, in 1975 females also accounted for a significantly larger proportion of the unemployed pool, at 39.6%. Another part of the story concerns the participation rates of teenagers. In 1955, workers and those counted as officially without work (but searching) in the 16-19 age group constituted 6.3% of the civilian labor force. By 1975, the percentage of "participant teenagers" had risen to 9.4% — but by 1985, that percentage was down to 6.8% again, and fell to 5.9% by 1995. As can be seen by a closer look at the numbers, more than half of the unemployed in 1975 were secondary or tertiary workers, who were much less likely to put strong downward pressure on wage rates. Still, the overall unemployment picture was rather bleak — there were also large increases in the unemployment rate for experienced workers (from 4.8% to 8.2%) and the average duration of joblessness lengthened perceptibly.

By 1985, the difference between the representation of women in jobs and the unemployment pool narrowed — 44.1% of those employed were females, and 45.6% of those out of work. Employed teenagers of both sexes averaged 3% of those with jobs, but nearly 9% of the unemployed. Demographic trends suggest that the relative importance of teenagers in the labor force peaked in the 1970's. By now, most have cut their hair, shaved, and started bathing regularly — perhaps they have even bought a tie or two! As the baby boomers reach their mid-twenties and get married, their participation rates among those employed increase rapidly. As can be seen in the table, the participation rates for women have continued to rise slowly, and the overall unemployment rate has fallen below six percent by 1996.

The final and most important explanation for the stagflation of the 1970's involves inflationary expectations. One of my favorite aphorisms, dutifully memorized by a generation of students, is: "Uniformly held expectations tend to be self-fulfilling." Let us spend a paragraph or two discussing this a bit. In the decade right after World War II, focusing on 1955, the average head-of-household probably expected neither inflation nor deflation on balance — many remembered the decade of the Depression, with falling prices, when debtors suffered greatly. Remember the villains of the silent films — they were bankers and other financial types with long waxed mustaches, who came to the farm to foreclose on the mortgage. The family was done in by falling commodity prices

— bankers seized the farm, and then the villain tied the farmer's daughter to the railroad tracks, for good measure. In the period right after the war, many prominent economists (Alvin Hansen, for example) forecast a return of falling prices, high unemployment, and insufficient aggregate demand. Thus, the average "G.I. Joe" coming back from Europe or the Pacific was not ready to mortgage his future to those mustache-twirling bankers, and prudently avoided indebtedness of any sort. In the early 1950s, the number of people expecting some sort of a serious deflationary episode was probably just about the same as the number expecting a continuation of the mild inflation of the late 1940s and early 1950s — the average expected inflation rate was equal to zero.

Most people probably use a fairly naive model to forecast next year's inflation. Unless inflation rates really accelerate, the past three or four years of price increases probably figure rather heavily in their assessment of what next year will probably bring. To simplify the arithmetic, I have constructed an expected inflation series, which uses last year's CPI change with a weight of 50%, two years ago with 30%, and three years back at 20%. (I could have used a more sophisticated distributed-lag polynomial function of some sort, but it did seem like a waste of computer time.) In the 1950's, there was only one year of a negative change in the CPI — 1954, when prices actually fell by 0.5 percent. For the decade as a whole, using the simple model just outlined, the expected inflation rate averaged just 2.1% per year — probably just about equal to the "quality improvements" taking place in a number of the products covered by the CPI (such as the shift from manual-transmission automobiles to automatics, for example). Still, we had only one year in which prices acutally declined (1954, as noted), and memories of the Depression decade grew dimmer and more distant.

As can be seen in Table 4.2, in the period 1974-1983, each year shows inflationary expectations of 5% or more—with both "oil shocks" contributing significantly in psychological terms. However, since 1984, we have generally experienced more years of "disinflation," where actual inflation rates have been well below the rates "predicted" by our crude expectations model (except 1987-1990). This has been particularly true since 1991, with inflationary expectations falling steadily.

To summarize the first section, Keynesian demand management policies can be used to stabilize the economy successfully only on the assumption that aggregate supply conditions are known or given. While it is not necessary to go so far as to draw a horizontal aggregate supply curve, as some textbooks do (Keynes himself would surely be horrified by this suggestion that this is what he really meant) — it does assume a relatively stable Phillips Curve trade-off between inflation and unemployment. Though this assumption worked quite well in the 1946-69 period in the U.S., we have discussed eight reasons or plausible hypotheses for the totally unreliable trade-off in the 1970s.

Table 4-2: Actual and Expected Inflation Rates, 1970-1985

Year	Actual	Expected*
1970	5.5	5.0
1971	3.4	5.5
1972	3.4	4.5
1973	8.8	3.8
1974	12.2	6.1
1975	7.0	9.4
1976	4.8	11.8
1977	6.8	6.9
1978	9.0	6.2
1979	13.3	7.5
1980	12.4	10.7
1981	8.9	12.0
1982	3.9	10.8
1983	3.8	7.2
1984	4.0	4.9
1985	3.8	4.0
1986	1.1	3.9
1987	4.4	2.5
1988	4.4	3.3
1989	4.6	3.8
1990	6.1	4.5
1991	3.1	5.3
1992	2.9	4.3
1993	2.7	3.6
1994	2.7	2.8
1995	2.5	2.7

* Calculates as $0.5\Delta P_{t-1} + 0.3\Delta P_{t-2} + 0.2\Delta P_{t-3}$ to yield next year's ΔP expectation.

These were, in approximate order of importance:

(1) Inflationary expectations;

(2) Changing labor force structure;

(3) Government policy errors (monetary, fiscal, and regulatory problems);

(4) Falling productivity (saving and investment trends);

(5) Unfavorable changes in international trade and finance (the ending of the Bretton Woods system and the rise of other countries as major exporters of manufactures and "high tech" products);

(6) Resource shortages and "bottlenecks" (especially OPEC and higher energy costs);

(7) The "market power" of labor unions and oligopolistic business firms; and

(8) "Malaise," which can be thought of as including everything else not specifically mentioned.

Some would argue that the Reagan Revolution of lower marginal tax rates, some reduction in the expansion of government spending and regulatory activity, and a remarkably successful "disinflation" of the American economy "saved the system just in the nick of time." Others would have a much more negative assessment of these policies. Is the Phillips Curve tradeoff being restored currently?

Milton Friedman and the Monetarists

Let us begin this section by a slightly provocative statement, to be explained a bit more fully later: "Just as Keynes would not want to be a Keynesian today, Milton Friedman is really not a Monetarist." If you are a bit puzzled, that's good, for economic analysis is not really as simple as presented by most texts today, where formal equations gloss over very important shades of meaning.

As outlined in the previous chapter, the essence of Keynesian analysis is the simple aggregate demand equation, $Y = C + I + G$, which implicitly assumes that $C + I$ will be less than $C + S$, and that the government will need to cure stagnation in the private sector by deficit spending, $G > T$. If the diagnosis is "inadequate aggregate demand," and the prescription is "compensatory fiscal policy," then the role of the central bank can be described very simply — "money does not matter." Note here that Keynes said "there's many a slip 'twixt the cup and the lip," but he himself discussed monetary theory and policy as serious and worthy issues. Many of his American followers went a good deal further, arguing that the only function for a central bank should be to keep interest rates low and stable. As a result of this view, the Federal Reserve was forced to "peg" the rate on long-term U.S. government securities at a very low 2.5%, up until about 1953 (eight years after the end of the war).

During these several decades of Keynesian orthodoxy, when it was considered to be quaint to talk seriously about the role of money, a small but increasingly loud voice somewhere in the Midwest was heard by the economics profession. At first, it was Milton Friedman himself saying: "Money matters!" Then, it was Uncle Miltie and several of his students repeating: "Money matters exceedingly!" But, as is often the fashion in such matters, the argument concerning money became dogmatic, turned into a theology, and today we have a rather large and very vocal body of monetarist opinion shouting: "money is all that matters!"

Let us talk (quite briefly, alas!) about Milton Friedman's contributions to economics. There have been many — theoretical, methodological, historical, and philosophical — but for purposes of a recapitulation in an undergraduate economics textbook, let me focus on just three areas. The first of these is macroeconomics, broadly speaking, the second is monetary history, and the third is economic philosophy. Before we get into some of the details of our discussion, a brief overview seems to be in order. Friedman fervently believes in the free market — as an institution for safeguarding individual freedom, for rational allocation of resources, for generating information, and for creating an impersonally fair distribution of income and power. This market as an institution is not interested in the color of your skin, your religious beliefs, how you spell your name, or your family background. It is sometimes said that economists are "people who know the price of everything, but the value of nothing." Let me suggest, without necessarily implicating Uncle Miltie, that the price established for a good or a service in a competitive market is a pretty good indicator of its value to that society.

First, in macroeconomics generally, it is important to acknowledge three of Friedman's contributions to that field. The philosophical aspect of these ideas should be noted as well — Friedman believes that the market economy is self-stabilizing, and that most governmental actions in monetary and fiscal policy are unnecessary at best, but destabilizing at worst. Friedman is well-known, even in standard Keynesian macro texts, as the author of the "permanent income hypothesis." In the late 1940s and early 1950s, as national income and product data were becoming available (GNP is a concept not used before World War II, but economists have since then made estimates for earlier years), a puzzling discrepancy was being noted by researchers working on the consumption-income relationship. One group of economists working with cross-section data were able to fit regression lines to their data points that were just like the textbook Keynesian consumption functions.For a straight-line graph, the MPC (or b) is constant — but the ratio of consumption to income falls, as income rises. Mathematically, the ratio C/Y (the Average Propensity to Consume, or APC) falls, as income rises — the APC approaches the MPC as income rises to infinity.

Therefore, in policy-making terms, if there is a secular tendency for $S > I$ at higher income, the role of the government will have to be expanded, in order to have a larger $G > T$ to offset contractionary tendencies.

On the other hand, Friedman and others investigating longer-run time series relationships between aggregate consumption and national income found a rather different consumption function. Nearly all time series data showed that consumption remained relatively constant with respect to GNP — the simple function, $C = bY$, was adequate to describe the relationship. According to Friedman, a distinction should be made between permanent and transient income. In the long run, consumption is primarily related to permanent income (or wealth). Thus, a medical student in the last year of his/her studies may well consume more than his/her current income, while an elderly Japanese worker in his last decade of well-paid employment (but facing a long retirement period with low income expectations) would save a lot. The marginal propensity to consume (MPC) out of permanent income is quite high — perhaps as high as 90%, while the short-run MPC is a good deal lower.

This has a couple of important policy implications. First, there is not secular or long-run tendency toward excessive saving as income rises; secondly, changes in disposable income, when viewed as temporary or transient, have a very low multiplier. In Keynesian terms, which a steadfast follower of Friedman would be reluctant to use, tax rebates and tax surcharges would not have much of a multiplier effect, and could not be relied upon for "fine tuning" the economy. (Of course, a loyal follower of Friedman would argue that virtually all cyclical instability is the fault mainly of monetary policy errors; thus, discretionary fiscal policy would not ever be needed.)

Friedman's second major contribution to macroeconomic theory involves his restatement of the demand for money. Just as we constructed a "straw man" of classical macroeconomics, let us return the favor to Keynes and the Keynesians — who have taught us that $M_d = f(Y, i)$. In the simple Keynesian world of standard macroeconomics texts, the demand for cash balances is directly related to the level of GNP (but it's a rather passive relationship, with the demand for transactions balances assumed to be a given fraction of whatever GNP, or Y, happens to be), but inversely to i, the rate of interest on long-term bonds. In the Keynesian world, an increase in the supply of money has just one effect —it creates an excess demand for bonds. If the Fed increases the money supply by 10%, the *only* permissible impact — in Keynesian theory — is on the market for long-term bonds, where prices rise and yields fall. In sharp contrast, Friedman posits a much more complex M_d function. This function says that money demand depends on wealth (or permanent income), the inflation rate (or yield on durable goods), the rate of return on equities (proxied by the overall earnings of investment in the stock market), the rate of return on bonds (the same as "i" in the Keynesian version of the demand for money), and the rate of return on "human investment" (e.g., health and education). Quite clearly, this is in many ways a superior formulation to that of the Keynesians. If we visit San Diego or Palm Beach, we are quickly convinced that a household's wealth is a much more important explanatory variable of money demand than current income — a retired couple with a low level of current *income* will have a large bank balance, if their permanent income *(wealth)* over their lifetime has been large.

In the classical view, money balances were demanded basically only for transactions purposes — an increase in the supply of money was viewed as creating an excess demand for goods and services. Thus, an injection of new money by the central bank would cause inflation. In the Keynesian world, money balances were held for either three or four reasons (discussed in the previous chapter), but transactions balances were viewed as strictly proportional to national income. An injection of new money would *not* cause a higher level of consumption spending — in the Keynesian system, one spends income not money. An increase in the money supply causes an excess demand for bonds — the interest on long-term government bonds will fall as a result of such an increase. Only if GNP eventually rises (and remember that there's "... many a slip 'twixt the cup and the lip"), will the demand for money for transactions purposes go up, but in a passive and predictable way. Milton Friedman's view of money demand seems to be a much more general and realistic one. An increase in the money supply exerts a powerful and pervasive influence on the economy, not easily specified empirically, which affects all financial markets as well as spending for goods and services. The Quantity Theory of Money is quite applicable — in the long run, inflation is rougly proportional to money growth. While the velocity of money is not constant, as suggested by some classical theorists, it may be a good deal more stable than the marginal propensity to consume, and hence, a better predictor of economic activity than the Keynesian multiplier.

A third macroeconomic contribution of Friedman's is the so-called "natural rate of unemployment hypothesis," already mentioned briefly in Chapter 1. This is often presented as a vertical Phillips Curve, denying that there exists a "trade-off" between inflation and unemployment. What Friedman has argued is that unemployment is affected more by supply-side considerations than by aggregate demand, which does not necessarily mean a vertical Phillips Curve. He has argued that monetary policy cannot be used to "peg" to a specific unemployment rate, since employment decisions at the micro level depend upon labor productivity, goverment regulations, and a host of other factors. It is impossibe to target unemployment rates in Wheeling, W.Va., or Detroit, for that matter, by the Fed buying government securities in the financial district of New York City.

In addition to his contributions to macroeconomic theory, which we have just reviewed very briefly, Friedman has also done a great deal of serious research in the area of monetary history. His co-authored volume (with Anna J. Schwartz), *A Monetary History of the United States, 1867-1960* (Princeton University Press, 1963), provides us with a meticulous examination of trends and cycles in monetary policy and economic activity. In response to the Keynesian claim that "money does not matter," Friedman and Schwartz argue that the Great Depression of the 1930's is itself "a tragic testimonial" to the power of money — from 1929 to 1933, the supply of money was cut by a third, nominal GNP also fell by a third, and unemployment soared. The Federal Reserve System, created to avoid bank panics and to serve as "the lender of last resort," was the principal culprit for allowing the money supply to shrink — thus, government policy errors and not instability in private sector spending is to blame for the Great Depression, says Milton Friedman. While it is beyond our scope to analyze the argument fully here, it may well be that Uncle Miltie is unduly harsh on the Fed in this connection. Considering the tools that the Congress had given to the central bank at its creation in 1914, the Fed acted promptly and courageously in 1930-31, cutting the discount rate from 6% to 1.5% in a number of steps. Still, perhaps they could have done more in 1929, as well as not *raising* the rate to 3.5% in the fall of 1931 (as the classical gold standard came to an end), but hindsight is always a good deal sharper. The general argument that the Depression was largely caused by a monetary contraction — with its deflationary expectations becoming cumulative — is certainly a plausible one.

While the power of money is very strong and pervasive, argues Friedman, monetary policy works with a long and a variable lag. If we examine monetary and real cycles over about a century, the average lag between a downturn in money growth and overall real economic activity (as measured by GNP) is eighteen months — but with a "standard deviation" of six months. Thus, the relationship between monetary policy changes and overall economic activity makes prediction and "fine tuning" very difficult — two-thirds of the time after a peak in money growth, other measures such as GNP will also turn down, but after either 12 months or 24 months after the change in monetary policy, says Friedman. What that statement leaves unspecified seems even more significant — one-third of the time the expected response will take place in the space of less than one year *and* more than two years later.

The relationship between money growth and changes in economic activity is a very powerful one — as Friedman says, the Great Depression was "a tragic testimonial" to the power of monetary policy, and "inflation is always and everywhere a monetary phenomenon." However, given that the lag between money growth and inflation is both rather long and quite variable, all hope of having an effective countercyclical policy by the monetary authorities must be forsaken —the central bank is probably more likely to be moving in the wrong direction than the right one, to be putting on the brakes after the economy had already turned down on its own, or hitting the accelerator after a boom has begun.

Finally, let's talk a bit about Friedman's economic philosophy. As was mentioned at the outset, Professor Friedman admires the virtues of the free market — the Chicago School, of which he is probably the best-known representative, is characterized by a fervent belief in the efficacy of private sector solutions. Both of his books on this topic, *Capitalism and Freedom* (1959) as well as the one, co-authored with Rose Friedman, *Free to Choose* (1982), are highly recommended — we cannot possibly do justice to their subtle and sophisticated argumentation in a couple of paragraphs in a textbook. They are to be savored, not summarized. But summarize we must — any economic system should be judged, first and foremost, argues Friedman, on how it treats liberty. The most desirable economic system creates institutional arrangements that maximize individual freedom, says Friedman. That's pretty strong stuff, isn't it? Many would probably favor trading a bit of freedom for a bit more equality — helping those less fortunate than we have been, even if forced to do so by the government's tax system rather than voluntarily through private charities. Still, Friedman is willing to consider other objectives, but freedom comes first and foremost.

Friedman argues convincingly that economic freedom under capitalism and the political freedoms of a democratic system go hand in hand. Under capitalism, the rights of all minorities are effectively safeguarded by the market. To paraphrase Friedman, the suppliers of newsprint sell it as eagerly to the publishers of *The Wall Street Journal* as to *The Daily Worker;* writers will willingly sell their work to either the *National Review* or the *Berkeley Barb* (or *Penthouse*); and printers will happily set type for any and all of the five. It is enough to have the money. The *Washington Post* will sell advertising space to the Republicans, the Democrats (though that's often provided free), the governments of Cuba and South Africa, the Moonies and the Hare Krishnas, the vegetarians and the Beef Council of America, in a word — the more, the merrier. Of course, such dissent and criticism are costly — a full-page ad in the *Post* will set you back a pretty penny, but it is enough to have the money to sponsor your viewpoint, no matter how bizarre or unpopular. As Friedman says, it is important that people are forced to make sacrifices for unpopular causes in which they deeply believe — otherwise, the freedom to criticize and to dissent becomes a license to attack the existing social order (as it did at times in the late 1960s and early 1970s).

Compare and contrast this "censorship by economics" to a centrally planned economy, where the State controls the means of production. Somehow, says Friedman, the advocates of "democratic socialism" have refused to face up to the fact that these two terms are fundamentally incompatible — or, at the very least, have refused to discuss how the fundamentals of democracy would be safeguarded in an economic system where most production decisions would be in the hands of the goverment. Imagine the plight of an idealistic student wishing to set up a Young Capitalists Club in Beijing — or advocate independence for Taiwan at the University of Hong Kong in 1998. She would have to ask the University printshop to print posters and leaflets to announce the first meeting, copy subversive propaganda on a state-controlled machine, ask a state-run radio station or TV studio for publicity, reserve a room in a government building, and secure Party approval for the speakers and their prepared texts. Impossible? Perhaps not, as we have seen in recent years. Difficult? Very.

As Friedman notes in *Capitalism and Freedom,* Winston Churchill was desperately trying to warn his countrymen in the late 1930's about the dangers of Nazi Germany. Here was an important public figure, a man of heroic stature, trying to do something important for his country. Yet, he was refused air time by the BBC, a government monopoly, because his viewpoint was "too controversial." In the United States today, it is still enough to have money to buy air time.

As Friedman says, the essential notion of a capitalistic society is voluntary coopera-tion and exchange — while the essential basis of a socialist society is force. To have him speak for himself:

> "... when you hear people objecting to the market or to capitalism and you exam-ine their objections, you will find that most of these objections are objections to freedom itself. What most people are objecting to is that the market gives people what the people want instead of what the people ought to want.

> ... In a market society, in a society in which people are free to do their own thing, in which people make voluntary deals, it's hard to do good. You've got to per-suade people, and there's nothing in this world that is harder. But the important thing is that in that kind of society it's also hard to do harm.

> ... The great virtue of a market capitalist society is that, by preventing a concen-tration of power, it prevents people from doing the kind of harm which concen-trated power can do.

> So I conclude that capitalism per se is not humane or inhumane; socialism is not humane or inhumane. But capitalism tends to give much freer rein to the more hu-mane values of human beings. It tends to develop an atmosphere which is more favorable to the development on the one hand of a higher moral climate

of responsibility and on the other to greater achievements in every realm of hu-man activity."[1]

Before we leave Friedman, we need to summarize by discussing briefly his most important policy recommendation: the Friedman Rule to increase the money supply by 3-5% per year. This idea is rooted in his theoretical, historical, and philosophical views just reviewed — and he would be happy to see a constitutional amendment to force the Federal Reserve to adopt this rule, and to adhere to it for a good long time, hopefully, forever. Friedman argues that "stop-and-go" monetary policy of Federal Reserve "fine tuning" is impossible because we cannot exactly specify money demand — thus, while monetary policy is powerful, it works with a long and variable lag. The Fed's messing around with monetary growth rates introduces elements of either deflation or inflation, hindering individual freedom in entering into private contracts, more or less randomly giving windfall gains either to creditors (as in the Great Depression) or debtors (as in the 1970's). Using $MV = PQ$ as the basic analytical framework, Friedman contends that a stable P-level is the most desirable target; velocity of money (V) can be expected to be constant, or fall slightly in the long run (though, in fact, it has risen rather significantly over the past thirty years), and real output (Q) is likely to be expanding, but at only about 3-4% per year. Thus, a stable price level would require an expansion of the supply of money at no more than 3-5% per annum. Initially, the rule could be set at 4% per year (which would mean 1% per quarter, making it easier for central bankers to understand). Then, after ten or twenty years or so, the rule could be discussed and reevaluated — adjusted slightly upward or downward, as the case may be. It may well be that the Friedman Rule is probably not sufficient in itself to restore both price stability and full employment — but, in conjunction with the ideas of the supply-siders, it should become an important ingredient of policy-making in the 1990's. Whether these economic ideas will find support in the political process is another matter, but I am already pleasantly surprised that political and economic freedom in the U.S. have survived for as long as they have, given the prevalence of "liberal" and "progressive" views in the worlds of media and academe.

The Emergence of Supply-Side Economics

It is difficult to provide a brief but useful summary of the so-called "supply-side school," because no such school presently exists, although it should. As the Reagan Administration's "chief ideologue," former Treasury official, Paul Craig Roberts, has pointed out, the supply-side argument developed mostly outside of academic economics — and has still not elicited much interest within academe, though some popular economic models are now beginning to take supply side effects into account a bit more seriously. The early advocates of supply-side ideas were a rather motley crew — a handful of journalists, a few economists at think-tanks and consulting firms, and very, very few

---

[1] Milton Friedman, *Bright Promises, Dismal Performance: An Economist's Protest,* edited by William R. Allen (San Diego: Harcourt Brace Jovanovich, 1983), pp. 89–90.

professors sort of operating at the margins of academe. Since people may actually be insulted by being either included or excluded, the definitive history of supply-side economic thought will not be offered here. It is a loose collection of important ideas which have emerged within the last ten years, and we cannot at this time present a coherent analytical framework. Supply-side economics is quite closely connected to the economic policies of "Reaganomics," and most discussion of supply-side ideas will be greatly influenced by one's political views.

In the heat of the early debate over supply-side principles in the late 1970s, a few good ideas and arguments were oversold and over-simplified. An example of this is the "Laffer Curve," reportedly drawn by Art Laffer (formerly with the Chicago and USC business schools, but more recently an unsuccessful Senate candidate in California) on a cocktail napkin. Plotting tax rates on the vertical and tax revenues on the horizontal axis, Laffer drew a parabola connecting zero and 100% on the vertical axis — and argued that the U.S. in 1979 had already moved beyond the tax rate at which maximum revenues would be collected by the government. "Support the Kemp-Roth bill, which proposes a 30% cut in tax rates, and the budget will be balanced shortly," was the message of its most enthusiastic advocates. While the tax cut bill proposed by Sen. Roth of Delaware and Rep. Kemp of New York provided the ideological underpinnings of rate cuts in both 1981 and 1987, tax collections did not go up sufficiently to balance the budget, while the savings rate has actually fallen. This has led to great rejoicing among economists and journalists opposed to the supply-side approach. "Voodoo economics is dead!" seems to be the cry — as you may recall, the Laffer Curve and other extreme supply-side arguments were called "voodoo economics" by George Bush in the debates of the 1980 campaign.

While a detailed assessment of the economic policies of and accomplishments of Reaganomics is also beyond our scope here, there is potentially much more to supply-side economics than the Laffer Curve argument. We now turn to a brief discussion of these much longer-term ideas. In the Keynesian model, all that matters is aggregate demand, $C + I + G + X - M$. Saving is a negative act, as we saw in the previous chapter. A rise in S means a fall in C and Y will fall by a multiplied amount. Taxes affect the level of Y through C. If the MPC = 0.8, the multiplier is 5; and in the world of Model II, the tax multiplier is minus four. If you need to boost Y by 100 billion, there are three sure ways to do this: (1) increase G by 20; (2) cut taxes by 25; or, (3) raise both G and T by 100. A supply-sider would probably react rather violently to suggestion No. 3 — after all, what kind of taxes are we talking about? Excise or sales, inheritance or property, income or import? In the world of Model II, it doesn't matter, but in the real world one would think that it matters a lot.

A reasonable general equation for developing a supply-side theory of the economy is given by:

$$Q = f(K, L, T, R, \Theta),$$

where Q is output of goods and services ("real GNP"), K is the stock of capital, L is the supply of labor, T stands for technology, R for resources and Θ is a "carpet-bag" variable, representing anything else that we may have left out (such as the entrepreneurial climate).

Like Friedman's demand-for-money function, this general production function is theoretically sensible, but probably impossible to estimate and measure statistically. For example, real GNP is certainly positively related to the stock of capital, which is presumably positively related to savings and sensitive to taxes — but it would be very difficult to specify the linkages exactly. The concept of the capital stock should capture both quantity and quality considerations — not just past spending on investment, but the present value of the expected stream of future earnings, which depends on capacity ultilization and all sorts of other factors. These will be influenced by the overall economic outlook, but also the sorts of policies are likely to be pursued. The variable L, also, should not be thought of as merely the number of man-hours per week offered by various occupational groupings, but should somehow include the concept of productivity. Technological progress and resource availability as well as the general "entrepreneurial climate" are certainly all affected by government policies, but it would be very difficult to specify very simply just how.

What does seem rather clear however, is that government policies were significantly reducing incentives to increase real output in the 1970's. A combination of inflationary pressure and governmental regulations, especially including high marginal tax rates, greatly reduced the attractiveness of productive effort — and increased the lure of the "subterranean economy." Even at rather low income, the tax ratio rose — the marginal income tax rate for the median income family rose from 17% in 1965 to 24% by 1980. Such "bracket-creep" or "taxflation" (as Paul Craig Roberts has termed it), was much more significant for families earning larger incomes. A family with twice the median income — which would hardly be considered as "the rich" — saw its marginal tax rate rise from 22% in 1965 to 43% in 1980. If we add in social security taxes as well as state and local income taxes, families of modest means (plumbers and college teachers) were paying more than half of each additional dollar of their earnings to the government. Tax considerations of economic activities often became more important than their expected returns.

This very significant upward drift in marginal tax rates greatly changed a number of significant relative prices. We can discuss briefly at least three such major changes — the first being what Craig Roberts calls the "work vs. leisure" tradeoff. Somewhat more broadly, the relative returns from officially recorded and taxable economic activity declined steadily in the 1970's, while the options of "leisure," do-it-yourself work, barter, tax shelters, and even illegal transactions became increasingly more attractive. If an electrician works on a Saturday in recorded employment and earns $300, of which the government gets more than half, he would not be likely to hire a painter to paint his house at $150 per day. A $50 bill to a dentist or a $20 cash tip to a waiter began to look twice as large in 1980, if they could conveniently arrange to "forget" to declare them to the IRS. The very rapid rise in $100 bills in circulation over the past twenty years is a pretty good indicator of the flowering of the "subterranean economy." While perhaps not as extensive as in the former Soviet Union or Eastern Europe, the American underground economy is often estimated to be as large as 15-20 percent of our GNP.

Writing about the underground economy appears to have become a growth industry in recent years, despite a paucity of good statistics concerning this subject. The term, the "subterranean economy," was introduced by Peter Gutmann, in a 1977 article of the same name in the *Financial Analysts' Journal*. By using some rather impressionistic statistics concerning the ratio of currency to checking account balances, Gutmann argued that unrecorded economic activity amounted to $176 billion in 1976 and $195 billion in 1977 — about 10% of officially recorded GNP, and "roughly equal to the official GNP of all of Canada." Edgar Feige has derived estimates that are roughly twice as large — $225-$369 billion for 1976, which then were 13-22 percent of measured GNP. Both of these initial estimates were based on rather crude macroeconomic techniques, derived from the monetary aggregates. More recently, we have also been provided rather more careful econometric and microeconometric studies, which still suggest that unrecorded economic activity amounts to a rather significant 8-10% of "official" GNP.

Some other aspects of taxflation in the 1970's involved its impact on the relative price of saving and consumption, as well as on the choice between consumption and investment. Prior to 1980, the combination of inflation and the prevailing tax system subsidized spending and penalized saving — in part, this was due to the general acceptance of a very simplistic Keynesian model, which views saving as a negative act (as in the "Paradox of Thrift"). Under existing tax rules in 1980, an upper-income taxpayer, in the 70 percent marginal tax bracket, would have paid an annual interest rate on a new mortgage of 10.78% — however, the federal government would have paid 7.55% of that, due to the deductability of interest payments from personal income. As a specific example, the District of Columbia government would have picked up an additional 1.18% in 1979 (D.C. had an 11% marginal income tax rate). Thus, the upper-bracket homebuyer could have borrowed at an after-tax rate of 2.05%! Partly because of this, real estate prices in tight housing markets soared in the 1970's — as long as property values in Georgetown were rising by 8-10% per year, why not borrow at 2%? Buy five or six houses there, two or three condos in Ocean City, why not? Uncle Sam would help you pay most of the interest (with Mayor Barry of D.C. chipping in a bit of small change as well). While housing expenditures, though only on new houses, are counted and viewed partly as investment, other forms of spending were subsidized as well. Most of people's interest on automobile loans was paid by governments. Even credit card charges at 18% per year would not be hard to bear, if governments paid 14.58 percent and your real rate, therefore, was less than four percent.

On the other side of the consumption-saving choice, the system heavily penalized interest income earned on one's savings. For small savers, Regulation Q — put in place during the Depression to prevent "cutthroat competition" among financial institutions — prohibited interest payments on transaction deposits (checking accounts) and put an upper limit on passbook savings accounts (at 5.25% for commercial banks, and 5.50 % for other depository institutions, mainly savings and loan associations). For higher income taxpayers, Treasury bills in 1979 were yielding a little more than 10 percent — however, this nominal yield was probably fully taxable at 70%, producing an after-tax return of 3%. Since the inflation rate in 1979 was 13.3% — "truth-in-advertising" advocates should have required all institutions selling T-bills to display a great big sign, preferably flashing in pink or purple neon, "minus 10 paid here!"

Closely related to the above argument is the consumption-investment choice as well. High marginal tax rates applied to investment income greatly lower the opportunity cost of consumption spending. Let us cite Paul Craig Roberts' famous Rolls Royce story:

> "... The 98 percent marginal tax rate, on investment income that applied in Great Britain until recently provides a good illustration. A person in that high bracket can spend $100,000 on a Rolls Royce or invest it at 17 percent. On a pre-tax basis the cost of the Rolls Royce is to forgo an income stream of $17,000 per year, a relatively high price for a car. After tax, however, the value of that income stream is only $340 per year (the 2 percent of $17,000 remaining after taxes), which is all the Englishman has to give up in order to enjoy a Rolls Royce — a very low price indeed. This explains the paradox of why there are so many Rolls Royces on London streets at a time when England is in economic decline. The Rolls Royces are mistaken for signs of economic prosperity, when in fact they are signs of high tax rates on investment income. The principle involved is most easily illustrated by this extreme example, but it operates across the spectrum of tax rates." [2]

This general principle is a very important component of the supply-side argument: taxflation in the 1970s greatly increased the attractiveness of conspicuous consumption, tax shelters and other non-productive investments, such as hoarding "collectibles," and decreased the real after-tax return of additions to plant and equipment. The dismal performance of the stock market during the "Malaise Decade" of the 1970's provides useful proof — owning a piece of American business equity was viewed as greatly inferior to buying precious metals, speculating in foreign exchange, participating in the real estate boom, and so on.

To end this chapter on a positive note, the expansion in economic activity to date has lowered unemployment rates remarkably (from more than 10% to just a bit more than 5%), without rekindling dangerous inflationary expectations. The stock market has reached ever greater heights — making a few of us dizzy. During the decade of the 1980s, the "Reagan Revolution" reflected supply-side ideas and was working rather well in creating jobs and reducing inflation. (And, the 1991-92 recession can be blamed on Bush.) The four principal tenets of "Reaganomics" announced early in 1981 were:

(1) A reduction in the growth of government spending, including an elimination of federal programs in those areas, where they were deemed duplicative or unnecessary;

(2) A lowering of the average federal tax burden, with particular emphasis on a long-term and permanent cut of marginal income-tax rates;

---

[2] Paul Craig Roberts, *The Supply-Side Revolution* (Cambridge, MA: Harvard University Press, 1984), pp. 36–37. Today, of course, marginal rates in most European countries are much lower — in large measure, due to the example of the U.S.

(3) The adoption of a more stable and decidedly anti-inflationary monetary policy;

(4) A significant lessening of federal government regulatory influence and reporting burdens on business.

While it is beyond our scope here to provide a comprehensive report card on the achievement of all of these goals, we can applaud the reduction of the top marginal tax rate from 70% to 50% by 1986 — and a further legislated reduction to 28-33% in 1988. Various tax shelters and "loopholes" have been made less attractive both by ruling them out entirely (the interest deduction for the third or fourth house, for example), or by the lower tax rate itself. Governmental intrusions in private business decisions seem to be less significant, and monetary policy has regained considerable "credibility." Still, government spending growth has not slowed very much — despite the fact that revenues have stabilized as a percentage of GNP — and budget deficits remain as a major problem even today. However, also at the present time, inflation remains low, and the dollar appears to be stabilizing. Relatively to what might have happened to American capitalism during the past decade, the Reagan administration gets at least a B in my grade book.

While the early claims of some supply-siders that cutting marginal tax rates will greatly increase tax revenues — balancing the budget within a couple of years — and lead to a veritable explosion of productivity gains and much greater private saving must be taken with several grains of salt, supply-side ideas are gaining adherents, including even Professor Samuelson in his latest two editions of the Principles text (now co-authored with William Nordhaus). It is very important to keep in mind that a serious supply-side argument emphasizes the impact of *long-run* changes in incentives. Let us conclude this overly long chapter at this time by highlighting the summary of supply-side ideas, as provided by Michael K. Evans:[3]

(1) Lower personal tax rates should raise the savings rate, because the after-tax rate of return on assets will be higher. In turn, greater saving should lead to lower interest rates and higher real investment. (Somewhat inexplicably, however, the savings rate has decreased in the 1981-1987 period and remains quite low.)

(2) A reduction in corporate tax rates should lead to higher investment by increasing expected rates of return. (Nevertheless, to some extent, the 1986 tax bill went in the opposite direction, though there are improvements in the relative treatment of various investment categories.)

(3) Higher investment should lead to higher productivity, which will enable the economy to respond to the stimulation provided to aggregate demand by the tax cut without inflationary pressures being unleashed.

(4) The transfer of resources to the private sector should also boost productivity, "... since productivity gains in the public sector are small or nonexistent."

(5) Lower marginal tax rates should moderate demands for wage increases, improve work effort and individual incentive.

(6) Lower inflation should cause an increase in net exports and strengthen the value of the dollar. It can be pointed out, however, that the U.S. trade deficit soared to more than record $150 billion in 1986 and 1987, when the American inflation rate was quite moderate and was at an even higher level in 1995 as well. In 1995, the U.S. dollar plunged to an all-time low against several important currencies, notably the Japanese yen and the German D-mark, but regained most of that loss by the end of 1996.

Let me finally conclude with a quote from Evans (which seems quite correct and to the point):

"... supply-side economics — the use of fiscal policies to shift resources from spending to saving and from the public to the private sector — represents the best hope for curing the ills of the economy in the longer run. In particular, the abandonment of supply-side principles — shifting resources back to the public sector and diminishing supply through tax increases — can only lead to stagnant or declining productivity and an eventual return to double-digit inflation."[4]

It is a matter of debate whether the Bush administration should be blamed for continuing Reagan's policies *or* abandoning them. Was the recession of the early 1990s a consequence of redistributing wealth toward the rich, as has been suggested by some, or the result of other policies? We can certainly now realize that limiting government revenues will not slow significantly the growth of federal spending. To put it slightly differently, by cutting marginal tax rates and by indexing the personal exemption, the Reagan administration attempted to "shame" the legislature into limiting overall spending. We have learned that politicians seeking reelection have little shame (indeed, the concept of shame may be disappearing in our society generally). President Clinton initially submitted budgets with a deficit averaging $200 billion per year "for as far as the eye can see." Since the 1994 takeover of the Hill by the Republicans, some compromises have been made — and the deficit is, in fact, coming down (from about $270 billion in 1993 to "only" $160 billion in 1995). Still, projected further cuts in spending are concentrated in the so-called "out-years," and there seems to be a lot of disagreement on changing the tax system. ∎

SUGGESTED READINGS

Arestis, Philip, and Thanos Skouras (eds.), *Post-Keynesian Economic Theory* (M.E. Sharpe, Inc., 1985).
Bawly, Dan, *The Subterranean Economy* (McGraw-Hill, 1982).
Boskin, Michael, *Reagan and the Economy* (ICS Press, 1987).

---

[3] Michael K. Evans, *The Truth About Supply-Side Economics* (New York: Basic books, 1983), pp. 253–256.

[4] *Ibid.*, p. 256.

Bronfenbrenner, Martin, *Macroeconomic Alternatives* (AHM Publishing Co., 1979).

Campagna, Anthony S., *The Economy in the Reagan Years* (Greenwood Press, 1994).

Cowen, Tyler, and Randall Kroszner, *Explorations in the New Monetary Economics* (Blackwell, 1994).

Evans, Michael K., *The Truth About Supply-Side Economics* (Basic Books, 1983).

Eisner, Robert, *The Misunderstood Economy: What Counts and How to Count It* (Harvard Business School Press, 1994).

Friedman, Milton, *Money Mischief: Episodes in Monetary History* (Harcourt Brace Jovanovich, 1992).

Hall, Robert E., and Alvin Rabushka, *The Flat Tax,* 2nd ed. (Hoover Institution Press, 1995).

Heymann, Daniel, and Axel Leijonhufvud, *High Inflation* (Clarendon Press, 1995).

Mattera, Philip, *Off the Books: The Rise of the Underground Economy* (Pluto Press, 1985).

McKenzie, Richard B., *What Went Right in the 1980s* (Pacific Research Institute for Public Policy, 1994).

Miles, Marc A., *Beyond Monetarism: Finding the Road to Stable Money* (Basic Books, 1984).

Roberts, Paul Craig, *The Supply-Side Revolution: An Insider's Account of Policymaking in Washington* (Harvard University Press, 1984).

Rousseas, Stephen, *Post-Keynesian Monetary Economics* (M.E.Sharpe, Inc., 1986).

Weitzman, Martin L., *The Share Economy: Conquering Stagflation* (Harvard University Press, 1984).

THE FUTURE OF CAPITALISM .

One can hardly imagine two more divergent views concerning the future of capitalism than those represented by Karl Marx and Joseph A. Schumpeter. I am tempted to separate them into two chapters, since they both may be spinning in their graves about being so paired. Still, I will keep them paired thusly, because of a delicious paradox. While Marx, to me, is completely wrong in his analysis, both in terms of fundamental theory, and historical assessment, his writings are read more avidly than those of any other economist, even today. Though I feel that Schumpeter's masterful insights about where we have been and where we are now headed seem to be remarkably clear and true, virtually no economist is likely to read any of his work today — most graduate students in conventional American Ph.D. programs are not even going to hear his name. Marx thought that capitalism would come to a violent end because of its failures — its economic "contradictions" were becoming impossible to bear — while Schumpeter argued that the immense economic success of the capitalist system would continue unabated, but, nevertheless also carry the seeds of its own socio-political destruction.

Marx and Scientific Socialism

Karl Marx (1818-1883) is arguably the greatest classical economist, and his ideas have probably had much greater influence on world politics than those of any other economist, except perhaps for Keynes. An obvious starting point for a very brief summary of Marxism is his "labor theory of value," which holds that the relative prices of commodities will be proportional to the "socially necessary labor time embodied in their production." A couple of points in that statement need a bit of elaboration. First, just spending more time on making a good will not increase prices — unnecessary or inefficient expenditures of labor time will not add value. Rather, Marx has in mind the labor time is that required to produce an article under the normal conditions of production, with average skill and intensity. Thus, if it takes me twice as long to complete this book as it would have taken the average economist, it will not be twice as valuable. Still, a thorough-going Marxist would maintain that the basic explanation for long-run or equilibrium price differences lies in labor time. Second, a bit more needs to be said about the word "embodied." If a table costs $100 and a chair $50, it must be because twice as much labor time has been spent in making the former. Such labor time would include not only that of the cabinet-maker making the finished product presently, but also the bits and pieces of past labor time that it took to make the hammer, the saw, and the sandpaper that were to construct it (and other pieces of capital). If we add up the total hours of present and past labor, says Marx, the table will inevitably represent twice as much "socially necessary" labor time. It seems to me that this is really a "weasel-word" — a way to chicken out, as it were. If we find, after careful reconstruction and analysis, that it actually took 2.2 times as much labor time to produce the table, and the price ratio is only 2 to 1, a good Marxist can always say — "well, that extra 10% of labor time wasn't really socially necessary, was it?"

Even a beginning student of "modern economics" should see two major criticisms of Marxian value theory — though there are enough qualifying words, such as "socially necessary," and enough general vagueness and obfuscation in Marx's writings to escape both accusations on a very simple level. The first objection that I would raise, continuing on a very simple level, is that relative commodity prices are as much influenced by demand (marginal utility) as by supply (marginal cost). When Marx published *Das Kapital* (in 1867), the marginal utility "revolution" of the 1870's had not yet taken place — so Marx was simply following the scientific path established by Adam Smith and David Ricardo, both of whom argued that the cost of production determined the "natural" price of a product. While it was possible for the actual market price to be different from the natural price in the short run, as Smith and Ricardo both noted, the "exchange value" would find equilibrium at the lowest production cost curve in the long run. Second, Marx's conception of capital as no more than "embodied labor" also has roots in Adam Smith's views in particular, later to be modified by the Austrian School's writing about the rate of interest.

Let us discuss this idea a bit more carefully. Even if we concede that natural resources ("land," as economists would call that input) should be, as socialists would claim, ought to be, owned by society as a whole. However, more should be said on this score. One of the major problems in the real-world socialist systems, which we shall examine, is the terrrible waste of natural resources and the degradation of the environment that they have experienced — probably due tho this fatal theoretical misconception. Marxian analysis seeks to reduce the contributions of capital and entrepreneurship to "embodied labor time." An important element in the contribution made by "capital" to the production process involves the "time value of money" — a capitalist entrepreneur had to forego his own consumption in order to advance the wages of workers making the hammer, the saw, and the sandpaper needed to make the table. Thus, the capitalist needs to be compensated for his *functional contribution* to the production of capital goods. Similarly, the entrepreneur (even if he is not the owner of all the capital used) takes a risk in organizing the production of a table, if everyone else has just been making chairs. Thus, the market price ratio of 2.2 chairs to a table may reflect the need for capital-owners and entrepreneurs to be compensated for the *opportunity costs* of their contributions, even if the precise ratio of embodied labor hours is something different.

To continue Marx's main theme, all value is due to labor time input. However, the difference between the value of labor and the "price of labor-power" is called "surplus value." Notice the rather insulting and demeaning term Marx used for "wage payments" — they are merely the price of labor power. The capitalist exploiter is not at all interested in you as a human being, as an individual, as a clever and contributing member of society — all he seeks to do is to buy and use your labor power, at a wage rate as low or cheap as possible. The price of labor power is kept very low, driven down toward mere subsistence, by the existence of the "industrial reserve army" (a Marxian term for the unemployed). As time goes on, the amount of surplus value appropriated by the capitalists (or, as Marx called them, the "bourgeoisie") rises steadily — as wages get pushed down even further, as the length of the working day increases, and as production processes or techniques become more capital intensive. I must confess that this last point has remained a bit of a mystery to me still. Marx talks rather vaguely about "killing the goose that laid the golden egg" — about substituting capital for labor, which is the ultimate source of surplus value, but I am willing to leave it a bit vague and confusing for our purposes here. What is clear, however, is Marx's insistence on growing concentration of economic power and increasing contradictions between the productive capacity of the capitalistic system and the purchasing power of the working class (the "proletariat" in Marxian terminology).

Under capitalism, as analyzed by Marx, business cycles over time grow increasingly severe — each depression is worse than the previous one, and the "industrial reserve army" of the unemployed grows larger and larger. In each cyclical downturn, smaller capitalists get gobbled up by the larger ones. For a short period of time, the ultimate collapse of the system, which is scientifically inevitable of course, can be delayed by "imperialism" — sending off the industrial reserve army to conquer and manage colonial areas — but the inherent contradictions in capitalism can only end in a violent overthrow of the bourgeoisie. ("Up against the wall!") While Marx was grudgingly admiring of the rapid growth rates realized by capitalist societies, he felt that growth would in fact be greatly accelerated by the full liberation of "socially necessary" labor — as workers were transformed from being wage slaves selling their labor power to greedy exploiters to fully liberated members of a socialist society working for the common good ("all power to the people!"), their full human consciousness would begin to flower and bloom — and scarcity/want would soon disappear entirely.

The historical dimension in Marxian analysis is that of "dialectical materialism." Borrowing the concept of dialectics from the German philosopher Georg Hegel, Marx taught that history proceeds through (scientifically inevitable) stages. Progress takes place as the result of a clash between a *thesis* and an *antithesis,* which form a *synthesis.* The synthesis, in turn, emerges as the new thesis and proceeds as the dominant force until a change in the underlying conditions of production produces a contradictory antithesis, and so on. However, Marx's utilization of this "stages of historical evolution" approach is really quite brief. As we shall see momentarily, there are really only three or four such epochs, before the process comes to an end — as in most fairy tales, with "everyone living happily ever after."

Mankind's history begins with the thesis of "primitive communism," a setting much like the Garden of Eden, with tribal groups engaging in community hunts and cooperating cheerfully. Everyone pitches in to gather berries, edible plants, mushrooms, and so on — while the young hunters go off to kill a buffalo or a mastodon. All contribute to productive activity on the basis of their ability, and all eat their fill after the successful hunt is over. The antithesis of "private property" — the snake in the Garden of Eden — comes slithering on its belly into the primitive communal society. Caveman Zog now finds a small, snug cave, and a curvaceous maiden (you may think of Raquel at this point, but briefly, please). He hangs around the cave entrance with a fearsome club — "no, Charles, don't you do that — she's *my* wife!" — and begins to enforce his property rights. (Apologies for the politically incorrect tone of this paragraph are hereby offered.) The synthesis that emerges from this clash of "primitive communism" versus "private property" is, of course, *feudalism*. Those individuals most successful in asserting their property rights, usually by force, emerge as a leading class, eventually becoming a hereditary nobility, while everyone else joins the peasantry — bound to the land and obedient to their masters.

In turn, the thesis of feudalism, with its emphasis upon tradition, personal loyalties, and a production system closely tied to the land, is challenged by the antithesis of the market as an institution. As noted in Chapter 2, the full development of a market economy had a number of significant prerequisites — a nation-state strong enough to enforce law-and-order provisions and improve transport and communications, a developing monetary and financial system, and a philosophical model justifying money-making as an acceptable, a bit later even an admirable, realm of human activity. The clash between feudal institutions and the existing sociopolitical order, and the idea of free-market allocation and profit-seeking, produced the synthesis of primitive capitalism. The old order of static status relationships, tied to a specific piece of land and hereditary in nature, was challenged by a very mobile and unstable definition of wealth and status — entire family fortunes could be made and lost in a few decades, and eventually (as capitalistic relations developed further) a few years or even a few months. The enormous gains and losses of plunder and trade, available to nobility as well as commoners in the "new order," dwarfed the land-based fortunes of those participating in the old, feudal scheme of things. The market was an impersonal institution, emphasizing mobility, information, and innovation. The dynamics of the emerging trading system soon led to a much greater importance being granted to "capital," an input that could readily be switched from one plant to another, from a failing industry to a profitable one, than to "land," which was generally associated with static and traditional production processes. Labor was no longer tied to land as a result, and quickly followed capital (and entrepreneurship) in a search for the highest returns.

As capitalism developed, according to Marx, it became more and more vulnerable. Due to an inherent contradiction between its enormous productive capacity and the niggardly amounts that capitalists paid as the "price of labor power," capitalism was subject to more and more violent business cycles. In each business cycle downswing, two things would happen — more workers would lose their jobs, adding to the growing ranks of the "industrial reserve army" of the unemployed. Second, smaller capitalists would be "gobbled up" by the larger business firms, leading to a growing concentration of economic power in fewer and fewer hands. Workers would inevitably become increasingly alienated, and develop the realization that there was no hope of improving their lot under the capitalist order. Further "immiserization of the proletariat" was inevitable, wrote Marx — and a thoroughly alienated and an increasingly unified working class, "the proletariat," would emerge as an antithesis to the capitalist system, the prevailing thesis of the day. Indeed, the "proletariat" would soon develop an international consciousness, realizing that the class struggle had a world-wide dimension (the theme song of countless Comintern meetings was, of course, called the "Internationale"). As Marx and Engels call for in their *The Communist Manifesto* (1848): "Workers of the world, unite! You have nothing to lose but your chains!"

Marx on the Future of Capitalism

The internal contradiction of capitalism consists of an enormous increase in its productive capacity and its tendency to starve the share going to the working class, i.e. the problem of underconsumption. Marx was grudgingly quite positive, indeed even poetic, about the productive accomplishments of the capitalistic system. In an often-quoted passage, Marx points to this:

> *"The bourgeoisie has played a most revolutionary role in history ... The bourgeoisie, during its rule of scarce 100 years, has created more massive and more colossal productive forces than have all preceding generations together. Subjection of nature's forces to man, machinery, application of chemistry to industry and agriculture, steam-navigation, railways, electric telegraphs, clearing of whole continents for cultivation, canalization of rivers, whole populations conjured out of the ground—what earlier century had even a presentiment that such productive forces slumbered in the lap of social labor?"* [1]

Many of us would be tempted to add that these accomplishments did not "slumber in the lap of social labor," but in the dreams of individual entrepreneurs and the lure of the profit motive — nevertheless, the tremendous productive potential of capitalism is established by either interpretation.

However, said Marx, this immensely productive system would produce ever more violent business cycles, concentrate wealth in fewer and fewer hands, and cause the emergence of a thoroughly alienated, miserable, and also an internationally unified proletariat. When Marx was working on his *Das Kapital*, that was largely the way that it really was. Men, women, and children were working long hours at wage rates only barely above subsistence in much of Europe; sanitary and safety conditions in most factories and mines were marginal at best. Economic power was being concentrated in a small handful of closely-held companies in Europe as well as America — Rockefeller likened

---

[1] Karl Marx, *Manifesto of the Communist Party* (International Publishers, 1948), pp. 11–14.

his oil monopoly to the "American Beauty Rose" (of course, judicious pruning of competing buds was absolutely necessary). Ministers and priests were repeating the teachings of "Social Darwinism" from the pulpit — and many of us back then might well have been tempted to join a militant labor union and to learn the "Internationale" song.

As a prophet, Marx foresaw the clash of capitalism as the thesis and the proletariat as the antithesis producing a violent overthrow of the capitalist order, and the establishment of socialism, initially the "dictatorship of the proletariat," as taking place in the most advanced capitalist countries of his day, e.g., England, Germany, and France, very soon. Let us pause for just a moment to present one more important Marxian idea. We have mentioned that his view of history was summarized by the concept of "Dialectical Materialism" — but, up to now, have only explained the dialectical (thesis antithesis—synthesis aspect) component. Marx goes considerably further, which may explain his appeal to young economists. Any society's "mode of production," be it feudalism, capitalism, or socialism, will determine its ideological and social "super-structure" — in other words, economic arrangements dominate everything else. "Economic determinism," or materialism, teaches that political, social and even philosophical institutions and ideas all are derived from how economic activity is organized. As an example, here is one of Marx's best-known phrases, "religion is the opiate of the masses". In that, he is saying that all religious teaching is designed to keep the working class sedated and docile, with their sights set on a happier after-life, while their existence on this planet continues to be made more and more miserable by the exploitation of the capitalist class. The U.S. Constitution was framed by property-owners to safeguard their privileged status, say the Marxists, and the American family is only a temporary institutional invention. A nuclear family, consisting of husband, wife, and minor children, happens to be a convenient appendage of the capitalistic mode of production. It is entirely possible that under different economic arrangements, four husbands and twelve wives (or the other way around) would become a perfectly plausible family structure. Indeed, one of the more attractive "selling-points" for hot-blooded Russian youths in the early days of the Bolshevik revolution was the promise of "free love" under socialism.

After the violent overthrow of the small "bourgeoisie" class, there would be a brief period of socialism, characterized by the "dictatorship of the proletariat." Marx had relatively little to say about the actual workings of the socialist society — very little about production or pricing. However, the distribution of "total social product" would consist of the following seven categories:

(1)   A depreciation allowance;

(2)   An allowance for net new investment;

(3)   A reserve for contingencies, or an insurance fund;

(4)   The general costs of government;

(5)   A portion for the "communal satisfaction of needs" (schools, health services, and so on);

(6) "Funds for those unable to work;"

(7) Finally, there is the "... means of consumption which is divided among the producers of the cooperative society."

Under the auspices of the newly-organized cooperative society, as noted, there would occur a tremendous unleashing of human productivity and creativity — an end to "alienation of the worker." The worker would find a renewed pride in creating a product that would benefit society, and not simply enrich a capitalist exploiter. Furthermore, socialism will more or less rapidly transform itself into full Communism (always capitalized, just as Heaven should be), as there is a change in the superstructure. Marx says that there will be an accompanying dramatic alteration in both individual and social psychology, based upon affluence, education, greater free time, and as well there will be cooperative and creative reorganization of the work and production processes. "Full Communism" will mean the end of scarcity, and a distribution system based upon the noble principle of "*from* each, according to their abilities, and *to* each according to need." There will not really be any need for an "... exact calculation by society of the quantity of products to be distributed to each of its members." It is a wonderful vision, is it not? You, as a worker, would be free to do brain surgery in the morning, teach economics in the afternoon, and fix a leaking toilet in the evening. Thus, there would be an end to the "rigid division of labor," especially the distinction between manual and mental work. In turn, as a consumer, you would find most necessities — salt, bread, soup, gasoline, and vodka (?) — provided free by the public sector. With the full flowering of Communism, we can well imagine a fleet of open cars, with the keys still in them, to be parked right outside this building. If you're only going to Capitol Hill for your internship, you would choose a little red Geo or that orange VW for that trip, leaving the air-conditioned silver Jaguar for someone taking a longer trip, wouldn't you? At lunch, at the "Red 1789," you would surely opt for the healthy sauerkraut soup rather than the butter-dripped lobster tail, wouldn't you? (Your answers are, of course, strongly influenced by your recently-formed greedy, selfish capitalist personalities, as are mine...)

Marx as a Prophet

To recapitulate in a few sentences, Marx viewed capitalism as a historically necessary and inevitable stage in the evolution of mankind toward full Communism. Capitalism would be characterized by rapid growth and technological progress, which would cause the emergence of its antithesis — a unified working class, increasingly alienated and antagonistic to the rulers. While imperialistic adventures could utilize the "industrial reserve army" of the unemployed temporarily, the "immiserization of the proletariat" would continue (having both economic and psychological dimensions). Writing in the mid-19th century, Marx felt that a violent overthrow of capitalism was "just around the corner." Of course, he also did his utmost to hasten an international workers' revolution, organizing revolutionary groups throughout Europe and agitating tirelessly.

Why was Marx wrong? Why was there not a series of proletarian revolts, beginning with the advanced industrial countries of Europe, and then spreading to the rest of the world? Initially, and impressionalistically, let us cite Robert Heilbroner, an American socialist very sympathetic to Marxism:

> *"... One must begin with the clear recognition that the crowning event in the great drama of Marx's thought has not been realized. Not a single proletarian revolution has occurred in any industrialized capitalist nation. Moreover, there is no clear evidence that the system as a whole is now approaching a final 'breakdown.' For a period during the decade of the 1930s, it seemed as if the scenario of Capital was likely to be shortly fulfilled, as capitalism sank into severe depression, and revolutionary working-class movements appeared in Germany, France, and, to a lesser extent, in England. But that moment passed and capitalism emerged from World War II with rediscovered vitality. Economic growth at an unprecedented pace, expansion of capitalism around the world at a headlong rate, evaporation of the revolutionary mood, and the creation of welfare states in virtually all capitalist nations seemed to disprove, once and for all, the validity of Marx's laws of motion, and of the elaborations and extensions of those laws among his followers."[2]*

Indeed, in the early years of the 20th century, a genuine international consciousness of the working class failed to develop — this was especially the case in the United States (and Canada and Australia). While a number of Marxist-oriented groups functioned here briefly in the early days of the 20th century (notably the I.W.W., the "Wobblies"), rising wages and free land along the American frontier made Marx's story of "immiserization of the working class" appear quite ridiculous to people living in Milwaukee or Memphis around the turn of the century. On the continent of Europe, French and German workers put much greater emphasis on their *national* identity than on their membership in an international working *class*, the "proletariat," and both World Wars certainly proved and reinforced this tendency. Thus, the international character of the class struggle failed to emerge, and nationalism (along with religion, in a number of countries) became a much stronger force than initially envisaged by ("scientific") Marxism.

It can also be noted that the emergence of *labor unions* slowed (stopped, reversed) the exploitation of the working class. At the time of Marx's writing, labor unions were prevented from forming entirely or treated harshly. For example, in the U.S., unions were treated as "conspiracies in restraint of trade" even around the turn of the 20th century. Nevertheless, Samuel Gompers' American Federation of Labor (AFL) was at that time beginning to achieve some significant gains by using the simple motto: "More, now!" In America, labor unions emphasized *business* unionism from the outset, stressing *economic* gains from negotiations, rather than *political* goals. In Europe, powerful labor

---

[2] Robert L. Heilbroner, *Marxism, For and Against* (New York: W.W. Norton, 1980), pp. 127–128. See also F.R. Hansen, *The Breakdown of Capitalism: A History of the Idea in Western Marxism, 1883–1983* (Routledge & Kegan Paul, 1985).

groups emerged and contributed to the formation of political parties having a strong redistributional platform, and bargained successfully for wages and fringe benefits as well.

This brings us to a very key point in Marx's faulty forecast of class struggle and greater immiserization — the changing role of government and popular political participation in most market-type economies. "Scientific" Marxism suggests that political institutions would develop to serve the needs of the ruling class of capitalist owners of the means of production. However, here and everywhere, we see the emergence of governments and political parties chasing after the majority, trying to build pressure group coalitions of the workers and the debtors and the poor and the old, and so on. Here, again, a separate volume could be written on the emergence of "pressure-group politics" (and has been, e.g., Mancur Olson) and the economics of public choice and governing. Governments today have to pay attention to a very broad array of constituencies, and usually do not reflect narrow class interests, and certainly not those of the creditor class. A number of specific government policies of a redistributional nature might be mentioned:

(1) Anti-trust laws;

(2) Mandatory universal education;

(3) Infrastructure improvements;

(4) Pro-union legislation (collective bargaining, maximum hours, and minimum wages);

(5) Social security and income support provisions;

(6) Regulations affecting education (loan programs, affirmative action, and so on);

(7) Progressive taxes on income and wealth;

(8) Other laws and regulations.

On the whole, it would be most difficult to argue that all of the above are continuing to contribute to an ever-greater "immiserization of the proletariat."

A fourth point, closely related to the above, concerns the development of Keynesian economics itself — the argument that the public sector is to take an active role in economic stabilization. Or, to put it more strongly, if the diagnosis of mature capitalist economies is the deficiency of aggregate demand and private sector instability, then the prescription needs to involve an inevitable expansion of the government and a deliberate counter-cyclical fiscal policy. Marx wrote *Das Kapital* during the heyday of the international gold standard, a period characterized by *laissez faire* attitudes and a mild tendency toward deflation. While Marx felt that such institutional arrangements would tend to result in an under-consumption bias, which would eventually lead to a collapse of the system, Keynes came up with a similar diagnosis — but a vastly different prescription. Marx's emphasis on an inevitable *revolution* was replaced by the Keynesian *evolution* of a mixed capitalistic system, in which the government played an active role, often quite at odds with the interests of the owners of capital. For example, fiscal policies emphasizing high marginal tax rates and monetary policies leading to stabilization of interest rates at very low levels were followed by most Western industrialized countries in the period after World War II. Creditors would hardly approve of such tendencies. In the United States, as mentioned earlier, interest rates on long-term bonds were "pegged" at 2.5% percent until 1951, and remained at historically low levels until the 1960's.

Finally, echoing some of the material discussed in the first chapter, the development of financial markets and institutions greatly changed the ownership of the means of production. Instead of concentrating business equity into the hands of fewer and fewer "mega-capitalists," which was happening while Marx was scribbling away, the modern corporation has developed into a vehicle for de-personalizing ownership — possibly for the good or the ill of capitalism as an institution, as we shall see in the second half of this chapter. Business decisions were turned over to a self-perpetuating class of managers instead of being made by individual owners, with much greater priority being given to long-term sales growth and corporate survival than to short-term profit maximization.

Despite the fact that Marx's forecast of more and more violent business cycles, concentration of equity in fewer and fewer hands, and continuing immiserization of the working class has proven to be quite wrong, the number of books and articles using Marxist analysis (especially in the West) continues to expand remarkably rapidly. The library's collection of volumes devoted to Marx and Marxism is much larger than that focusing on any other economist, even Keynes, and certainly many times larger than the section occupied by the writings of Joseph A. Schumpeter, and books analyzing the Schumpeterian system. This seems rather curious, for Schumpeter's general prognosis concerning capitalism seems to me to ring remarkably true. Of course, as we shall see, there is some hope that Schumpeter was wrong as well.

J.A. Schumpeter: Lover, Horseman, Economist

Schumpeter is my own personal favorite among economists. Very much a European "gentleman of the old school," he taught at Harvard for many years and became sufficiently Americanized to develop a sense of humor. Upon his retirement from Harvard, he is said to have reported to those assembled that he had set himself three goals in his life. The first of these was to become "the greatest economist in the world;" the second goal was to be "the greatest horseman in all of Austria." And the third, according to this legend, was to be "the best lover in all of Vienna." He concluded by saying that he had certainly accomplished *two* out of the three.

Born in the same year as John Maynard Keynes, Schumpeter was a brilliant and immensely well-read scholar — his final book, *A History of Economic Analysis*, published only part-finished after his death, will probably never be matched by any other economist (in depth, breadth, or weight, and certainly not in the number of footnotes). However, it is certainly true that economic theory has developed in directions other than those taken by Schumpeter, and current writing is little influenced by his ideas. Some elementary textbooks do mention his name, but I fear that half of all Ph.D. candidates in economics today would not be able to identify his work at all. Since I feel that Schumpeter's analysis of "what makes capitalism tick" as well as where it is probably going is essentially right on the mark, I have chosen to divide this chapter rather equally between Marx and Schumpeter. (This is in sharp contrast to other comparative economics texts, which are likely to devote several detailed chapters to Marx, and perhaps a brief paragraph to Schumpeter.)

As Robert Heilbroner has written, Schumpeter was "... the most romantic of economists ... capitalism to his eyes had all the glamor and excitement of a knightly jousting tourney." Schumpeter himself likens it to a poker game, but not a game of roulette at all! Capitalism was not only an economic system based upon private property rights, it was a civilization, a "scheme of values" and an attitude towards life — it was *the* "civilization of inequality and the family fortune."

Schumpeter himself felt that a man's fundamental vision of the world, as well as contributions of real originality and significance to his field of study, were over by the time he reached the age of thirty. Thus, his *Theory of Economic Development* (first published in 1911 in German when he was 28) outlines his basic system of analysis, focusing on the role of the individual *entrepreneur*. As mentioned in the first chapter, the entrepreneur is an exceptional man of great ability — who enters the world of business with "the dream and the will to found a private kingdom." Maximizing profits is part of his motivation, but more important is "the will to conquer, the impulse to fight, to prove oneself superior to others, to succeed for the sake, not of the fruits of success, but of success itself." The entrepreneur is motivated mainly by "... the joy of creating, of getting things done, or simply of exercising one's energy and ingenuity." Economic growth is the result of *innovation*, of risk-taking, of carrying through new combinations of resources. The entrepreneur sets out on a "quest for boundless wealth."

A well-known German follower of Schumpeter (Erich Schneider) has identified five types of innovation (with typical Germanic thoroughness), which I will briefly paraphrase:

(1) Production of a new good, or a different variety/quality;

(2) A new method of production or marketing;

(3) Opening-up of a new market;

(4) New source of supply of raw materials or intermediate products;

(5) Establishment of a new organization, such as forming a monopoly or breaking one up.

A second important aspect of economic progress under capitalism involves *credit creation.* As Erich Schneider had put it:

"... In order to obtain command over resources to effectuate new combinations, the entrepreneur in a capitalistic market economy needs purchasing power. It is made available to him through bank credit. Along with the entrepreneur, the banker thus becomes the pivotal figure without whom no economic development is possible." [3]

While economic growth under capitalism is very rapid, indeed explosive, it is also necessarily cyclical. In Schumpeter's second major work, the prodigious two-volume *Business Cycles* (1939), he elaborated his famous "three-cycle schema." The capitalist world was always subject to three types of business cycles of varying duration. First, Schumpeter identified the so-called Kitchin cycle of 1.5 to 3 years length (named after a British investigator of short cycles, associated with minor innovations and swings in inventory accumulation). Second, there exists a medium-term Juglar (after a French economist) system of 7 to 10 year cycles — superimposed upon yet a third set of cycles, the long Kondratieff waves, lasting 54 to 60 years each. The first Kondratieff wave was the Industrial Revolution, associated with the steam engine, the cotton gin, and the mechanical reaper, lasting from the 1780's to 1842. The second Kondratieff cycle, caused by the railroads and other advances in transport and communications ran until about 1900. The third Kondratieff was moving upward until about 1930, fueled by the automobile, electricity, and innovations in chemistry, but then it peaked and headed down. It is important to note that Schumpeter called the Great Depression of the 1930's "The Disappointing Juglar," i.e., as yet simply another business cycle to fit into his grand schema of cycles — and not as a unique, extraordinary break with historical experience, necessitating a brand-new *General Theory*.

A thorough-going follower of Schumpeter might suggest that the third Kondratieff wave ended around 1960 — and that we may be on the downswing of a fourth long wave currently, perhaps associated with television, computers, and aero-space technology. However, few economists are willing to commit themselves to long-wave theories of this sort. It may well be that such swings are becoming shorter — so that we are now on the upswing of a wave caused by semi-conductors, advances in biochemistry, and innovations in marketing and finance. On the other hand, it may also be argued that the fundamental nature of capitalism has been so changed by now that Schumpeter's three-cycle schema no longer applies.

It is this last point that is worthy of careful discussion and analysis. Unlike Marx, Schumpeter saw nothing in the *economic* dynamics of capitalism that would portend its demise. Don't concern yourself about monopolies and market power, says Schumpeter, the "gale of creative destruction" will take care of them. Even if someone manages to establish a pool or a combination of firms to restrict the supply of a strategic resource or commodity (e.g., oil and OPEC), it will becomes immensely profitable to "chisel and cheat" on the agreement — and to develop innovations (energy conservation, solar and wind power, coal and gas derivatives) that cut into the excessively large profit margin.

---

[3] Erich Schneider, *Joseph A. Schumpeter* (University of Nebraska Bureau of Business Research, 1975), translated by W.E. Kuhn, pp. 15–16.

As long as entrepreneurial motivation is alive and well, market power associated with such monopolies will be very short-lived. Also, in a healthy capitalistic environment, there is no need to worry about the "poor," the masses of humanity, says Schumpeter. Writing in the 1930's, Schumpeter foresaw the elimination of poverty within the next fifty years — certainly in the U.S., and in much of Western Europe as well.

I would argue that his prediction is right on target, though this is the one point about which I have gotten the most vehement argument and disagreement from my students in this course. Let me spend a couple of paragraphs in elaborating my point of view — in defense of Schumpeter — which I may not be able to include in a heated class-room discussion. It is safe to say that we can also agree to disagree whether whatever poverty still remains is due to micro or to macro factors.

When Schumpeter forecast an end to poverty by 1980, say, he had in mind the kind of *absolute poverty* that was indeed encountered even in the United States in the 1930's, the kind described by Steinbeck in *The Grapes of Wrath* — families not having enough to eat, encountering problems of finding clothing and shelter, and not being able to afford to move from place to place. By 1980, or even earlier, such absolute poverty had been eliminated in the United States (and much of Western Europe and Japan). If we could actually find a truly needy family, not having enough to eat in Mississippi or Kentucky, they would have been on all network evening news shows very quickly, and would have gotten an enormously generous response to their plight by the next day. Oprah, Donahue, and Letterman would all have been there with their cameras — avidly filming footage on "poverty in midst of plenty."

Such families are getting harder and harder to find, however — there are food stamps, private charities, and special programs aplenty to take care of the majority of cases. Most churches would be absolutely delighted to find a well-behaved group of "poor" to sponsor and be-friend. What about the "homeless," you say? Have these poor unfortunates not been driven into the streets by the heartless shredding of the "safety net" by the true believers of the Reagan Adminstration — and now Gingrich and his ilk? Hardly, say I. While there may be a few cases of people "down on their luck" having to sleep in their cars — or even losing them and being forced into the streets temporarily — the vast majority of the "street people" are mentally ill, alcoholics, or drug addicts. I am not suggesting that we should not try to help them, but I certainly do want to say: (1) that their plight is not due to "a failure of the system" to provide opportunities and ways of escaping poverty (rather easily and quickly — witness the Cubans in Florida and the Asians in California),[4] and (2) that the problems of the street people can most easily be addressed by private volunteer efforts, and not by the federal government. Still, on balance, I would personally not object at all to using my D.C. tax money for food, shelters, and medical care, although I have some serious doubts about a large city's governmental machinery being able efficiently to do much along those lines, in comparison with the Salvation Army, say.

---

[4] For some further discussion, see Charles Murray, *Losing Ground: American Social Policy, 1950–1980* (Basic Books, 1984).

Another interesting contrast between Marx and Schumpeter is the more general issue of alienation and immiserization, which the former thought to be an inevitable part of the development of capitalism. Here again, the Schumpeterian view would echo that of Smith — there will be such enormous growth in output and income that the wasteful consumption of the rich can be ignored, for the working people will be taken care of abundantly. A key idea, after all, is that mass production benefits the masses. The rich nobles always lived pretty well — freshly killed meat was brought in for their feast, servants would light torches in the great hall, and the ladies would dress for dinner in finery imported from all over the world (including silk stockings, of course). The invention of a refrigerator, an electric light bulb, and nylons (for the "working-girls" says non-PC Schumpeter) clearly did not mean much for the upper five percent of the population, but benefitted the rest of us a lot. The entrepreneur, setting out on his "quest for boundless wealth," does not seek to publish a volume of erudite scholarship or the great American novel — no, some scripts for "Married with Children" and a couple of historical romances (what I call the *Please, Sir, No, No, Not Again,* books!) will do the trick.

To return to the main thread of the story, Schumpeter greatly admired the capitalistic system, viewing the business entrepreneur as a dynamic and romantic figure, and saw nothing to criticize seriously in its economic performance — on either efficiency or equity grounds. Yet, paradoxically, the economic success of capitalism seems to carry within itself the seeds of its own destruction. "Can capitalism survive?" asks Schumpeter. His answer: "No, I do not think it can." Capitalism will certainly not end with a violent *revolution,* since its tremendous benefits have greatly improved the standard of living for everyone, but certain trends in its *evolution* will lead to its permanent and irreversible transmutation.

In his powerful book, *Capitalism, Socialism and Democracy* (1942), Schumpeter argues that the success of capitalism leads to political and sociological changes that will, more or less inevitably, destroy the system in the long run. The capitalist entrepreneur functions best in a pre-capitalist social framework — he needs to challenge feudal rules and institutions, to compete against the old aristocracy for status and recognition, and to substitute merit and rationality for tradition and authority as decision-making principles. To summarize the main themes of his book briefly, Schumpeter mentioned four factors as contributing to the fatal transformation of capitalism as an economic system, and also "the civilization of inequality and the family fortune."

The first of these factors is the inevitable "obsolescence of the entrepreneurial function." Large business firms grow ever larger — the modern corporation evolves from the family firm — and innovation becomes a matter of routine. Nowadays technical progress is entrusted to the research departments of IBM, Sony, and Phillips, while marketing and accounting staffs are responsible for transforming inventions into new and better ways of doing things. To be sure, a few individual "knights" ride forth to do combat in the world of business today — quite a few computer companies and software firms have started out as being identified with a single individual. Still, the number of firms having a particular family connection is shrinking rapidly, particularly among the

Fortune 500 or those listed on the New York Stock Exchange. The role of individual decision-making is quite severely circumscribed in any large organization, be it a profit-making corporation, a government body, or a university. Today most decisions are made by meetings or committees, which pay a lot of attention to public relations and legal ramifications. While the "bottom line" in business decisions is often mentioned, one would have to be very naive to believe that any business decision hinges only on the management's desire to maximize profits. Attempts to assert pure entrepreneurial authority — "I know best, and that's what we'll do" or "I'm in charge here!" — will be treated with suspicion and downright hostility in most large institutions. But, even more importantly, such individual assertiveness is becoming unnecessary, since progress is automatic, impersonal and routine.

Second, Schumpeter argued that capitalism as economic system becomes vulnerable to a transformation due to "the destruction of the protective strata." As noted before, the capitalist entrepreneur functions best in a pre-capitalist, semi-feudal environment. While capitalist rationality goes hand-in-hand with rational political systems — representative government and democracy. Indeed, it is convenient for the entrepreneur to have a stable political order, to have someone else "manage the affairs of church and state," in Schumpeter's words. Historically, in pre-capitalistic Europe, this function was performed by the hereditary aristocracy, which is what Schumpeter meant by the "protective strata." To some extent, even in the United States, a "nobility of sorts" developed about a hundred years ago — "old money" owned by those whose ancestors came over on the Mayflower, that of the New England WASP families, was somehow viewed as noble in itself. In some of today's less developed countries (LDC's), there also exists an "oligarchy" of several hundred powerful families, which are tempting for an entrepreneur to challenge. But, in the older capitalistic countries, Europe and the U.S., for various reasons, the protective strata seem to be withering away. As I said in my *National Review* article:

> *"...where is European nobility today? Working as waiters in New York, or jetsetting from Nice to Bangkok, depending on the skill or luck of their lawyers and accountants, but certainly not tending to the affairs of state. What of the Eastern Establishment in the United States? The affairs of state are left to parvenus from Texas and California, or even former football players from Ann Arbor. The care and feeding of American culture and education is often left to minority group members, and the hold of the Establishment is diminished even in the world of business and finance. The abdication and elimination of the protective strata of the upper class forces the prospective entrepreneur to look after matters of church and state — giving speeches to the Kiwanis, serving on foreign policy councils and presidential commissions, and filling out endless governmental forms. This saps his energy and destroys his profit-maximizing soul."*

I disagree

A third, rather closely related, factor might be called the "modification of the institutional framework." It is difficult to do full justice to Schumpeter's subtle and profound discussion of this point, but let me try. In the heyday of pure capitalism, the dominant form of business enterprise was the family firm, a man's "private kingdom"

consisting of physical assets, such as the factory, the mine, and the farm. Today, the modern corporation still has a physical dimension, but exists mainly on paper — and there is a very distinct separation of management and ownership. Capitalist rationality "turns upon itself" — destroying old loyalties and "habits of super-and-subordination." To cite my brilliant article again:

> "...Such habits, or class relationships if you will, are 'essential for the efficient working of the institutionalized leadership of the producing plant.' Worker loyalty and a certain 'fear of the boss' as well is very much a thing of the past, as workers accumulate assets (including investment in the education of the next generation as an important part of the portfolio), union seniority, and unemployment benefit rights." [5]

To continue to elaborate this third point a bit more, as Heilbroner says,

> "...The once daring, independent, perhaps unscrupulous, but always energetic knight of business was being replaced by a very unknightly figure in a lackluster costume." [6]

Professional managers today are much more motivated by a large, steady income and a secure niche in society rather than "the quest for boundless wealth," says Heilbroner. They become "satisficers," to use Herbert Simon's term, and their decisions in the business realm will be affected by market share, stability of employment, geographic diversification goals, environmental impact, affirmative action, "good corporate citizen," and even foreign policy considerations as much if not more than a healthy "bottom line."

(4) A fourth, and final factor noted by Schumpeter (most perceptively, since there was not at all that much of it around in the 1940's) is the "growing hostility of the intellectuals." This is such a delicious topic I hardly know where to begin. Let me initially be quite serious and straightforward — in the early days of capitalism, entrepreneurs and "men of letters" were often allies. Poets and novelists mocked the pretensions of aristocrats, lampooned the follies of royalty, and criticized the excesses of the Church. Popular literature often celebrated the success of the hard-working, honest, thrifty, and ambitious lad (the *Horatio Alger* genre) and business leaders were often celebrated as heroes in the press and the history books. Slowly this all started to change — the "muck-raking" literature around the turn of the century depicted graphically the exploitative nature of

---

[5] George J. Viksnins, "Joseph A. Schumpeter: Lover, Horseman, Economist, " *National Review,* August 15, 1975, p. 885. A few years later, I certainly would also have included a slighting reference to a peanut farmer from Georgia, and an elderly actor from California, but George Bush shot some large holes in my argument. Still, perhaps the exception proves the rule.

[6] Robert L. Heilbroner, *The Worldly Philosophers, op. cit.,* p. 220.

capitalist enterprises. Dos Pasos and Steinbeck provided vivid descriptions of the plight of the poor, and *Babbit* became the synonym for the uncultivated greedy businessman.

This trend has taken off exponentially in recent years. I often tell my students that a European intellectual today is defined by three main characteristics — he or she will be anti-business, anti-technology, and anti-American. It matters not at all if he or she has never heard of Milosz or Solzhenitsyn, knows nothing about the location of Riga or Kabul, and is woefully ignorant about the Pythagorean Theorem — as long as the above three "anti's" are firmly in place, a position of honor in European "salons" or "cafes" is assured. In the United States, there is a strong tendency — among college sophomores at least — to copy our more "worldly" and "sophisticated" European brethren on this score. Thus, it is perfectly plausible to meet a nice young man or woman from Nebraska holding profoundly anti-American views — e.g., that American living standards are based upon "the rape and plunder of Third World resources." (When the fact that our well-being is so often the result of the toil and thrift of their grandparents is an idea that seems strange to them.)

The hostility of intellectuals to capitalism is certainly easily seen by any careful analysis of the media and popular entertainment. Progressive opinion continues to approve of government intervention as the best way to deal with problems, and society has placed sharp limitations on private property. Although capitalism-bashing is a bit less popular than it used to be, due to the collapse of most socialist governments, it is still vaguely shameful for an intellectual to be a Republican. How many do you know? In books and movies, any obscenity seems fair game today — the only terms to be censored are: the "profit motive," the "free enterprise system," and a handful of others. Any act between "consenting adults" can be shown on the Silver Screen or discussed on a talk show, without any visible signs of disapproval, except an economic transaction. If someone gains in a business deal, the other person loses, right? I'm exaggerating slightly here, for the sake of emphasis, but isn't that basically true? Who are the villains of our films and novels? To be sure, there are a few Nazis still around — but isn't it usually an American businessman? J.R.Ewing? Would it be possible to have a black, a Jew, a woman, or a Hispanic as "the heavy" in a TV series? Of course not — it has to be a white male businessman (well, it could be a cop or a preacher or a principal "gone wrong," all authority figures...). I rest my case.

Actually, I'm being overly dramatic. Capitalism may be dying of boredom even more than because of active intellectual criticism. As Heilbroner has put it:

> "...And so, in the end, capitalism would become old-fashioned. It would no longer be a meaningful word, an idea that could move men to action or rally supporters in a time of crisis. In time it would disappear before the oncoming march of social-ism and its disappearance would be marked by neither a bang nor a whimper. Capitalism would fade away with a resigned shrug of the shoulders." [7]

---

[7] *Ibid.*, p. 291.

I am certainly tempted to end this chapter at this point with a fatalistic flourish — to say nothing about Reagan and Thatcher, not to comment on the dismal failure of collectivism, and not to support the resurgence of neo-conservative theories and ideas. Before turning to the concluding section, I would suggest a class discussion of what *one* event, noted in a headline by the *New York Times* and the *Washington Post,* will in fact signal the end of capitalism in America.[8]

Conclusion

Capitalism as an economic system will vanish by the end of this century, predicted Schumpeter. The demise of the market system will not be caused by the concentration of economic power and violent crises (Marx and the Marxists) or a "drying up" of investment opportunities and secular stagnation (Hansen and, to some extent, Keynes), but by inflation and a failure of political will in the Western democracies. To cite Arthur Smithies, a Harvard colleague and Schumpeter's friend:

> *"...the modern mixed economy is bound to create demands for public expenditures which will increase aggregate demand and raise employment above its 'natural' rate. That in turn will set in motion the all-too-familiar wage-price spiral, with the consequence of general inflation. For all this to happen, the central bank must be willing to 'accommodate' the inflation by creation of money. But this is likely to happen since the bank itself will be under continual attack. It may be nationalized, as in England, or it may be harassed by a democratic legislature, as in the United States..."* [9]

Under "endemic" inflation, wage and price controls become necessary. This leads to ever-greater efficiency losses, which will create the conditions for the emergence of centralized socialism — first, governmental allocation of credit (another name for "industrial policy" currently being advocated?) and, lastly, government planning and allocation of most resources.

In his preface to the second edition of *Capitalism, Socialism and Democracy* (1947), Schumpeter tried to answer the charge of "defeatism" that had been made against him:

---

[8] In my opinion, it is a close tie between "Big Board Suspends Trading" and "Chicago Board of Trade Ordered Closed." A system of wage and price controls, and socialist resource allocation, would be incompatible with "auction markets" for financial instruments and commodities — the New York Stock Exchange and the "commodities pits" in Chicago would have to close.

[9] Arthur Smithies, "Schumpeter's Predictions," in Arnold Heertje (ed.), *Schumpeter's Vision* (Praeger, 1981), p. 145. It is interesting to note that John Kenneth Galbraith's diagnosis of a stable capitalistic order due to "countervailing power" of groups breaks down under inflationary conditions. See John Kenneth Galbraith, *American Capitalism: The Concept of Countervailing Power* (M.E. Sharpe, Inc., 1980).

"... The report that a given ship is sinking is not defeatist. Only the spirit in which this report is received can be defeatist: The crew can sit down and drink. But it can also rush to the pumps!"

The late William Fellner has argued that there has indeed been a rush to the pumps, in part because of Schumpeter's analysis — perhaps not to rescue the ship of "unfettered" capitalism of the 19th century (or even the 18th), but to keep the "fettered" version from sinking. To cite Fellner:

"...What our author has probably underestimated, however, is the efficiency with which many Western-type advanced economies continued to function until not long ago despite the Schumpeterian tendencies. This is one of the reasons that make one wonder whether the structural relations that have evolved in the post-war world need really to be viewed as representing a series of milestones on the road to centralized socialism. The facts do not so far contradict the interpretation that these structural relations describe a 'system' in its own right that may prove viable for an extended period and the further evolution of which may lead toward less as towards more governmental power.

... There does seem to be a growing inclination to move to the pumps, and this leaves the question wide open whether the ship that was sailing during the greater part of the postwar period — not the ship of the 'heyday of capitalism' — will be rescued." [10]

It is certainly true that the advocates of greater government intervention face a hostile audience in the United States — and even in Europe, some "Green" intellectuals have added a fourth "anti" (they are often anti-business, anti-technology, anti-American, and anti-government). While the Reagan Revolution has not succeeded in reducing the size of the government, the growth of government spending and regulations has slowed considerably. Inflation has decreased remarkably, and taxes have been reduced some-what — so that politicians no longer have to deal with spending a rising "fiscal dividend," but have to worry about higher "fiscal deficits" instead.

Another important aspect of slowing down the "march into socialism" has been the dreadful experience of previously-centralized countries subjected to central planning. Even in the Third World, the experience of Vietnam, Cuba, Mozambique and South Yemen can be contrasted to Korea, Taiwan, the Ivory Coast, and Singapore. In Europe, the contrast between East and West has been quite stark. To quote "Sovietologist" Peter Wiles of LSE who grudgingly admits that the West is doing a bit better:

"... Today nationalism in its commonest form is associated in the minds of people who live under advanced capitalism with military aggression, the GULAG and the KGB. Today it remains the case, as it always has since 1917, that political emigrés flow in their vast majority from countries that have nationalized a lot

---

[10] William Fellner, "March into Socialism, or Viable Postwar Stage of Capitalism?" in Arnold Heertje (ed.), *op. cit.*, pp. 60–61.

(whatever their detailed economic policies) to countries that have not. Economic emigrés flow, of course, from poor to rich, which is another matter, but even they feel a severe political constraint: there are no Portuguese in Latvia, but there are in France."[11]

I cannot resist a little tangent concerning capitalist ideology, put so beautifully by Wiles:

"... There is no capitalist ideology any more, or only amongst marginal groups. I think here of all those brash young executives from the less well-known business schools; the ethnic minorities coming up, and the immigrant bourgeois of the second and indeed the first generation. I think of certain fashionable new fields: pornography, television, advertising, pop music, Chicago economics. It is evident that driving, unscrupulous self-dedicated people have not disappeared ... but it is true that they have no ideological stability. In addition, they are not gentlemen, they are not upper middle class ... Though surely that is less important, it still matters. You cannot lead people if you have no style, and are wholly wrapped up in yourself."[12]

As a bourgeois first-generation immigrant from a very small ethnic minority, I certainly appreciate Dr. Wiles' admonitions concerning style. I have read Dale Carnegie and Miss Manners. What do I do next?

Though I would like to continue discussing Schumpeter's vision, for and against, for another hundred pages at least, it is time to close this chapter and to move on. Robert L. Heilbroner in his contribution to Arnold Heertje's book, asks "Was Schumpeter Right?" — and answers: "No. I do not think he was." Heilbroner continues:

"... at the innermost core, I think his analysis is flawed, incomplete and inadequate. On the surface of things, however, and certainly compared with the vast majority of the writers of his time, it is a bravura performance, closer to the subsequent trends of history than the heady expectations of the contemporary Left, the naive hopes and fears of the liberal middle, and the black forebodings of the believers in the Road to Serfdom."[13]

A rather ambivalent assessment is also offered by Paul Samuelson's contribution to the same volume:

"... In concluding, this needs to be said: what capitalism is succeeded by is not necessarily 'socialism' in any of the conventional senses of that word.

Speaking for myself, what I find to wonder at is not that the considerable efficiencies of the market mode of organizing society have been interfered with in this

---

[11] Peter Wiles, "A Sovietological View," in Arnold Heertje (ed.), *op. cit.*, p. 156.

[12] *Ibid.*, p. 153.

[13] Robert L. Heilbroner, "Was Schumpeter Right?" in Arnold Heertje (ed.), *op. cit.*, p. 95.

century. What is to be wondered at is how restrained and orderly that process has been for the advanced nations in the mid-20th century. To say this is not to express optimism. On the contrary, as I look around the world at the recent developments in the mixed economies, I confess to some anxiety whether the coming of equity and progress may not be in jeopardy at the century's end." [14]

But it would not do for us to end on such a troubled note; the entrepreneur is still with us and doing his thing. Let us hear instead (with violins playing) from George Gilder:

"... Beyond the horizons of calculation or prophecy, at last the mountain moves; and there unfurls a great returning tide of vindication that overflows all plans and expectations. It is an irrational process, but it is the classic experience of the entrepreneur, the endlessly recurrent miracle of capitalism, by which orphans and outcasts vastly and repeatedly excel the works and wealth of emperors, the reach and rule of armies, the dreams of kings, the calculus of expertise, the visions of state." [15] ∎

SUGGESTED READINGS

Gilder, George F., *The Spirit of Enterprise* (Simon and Schuster, 1984).

Hansen, F.R., *The Breakdown of Capitalism: A History of the Idea in WesternMarxism, 1883-1983* (Routledge & Kegan Paul, 1985).

Heertje, Arnold (ed.), *Schumpeter's Vision: Capitalism, Socialism andDemocracy After Forty Years* (Praeger, 1981).

Heilbroner, Robert L., *Marxism, For and Against* (W.W. Norton, 1980).

Howard, M.C., and J.E. King, *A History of Marxian Economics* 2 vols. (Princeton University Press, 1992).

King, J.E. (ed.), *Marxian Economics* (E.Elgar, 1990).

Nove, Alec, and I.D. Thatcher (eds.), *Markets and Socialism* (E. Elgar, 1994).

Schneider, Erich (translated by W.E. Kuhn), *Joseph A. Schumpeter: Life and Work* (University of Nebraska Bureau of Business Research, 1975).

Schumpeter, Joseph A. (with a new introduction by Tom Bottomore), *Capitalism, Socialism and Democracy* (Harper & Row, 1976).

Shionoya, Yuichi, and Mark Perlman (eds.), *Schumpeter in the History of Ideas* (University of Michigan Press, 1994).

Sixel, Friedrich W., *Understanding Marx* (University Press of America, 1995)

Stolper, Wolfgang F., *Joseph Alois Schumpeter: The Public Life of a Private Man* (Princeton University Press, 1994).

Wood, Ellen M., *Democracy Against Capitalism* (Cambridge University Press, 1995).

---

[14] Paul A. Samuelson, "Schumpeter's Capitalism, Socialism and Democracy," in Arnold Heertje (ed.), *op. cit.*, pp. 19–20.

[15] George Gilder, *The Spirit of Enterprise* (Simon and Schuster, 1984), p. 257.

C H A P T E R   S I X

SOCIALISM IN PRACTICE:
THE STALINIST MODEL

*I*n *Das Kapital,* Marx expressed a great deal of admiration for the rapid economic progress under capitalism, as we have seen in the previous chapter, viewing the build-up of a sophisticated industrial infrastructure as a "historically necessary" stage on the road to socialism. However, there is very little in Marx on how a socialist economy will operate after the inevitable collapse of capitalism. When the Bolsheviks seized power in Russia, they went back to Marx to look for instructions about how a socialist economy would function in practice — and found very little indeed. Marx had devoted most of his energy to explaining the various "internal contradictions of capitalism" that would eventually lead to its demise and replacement by socialism — which he viewed as a vastly superior form of economic organization, a higher stage in the history of mankind. Marx provided no systematic demonstration of the superiority of socialism and was quite cryptic about the functioning of such an economy. Indeed, it was long debated in the Soviet Union in the early years whether Marx's labor theory of value was meant to apply to socialism.

Certainly, Marx assumed that a high level of capital investment and a great deal of technological progress would have already taken place at the time of the proletarian take-over of the economic·system. The bulk of *Das Kapital* was devoted to trying to discover and analyze the "laws of motion" of capitalism. There is no blueprint for the socialist economy in that monumental work. Writing during the latter half of the 19th century, Marx seemed to feel that a violent overthrow of the decadent and exploitative capitalist order was "just around the corner." Since capitalism was viewed as a "historically necessary stage" by the theory of dialectical materialism, there is a strong presumption that a socialist revolution would *first* have to take place in the most *advanced* capitalistic nations — at the turn of the century, therefore, in Great Britain, France or Germany. Or, for that matter, the United States might have been ripe for such a revolution, since American's eastern seaboard, at least, had an industrial base roughly equal to that of Western Europe. Yet, the overthrow of the capitalistic order first took place in a rather primitive country, Russia, with an underdeveloped industrial proletariat—which was rather difficult for the theorists of Marxism to explain.

When Lenin arrived back in Russia on April 16, 1917, he addressed the welcoming crowd thusly:

> "... *Dear comrades, soldiers, sailors and workers, I am happy to greet in you the victorious Russian revolution, to greet you as the advance guard of the international proletarian army. ... The war of imperialist brigandage is the beginning of civil war in Europe. .... The hour is not far when the people will turn their weapons against their capitalist exploiters. .. In Germany, everything is already in ferment! Not today, but tomorrow, any day, may see the general collapse of European capitalism. The Russian Revolution you have accomplished has dealt to it the first blow and has opened a new epoch. .. Long live the International Social Revolution!*"[1]

Vladimir Ilyich Ulyanov (1870-1924), who took the revolutionary code name Lenin, was now faced with the formidable task of building "socialism in one country," since Western European capitalism did not in fact collapse after World War I, when the Bolsheviks seized political control in Russia. Essentially learning by doing, Lenin has contributed a great deal to communist theory and practice, so that today he is mentioned as nearly equal to Karl Marx in the doctrines of Marxism-Leninism—an ideology, even a theology of continuing importance in today's world. Of course, the events of the past few years have greatly diminished its credibility.

A few of Lenin's most important contributions can be discussed briefly here—many were formulated in jails (in comparison to Stalin's "gulags," these were quite civilized under the Czar—it seems that Vladimir could still buy his brand of mineral-water). Lenin worked on his various pamphlets during a brief sojourn in Siberia, and in exile from Russia right before World War I. Despite some loss of relevance, some of them are still being studied today by bright members of disaffected groups in Africa, Asia, and Latin America (and quite a few curiously dissatisfied young people of the prosperous "First World" as well). Lenin repeatedly emphasized the role of *party cadres*—a secret, tightly-knit and well organized group of professional revolutionaries, whose task is to implant a *socialist consciousness* in the society as a whole. After the October Revolution in the Soviet Union, great emphasis was put on the role of the Communist Party in developing a "system of thought control," a society which relied on a great deal of both explicit and implicit censorship. It is difficult for us, living in an open society awash with information and dissent, to picture the approach to daily life of a Soviet citizen just a few years ago. It is hard to imagine mothers and fathers teaching little Ivan to "be careful of what you say in school" at a very early age, of having to be always on guard with one's co-workers, and being cautious even with family members (there were some well-documented cases of children "turning in" their parents). Rigid control of literature and the media, coupled with the threat of the prison camps, up until the mid-1980s fashioned a society almost impossible for us to imagine. A flavor of life under communism is given by the following passage:

---

[1] Edmund Wilson, *To the Finland Station*, (Doubleday & Company, Inc., 1940), p. 469.

". . . The system of secrecy is one of the essential features of Communist power. It penetrates the whole life of society. Closed sessions, meetings, directives, councils, and deliberations, signed statements about non-disclosure, passes, rights of entry. The functions of secrecy are fairly transparent. The first aim is to hide what happens from strangers and from one's own people and to reduce to a minimum the extent to which people are informed. The badly-informed individual is easier to rule and manipulate. Further, secrecy renders demagogy as well as disinformation and the lies of propaganda less open to attack. It confers more significance on the powers-that-be in the eyes of the uninformed mass. Secret decisions work more powerfully on the masses. Rumors of them get about in one way or another anyway, and are sometimes spread on purpose by the authorities. In conditions of secrecy and of exclusivity and with the operation of a pass-system one can call people to justice on charges of 'divulging state secrets,' 'slander,' and 'collecting information.' People live under the threat of such actions, which is more effective than the actions themselves. . . " [2]

The major contribution of Lenin to "communist theory" was the ruthless subordination of all other goals to keeping the Communist Party in power. The Bolsheviks were initially incredibly optimistic about how the economy would keep on running itself. Once the exploitative capitalist class had been removed, workers would take over the tasks of management—and everyone would live happily ever after.

A second point which needs to be mentioned is Lenin's "law of uneven development." This is the argument that socialism can initially emerge as the result of a political revolution in an underdeveloped country. This will be followed by revolutions in more advanced countries, but might be delayed a bit by the further development of imperialism—the exploitation of less developed "periphery" areas by mature capitalistic states as sources of raw materials and markets for manufactures. In his 1916 pamphlet, *Imperialism—The Highest Stage of Capitalism,* Lenin argued that capitalism in Europe and America had entered a new evolutionary period, of imperialism as monopoly capitalism, where production was concentrated in a few large enterprises. Monopoly capitalism will be controlled by financial institutions, mainly multinational firms. As Harry Schwartz has put it:

". . . Because of the uneven development of capitalist countries, he (Lenin) argues, imperialism is marked by the great export of capital from highly developed countries, where rates of profit are relatively low, to backward countries, where profits are high because land, wages, and raw materials are cheap. The export of commodities is greatly facilitated by these capital exports, since loan agreements often stipulate that money may be spent only in the country where capital has been obtained. In this period world

---

[2] Alexander Linoviev, *The Reality of Communism* (Victor Gollancz, Ltd., 1984) pp. 210–211. Even during the summer of June 1991, the official Moscow version of what transpired in Lithuania and Latvia in January of that year shows clearly that the "Big Lie" lived on in the USSR, up until the dissolution of the Soviet Union in the fall.

markets are characteristically divided into spheres of exclusive influence by the huge corporations of the advanced powers."[3]

For a while, profits earned by these huge corporations will also be used to "bribe" certain groups of workers, in order to divide and rule the proletariat, but Lenin did not doubt the fact that the ultimate collapse of capitalism was just around the corner. However, Lenin and his followers failed to foresee the development of financial and other institutions for the dispersal of economic and political power. They also failed to recognize the important role played by America in shaping a truly democratic, market-oriented world economic system, which a hundred years later was so vastly different from European capitalism of the 1860's analyzed by Marx. America's dominant role in the world after World War II also greatly contributed to ending the colonial system of "spheres of influence," with the United States itself taking the lead in its only "colony," the Philippines (which was granted independence on July 4, 1946).

A third important aspect of Leninism is his sharpening of the distinction between the "lower" stage of socialism and the "higher" one of full communism—with the former being of more or less indefinite length. In his *The State and Revolution*, published shortly before his coming to power in 1917, he defines "full" communism thusly:

> "*. . . For when all have learned to manage, and independently are actually man-aging by themselves social production, keeping accounts, controlling the idlers, the gentlefolk, the swindlers, and similar 'guardians of capitalist traditions,' then the escape from this national accounting and control will inevitably become so in-creasingly difficult, such a rare exception, and will probably be accompanied by such swift and severe punishment (for the armed workers are men of practical life, not sentimental intellectuals, and they will scarcely allow any one to trifle with them), that very soon the necessity of observing the simple, fundamental rules of everyday social life in common will have become a habit...The door will then be wide open for the transition from the first phase of Communist society to its higher phase, and along with it to the complete withering away of the state.*"[4]

War Communism and the NEP

When Lenin and his band of professional revolutionaries came to power, after the October Revolution, the Communist Party became the state, and embarked upon a series of land reform and nationalization measures. Armed workers were encouraged to seize the houses and the apartments of the middle class. Factories were taken over by the local "Soviets." Initially, money was abolished, to be replaced by labor certificates, all wages were to be equal, and attempts were made to abolish all private trade. To be sure, the Civil War also greatly affected economic activity, with important segments of the Russian empire breaking away from the Soviet Union. This period of so-called "War Communism"

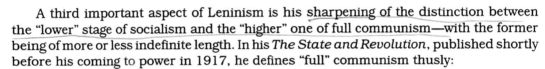

---

[3] Harry Schwartz, *Russia's Soviet Economy*, Second Edition (Prentice-Hall Inc., 1961), p. 89.
[4] Cited in *Ibid.*, p. 92.

lasted until 1921, with predictably disastrous results. Agricultural production fell by about 40%, even after allowing for the effects of the war—as Gregory and Stuart summarize:

> "... there was a sharp decline in both agricultural output and marketings to the state during the 1918 to 1921 period even after adjustment for war devastation. Peasants were holding back grain in storage, were planting less, and were selling to private traders. The area of Siberia sown in wheat was halved and in the Volga and Caucasus regions was reduced to as little as one-quarter of previous levels. Actual sowing concealed from authorities was reported as high as 20 percent of the sown area in some regions. Since agricultural surpluses in excess of family subsistence were requisitioned, there was no incentive to produce a surplus. Instead, the peasant, if he could not conceal his surplus from the authorities, restricted output to the subsistence needs of his family. Thus, War Communism's agrarian policy estranged the Russian peasant from the Bolshevik regime and encouraged him to engage in dysfunctional behavior, such as restricting output and hoarding or concealing surpluses during a period of agricultural shortages." [5]

The secret police (*Cheka*, the great grandfather of today's KGB) and the army had to be used to requisition food supplies for the cities, inflation was rampant, and major cities were becoming depopulated. The sailors of the Baltic fleet, who had been quite instrumental in bringing the Bolsheviks to power, revolted in sympathy with the hungry workers of Petrograd (yesterday's Leningrad and today's St. Petersburg) in the famous Kronstadt Revolt of 1921, only to be massacred by loyal Red Army troops.

Lenin beat a strategic retreat by instituting the New Economic Policy (NEP) of 1921-1928. NEP involved considerable reliance on market-oriented allocation and distribution, with the state retaining control over the "commanding heights" of heavy industry, banking and finance, transport and communications. The purchasing power of the ruble was stabilized by the reopening of the State Bank in 1921, which began to phase out the old depreciated paper ruble and instituted a new currency, the *chernovets*. The NEP worked reasonably well, as limited property rights were restored. In trade and services, market principles were once again allowed to work — food reappeared in restaurants and one could get a haircut in a barber shop. Peasants were willing to work harder again — effort and reward were linked. By 1928, both industry and transportation had surpassed their prewar levels by modest amounts, while agricultural output was nearly 20 percent higher. During the 1920's (Lenin died in 1924), the Soviet Union was engaged in both a fierce leadership struggle and a grand theoretical debate about the course to be followed, since the task ahead was building socialism in a single country, because the expected proletarian revolution in the advanced capitalistic countries had failed to materialize.

---

[5] Paul R. Gregory and Robert C. Stuart, *Soviet and Post-Soviet Economic Structure and Performance* Fifth Edition (Harper Collins, 1994), p. 51.

The Great Industrial Debate

Since the period of War Communism had nearly brought down the Bolshevik regime, as shown by the Kronstadt Revolt, the decade of the 1920's provided a "breathing spell" of sorts. With the advent of the New Economic Policy, a number of Bolsheviks, including Lenin himself, experimented with various techniques of "scientific management" in state enterprises, including Taylorism (developed in the United States), which involved the use of time-and-motion studies. Great emphasis began to be placed upon the development of output quotas (which became known as "norms" in Russian), and the use of differential piece rates for the overfulfillment of quotas, especially in heavy industry. This placed Soviet labor unions in a rather difficult position. As Donald Filtzer points out:

> ". . . The unions were clearly in a compromised position, for as arm of the state and of the latter's industrial policy, they were hamstrung in any attempts they might make to defend the interests of their members which might run in a contrary direction. The unions were not unaware of this political schizophrenia. At the start of the NEP, they openly complained of a return to capitalist-style management—replete with the emergence of mass unemployment. But the opposition was short-lived. Tomskii, head of the trade unions, resolved the problem by identifying the 'interests' of the working class with the restoration of productivity, and thereby with the interests of the state. Henceforward, the direction of the trade unions' allegiance was unambiguous. By 1924, they were offering little more than token opposition to the drive to extend the application of piece rates or to the massive rises in output quotas being imposed by many managers." [6]

After the death of Lenin in 1924, the Bolsheviks were engaged in both a leadership struggle mainly between Stalin and Trotsky, but also in an extensive theoretical debate about the strategy to be followed in building "socialism in a single country." The "right wing" of the Party, led by N. I. Bukharin, who was also a strong potential candidate for Lenin's mantle, counseled gradualism and balanced growth—essentially a continuation of the New Economic Policy with its emphasis on market mechanisms. Extending the NEP principles to the countryside in 1925, Bukharin hoped to speed up economic growth by encouraging private peasant accumulation—broadening total demand for industrial products and increasing the marketable surplus of agriculture. To cite Stephen F. Cohen, Bukharin's biographer:

> ". . . The larger aim of the reforms was 'unleashing commodity turnover,' a goal which Bukharin termed 'the general line of our economic policy.' He believed that a flourishing of trade would result in the fastest and surest economic growth. Broadening the absorption capacity of the market, raising the total volume of commodities, and accelerating their circulation between industry and agriculture, 'is the main method of accelerating the tempo of our economic life.' It 'would

---

[6] Donald Filtzer, *Soviet Workers and Stalinist Industrialization: The Formation of Modern Soviet Production Relations, 1928–1941* (Pluto Press, 1986), p. 23.

provide space for the fullest development of productive forces.' For this reason, manufactured goods originating outside the state sector were to be welcomed. The reforms applied not only to peasant farming but also to the vast network of small handicraft industries, which manufactured a great variety of goods and whose development would contribute to the total national income. Similarly, Bukharin urged that industrial products be imported if necessary to meet internal demand, because an imported tractor, to use his example, would increase the capacity of the home market and eventually generate additional demand for Soviet industrial products." [7]

Rightists

Thus, to put it very simply, the Rightists argued in favor of "balanced growth," based upon an improving agricultural sector, private enterprise in services and light industries, and greater economic interdependence with other countries, if need be. Such a policy would have involved basic principles very much like the initial economic reform programs in some East European countries in the fairly recent past, notably Hungary's "New Economic Mechanism," sometimes called "Goulash communism."

Leftists

The Leftists, led by Leon Trotsky, based the core of their argument on the ideas of economist Eugene Preobrazhensky. To simplify somewhat, their theoretical approach was to rely on "unbalanced growth" with an emphasis on heavy industry. A "big push" to expand the economy's capacity to produce capital goods was needed, said Preobrazhensky, ". . . for a spurt below the crucial minimum effort of investment would be self-defeating." In turn, the potentially inflationary effects of a large increase in investment spending should be offset by changing the structure of effective demand toward forced saving. The development of the country's infrastructure (railroads, electric power, transport and communications) as well as extractive industries should be stressed, since the long-run linkages provided by investments in heavy industry would be more important than short-term returns from agriculture and consumer goods industries.

The fact that investments in heavy industry and infrastructure have a low current return and a "long gestation period" is relatively unimportant, according to the Leftists. In 1928, G. A. Feldman developed a two sector mathematical model, which showed the long-run advantages of re-investing industrial profits in capital accumulation rather than allowing consumption to rise. Sometimes called the "Turnpike Theorem" (the quickest way from point A to B may not be a straight line—if a "beltway" is available for your trip), Feldman's model assumes a closed economy and a zero interest rate. To put this latter point a bit more formally, the state determines the society's rate of time-preference—in the absence of financial markets, consumer preferences for present consumption do not perform a signalling function. In addition to the "Turnpike Theorem," the Leftists also spoke practically about the need to replace Russia's obsolete and depreciated capital stock, and to switch over to the latest technology and capital-intensive methods. The need to develop input-output linkages, e.g., vertical integration of production processes, was also discussed as an argument in favor of a decided emphasis on industrialization.

---

[7] Stephen F. Cohen, *Bukharin and the Bolshevik Revolution*(Alfred A. Knopf, 1973), p. 177.

Roughly at this same time, a formal input-output table was developed by Vassily Leontieff, later a professor at Harvard and a Nobel laureate.

Since Russia had not gone through a significant period of full-blown capitalist accumulation before the Bolshevik take-over, the concept of "primitive socialist accumulation" was devised by the Leftists—which essentially entailed treating agriculture as an "internal colony." Modernization and "true" economic development and progress were to be viewed as essentially synonymous with industrialization and urbanization. Indeed, perhaps even today in much of Eastern Europe, the "country bumpkin" is still the butt of cruel jokes made by their "sophisticated" citified cousins. The ruthless exploitation of peasants—especially the more successful farmers, called *kulaks* (a Russian word meaning fist)—made sense both economically and politically. The *kulaks* were the sober, thrifty, and hard-working people of the land, who had little in common with the militant armed workers of the cities,[8] and who had even less sympathy for the pseudo-intellectual socialists active in the Bolshevik revolution. The moderately successful owner-operator of a family farm in Eastern Europe was a natural enemy of the communal production arrangements favored by the Bolsheviks.

To recapitulate briefly, the essence of the Leftists' argument in the "Great Industrial Debate" of the 1920's involved:

(1) An emphasis on heavy industry and infrastructure development;

(2) A high level of investment and savings, with the savings rate to be determined by the state;

(3) Autarky, i.e., an emphasis upon self-sufficiency and minimizing foreign trade and contacts;

(4) The use of the "Turnpike Theorem" and input-output "linkages" to *plan* economic growth and development; and

(5) The treatment of agriculture as an "internal colony."

The Stalinist Model

After the death of Lenin, Leon Trotsky appeared an obvious choice to assume the leadership of the Bolsheviks. Some of the power struggles, alliances and betrayals, and the arguments and purges of the 1920's and the 1930's are just now being clarified—for there is an enormous difference between what actually happened and the official Soviet version of early history. As we know, Stalin initially sided with the "Rightists," such as Bukharin and appeared to be willing to continue a NEP-type plan. However, with Trotsky leaving the USSR in 1927 (Trotsky was later killed by a Stalinist agent, while in exile in

---

[8] On this cultural divide, cf. Lynne Viola, *The Best Sons of the Fatherland* (Oxford University Press, 1987).

Mexico in 1940), Stalin in fact chose the model of rapid industrialization developed by Preobrazhensky, Trotsky, and others, and launched the Soviet Union into the First Five-Year Plan in September 1928 (though the plan document was formally approved by the Sixteenth Communist Party Congress only in April 1929). The plan was officially announced as completed a little more than four years later, as of year-end 1932. As Harry Schwartz has pointed out, substantial but uneven progress was made (1) output of machinery and electrical equipment was nearly 60% more (in ruble value) than the plan goal; (2) consumer goods output was only 73.5% of the target; (3) the 1932 grain harvest was projected at 106 million metric tons while actual output reached less than 70 million tons; (4) steel production was to be more than 10 million tons, but only 6 million tons were produced. As Schwartz says:

> ". . . *The First Five Year Plan may be considered to have been fulfilled, if one de-fines fulfillment solely in terms of some over-all indicator that balances failure in one area with unexpectedly good performance in another. In retrospect, however, there can be no doubt but that the First Five Year Plan gave only a poor forecast of what actually did happen after its adoption, except, in the most general sense, that the plan did call for an intensive program of capital investment and greater socialization in all major areas of the economy.*" [9]

Future plans in the Soviet Union were generally couched in terms of physical output targets—delivery times and quotas are drawn up by the central planning agency, the Gosplan, and given to the various ministries. Initially, the problems of input-output coordination were considerable and work stoppages due to a deliberate wearing-out of capital equipment took place frequently. Quality of output deteriorated, especially in the consumer goods area (shoes falling apart in the rain, sausages with bolts in them, and other problems). In order to speed up fulfillment of the plan, quotas are revised in only one direction, upwards. The use of "socialist competition" developed new methods of exploiting the working class by using special designations.

> ". . . *Shock workers (udarniki) were those who exceeded their production quotas and/or 'volunteered' for extra work (overtime was technically illegal), to work so-called 'Communist Saturdays' (subbotniki) helping to gather crops on nearby col-lective farms, or to raise their work norms. At first the incentives offered to shock workers were quite modest, but as the policy of intensified piece work and wage differentiation took hold shock workers became a privileged elite entitled to quite substantial bonuses and access to scarce foodstuffs and consumer goods. The re-gime, of course, insisted that workers participated in shock work campaigns out of socialist enthusiasm, but the reality was that for the vast majority the overrid-ing incentive was the need to boost earnings at a time of extreme hardship and high inflation.*" [10]

---

[9] Harry Schwartz, *op. cit.*, pp. 121–122.
[10] Donald Filtzer, *op. cit.*, p. 70.

The work speed-up and quota over-fulfillment policy received quite a boost on August 30, 1935, when a miner named Aleksei Stakhanov mined a record 102 tons of coal in a single shaft—an achievement "highly orchestrated and well prepared." A special designation, "Stakhanovite," was quickly developed by Stalin's regime—and workers were pushed to join the ranks of this elite super-worker category. The basic strategy of raising output norms and dividing the workers into the "haves" and all others was relatively successful. As Filtzer points out, the incentives to become a Stakhanovite were quite strong.

(1) While a wage reform in 1934 had raised the basic pay of the most lowly paid workers, the new policy greatly raised bonuses for plan overfulfillment.

(2) Stakhanovites received "special privileges in the form of goods and services which their wages — no matter how high — could not provide them." (Some received specially built, furnished homes, a few others free cars.)

(3) For "leading Stakhanovites," national publicity and upward social mobility were also considerations.

(4) ". . . At a time when the average monthly industrial wage in 1936 was about 225 rubles, Stakhanovites could earn 600 to 700 or even over 1000 rubles."[11]

In addition to a policy of large investments in heavy industry and infrastructure, the concept of treating agriculture as an "internal colony" was put into practice in the 1930's — with a vengeancence! Let me digress a bit on a personal note — perhaps a bit out of place in a textbook — but possibly a better use of time than several tables on the number of farms collectivized and the decline in output. Somewhere in central Latvia there once existed a family farm bearing a designation with my last name — a place called "Viksninas." My parents told me that I visited there as a boy of four or five, but for many years it was merely a part of my imagination, not as a memory as such. Let us imagine it as of 1949, say. There is a dirt road leading to a white clapboard house, sheltered by some fruit trees — some apples, pears and cherries catch the sun's rays. Across the yard from the modest family dwelling, there is a storage building and a small barn. The barn housed two horses and four cows — and all six animals have names. A dozen or so chickens are scratching about near the barn — to the best of my knowledge they don't have names, though the rooster might. There are a few acres planted in potatoes and a few more in wheat — with a shade tree here and there planted by an ancestor with the same last name. There are a few paths, to the neighbors and to the little river, all trod by family, close friends, and neighbors in that rural district of Latvia. This sort of an agricultural production unit is characteristic of much of Eastern Europe, Russia and the Ukraine — the cows have names. . .

---

[11] *Ibid.*, pp. 185–186.

Collectivization .

I went back to Latvia in 1970 for a four-day visit, and had a chance to meet my uncle Aleksis, who had remained behind when many Latvians fled in 1944-45. As we talked about the collectivization of "our place" when the Russians came again, after World War II was over, my old uncle became more and more agitated, more and more incensed — about the utter unfairness of it all, its simple "wrongness." They took his cows and chickens, and seized the output of his fields. The small farm still exists — my cousin still lives in the house — but virtually all of the land was incorporated in the collective farm. I have indulged myself with a bit of melodrama here — "the cows have names" — in order to ty to get you to appreciate the micro, the "human" side of what the collectivization drive of the 1930's meant for the peasantry of the Soviet Union. The visceral dislike that most Ukrainians have for their Russian masters can probably be traced back to the forced collectivization and the famine of the 1930's, for example. This hatred was even fresher in the three Baltic republics — Estonia, Latvia, and Lithuania — which had been independent countries in the inter-war period (and are once again), and where agriculture was collectivized in the late 1940's. (In the "Viksninas," I am told that the collective farm chairman tried to take the second cow — of a total of two. My cousin said — that one belongs to my mother, and then you better take her along too. He blinked, and said: "never mind...")

During the collectivization drive of the 1930's, under Stalin's direction, more than half of all farms were collectivized by the end of the First Five Year Plan, the end of 1932. By 1936, virtually all of the arable land was amalgamated into about a quarter of a million collective farms (called a *kolkhoz*) or a much smaller number of even larger state farms (*sovkhoz*). The latter are state enterprises, "factories in the field," of a very large size (even by California standards) — usually larger than 10,000 acres. There was one such farm, called "Gigant," set up in 1931 with 239,000 hectares (about half-a-million acres!). Workers on state farms are essentially government employees, and the state farms have been favored historically by government policy in setting of wage rates, provision of new agricultural machinery, and the location of transportation facilities. The *sovkhoz* were often established on large feudal estates or church lands taken over by the Soviet state, or on land previously not under cultivation (similar to Nikita Khruschchev's "virgin lands" program in Siberia and Kazakhstan).

However, in the 1930's, most farmers in the Soviet Union were forced to surrender their land and capital to the local *kolkhoz*, being forced to join the collective literally at gunpoint. The response of the rural people can well be imagined — Ukraine, the "bread basket of Eastern Europe," was singled out for particularly harsh treatment, partly designed to finish off Ukrainian nationalism. Eventually, the government won.

". . . But the cost had been heavy, being estimated by one competent observer to have included the loss of half the nation's livestock, much of its other agricultural capital, and a disruption of agriculture that helped bring on the poor harvests of 1931 and 1932 with their accompanying famine. Perhaps as many as five million kulak families may have been deported to Siberia and the Far North for their resistance. Only by importing larger numbers of American tractors was the

> *Soviet government able partially to replace the large number of horses slaughtered during its struggle with the peasants."* [12]

The generally cited figure for famine deaths — as noted, mainly in the Ukraine — is 4 to 5 million people, but a more recent estimate has put it in the 7 to 8 million range. Whatever the exact figures, a matter of considerable controversy in the literature, collectivization amounted to a social disaster with inestimable suffering.

After the collectivization drive was completed, the process of treating agriculture as an "internal colony" began in earnest. The basic approach in doing so involves twisting the terms of trade, the ratio of industrial to farm prices, against agriculture. This has sometimes been termed the use of "price scissors"—keeping agricultural prices low, while allowing the prices of the products bought by the rural population to go up over time (the price of sugar and soap was raised 5-6 times for example). The *sovkhoz*, the state farm, automatically turns over all its agricultural output to the government, and its workers receive a salary not tied to their productivity but to the classification of their jobs and number of years of experience. On the other hand, the collective farm workers, the *kolkhozniki*, were badly squeezed by mandatory deliveries of about half of their output to the government, and low prices being paid for deliveries above the quota target. One rather clever device used by the Soviet government was the establishment of a network of Machine Tractor Stations (MTS) in the 1930's.

Up until 1958, when the MTS system ended, the collective farm, or *kolkhoz*, was paid a fixed price for the delivery of compulsory crops, such as grains, which was not even adjusted to cover the rising costs of production. Such compulsory deliveries were based upon the size of the planted area, ". . . shifting the burden of unpredictability of agricultural returns on to the agricultural sector and away from the state." In addition, in-kind payments had to be made for the services of the MTS machinery and agricultural specialists, in many cases, leaving relatively little for sale at higher above-quota prices as in the so-called "kolkhoz markets." In case of a bad harvest, the residual claimants, the "kolkhozniki" themselves, would not have much left over.

Any discussion of the Soviet economy in the period before World War II would be seriously incomplete, if it did not mention the instruments of state terror developed under Stalin. We have mentioned the "carrot" of special incentives given to the "stakhanovites" in the 1930's—higher wages, access to housing and other benefits, and public recognition. Equally important, and probably more so, was the "stick" of punishment, often random and capricious, of executions, torture, slave labor camps, psychiatric hospitals, and exile. Some aspects of this system of repression have been described by people who have escaped the Soviet Union, notably Alexander Solzhenitsyn in his *Gulag Archipelago*. It seems a bit out of place to talk about such things in an "objective-scientific, Western-optimistic" economics text, but my colleagues and compatriots on the other side of the historical "Iron Curtain" should not ever forgive me, if I did not. In the West,

---

[12] Harry Schwartz, *op. cit.*, p. 115. See also Alec Nove, *An Economic History of the USSR, 1917–1991*, New and Final Edition (Penguin, 1992), pp. 101–197.

we are tempted to think about courts and investigations in very polite and civilized terms — "innocent until proven guilty," "due process," "jury trial by one's peers," and "rights of the accused." The concepts of "justice" and "law" are ludicrous in the view of the *Soviet reality*—a little less so today, but certainly historically. The purges of the 1930's got rid of *all* Soviet leaders not personally devoted and indebted to Stalin the great "leader, teacher, and friend of all the Soviet people." When the USSR occupied the Baltic countries (Estonia, Latvia, and Lithuania) initially in 1940, and then again in 1945, hundreds of thousands were imprisoned, exiled and executed, to create a docile population. I may be a bit subjective on this point, since my earliest memory is waking up in a hut in the middle of a forest outside Riga in June 1941 (being nearly four at the time), for my father had learned our family was scheduled for deportation to Siberia. We were able to escape this then, and managed to get out a couple of days ahead of the Red Army in the autumn of 1944.

In the last years of the USSR, the "apparatus of terror" was less capricious and random, "evidence" was examined a bit more carefully, and people were murdered and/or tortured a good deal less often. Certainly, a few highly-placed and visible dissidents were allowed to leave. Would you or I have been very outspoken in a society where dissent would often be branded as treason, and the chance for overseas travel or similar benefits be forever denied to those with any "black marks" in their dossier? I suspect that I would have been very quiet and careful, if my family had not escaped in 1945, and I had gone through the educational system of the Latvian SSR. Even today, it may be useful to keep your innermost feelings to yourself in the "transitioning countries." This has changed remarkably in recent years, as is discussed in the next chapter, but the historical context has to be kept in mind.

The main emphasis of the Stalinist model was on central control and a disciplined hierarchy. The Second Five Year Plan (1933-1938) was devoted primarily to the development of infrastructure, and the Third Five Year Plan (1938-1942) was modified to fit the military requirements of the "Great War to Defend the Fatherland," which is the Soviet term for World War II. The Fourth Five Year Plan (1946-1950) involved a thorough currency reform — Soviet citizens exchanged government bonds on a 3 for 1 basis, and had their cash money holdings reduced even more severely, on a 10 for 1 ratio. Monetary policy carried out by the Gosbank (the chief banking organ in the Soviet Union) was quite effective since the authorities had the power to simply cross out the last digit in your bank balance. Protesting against such an arbitrary action would have been futile, since your balance undoubtedly reflected "profiteering" activities during the war, though some smaller bank balances were exempt from this massive devaluation.

Post-War Developments

The "Stalinist Model" of economic development produced rapid growth in certain branches of industry, particularly those connected with military mobilization, capital goods industries, and infrastructure. These industrial accomplishments are aptly summarized by Harry Schwartz:

> "... In little more than a third of a century, despite the destruction of one civil war
> and two World Wars, coal output has been increased about tenfold, pig-iron pro-
> duction about sevenfold, steel about ninefold, petroleum almost sixfold, and elec-
> tric power generated over sixtyfold. Along with this has gone the comprehensive
> development of every other branch of heavy industry: machine-building, arma-
> ments, chemicals, and the like. On the other hand, the gains made in agriculture,
> though appreciable in some fields, have been of no such magnitude as those in
> industry, and the disproportions between industrial and agricultural growth have
> often caused difficulty." [13]

We can discuss four main areas in which the Stalinist approach was encountering
systemic problems by the mid-1950's. After Stalin's death in 1953, some discussion of
these problem areas began to appear in Soviet literature as well. It is certainly true that
the system of brutal political repression, known as "Stalinism," was moderated under
Nikita Krushchev, who eventually emerged as Stalin's successor. Still, Soviet economists
and policy-makers had to keep in mind very carefully the possibility that any criticism
of the system could be taken as punishable dissent, i.e., "the spreading of lies about the
Soviet state," which could earn you a "tenner" or even a "quarter" in the special regime
camps.[14]

First, as noted in the citation from Schwartz, agriculture was not doing very well.
Despite population growth, and the occupation of the three Baltic countries (Estonia,
Latvia, and Lithuania) in 1945, which had exported substantial quantities of agricultural
produce in the inter-war period, it is estimated that grain production in the mid-1950's
was about the same as in the 1925-26 harvest. Losses due to the collectivization drive
were also very significant in other areas of agricultural production — Schwartz points
out that in the 1930's output of eggs fell to about one-third of the 1927-28 level, and that
milk and meat output was cut in half. In 1938, for example, this would have allowed the
consumption of one egg per week by each Soviet citizen, and meat consumption of less
than one pound per week. In the post-Stalin era, it became evident that the treatment of
agriculture as an "internal colony" had been unduly harsh.

After the death of Stalin, it was clear that the agricultural sector needed infusions of
human capital as well as money to show any sort of significant improvement. Nikita
Khrushchev associated himself with three major initiatives in agriculture: (1) the "Virgin
Lands" program; (2) the corn programs and (3) the "Plow-Up Campaign." The virgin
lands program involved cultivating a large tract of land in Kazakhstan and Siberia.
Beginning with about 13 million hectares in 1955, the virgin lands scheme grew to 42
million hectares by 1960, accounting for about one-fifth of all area sown by all farms
in the Soviet Union. While the program was effective on a short-term basis, reducing
the need for imported grain, it did not accomplish much in terms of a longer-term

---

[13] Harry Schwartz, *op. cit.*, pp. 622–623, when Lenin was asked to define "communism," he
responded: "Government by the communes plus electricity."

[14] A "tenner" referes to a ten-year sentence and a "quarter" to a 25-year one in the Gulag Archipelago.

perspective. When Khrushchev visited Iowa, he fell in love with modern corn production methods (and yields there). It is also true that corn gives more fodder per acre than other feed grains, and the Soviets increased the area planted in corn from about 4 million hectares in 1954 to nearly 40 million by 1962. However, the planners neglected to consider the many years of scientific effort devoted to the development of special seeds suitable for the conditions of American agriculture, but not readily adaptive to Soviet conditions. The Russian word for corn or maize is "kukuruza." This word has become a symbol for "hare-brained schemes," which eventually led to Nikita's downfall. (When I mention planting corn to people in Latvia, I get sarcastic smiles — "we've tried that...") The third element of Krushchev's attempt to improve agricultural production involved a drastic reduction in the amount of land allowed to lay fallow. Clearly, such a policy involves a trade-off of short-term gain for a good deal of longer-term harm.

Throughout the post-war period, Soviet agriculture was characterized by a trend toward greater centralization. In numerical terms, first of all, the state farms ("sovkhoz") have grown from about 5000 in the mid-1950's to 21,000 such organizations at the end of 1980, while the share of these "corporate farms" has risen from 12% of the sown area to 54%. Over this same period, the number of collective farms ("kolkhoz") has dropped steadily — from nearly a quarter of a million in 1940 to 97,000 in 1953, and only 25,800 units in 1980. The average size of a sovkhoz in 1980 was about 17,000 hectares (or 42,000 acres), while the average kolkhoz increased from only about 1000 hectares in 1940 to more than 10,000 hectares in 1987. In recent years, the distinctions between a state farm and a collective farm have been reduced and some private farming is permitted. The MTS structure was eliminated in 1958, with agricultural machinery and tractors being sold to the collective farms, and minimum wages for the workers on the collective farms (the "kolkhozniki") were linked to wages paid at the sovhoz after 1966.

Still, living conditions in the rural areas of the former Soviet Union are quite stark — an all-weather network of roads has not yet been developed, and communal residences are cheap and shabby. D. Gale Johnson recounts an experience in attending a conference in Alma Ata in 1981 —

> "Within no more than twenty-five miles from one of the most modern and prosperous cities in the Soviet Union, our bus became stuck on a dirt road leading to a picnic site prepared for visiting foreigners! The Soviet rural road system can only be described as a disgrace, the result of decades of socialist neglect."

Johnson provides a very interesting translation from a 1981 article by Boris Mozhayev, which paints a most vivid contrast:

> "... Wherever I have seen peasant farmers attached to 'their own' land and freed from the sort of petty supervision that hampers initiative, I have always found people of lofty culture, vast knowledge and remarkable skill. They can not only handle but repair and even rebuild complex machinery. They are very well versed in agronomy. Many are real selection specialists who develop new varieties of fruits and berries in their own gardens and orchards. They visit clubs and

take part in amateur arts. They vie with one another in trimming their homes and landscaping their yards. It is no wonder people say that you can tell the culture of such home owners from the street.

In contrast, how sad it is to see rural apartment buildings, so-called communal residences, surrounded by impassable mud and bare yards with rickety little tables where zealous smokers sit killing time by playing dominoes. You won't even find a sapling, much less an orchard, around such buildings. This is an example of what happens when the vital ties between the peasant and the land are severed."[15]

To recapitulate briefly, a key problem facing Soviet planners in the post-Stalin era was how to revive an agricultural sector drained by several decades of ruthless exploitation. It is also very important to recognize the human capital dimension here— literally millions of the best farmers ("Kulaks") were killed by the state as a matter of policy, and the best and the brightest of rural young people were lured away by greater opportunities in the cities. Despite massive investments in infrastructure and new initiatives during the 1960's and the 1970's, such as the virgin lands program, the agricultural sector presents a continuing problem area.

 A second systemic problem area is that of investment efficiency. One of the main arguments of the so-called "Austrian School" is that calculations involving economic efficiency are fundamentally impossible in a socialist system.[16] Public ownership of the major means of production essentially abolishes financial markets and institutions. In a capitalistic economy, a system of financial markets and institutions provides two very important functions: the mobilization of saving and the allocation of investment. In a planned economy, the first function can be provided rather more easily by central authorities — at the limit, they can provide a level of wages just high enough to keep workers alive, sell whatever is produced to foreign countries, and "save" the difference. Annual national saving, thus theoretically could be 80-90% of total output. In the USSR, outside of the prison camps, personal consumption has been allowed to rise above the biological minimum for most people, but the state was still able to save and invest nearly a third of national output, essentially by using the so-called "turnover tax." The central authorities have a second chance to mobilize savings. If they did raise people's incomes above subsistence, but did not produce a correspondingly higher level of consumer goods, either in quantity or quality terms, then funds will return to the Gosbank, the state bank, in the form of increased private deposits. This will be discussed a bit further in the next chapter.

---

[15] D. Gale Johnson and Karen McConnell Brooks, *Prospects for Soviet Agriculture in the 1980's* (Indiana University Press, 1983), pp. 9–11. Prospects have not improved in the 1990s either.

[16] For considerably more on this free-market-oriented approach, see Wolfgang Grassl and Barry Smith (eds.), *Austrian Economics* (Croom Helm, 1986)

Although, as has been argued above, a socialist state can mobilize savings quite effectively, it runs into considerable difficulty in allocating available investment funds. We need to go off on a brief tangent to discuss this fully — but this is quite a key point. In a market-type economy, investment funds will be allocated by financial intermediaries to the most credit-worthy borrower for their most productive new projects. Put yourself in the position of a commercial bank loan officer — you have been assigned to deal with Obfuscation Interface, Inc., a new computer software company near Reston, and are told that OI wants to borrow $30 million. Your first task would be to make very sure that OI will not go "belly-up" (bankrupt) during the term of the loan — in a socialist regime, that would not be a serious consideration, since state enterprises do not generally fail. A second task for the bank officer would be to take a very careful look at the projects being proposed by OI for financing. Let us assume that the "prime rate" (the rate that banks charge for short-term loans to their very best customers, such as IBM or the local Catholic Diocese) is currently 10%, and that OI is proposing to borrow the $30 million for Projects A, B, and C, each of equal size and maturity, to keep matters simple. Your job will be to go through OI's projected numbers with a fine-toothed comb, check all the assumptions about prices, costs, and so on — to do what? What's the bottom line?

Yes, of course, you will be calculating each project's "rate of return," the expected return on investment. Let us assume that Project A shows a 30% return per year (on an appropriately discounted basis). Project B, an 18% rate, and Project C, 12%. The final report that you make to the loan committee will be something like this: (1) Approve Project A for the full $10 million, with your bank acting as the "lead bank," advancing $6 million and arranging for other lenders to come up with the rest; (2) Give partial approval to Project B, committing about $2 million, but telling OI to look for other sources for the rest; and (3) Turn down Project C entirely, since the expected rate of return is 12%, and OI would have to pay your bank a rate equal "prime plus three," i.e., 13%, and the project would not be viable (it would need to be modified or perhaps postponed until the prime comes down a bit). Now, of course, this is a bit of a fairy tale — it could be that OI's president and you were classmates at Georgetown, or that OI's president is a cousin of the State Banking Commissioner, or that you're dating his daughter. Still, if you allow such other considerations to overrule economic efficiency quite often, your performance as a bank loan officer will suffer, and you'll be looking for a government job pretty soon. . . Did the Gosbank lending officer have to do rate of return calculations? Probably not very carefully, if she was lending at a zero interest rate — then a million rubles earned by a Leningrad housing project in 1992 looks the same as a million rubles derived from a Siberian hydroelectric project, which begins to pay off in 2012. In practice the Gosbank would probably have allocated investment funds based on the political clout of the various ministries asking for credit, possibly with an eye to some sort of balance among the republics as well. Enterprise managers would generally have asked for more than they needed, since quotas would have been used to allocate credit.

As has been pointed out, lending officers of financial intermediaries — such as commercial banks, savings and loans, insurance companies, pension plans, and so on—must make sure that the projects in which they participate *directly* will earn at least the competitively determined interest rate. They are likely to be rather more generous in lending for investments where the internal rate of return that is expected exceeds "the market interest rate" by a considerable amount — enforcing allocative efficiency rules. The organized financial markets for stocks and bonds do the same a bit more *indirectly,* but also provide a test of market discipline that is difficult or impossible to duplicate under socialism. This time, put yourself in the role of a financial analyst with a pension fund having $30 million to invest. What stocks will you buy? What bonds? In the stock market, you will again fundamentally look for shares with the highest prospective return. If you are looking for income, you will look for companies paying high dividends — better yet, for stocks with a record of increasing dividend yields as well as rising share prices. By buying such stocks, and bidding up the prices of successful, profitable companies, you are indirectly signalling the management of such firms that they will be able to attract additional venture capital on favorable terms. If you are primarily looking for growth in the funds entrusted to you, you will focus on expanding sectors — computer services, health care, biological research, and defense recently — in which some companies may have been overlooked by others. You will spend some of your time computing and evaluating price-earnings ratios. All other things being equal, you will look for a *low* ratio or price per share to the annual earnings per share — a P/E ratio of 5 means a 20% return on your funds, while a P/E ratio of 10 is a 10% return. If you find a low P/E ratio, as we said, overlooked by others, your act of buying shares in that firm will raise the price of the stock, and probably attract other investors (especially those using computer-driven buying programs). In the bond market, investment funds are allocated on the basis of rating systems, such as those maintained by Standard & Poor's and Moody's. A company receiving a AAA bond rating, the best, will be able to borrow at a lower interest rate — again, indirectly signalling the availability of funds to creditworthy borrowers for projects having expected returns above the market-determined bond interest rate.

To return from this somewhat peripheral, but very important and interesting tangent, there were no competitive stock or bond markets in the Soviet Union, of course, and the exchanges in 1996 are still fairly primitive. The Gosbank was used to mobilize savings to some extent, but the allocation of investment funds was determined by a very complex system of bureaucratic negotiations involving enterprise managers, ministry officials, "nomenklatura" members at the republic level, and the central planning authorities.[17] Under the Stalinist Model, the dysfunctional features of socialist credit allocation were not as apparent as in the 1960's and 1970's. In a poor country concentrating on the buildup of infrastructure and the military, most allocation decisions can be made on the basis of *engineering considerations.* If you have found an oil deposit or a gas field, an engineer can tell you what size pipeline will need to be laid to get these resources to the nearest population centers. Setting up generating facilities for electric power may involve some economic calculations, but once you have decided on a particular dam on a given

---

[17] The "nomenklatura" is the managerial elite of the U.S.S.R., numbering around half-a-million, consisting of Party members occupying key positions in the governmental "apparat" and in enterprises.

river, engineers can tell you what the transmission network should be. Telephone lines are also likely to be determined by population density — as well as military-security considerations. Railroads and canals can also be drawn on a map, without much market research being necessary — although Alexander Solzhenitsyn mentions visiting one of Stalin's pet projects, the White-to-Baltic Sea canal, in the mid-1960's. On this canal, built by "zeks" (slave labor camp inmates) in a real hurry, Solzhenitsyn saw only two pitiful barges — one hauling pine logs in one direction, the other hauling the same kind of logs North.

As the Soviet economy grew and began expanding its trade with other countries, first with the COMECON[18] countries and later the West, and consumption levels in the USSR itself improved, the necessity for more economic efficiency became more evident. However, the absence of competitive markets for consumer goods as well as financial instruments makes it very difficult to judge which sectors of the economy to expand and which ones to contract, even to assess whether "Enterprise A" is performing better than "Enterprise B" in a single sector. Put yourself in the shoes of the manager of a Leningrad factory making ladies handbags, some time in the late 1960's. You have survived the purges, you live in a comfortable apartment on the top floor of the 10-story building recently built for your ministry, and your kids are studying engineering and chemistry respectively at Leningrad State U. (it isn't Moscow, but things could be a lot worse). You have been "the boss" for six years now, you earn 800 rubles per month, and your subordinates bring you nice gifts on your birthday and New Year's (a number of them seem to have relatives in the West, and imported luxuries turn up quite often). Your primary goal at work has been to meet quantity quotas negotiated with your ministry — say 100,000 pocketbooks of a large size and 50,000 of a smaller one. This is subdivided into monthly deliveries, but you better not come in *under* the annual goal—however, it would be stupid to produce a 200,000 total ever, because those meddling fools at the ministry would quickly raise your quota to that level — after all, their goal is to maximize output for their division or geographic area. A year ago, new machinery arrived, but it is still sitting in crates, since the new building has not been finished yet; you have got about four years' worth of plastic (black *and* red) in inventory, and a year of zippers (must talk to Ivan about getting more).[19]

You have vaguely heard about some fellow called Evsey Liberman, a professor at the Kharkov Institute for Engineering and Economics, who has proposed some sort of

---

[18] The Council for Mutual Economic Assistance (also sometimes CMEA) was established in 1949 to promote the integration of the planned economies of the USSR and Eatern Europe; Albania was a member until 1962, but Cuba joined in 1972 and Vietnam in 1978. Other members included Bulgaria, Czechoslovakia, East Germany, Hungary, Poland, Romania, and Mongolia. See Klaus von Beyme, "Economic Relations as an Instrument of Soviet Hegemony over Eastern Europe?" in Hans-Hermann Höhmann *et al, Economics and Politics in the USSR* (Boulder: Westview Press, 1986). The Comecon was formally dissolved in early 1991.

[19] Ivan is a "tolkach," a Soviet term meaning "expediter," who uses his personal contacts with various industry and ministry officials to get things done outside strictly official channels.

reforms in enterprise management. Indeed, in 1967 your enterprise will have to pay a 6% annual interest charge to the Gosbank for all fixed and circulating capital, you are given a profitabilty "norm" of 4% of the value of total yearly deliveries, and are told that any earnings above this 4% can now be used to make bonus payments to you yourself and to your workers (though the state will take half of "excess profits" first). While some Western media greeted Libermanism as return of capitalism to Soviet industry, a re-introduction of "interest" and "profit," Soviet managers were not overly impressed. You probably requested permission to raise the price of your ladies' handbags to cover the interest payments, which was eventually granted. Maybe you decided to make a few brown medium-sized ones, since the big red ones were not moving at all, but the prospect of an annual bonus probably did not move you to double your output. You recently bought a car, and there are 3500 rubles in your personal savings bank account already. The new building was finally finished, and the machinery installed — but after a few months of operation, it broke down, and you have to wait for spare parts and an engineer from East Germany. There has been some talk about exporting the new brown ones to Poland, but Ivan has only been able to get six months' more of zippers. Some eager-beaver actually mentioned making real leather brown handbags — now, those would sell, but could we get leather on a steady basis? Better not rock the boat . . .

The above hypothetical story has summarized some of the problems of relying primarily on physical "success indicators" in the recent past of Soviet industry:

(1) Overinvestment in plant and equipment, with a considerable amount of idle machinery;

(2) Hiding true output capacity, due to a fear that output quotas would be "ratcheted up";

(3) Hoarding of labor and other inputs because of periodic "storming of targets" will be required (quota overfulfillment to celebrate Lenin's Birthday, for example);

(4) Low quality of output and inflexible pricing policies;

(5) Lack of attention to "negative externalities" — pollution, worker safety, and so on;

(6) Resistance to innovation and technological progress (though industries dealing with the military and aerospace exploits seem to be an exception).

A third general problem area in the slowing down of Soviet growth involves labor and resource bottlenecks, which were becoming increasingly evident by the 1970's. The Stalinist Model of economic mobilization was based upon a more *extensive* use of the factors of production, but what is now needed is an increase in their productivity, their more *intensive* utilization. The Soviet industrialization drive was based upon a rapid and large-scale mobilization of capital, as already noted. It also involved a large shift of labor out of agriculture into industrial employment, as well as the entrance of many women in the urban labor force. Considerable productivity gains are possible, when a farmer, who had been working intensively only during parts of the short Russian growing season, gets transformed into a 48-hours-per-week factory worker — and his wife enters full-time employment in the city as well. (As an aside, the lot of Soviet women is not an enviable one. While many are doctors, dentists, teachers and scientists, they often rise very early to do food shopping for the family everyday — and return to do all of the cooking, dishes and laundry. Few families have refrigerators, fewer still dish- or clothes-washers, and the frozen TV dinner was yet to be invented a few years ago. In a typical household, the woman is doing all of this, while the man of the house drinks and plays chess with a friend. This may all be going on in a communal apartment, where several households have to share a stove and a sink. Small wonder about divorce rates!) Thus, a second extensive source of labor supply growth was the entrance of a majority of women into full-time employment. During the past two decades, there has been a large expansion in the labor force participation of women in the United States as well, but the Soviet participation rate is much higher on average (about 50% in the U.S. and 85% in the U.S.S.R.). Finally, while the Soviet Union is very rich in natural resources, the most easily accessible sources of energy, for example, were used up during the Stalinist growth period — and now additional deposits of coal, oil, and gas can be exploited only at a much higher marginal cost. Similarly, new land being brought under cultivation is much less suitable for agriculture, and requires costly irrigation schemes. Thus, the third systemic problem area facing the Soviets in the post-war period involved increasing the *productivity* of the factors of the production, since factor supply growth was slowing down.

autarky

(4)   The fourth and final factor to be considered briefly is foreign trade. An important component of the Stalinist Model, as noted, was the policy of "autarky," meaning a policy of self-sufficiency — not ever really completely achieved, of course. Still, foreign trade involves contacts with foreigners — and may involve allowing Soviet citizens to travel and to see what life is like outside. Under Stalin, as Solzhenitsyn notes, upon repatriation, Russian P.O.W.'s were sent off to the camps, so as to minimize information about living standards in the West (even in prison camps!) from entering Soviet society. However, advances in communications technology — radio, telephones, television, and films — have been such that it had become impossible to seal off the USSR from the rest of the world completely. Also, the benefits of an "international division of labor," so to speak, were becoming more obvious — the Soviet Union could trade some of its abundant resources for Western grain and technology.

While the population of the Soviet Union was about six percent and its output about ten percent of the world total, its share of world exports was only about 4 percent, and its imports about 3.5 percent of the world total. In value terms, total Soviet trade is not much larger than that of the Netherlands. As Buck and Cole point out:

> ". . . *Soviet foreign trade is relatively limited in scale for at least three distinct major reasons. First, very large size, other things being equal, minimizes the need to trade, a feature shared with the USA, China and India, all of which have low import coefficients. Secondly, Soviet leaders have been preoccupied with the pros-*

pect of hostile neighbours, the risk of economic sanctions and the threat of military attack, reasons enough to encourage considerable economic self-sufficiency at both national and regional levels. Third, since the USSR has a centrally planned economy, imports and exports have to be allowed for in national plans. it is not easy, however, and in some cases not possible at all, to allow for, let alone control, the prices and requirements of Soviet products in foreign countries, and to guarantee the availability of products that need to be imported. The co-ordination of plans within CMEA, however, ensures a reasonably captive and predictable market for much of Soviet trade." [20]

In 1950, 80 percent of all Soviet foreign trade was with socialist partners, and only 16 percent with industrial capitalist countries. The decade of the 1970's saw a significant expansion in East-West trade, largely financed by Western banks wishing to recycle their "petrodollar" deposits, and trade with Western industrial countries reached 32.2 percent of the total. In more recent years, however, when total CMEA debt to the West reached nearly $ 100 billion, there was a return to greater intra-CMEA trade — which rose from 47.6 percent of total Soviet trade in 1981 to 52.1 percent in 1984.[21] With Soviet planners emphasizing the production of capital goods under the Stalinist model, 30-40 percent of total imports consists of machinery, mostly from its CMEA trading partners, but also from Western Europe and Japan. Since the mid-1960s, about 20% of total imports have been food imports, whereas food exports in the 1980s averaged less than 2% of total USSR exports. Consumer good imports in the 1980s accounted for 11-12% of the total, down from about 18 percent in 1970— while consumer goods exports, largely due to quality considerations, did not exceed 2-3% of total exports. More than half of the total value of Soviet exports in the 1980's was derived from the sale of fuels and energy — oil, natural gas, coal and electricity. Official Soviet trade statistics do not include transactions in the military hardware, gold, platinum, and diamonds, which provided considerable earnings as well. The enormous price increases for oil and gas provided large windfall gains for the Soviets in the 1970's though they did not initially charge the "full price" to to their CMEA satellites — providing a subsidy estimated at more than $ 10 billion per year in the early 1980's.

To summarize this final section very briefly, growth in the USSR was quite rapid under the Stalinist model. The planning process stressed meeting and exceeding physical output targets set up in a series of five-year plans. The growth strategy was based on a high savings rate, in part achieved by exploiting millions of slave laborers in Stalin's camps as well as the rural peasantry. Investment funds were allocated to the military, heavy industry, and infrastructure. In the post-Stalin period, political repression lessened — presumably the strongest and most vehement opponents of the system had all been killed by the 1960s — and discussion of future goals and strategies began to appear in the Soviet literature. We have discussed four systemic problem areas:

---

[20] Trevor Buck and John Cole, *Modern Soviet Economic Performance* (Oxford: Basil Blackwell, 1987), p. 65.
[21] *Ibid.*, p., 68

Problems !

(1) Additional investments were needed in agriculture, where productivity was very low and living conditions quite miserable;

(2) Allocation of investment on the basis of engineering considerations was encountering diminishing returns and it was necessary to seek greater economic rationality;

(3) Output gains due to the use of more *extensive* factor inputs (such as the absorption of farmers and women into the industrial labor force) were slowing, and efforts needed to be made to use factors of production more *intensively* (increase productivity);

(4) The USSR found it necessary to increase its foreign trade contacts with the West, especially in food and feed grains as well as machinery.

In general, all of these issues are inter-connected to some extent — economic progress seems to cry out for greater decentralization and flexibility, especially in agriculture. However, that may also imply greater individual freedom and more regional autonomy — as in Khrushchev's attempt to abolish centralized ministries and institute 105 regional economic councils (the so-called "sovnarkhozy") in 1957. In 1965, after the fall of Khrushchev, Kosygin and Brezhnev went back to the ministries, however, since the "sovnarkhozy" often had "placed the needs of the region above that of the national economy." The Liberman reforms of 1967, which reintroduced interest and profit to some extent, were just the beginning of a "treadmill of reforms." ■

SUGGESTED READINGS

Cohen, Stephen F., *Bukharin and the Bolshevik Revolution* (Alfred A. Knopf,1973).

Danilov, V.P., *Rural Russia Under the New Regime* (Indiana University Press, 1988).

Davies, R.W., *et al*, *The Transformation of the Soviet Union, 1913-1945* (Cambridge University Press, 1994).

Filtzer, Donald, *Soviet Workers and Stalinist Industrialization* (Pluto Press, 1986).

Gregory, Paul R., and Robert C. Stuart, *Soviet and Post-Soviet Economic Structure and Performance*, Fifth Ed. (Harper Collins, 1994).

Hedlund, Stefan, *Crisis in Soviet Agriculture* (Croom Helm, 1984).

Hunter, Holland and Janusz M. Szyrmer, *Faulty Foundations: Soviet Economic Policies,1928-1940* (Princeton University Press, 1992).

Hutchins, Raymond, *The Structural Origins of Soviet Industrial Expansion* (St. Martin's Press, 1984).

Linz, Susan J. (ed.), *The Soviet Economic Experiment* (University of Illinois Press, 1990).

Navrozov, Lev, *The Education of Lev Navrozov* (Harper's Magazine Press, 1975).

Owen, Thomas C., *Russian Corporate Capitalism from Peter the Great to Perestroika* (Oxford University Press, 1995).

Rutland, Peter, *The Myth of the Plan* (Huthinson, 1985).

Schwartz, Harry, *Russia's Soviet Economy* (Prentice-Hall, Inc.,1961).

Solzhenitsyn, Alexander, *The Gulag Archipelago* (Harper Collins, 1985).
Viola, Lynn, *The Best Sons of the Fatherland* (Oxford University Press, 1987).
Wilson, Edmund, *To the Finland Station* (Doubleday & Co., 1940).
Zinoviev, Alexander, *The Reality of Communism* (Victor Gollancz, Ltd., 1984).

CHAPTER SEVEN

WHAT COMES AFTER THE CMEA?

*I*n the 1970s, when I first taught this course, there was a fair amount of actual comparing of systems taking place. Twenty years ago, it was not completely obvious that the living standard for the average Soviet family was significantly lower than in West Europe, or even the United States. Of course, then many liberals viewed socialism as a more meritorious system. As mentioned below, various Western "Kremlinologists" provided rather generous estimates of GNP per capita for the various Comecon (or CMEA) countries. It can also be pointed out that the Soviet system statisticians steadfastly refused to accept the GNP concept — all Comecon countries adhered to their Net Material Product concept — and that many Western economists were increasingly troubled by the systemic shortcomings of the GNP measure, some of which were mentioned in Chapter 1. Government spending is included in GNP on a simple money outlay basis — missiles and computers, toilet paper and government salaries, research contracts and highways are all treated the same in adding up GNP. A new papermill's output will enter this year's GNP, as will the expenditures of a sewage treatment plant downriver, which are needed to remove the mill's waste. Goods and services are entered on the basis of market price. A semi-pornographic hit movie, the salary increase of a sports star, and a rap video featuring Beavis and Butthead will all increase GNP — and happiness, right? Finally, the potatoes harvested in November and December will get counted in that year's GNP, regardless of whether they become McFries that month or get eaten by rats or rot in storage. GNP is a production-oriented statistic, which also ignores the using-up of resources (just like the Soviet NMP). Thus, a closer look at consumption may be preferable to the GNP per capita comparison with which we wrestled a bit earlier.

A comparison of consumption levels for the average American family and an average Soviet family is not very easy to summarize, either, because of great differences in consumer good prices and their availability under the two systems. But let us go back to the early 1980s, when the classical socialist model was at its best, and try to do that. An impressionable American student visiting the USSR on a summer tour in the 1980s learned that an average family in Moscow or Leningrad earned 300-500 rubles per month — which was realized by husband and wife both working full-time. Their rent for a small, but perfectly charming one-bedroom apartment, in a rather new eight story apartment block controlled by the ministry employing the husband, was only 36 rubles per month or even less, with all utilities included (though the elevator was not very reliable). The student was also told that the couple's two children will receive free education, if they qualify, all the way through university — as well as postgraduate study. (This would certainly strike a very responsive nerve in a Georgetown senior soon to be graduating in a happy frame of mind, but deeply in debt!) Our student will also have been told about free medical care, would find out first-hand that a subway ride on the Moscow Metro then was still about a nickel (while the Washington Metro was already about a dollar), and that the price of bread and potatoes is but a fraction of their cost back home. When young Steve or Jennifer learned about the price of a Moscow theater ticket (a couple of rubles *versus* $28 at the Kennedy Center, even in the balcony), a popular hard-cover novel (around a ruble versus $8.95 even at Crown books), or even the fairly good and cheap beer, they were probably all set to conclude that Ivan and Irina, our hypothetical Moscow couple, seemed to live a good deal better than Steve and Jennifer would, settling down in the Washington suburbs.

While the situation outlined above would be stressed by Soviet propagandists, and it includes no falsehoods as such, the standard of living for a middleclass Soviet family — even in Moscow, Leningrad, Riga or Tashkent (e.g., cities which had been open to foreign visitors) — was and is still so low as to surprise Western visitors, when they learn more about the situation. While the price of bread and potatoes was kept constant at a very low level until very recently, the total cost of a market basket mainly of food and beverages was quite high — most Soviet families spent over one-half of disposable income on such items, while these expenditures account for only about one-third of the total in the United Kingdom and Italy, but only about 20% of total household consumption goes for food in the United States. This reflects Engel's Law, which says that the percentage of family income spent on food falls, as income rises.

An instructive comparison of living costs — and, by implication, overall living standards — is provided by Table 7-1, which shows the work-time equivalent of various consumer goods and expenditure categories, for Moscow and four Western cities in March 1982. The first line confirms the point made in the paragraph above — since it took more than 40 hours of work-time in Moscow to buy a standard weekly basket of food, drink, and tobacco for a family of 3.5 persons, a household of 1.6 wage-earners did not have a standard of living close to Western standards. The basket used for this calculation consisted of 23 basic goods, and the Moscow work-time was not the lowest one for any of the items included. As a rough order of magnitude, this standard basket of "necessities" took three times more labor time in Moscow than in Washington, and more than twice as long as in the other three cities shown. For services, in many cases, the reverse was true. As has been noted above, rent was heavily subsidized in the Soviet Union — an unfurnished "flat" in Moscow "cost" only about half the labor time of such an apartment in Munich, but less than one-fourth of Washington rentals. It is also true that a month's worth of gas for heating or cooking (mainly the latter) was much cheaper than in the West, as was bus fare. However, housing seems to have received quite a low priority in the Soviet system (the size, on average, was very small) and also created perverse distributional consequences in real terms. For example, a division chief earning 500 rubles per month may have had access to a ministry-controlled apartment costing 30 rubles per month within easy walking distance, while one of his underlings making a third of his monthly salary would have had to pay twice that much in rent, and pay to commute over a long distance as well. Many young workers simply could not afford a place of their own, even if both husband and wife worked, and were forced to sublet with a set of parents — usually the husband's, which put the bride in a "really nice situation," having to share mother-in-law's kitchen and bath.

Table 7-1 clearly shows very large disparities in the real cost of consumer durables. A small car in Moscow took ten times as much labor time in Moscow as in Washington, and gasoline to run it was about six times more expensive in the Soviet Union. These relative costs seem to reflect the well recognized antipathy of the Soviet rulers to the private automobile. As Raymond Hutchings has noted:

> *"...It is certainly possible to find other reasons for the preferential growth of electric power generation, or of rail transport, in socialist states. These would include, as regards to the former, Lenin's aphorism about electricity and Soviet power, and as regards the latter, that an authoritarian state may well prefer that its people should move about along fixed alignments, rather than less predictably and more independently in their own motor car."* [1]

However, the real cost of a T-shirt, a pair of jeans, and a color TV set was also about ten times as high as the Washington level — and the cost of aspirin was nearly 500 times as high! The rest of the figures in Table 7-1 seem to be self-explanatory — though it is quite surprising that a 60 mile train fare would be 2 to 3 times as expensive as in the West.

The issue of income distribution in the USSR is quite a complex one — and comparisons of statistical measures of inequality, such as the Gini Coefficient (discussed briefly in Chapter 1), with Western countries are even more difficult to make. For example, there is the important problem of pre-tax versus post-tax income — clearly, if we were trying to make welfare comparisons between the bottom 10% in the US and the USSR, we would prefer to use the latter measure. However, the U.S. uses mainly *direct* taxes on income and property to collect revenue (which are relatively easy to measure), whereas the USSR relied primarily on the *indirect* turnover tax. It is beyond our scope to get into a detailed discussion of problems of measurement, data availability, and disagreement among scholars on this score. These problems are all discussed in great detail in Abram Bergson's survey article written about ten years ago on this issue, who concluded:

> *"...In sum, any definitive judgement on comparative income inequality in the USSR and the West is obviously excluded but Soviet income inequality probably*

[1] Raymond Hutchings, *The Structural Origins of Soviet Industrial Expansion* (Macmillan, 1984), p. 195.

Table 7-1: Work-time Equivalents of Selected Goods, Five Cities, 1982

	Washington	Moscow	Munich	Paris	London
Standard weekly 'basket' drink & tobacco for a family of 3.5 persons (hours)	16.3	46.8	20.4	19.4	22.5
Cosmetics, drugs, etc (in minutes)					
Toilet soap (sm. bar)	4	20	6	7	5
Toilet rolls (2)	7	32	5	13	10
Aspirin	5	246	64	21	9
Lipstick	30	69	80	76	60
Transport (in minutes)					
Petrol, 10 litres, reg.	32	185	61	87	85
Taxi fare, two miles	21	27	35	27	52
Bus fare, two miles	7	3	8	9	11
Train fare, 60 miles	104	258	86	87	119
Small car (months)	5	53	6	8	11
Clothing					
Tee-shirt (in minutes)	19	185	50	53	40
Pair jeans	3	46	7	6	6
Pair men's shoes	8	25	5	7	7
Consumer durables					
Small refrigerator	44	155	42	53	40
Automatic washing machine	47	165	96	56	81
Colour TV	65	701	143	106	132
Housing & services					
Monthly rent, subsidized unfurnished apt, 50m^2	51	12	24	39	28
One month's gas (in minutes)	290	39	125	369	568
One month's water (in minutes)	32	123	37	95	97
Family medical insurance	22	nil	33	nil	nil
Men's haircut (in minutes)	63	37	60	108	34

Source: Trevor Buck and John Cole, *Modern Soviet Economic Performance* (Basil Blackwell, 1987), Table 9.6, p. 160, adapted from a Radio Liberty Study.

has been found to be greater than often supposed. It is very possibly as great as or greater than that in Sweden, and not much less than that is some other Western countries such as Norway and the United Kingdom. Income inequality in the USSR is commonly assumed to be less than that in the U.S. That is doubtless so, though not by as wide a margin as sometimes imagined. Elsewhere in the West, however, inequality is sometimes greater than in the United States. [2]

Bergson's conclusion that the degree of inequality in the Soviet Union is somewhat surprising is reinforced by interview data of the Soviet Interview Project (SIP), based on three-hour face-to-face interviews with nearly 2800 emigrants from the Soviet Union (during 1979-1982).[3] These SIP data report that the highest tenth of urban households received about a third of all income, while the bottom tenth had only about a three percent share. The so-called "nomenklatura" (approximately half-a-million persons in party-controlled positions of influence) lived quite well in those days — the availability of goods in special shops and privileged access to imports "through channels" was becoming vastly more important than money income in the shortage economy. Barter transactions and the widespread use of "blat" are also very difficult to measure. ("Blat" is roughly translated as "pull," or influence.) *disparity*

To be a bit more fair in our assessment of the USSR in the old days, we should mention that there was a sort of "social contract" between the Soviet population and the Party rulers. The "nomenklatura" was quite careful to keep its higher real standard of living quite inconspicuous. The number of luxury automobiles was quite limited (while Brezhnev allegedly had about a dozen, they were seldom parked on the street), and the highest officials lived in comfortable "dachas" in walled compounds behind locked gates. The standard of living for the bottom quarter was pretty stark, but the prices of staples, such as bread, milk, and potatoes were low, and the cost of urban transportation was kept constant at a few cents for a long time. Deficit products were often allocated on the basis of the 2Q principle (standing in a *queue* for meat, and being limited to a *quota* of two kilos) had a distributional effect that was positive for the pensioners and the poor — the opportunity cost of their time was very low, if not zero.

---

[2] Abram Bergson, "Income Inequality Under Soviet Socialism," *Journal of Economic Literature*, September 1984, p. 1073. Bergson also points out that the upper 10% of urban households received 24.1% of total income, while the corresponding share of the lowest tenth was 3.4%. See also Gregory Grossman, "Roots of Gorbachev's Problems: Private Income and Outlay in the late 1970s," in Joint Economic Committee, *Gorbachev's Economic Plans*, Vol. 1, pp. 213–230.

[3] For further details, see James R. Millar and Peter Donhowe, "Life, Work, and Politics in Soviet Cities — First Findings of the Soviet Interview Project," *Problems of Communism*, Jan.–Feb. 1987, pp. 46–55. A thorough discussion of the second economy can be found in Jim Leitzel, *Russian Economic Reform* (Routledge, 1995), chs. 1–2.

"Prison of Nations"

Many people in the West, even social scientists have used the word "Russia" in speaking about the Soviet Union, and have often tended to refer to all inhabitants of the U.S.S.R. as "the Russians." This always was quite incorrect and sloppy, since an understanding of that society and the problems faced by the economy of the former Soviet Union (FSU) requires an appreciation of the "nationalities issue" and its role in the disintegration of the empire. By the end of this century, ethnic Russians will be less than 50% of the total population of the FSU area (so-called "Great Russians" accounted for 52.4% of the total in the 1979 census). The next largest national group, the Ukrainians, opted to set up an independent state in 1991, and their future political and economic ties with their Slavic neighbors are a matter for debate. As noted in the previous chapter, the famine of the 1930s affected the Ukraine particularly harshly and, therefore, many Ukrainians greeted German tanks and troops in 1941 with flowers. Nationalistic Ukrainians wanted at that time to establish an independent country, and fight alongside the Germans against the Red Army. To make a long and complex story very short, the Germans would have none of it, probably because they considered western portions of the Soviet Union to be very suitable as living space ("Lebensraum") for the "master race" ("Herrenvolk") itself — eventually resettling Ukrainians and other lesser races somewhere else on less fertile and pleasant land. Still, despite factional infighting, assassinations, coups and countercoups, a Ukrainian government in exile functioned in Paris for many years, later moving to Germany. It should be also noted that Ukraine along with Belarus (White Russia) continued to have separate seats in the United Nations, even when the USSR existed.

Since I was born in Riga in 1937, before Latvia's occupation by the Soviets, I am probably guilty of placing too much emphasis on the role of the three Baltic republics (Estonia, Latvia, and Lithuania). At the time of the formation of the Soviet Union, when the consolidation of Bolshevik power was helped enormously by the personal loyalty of the red Latvian rifles ("strehlnieki") to Lenin, whose leaders generally thought that autonomy, or even independence, for the Baltic peoples had a better chance under the "Reds" than the "Whites." Indeed, Lenin himself referred to the Czarist empire as "the prison of nations." Nevertheless, despite these early sympathies, in a few years, the Bolsheviks in Latvia itself were ousted and all the western areas of the Russian empire eventually broke away successfully. As David Lane says:

> ". . .After the revolution the political fate of these national areas depended partly on geography, partly on the popular support enjoyed by the Bolsheviks and partly on the ability of the new Soviet government to enforce its decisions. Poland, Finland, Lithuania, Latvia, and Estonia all became established states. They were all (except Finland) under German occupation at the time of the revolution and many expressed anti-Russian sentiments. Their geography allowed for successful intervention by the Western powers in support of their independence. Despite the presence of Russian immigrants in some of the Baltic provinces, grass roots

support for unification with Russia was not large. In these countries, national so-cial-democratic parties were strongest and they favored separation." [4]

During the inter-war period of independence lasting a little more than twenty years, the Baltic states developed fairly successful economies and were generally integrated into the Western-oriented world economy. Significant gains were made in developing their national cultural activities and educational systems, though the Depression of the 1930's hit the export-oriented Baltic countries quite hard. As it has now been learned, however, Nazi Germany and the Soviet Union had divided Eastern Europe into "spheres of influence" in the Molotov-Ribbentrop Pact of 1939 — with Hitler getting Poland and Stalin taking Finland and the Baltic countries. The Soviet Union initially set up military bases in the three countries in 1940, and then sent a larger force — the Balts did not fight the invaders. However, Finland fought the attempted take-over heroically in the so-called "Winter war" (on December 14, 1939, the League of Nations expelled the U.S.S.R. for this aggression). Although Finland wound up losing about one-tenth of its territory, most of Karelia, it managed to maintain its national existence. In contrast, the three Baltic countries were forced to hold Soviet-run elections in 1940, electing representatives of the "Bloc of the Toiling People" by more than 95 percent of the vote. These puppet governments in turn requested permission to join the USSR soon thereafter (maps printed in Moscow *before* these elections showed the three as SSR's already...).

Latvians call 1940-41 the "Year of Horror," with its awful memories of Soviet-spon-sored murder, state torture (the pulling out of fingernails by pliers apparently was a KGB specialty), and large-scale deportations. In response to this year of repression, in the Baltic countries German troops were also greeted as liberators in 1941. However, as in the Ukraine, the Germans did not permit Baltic national governments to be re-estab-lished, having their own plans for this part of the world as well. Still, along with the Finns and a number of others, the Estonians and the Latvians fought against the Soviet Union in World War II in semi-autonomous national military units on the side of Nazi Germany. As World War II was coming to an end, many Balts fled into exile, with most eventually making their way to the U.S. and Canada. (Soviet disinformation was remarkably successful in maintaining the equation of Balt equals Nazi, with some help from "progressive" public opinion in the West as well.) There were reliable reports of rather large-scale and persistent guerilla warfare in the Baltic region against the Soviets during the postwar period, lasting well into the 1950's. The local languages in the Baltic republics are quite distinct from Russian — Estonian is not an Indo-European language at all (it is a Finno-Ugric language akin to Finnish and Hungarian). Latvian and Lithuanian are Baltic languages of considerable linguistic similarity, but both are about as far from Slavic languages as they are from English. Lithuania is predominantly Catholic, with close historical ties to Poland, while Estonia and Latvia had large Lutheran populations before the war, in part due to history shared with Sweden. All three Baltic states regained independence in 1991, after the failure of the August coup in Moscow

---

[4] David Lane, *Soviet Economy and Society* (New York University Press, 1985), p. 208.

(one of the leaders of the coup was a thoroughly Russified Latvian, Boris Pugo), and joined the U.N. and other international organizations. At the present time (1996), NATO membership for the three Baltic countries is being debated, and the outcome appears uncertain.

As mentioned above, Belarus has a separate seat in the United Nations and a long history of partitions, alliances and struggles for autonomy. A 1921 peace treaty between Poland and the USSR left much of the western half of "White Russia" under Polish rule, but the Molotov-Ribbentrop Pact in 1939 gave that back to the USSR — with a 97% "plebiscite" voting in favor of joining the USSR in November 1939. While linguists regard "White Russian" as being closer to Russian than Ukrainian, its vocabulary also manifests considerable influences from Polish and Lithuanian. About 80% of the population of Belarus is listed as having that nationality — so that here too we have a sizeable population (nearly ten million) in a specific geographic area, with a separate language and culture, which has now also set up an independent state, although strong sentiment in favor of re-unification with Russia has surfaced in 1996.

To round out the European portion of the former Soviet state, we have Moldova, which initially was a part of Ukraine. Historically and linguistically, it is essentially a part of Romania, from which it was seized a piece at a time in 1924 and 1944. The Romanians also fought against the Soviets in World War II and had then recovered all of Bessarabia from the control of the USSR. After the war, however, the Moldavian S.S.R. was re-established and some 500,000 Romanians deported to Siberia and Kazakhstan. (At this same time, Stalin also deported whole populations of other "untrusted" ethnics — with the Volga Germans and the Crimean Tatars being the best-known cases.) Essentially there is no such thing as a "Moldovian" — they were simply a couple of million Romanians who were living under Soviet rule. On the whole, they may eventually prefer to be unified with Romania. Today, at least economically, there is probably not much to choose between the two sides of that border, and Moldova has remained a separate state to date. Finally, the former Union-Republics in the European part that we have discussed are ringed by an arc of areas inhabited by smaller ethnic minorities.

The remainder of the former empire is even more heterogeneous than the European part. To the south, the Georgians and the Armenians, each a nationality of about two million people, have ancient Christian civilizations and a long, complex history. Both were once members of a Trans-Caucasus Federation along with Azerbaijan, but that Federation was dissolved in 1936. The Armenians suffered a holocaust at the hands of the Turks, and they have been fighting the Azeris off and on in recent years. In 1990, the Red Army's massacre of women in Tbilisi, the capital of Georgia, was a key step in the collapse of the USSR. On the other side of the Caspian, there is sparsely populated Kazakstan, the second largest Soviet republic, roughly equal in size to Western Europe. Despite the fact that Kazaks comprise approximately 30% of the population, there were serious riots in Alma Ata (now Almaty) when a Russian had been appointed party boss of the republic.

Of the four Central Asian countries, former S.S.R.'s, three border on Afghanistan, with which they share many historical similarities, not the least of which is Islam. Regarding the "Southern Tier" Jan Ake Dellenbrant says:

> *"...The Central Asian republics, i.e., the Uzbek SSR, the Kirghiz SSR, the Tadzhik SSR, and the Turkmen SSR have many features in common: all have basically agrarian economies despite considerable industrial development in the recent period; cotton growing is an important sector especially in Uzbekistan; the level of socioeconomic development is lower than elsewhere in the Soviet Union; and population growth is extremely rapid."* [5]

Table 7-2 tries to show a number of facts about the Soviet Union in the fairly recent past, and the so-called "Newly Independent States" (NIS countries, in World Bank terminology) currently. The ruble statistics for 1970 and 1982 showed substantial disparities among the fifteen "fraternal republics." Back then, Estonia and Latvia usually ranked first and second in the USSR by most socioeconomic indicators, quite often by as much as 30-35%, while some of the "Southern tier" republics were some 50% below the mean. As Soviet growth slowed in the 1980s, regional inequalities increased somewhat - the growth in republic per capita income was the lowest in Turkmenistan and Tajikistan. Soviet planners faced a formidable task in trying to deal with what was called "the Triangle Problem." First, jobs were "in the West" — in the European part of the USSR, and in the Trans-Caucassus republics, often in "captive nations" worried about their ethnic survival, or in Russia itself. Second, resources were "in the North," in Siberia and Kazakstan, and they would have to be transported over several time zones, either to the jobs or to the people. And, third, the people were "in the South," with significant increases in population growth taking place only there — the fastest being among rural Muslims in, say, Turkmenistan. This problem was aptly summarized by geographer Leslie Dienes:

> *". . . Varied and divergent regional endowment can, of course, promote regional specialization and trade, a multifaceted economy, and vigorous growth. But distances, physical geography, cultural and ethnic heterogeneity, especially when coupled with distinct geographic subunits within the confines of a single state, can also present obstacles to economic development and national cohesion. Economic growth in the USSR increasingly involves the successful linking of the European core with a vast raw hinterland plus a broad arc of non-European periphery. Each of these three worlds shows a great diversity within itself. Yet broadly speaking the first possesses the established industrial capacity, infrastructure and skill and the location for foreign trade, the second the great bulk of natural resources, the third all future increments to the labor force for the next 10-15 years. Combining the increments in production factors from these incongruous*

---

[5] Jan Ake Dellenbrant, *The Soviet Regional Dilemma: Planning, People, and Natural Resources* (M.E. Sharpe, Inc., 1986). See also Boris Z. Rumer, *Soviet Central Asia: "A Tragic Experiment"* (Unwin Hyman, 1989).

worlds across the breadth of a land one-sixth of the earth surface would surely tax the ingenuity even of the most flexible and imaginative leadership." [6]

As we shall see shortly, neither "flexible" nor "imaginative" would be particularly precise definitions.

A second observation about the numbers in Table 7-2 concerns the figures for 1989. During the entire "Cold War" period, which roughly overlaps my twenty-plus years of teaching this material, a large amount of time was devoted to an analysis of Soviet macroeconomic statistics. With the advantage of hindsight, most Western "experts" on the USSR tended to be overly generous in presenting a GNP per capita figure. In the late 1980s, as a great thaw began in American-Soviet relations (the first student from the

Table 7-2: National Income in Rubles per Capita, 1970–1982
(and in U.S. dollars, 1989 and 1994)

Republic	1970	1982	Percent Change	1989*	1994
RSFSR	1,335	2,171	+63	$5810	$2650
Estonia	1,622	2,473	52	6240	2820
Latvia	1,565	2,469	58	6740	2320
Lithuania	1,343	1,957	46	5880	1350
Ukraine	1,161	1,708	47	4700	1910
Belarus	1,100	2,155	96	5960	2160
Moldova	981	1,540	57	3830	870
Georgia	875	1,686	93	4410	n.a.
Armenia	923	1,704	85	4710	680
Azerbaijan	743	1,380	86	3750	500
Kazakstan	984	1,233	25	3720	1160
Uzbekistan	737	1,103	50	2750	960
Tajikistan	690	850	23	2340	360
Kyrgiz Rep.	818	1,047	28	3020	630
Turkmenistan	880	943	7	3370	n.a.
USSR	1,199	1,887	57	5000	n.a.

Source: J.A. Dellenbrant, *op. cit.,* p. 153

* Dollar estimates from *Geonomics* Jan./Feb 1991, p.3.

**World Development Report, 1996,* Table 1.

---

[6] Leslie Dienes, "Regional Economic Development," in Abram Bergson and Herbert S. Levine (eds.), *The Soviet Economy: Toward the Year 2000* (Allen & Unwin, 1983).

USSR attended the Institute for Political and Economic Systems at Georgetown in 1989), various academic contacts and cooperative efforts got under way. Table 7-2 gives a representative set of dollar estimates for the republics from a newsletter called *Geonomics* published at Middlebury College in Vermont. (In passing, it might be noted that the Joint Economic Committee cited a figure of $7700 for 1985, and even higher numbers have at times been used by other U.S. government agencies.) Thus, the *Geonomics* figure of USSR GNP per capita of $5000 is near the mid-point of a range of estimates circulating in the West around 1989. The final column of Table 7-2 shows the World Bank estimates for the NIS countries for 1994. The Russian Federation at $2650 can be compared to the U.S. at $25,800 and Japan at $34,630 (these are at official exchange rates — the range is smaller when PPP statistics are used). It can be pointed out that all of these numbers in the last column are less than one-half of the 1989 figures — pointing out that those figures had been slightly inflated, but also showing the enormous collapses in income, output, and even average consumption measured in calories, which have taken place since the collapse of the Soviet Union in 1991.

Glasnost, Da! Perestroika...

When Mikhail Gorbachev became the General Secretary of the Communist Party in March 1985, he faced a rapidly collapsing system of traditional central planning. Total industrial production — which is at the heart of a standard Stalinist assessment of economic success — had grown at a solid 6.2% annual rate in the 1966-70 period, and reached still a most satisfactory 5.4% in 1971-75. Mancur Olson's concept of an "encompassing interest" is of great relevance here. As Olson has put it:

> *"...Stalin was, in effect, the owner of the Soviet Union. He therefore had an interest in the productivity of his domain similar to the interest an owner of a business firm has in maximizing the value of the firm's output. Stalin and some of his successors could use a large portion of any increase in Soviet output to increase their military power, international influence, and personal prestige."* [7]

Over time this "encompassing interest" of the totalitarian dictator tends to weaken. Central planning requires very strong discipline — the threat of brutal punishment remained credible for a long time. However, the "narrow interests" of the *apparatchiks* do not involve the enthusiastic support of a growth-maximizing strategy. The typical Soviet manager's behavior was discussed in the previous chapter — he works with a "soft budget constraint," which led to a chronic worsening of the "shortage economy." Overall industrial growth rates fell to 2.6% in 1976-80 and to only two percent per year in the 1981-85 period. [8] Since rapid growth in industrial production was perhaps *the*

---

[7] Mancur Olson, "The Hidden Path to a Successful Economy," in Christopher C. Clague and Gordon C. Rausser (eds.), *The Emergence of Market Economies in Eastern Europe* (Blackwell, 1992), p. 57.

[8] Central Intelligence Agency, *Handbook of Economic Statistics,* 1990, p. 67.

central planning fails

key indicator that communism would win, the slowdown was very embarrassing to the planners. For example, in the 1961-80 "Perspective Plan" steel output was targeted to reach 250 million tons by the end of the period, but the actual was only 148 million; in synthetic fibers and plastics, the shortfalls were relatively much greater.

It is difficult to quantify the influence of the communications revolution that was gathering speed in the early 1980s. The Soviet regime had been moderately successful in jamming Voice of America, BBC, and other broadcasts beamed at audiences behind "the Iron Curtain," but this was just one area of access to information. Tourism was increasing significantly, quite a few Soviet academics were allowed to attend conferences in the West, and the use of television and computer networks was getting underway. As Roy D. Laird has noted:

> "...there was the increasing penetration of the iron curtain by formerly forbidden information. Particularly important was the introduction into the USSR of the ideals expressed in the Universal Declaration of Human Rights and a heightened knowledge of the standards of living enjoyed in the developed market economies, standards of living that were undreamed of by the Soviet masses."[9]

Another significant development in the 1980s was the startling shift in leadership in both America and England. Neither Ronald Reagan nor Margaret Thatcher could be regarded as "soft on communism." As has been said of Gorbachev, the same could be applied to them both: "nice smiles, but iron teeth." After decades of Western appeasement and detente, it must have been quite shocking to hear the descriptive term, "evil empire." A final consideration was perhaps the most important — it was clear that the Soviet Union was beginning to lag behind the fields of science and technology, especially in computers and telecommunications, which had very telling implications for the strategic balance.

Thus, Gorbachev decided to embark on a program of radical reforms in many areas of life simultaneously. The themes of his early efforts included the retooling and modernization of industry, using sharply higher investment, a heightened emphasis on quality control, the anti-alcohol campaign, and the encouragement of cooperatives. The "Law on State Enterprises" replaced obligatory output targets with so-called state orders ("goszakaz") — centrally directed orders for firms to deliver specified quantities of goods. This law also allowed some horizontal contacts with other enterprises reminiscent of the "sovnarkhoz" experiment, and gave managers somewhat more autonomy in the allocation of internally generated funds in the payment of wages and bonuses. There was also some legalization of private economic activity, but initially the labor to be employed in services or light industry was to be limited to "jointly-residing family members," which implied that a couple of brothers living in separate apartments could not legally operate a joint shoe-repair shop. The new "perestroika" regulations emphatically excluded gambling establishments, massage parlors, and photocopying services. In the area of

---

[9] Roy D. Laird, *The Soviet Legacy* (Praeger, 1993), p. 22.

economic reform, cynical Soviet citizens looked upon "perestroika" as simply another marginal adjustment in the rules of the game. The half-hearted effort to reorganize the financial system — splitting up Gosbank into five specialized institutions — weakened the control system. In 1989-90, managers discovered that rubles in enterprise accounts could sometimes be used in cooperative ventures and sometimes even turned into cash! In the final days of the system, there was no shortage of plans — in 1990, for instance, S. Shatalin, G. Yavlinsky, and others drafted a so-called "500-day programme," with support of Western colleagues. At the same time, prime minister Ryzhkov, assisted by Abalkin, was drafting a less radical alternative. They all called for macroeconomic stabilization and the legalization of private enterprise, but they failed to convince the Supreme Soviet, which did not have a "reliable reform-minded majority."[10]

In the other area, political liberalization, associated with the words of "glasnost" and "democratizatsiya", Gorby succeeded beyond his wildest dreams. People took him quite seriously, and began telling the truth, especially about history. First Bukharin and then even Trotsky emerged ghostlike from the mists of the past, then the signing of the Molotov-Ribbentrop Pact comes up on the memory screen, as do millions of Solzhenitsyn's "zeks," clutching at one's conscience...The Poles got away with Solidarity, the Berlin Wall came tumbling down, and Western airlines began flying to the Baltic republics. In 1989, I received an official invitation from the head of the University of Latvia to come to Riga for a series of lectures. There I stood — in the main auditorium of the Marxist-Leninist University of the Central Committee of the Latvian Communist Party — talking enthusiastically about Latvia's economic independence and the market economy, while "Uncle Lenin" smiled down on me benignly. I knew for sure that the Communists' game was over — for me, a Reagan Republican and a Voice of America "stringer" since 1964, to be invited to speak meant that the threat of a "visit to the land of the white bears" was no longer very credible for my hosts even in 1989. But it took another two years for the Soviet Union to implode.

It is an interesting question — what led Gorbachev to do it? He probably felt that political liberalization would lead to improved economic efficiency. Participatory democracy would be associated with a lessening of dysfunctional behavior discussed in the previous chapter — the hoarding of inventories, low quality output, theft of state property, and so on. The people would become more optimistic about the future — progress in science and technology would be revived, and relations with the Western democracies would be improved. A very important sign of this latter point was an exchange program set up with a consortium of (mainly) New England colleges and universities, headquartered at Middlebury College in Vermont, which brought fifty of the "best and brightest" Soviet university students to study in the U.S. in 1989. All that was really needed to finish off the "evil empire" was to show an average American super-market to enough young

---

[10] "It was elected by the freest ballot since 1917, but it was made up of officials nominated by various bodies controlled by the Communist party." See Alec Nove, *An Economic History of the USSR, 1917–1991*, New and Final Edition (Penguin, 1992) p. 408.

leaders from there. "Glasnost" was especially avidly embraced in the Baltic countries, whose incorporation into the USSR had not been recognized "de jure" all along![11]

The Transition

Someone has described going from the market economy to Stalinist socialism as making a fish soup from an aquarium — but the way back may be as difficult as reversing the process. As Eastern Europe began to move away from socialism (the Comecon trading system ended in 1991) and the republics of the USSR became independent countries, there was a heady atmosphere of optimism surrounding the process of change. Dismantling socialism was relatively easy; production targets and five-year plans no longer existed. However, the establishment of the institutions of a market economy will take a lot longer and will apparently be more difficult than we once thought. These countries are passing from one mode of economic organization to a thoroughly different one; institutions tend to resist change. In the words of the *1996 World Development Report*:

> "...Paternalistic and restrictive, these institutions delivered goods and services to meet basic needs while setting severe limits on individual choice and indoctrinating citizens with antimarket propaganda. Thus, for the transition to succeed it must transcend economic engineering, restructure the institutional basis of the social system, and develop civil society — an enormous agenda that will take many years to complete." (pp. 3-4)

There is no general theory of the transition, despite the thousands of books, articles, special studies, and conferences which have been employing experts, consultants, and academics from both West and East. As the Comecon system of trade and the rules of central planning were abandoned, output fell precipitously and prices rose. Attempts to maintain the status quo and to print money to "paper over" political compromises — as in Ukraine and the "Southern" tier — have led to worse consequences, although the consequences of armed conflicts (Armenia, Azerbaijan, and Georgia) are even more disastrous. In Russia itself, the level of GDP is estimated at about 50% of its 1989 value, 25% in Georgia, and the authorities do not yet have a number for Turkmenistan. It is, of course, true that eliminating activities having a "negative value-added" is a good idea, and slaughter of cows no longer giving milk is sound policy. The World Bank has estimated a "Cumulative Liberalization Index," which has enabled it to identify (1) Advanced Reformers, with an index above 3.0 — Slovenia, Poland, Hungary, Czech Republic, and Slovakia, and (2) High Intermediate Reformers, with a CLI above 2.0 — Bulgaria, Estonia, Lithuania, Latvia, Romania, Albania, and Mongolia. Most of these countries have moved quite resolutely in the direction of a "market economy without adjectives." Janos Kornai has suggested that it is less painful to amputate a leg with one

---

[11] See Anatol Lieven, *The Baltic Revolution* (Yale University Press, 1993), and Juris Dreifelds, *Latvia in Transition* (Cambridge University Press, 1996).

chop rather than dozens of small slices. Following Vaclav Klaus, the "hard core" of reform measures, all of which must be taken together, without any particular sequencing being needed, includes:

- early, rapid, and massive privatization;

- price deregulation;

- foreign trade liberalization and currency convertability; and

- monetary and fiscal conservatism.[12]

return

As mentioned above, the reform process began in a very upbeat fashion. I became a consultant to the Bank of Latvia in August 1992, and helped my native country to embark on a rather strict stabilization program at that time. I also assisted the largest political party ("Latvia's Way") with the drawing up of its economic program, then called "Latvija 2000," a very reform-oriented document. The party won 36 seats (out of 100) and set up a coalition cabinet with the centrist Farmers' Union to move Latvia as quickly as possible toward competitive capitalism and eventual entry into the European Union. Trade was to be quickly reoriented toward the West (it had been tied to the Comecon before, almost entirely), our currency would be completely convertible, and prices would be allowed to move toward world market levels quickly. Subsidies would be phased out, and imports liberalized. We were quite successful in some fields. For example, the permanent currency, the Latvian "lats," the name is the same as the pre-Soviet monetary unit, was returned to the pockets of Latvians in March 1993. It was probably the world's strongest currency over the subsequent twelve months appreciating steadily, until it was decided to peg it to the SDR in the spring of 1994. The rate that was selected was 1 SDR = 0.7997 lats (which comes out at about one U.S. dollar equals 0.55 lats).[13] However, we learned that a strong and stable currency does not in itself assure economic progress. As trade with the East collapsed, output and income fell drastically — indeed it was estimated that average daily caloric intake in 1993 was about one thousand calories lower than it had been in 1991. The Baltic countries were transformed from being "show-case" republics of the resource-rich Soviet superpower empire into three small markets with very few resources, save a relatively well-educated but now embittered labor force. While the main reason for the contraction was the "trade crash," many people blamed the reformers — and in all three countries a distinct backlash took place.

In Latvia, it was a two-stage process. The coalition with the Farmers' Union fell apart, and my one-time tennis buddy, Valdis Birkavs resigned as the Prime Minister (I had

---

[12] Vaclav Klaus, *Dismantling Socialism: A Preliminary Report* (a Road to Market Economy II), Praha, Top Agency, 1992, p. 27.

[13] For further detail, see George J. Viksnins and Ilmars Rimshevitchs, "The Latvian Monetary Reform," in Thomas D. Willett *et al* (eds.), *Establishing Monetary Stability in Emerging Market Economies* (Westview, 1995).

actually been officially approved as an adviser to Birkavs, but never actually gave any private advice). A new cabinet was formed by Maris Gailis, without any of the three ministers, who had studied at Georgetown under the auspices of our Pew Economic Freedom Fellows Program. This led to a well-known historian, and a distinctly left-wing member of the Saeima at the time, Ilga Grava (now Kreituse) to say that she was thankful that Latvia was finally getting rid of the "Georgetown University Syndrome." Unfortunately I did not have a chance to respond on the spot that it was too early to give up on the market in Latvia, and to return to the "Moscow U. Model." The centrist LC party set up a new coalition with a splinter faction of a pro-Russophone group, but economic policies did not change very much. The second stage of the backlash against the reformers began in the "Saeima VI" elections in the fall of 1995. A new party, the Democratic Party "Saimnieks" (DPS — the word "saimnieks" can be translated, somewhat unkindly, as "boss"), was formed, attracting quite a few KGB and Komsomol types as well as the aforementioned Ilga and her new husband, Aivars Kreituss. This "party of discontent," to borrow a term from Leszek Balcerowicz, won 18 seats, while the LC saw its deputies shrink from 36 to 17. The party called "For Fatherland and Freedom," quite rightist on the citizenship issue, but holding moderate economic views, took 14 seats, one less than the real surprise — TKL. TKL stands for "People's Movement for Latvia," and is controlled by a German adventurer named Zigerists, who does things like handing out boots and bananas to pensioners, and holding fireworks shows in the provinces. Initially, both parties of discontent put forward a government, which failed to be approved in the Saeimia by a single vote. Shortly thereafter, a businessman (and a former deputy minister) named Andris Skele took on the task of assembling a government on the basis of cooperation among the first three of the parties mentioned above.

Latvia is a fairly representative case. — I apologize for bringing up my personal experience, which probably interests me more than you, but it may be as instructive as a table of output statistics. Let us conclude this chapter by following the seven "tendencies" enumerated by noted Hungarian economist Janos Kornai in his latest collection.

(1) Marketization — most of the transition economies, including China and Vietnam, have allowed supply and demand to determine price levels, although we are not seeing a "triumphant advance toward perfect competition." The state often engages in regulation, when there is no reason to intervene, and fails to intervene when it properly should.

(2) Evolution of the private sector — Kornai argues strongly that there is no "Third System," which could prove its superiority over Stalinist socialism and modern capitalism. Thus, it is necessary to permit the state sector to contract — some firms simply close, others are weakened through "decapitalization" and the theft of state property, and some others improve their efficiency under the pressure of the private sector.

(3) Reproduction of the macro-disequilibria — there exist at the turning point, the following four problems: "chronic shortage, open or repressed inflation, budgetary deficit, and foreign debt."[14] All are really interrelated, and both inflation and unemployment may worsen "for a long time to come." It is probably most important to bring inflation under control first, and to establish the credibility of the monetary authorities, but this requires the sort of resolve demonstrated by very few East European leaders.

(4) Development of a constitutional state — a market economy, based primarily on private ownership, cannot operate in a lawless environment. Why produce more than you can eat, if a man with a gun will take it from you? Kornai talks about the need for three levels of state activity: legislation, enforcement of the law, and — probably most importantly — the alteration of the mentality of citizens. As Kornai says:

"...The previous illegitimate system destroyed people's honest respect for the law; instead they were influenced only by fear of erratic repression. ...Those who cleverly circumvented some regulation or other were really admired, since that was a way of surviving. It will be a long time before public morality improved in this respect, before a state is reached where a breach of the regulations, betrayal of public trust, tax evasion, business dishonesty or corruption is condemned."[15]

(5) Development of democratic institutions — Kornai presents three observations on this score. The ruling Communist party, with its anti-capitalist ideology and program, must be destroyed — but this does not guarantee the development of democratic institutions. Second, for democratic arrangements to be stable, the economic system must be based on private property and contracts. As "...state ownership inevitably leads to a totalitarian political system." However, not all market economies are democracies, and the authoritarian temptation is strong. Very few of the post-communist countries had any historical experience with a stable and long-lived democratic system. And, yet, those of us who believe in democracy must now be especially vigilant in defending it. A very thought-provoking citation on this score:

"...democracy will make the transformation of Soviet-type economies into private enterprise market economies more difficult, but without democracy it would be altogether impossible. Democracy is primarily a truth-seeking procedure of social praxis. It is the only way to discover the extent of tolerable burden and dislocation that the transition to a new system must cause. It also reveals the necessary

---

[14] Janos Kornai, *Highway and Byways: Studies on Reform and Post-Communist Transition* (The MIT Press, 1995), p. 215.

[15] *Ibid,* p. 218. On this score, see also Alice Amsden, Jacek Kochanowicz, and Lance Taylor, *The Market Meets Its Match: Restructuring the Economies of Eastern Europe.* (Harvard University Press, 1994).

adjustments in the pace and scope of changes, and in the distribution of the so-cial cost of transition. Most important, without democracy it is impossible to legiti-mize a society's basic institutions and policies. And without this legitimacy the traumatic but necessary overhaul of Soviet-type economies is unthinkable."[16]

(6) The redefinition of a national community — Kornai notes that in the West, there is a movement toward integration into a larger community. In the East, however,

"...Comecon collapsed because it was imposed on the other Eastern European countries by the Soviet Union; the Soviet Union and Yugoslavia have fallen apart because in many respects they were artificial creations thrust with merciless op-pression upon smaller communities that yearned for sovereignty."[17]

The newly sovereign states will show considerable resistance to greater integration, despite positive official rhetoric on the part of centrist political parties and coalition governments. Influential groups will continue to stir up feelings against "Westernization" (called "bourgeois spiritual pollution" in China) and appeal to nationalism, when the demands of the IMF or other international organizations interfere with their interests.

Indeed, some view the nationalistic tendencies in these countries as much more powerful and dangerous forces than does Kornai. It may be a bit extreme, but here is the view of Stjepan Mestrovic:

"...postmodern forces in the sense of post-Enlightenment narratives are clashing with genuinely post-modern or anti-modern forces such as tradition, nationalism, fundamentalism, racism, and what the West calls human rights abuses. The Dis-neyworld dream of a united Europe is slowly but steadily unraveling as Britain, France, Germany, and other EC states bicker on issues ranging from a common currency, open borders, and especially — Bosnia-Hersegovina. Balkanization is affecting the West, not just the Balkans: the large trading blocs desired by the West are becoming smaller; metaphorical wars are waged by the West against Japan and other nations in the economic sphere and against drugs, violence, and other fictions within their own borders..."[18]

Even if the countries of the USSR avoid going the route of the former Yugoslavia, what will happen in Russia itself is difficult to predict. While Boris Yeltsin has managed to survive up to now, both physically and politically, there is plenty of discontent in Russian society for demagogues to exploit. In the 1993 parliamentary campaign,

---

[16] Andrzej Brzeski, "Post Communist Transformation: Between Accident and Design," Robert W. Campbell, (ed.), *The Post-Communist Economic Transformation: Essays in Honor of Gregory Grossman* (Westview Press, 1994), pp. 11–12.

[17] Janos Kornai, *Highway and Byways..., op. cit.*, pp. 222–223.

[18] Stjepan G. Merstrovic, *The Balkanization of the West: The Confluence of Postmodernism and Postcommunism* (Routledge, 1994), p. 192.

Vladimir Zhirinovsky, spoke of Russians regaining a place of honor in the world in very vivid terms — "dining in the proper manner in the grandest restaurants in Europe and America;" and having "every girlie *(devchonka)* in Australia...physically aroused by the word 'Russian' because she would know that the Russians are the liveliest, the wealthiest, the most generous..." It should be kept in mind that pre-Soviet development in the larger cities was often carried out by non-Russian entrepreneurs. Partly because of the corruption and the uncertain legal framework, but also partly because of the xenophobic attitudes of prospective Russian joint venture partners, foreign investments in Russia have been relatively small. These investments have been largely concentrated in the energy and tobacco sectors, making demagoguery childishly easy — the Americans have come to rape Mother Russia's resources and to destroy the lungs of our young. The non-Russian theme can also be played again and again. As Owen has pointed out:

> "...Strong parallels existed between the reactionary version of post-Soviet Russian capitalism — virtuous entrepreneurship, ethnic pride, religious devotion, family solidarity, and physical violence — and the similar ideological system articulated six decades before the Nazis which contrasted the allegedly healthy capitalism of Aryans to the dangerous capitalism of despised minority groups, especially the Jews."[19]

(7)   An unequal increase in welfare — getting back to Kornai, there will be a fairly broad stratum of winners in the transition process, particularly those tied to private business. A much smaller group becomes conspicuously rich very quickly — the BMW, the leather jacket, the Adidas, the mobile phone, and a miniskirted redhead are all trappings of the successful "free marketeer." In all of the post-communist countries, the new governments inherited social safety nets featuring free medical care, subsidized education (college students receiving stipends rather than paying for education), enterprise-supported vacation facilities, early retirement with full pensions, and so on. As public sector revenues shrink due to privatization, restructuring, and tax holidays for joint ventures, the governments are hard pressed to deal with these implicit obligations. We conclude, along with Kornai:

> "...For all these reasons, deep dissatisfaction among broad strata of people over the stagnating or falling material standard of living, and the unemployment and social insecurity suddenly falling on them, must be expected for a long time to come. It will be hard under the circumstances to ask people to make further

---

[19] Thomas C. Owen, *Russian Corporate Capitalism from Peter the Great to Perestroika* (Oxford University Press, 1995), p. 164. A very perceptive analysis of where Russia stands today is in Vladimir Bukovsky, "Yeltsin's First Hundred Days," in Richard M. Ebeling (ed.), *Can Capitalism Cope? Free Market Reform in the Post-Communist World* (Hillsdale College Press, 1994).

sacrifices. That is another reason why the rectification of the macro-disequilibria will be protracted, not to mention the dangers the discontent poses from the point of view of maintaining democracy." [20] ∎

SUGGESTED READINGS

Amsden, Alice H., Jacek Kochanowicz, and Lance Taylor, *The Market Meets Its Match* (Harvard University Press, 1994).

Aslund, Anders, *How Russia Became a Market Economy* (The Brookings Institution, 1995).

Aslund, Anders (ed.), *Russian Economic Reform at Risk* (Pinter, 1995).

Buck, Trevor and John Cole, *Modern Soviet Economic Performance* (Basil Blackwell, 1987).

Colton, Timothy J., *The Dilemma of Reform in the Soviet Union* (Council on Foreign Relations, 1986).

Cook, Paul and Frederick Nixson (eds.), *The Move to the Market? Trade and Industry Policy Reform in Transitional Economies* (St. Martin's Press, 1995).

Dellenbrant, Jan Ake, *The Soviet Regional Dilemma: Planning, People, and Natural Resources* (M.E. Sharpe, Inc., 1986).

Gregory, Paul R. and Robert C. Stuart, *Soviet and Post-Soviet Economic Structure and Performance*, Fifth Edition (Harper-Collins, 1994).

Gros, Daniel and Alfred Steinherr, *Winds of Change: Economic Transition in Central and Eastern Europe* (Longman, 1995).

Johnson, D. Gale and Karen McConnell Brooks, *Prospects for Soviet Agriculture in the 1980's* (Indiana University Press, in Association with the Center for Strategic and International Studies, Georgetown University, 1983).

Johnson, Simon and Gary Loveman, *Starting Over in Eastern Europe* (Harvard Business School Press, 1995).

Kornai, János, *Highway and Byways: Studies on Reform and Post-Communist Transition* (The MIT Press, 1995).

Laird, Roy D., *The Soviet Legacy* (Praeger, 1993).

Landesmann, Michael A. and István Székely (eds.), *Industrial Restructuring and Trade Reorientation in Eastern Europe* (Cambridge University Press, 1995).

Lavigne, Marie, *The Economics of Transition: From Socialist Economy to Market Economy* (St. Martin's Press, 1995).

Leitzel, Jim, *Russian Economic Reform* (Routledge, 1995).

Liu, Guoli, *States and Markets: Comparing Japan and Russia* (Westview, 1994).

Matthews, Mervyn, *Poverty in the Soviet Union* (Cambridge University Press, 1986).

McMahon, Gary (ed.), *Lessons in Economic Policy for Eastern Europe from Latin America* (Macmillan, 1996).

Meštrovic, Stjepan G., *The Balkanization of the West: The Confluence of Postmodernism and Post-communism* (Routledge, 1994).

Nove, Alec, *An Economic History of the USSR: 1917-1991*, New and Final Edition (Penguin, 1992).

Stiglitz, Joseph, *Whither Socialism?* (The MIT Press, 1994).

Wyzan, Michael L. (ed.), *First Steps Toward Economic Independence: New States of the Postcommunist World* (Praeger, 1995).

---

[20] Janos Kornai, *Highway and Byways...*, op. cit., p. 225.

LESS DEVELOPED COUNTRIES: THE "WORLD ECONOMY" VIEW

*T*hough economics as a science itself has a relatively short history of a little more than two hundred years, dating back to Adam Smith's excellent and oft-cited development text, the subfield called "economics of less developed countries" is even a much more recent field of study. Development economics or the "economics of the LDC's" has been offered as a separate course in most major economics departments only during the past thirty or forty years, and perhaps even for a shorter time period in many colleges and smaller universities. The best-known and oldest journal in this field, *Economic Development and Cultural Change,* published by the University of Chicago Press, began about forty years ago. The first textbook addressed to the special problems of the underdeveloped countries, written by Meier and Baldwin, came out in 1957. As an initial generalization, academic research interests in the economic problems of the so-called "Third World" are of quite recent vintage. Nevertheless, and somewhat surprisingly, but also as perhaps an even greater simplification—the basic attitude this subfield seems to have switched in a fairly short time from one of rather naive optimism to one of profound pessimism.

This chapter and the subsequent one contrast two differing approaches to the problem of "Third World" development. But before we get into this contrast of theoretical approaches, a few matters of classification and definition need to be discussed briefly. What is the "Third World?" It can be pointed out, first of all, that this concept covers a very heterogeneous group of countries, from Singapore to Afghanistan and Brunei to Zimbabwe, and that there is probably no single characteristic that all of these countries share. Thus, a short definition is difficult to provide — especially after the fall of the Berlin Wall.

As a leading development economics text nearly ten years ago put it:

"...Perhaps the best way to define it is by elimination. Take the industrialized market economies of Western Europe, North America, and the Pacific (the 'first' world), and the industrialized but centrally planned economies of Eastern Europe (the 'second' world); the rest of the countries constitute the third world. All third-

world countries are developing countries and these include all of Latin America and the Caribbean, Africa, the Middle East, and all Asia except Japan. The geographic configuration of this group has led to a parallel distinction—north (first and second worlds) versus south—that is also in current vogue. But the south or third world encompasses a wide variety of nations. The obvious differences between the wealthy (if structurally underdeveloped) oil exporters and the very low-income, poorly endowed countries have led some to add fourth and fifth worlds to the classification. Political motivations create further exceptions: South Africa and Israel are usually not considered part of the third world; nor are Spain and Portugal, former colonial powers, although in many respects they are less developed countries.[1]

For our purposes, possibly the simplest way to define what we mean by "the LDC's" is to say that we are talking about all countries still eligible for official World Bank assistance today, or which have received World Bank aid since the founding of that institution (at Bretton Woods in 1944).

The World Bank Atlas classifies all countries on the basis of GNP per capita; the "low-income economies" category covers 51 countries with a population of more than 3.2 billion people—the ten largest countries (in terms of population) are briefly described by Table 8-1. All had a per capita GNP below $750 in 1994 — the majority of mankind is very poor. China's population at more than a billion people, accounts for nearly one-third of the total included in this grouping and had an official per capita GNP of $530 in 1994. According to World Bank statistics, India's GNP per capita was slightly lower at $320, and its growth rate in the 1985-94 period was considerably lower. Still, even if we make the customary upward adjustment for exchange rate problems and price structures and we get $1280 for India and $2510 for China, it is clear that, the average Chinese or Indian is eking out a living standard just barely above subsistence. And, the situation in Bangladesh and Ethiopia is a good deal worse—and only slightly better in Pakistan. The two largest African countries, Nigeria and Tanzania, are essentially standing still. As we argue over minute and marginal economic policy differences in the U.S., incensed by the insensitivity of the Republicans or the foolishness of the Democrats, we should keep in mind the daily struggle of existence that faces more than three-quarters of mankind.

The next World Bank category, the "middle-income economies," account for another billion-plus people, with a 1994 GNP per capita of $2520. The largest of the "lower middle-income economies," Indonesia, is experiencing rapid growth—while the Russian Federation (a newcomer to World Bank statistics) has experienced a decade of negative growth. The "lower middle-income" category includes 39 nations, ranging from Bolivia (GNP per capita of $770 in 1994) to Botswana and Estonia at about $2800 (no statistics for Iran or Lebanon are given). Turkey, at $2500, has been losing ground in terms of overall growth, while Thailand has been gaining.

---

[1] Malcolm Gillis, Dwight H. Perkins, Michael Roemer, and Donald R. Snodgrass, *Economics of Development*, Second Edition (W.W. Norton & Co., 1987), p.6.

Table 8-1: Ten Largest Low-Income Countries

Country	Population (millions)	GNP per capita (US$, 1994)	Real GNP growth rate, 1985–1994	Life expectancy
China	1190.9	$530	7.8	69
India	913.6	320	2.9	62
Pakistan	126.3	430	1.3	60
Bangladesh	117.9	220	2.0	57
Nigeria	108.0	280	1.2	52
Vietnam	72.0	200	n.a.	68
Egypt	56.8	720	0.6	61
Ethiopia	54.9	100	n.a.	49
Myanmar	45.6	n.a.	n.a.	58
Tanzania	28.8	140	0.8	51

Source: *World Development Report, 1996,* pp. 118–119.

The final category of LDC's, "upper middle-income economies," ranges from Brazil with a GNP of $2970 per capita in 1994 to Korea with $8260; Singapore, Hong Kong, and Israel have all graduated to the "high-income economies" group in the World Bank measurement system. Most of the countries in this category have become aid donors rather than recipients (though Israel is probably both), and a few of the upper middle-income category also have "graduated" from being permanently "Third World." As one prominent critic of foreign aid has put it, the Third World is "a collectivity confronting the West," which is also generally "hostile to it." Further,

> "...Foreign aid is central to the economic relations between the West and the Third World. It will remain so long as there is a Third World. The Third World and its antecedents and synonyms, such as the underdeveloped world, the less devel-

Table 8-2: Ten Largest Middle-Income Countries

I. "Lower Middle-Income"

Country	Population (millions)	GNP per capita (US$ 1994)	Real GNP growth rate 1985–1994	Life expectancy
Indonesia	190.4	$880	6.0	68
Russian Federation	148.3	2580	-4.1	64
Philippines	67.0	950	1.7	65
Turkey	60.8	2500	1.4	67
Thailand	58.0	2410	8.6	69

II. "Upper Middle-Income"

Country	Population (millions)	GNP per capita (US$, 1994)	Real GNP growth rate 1985–1994	Life expectancy
Brazil	159.1	$2970	-0.4	67
Mexico	88.5	4180	0.9	71
Iran	62.5	n.a.	n.a.	68
Korea	45.5	8260	7.8	71
South Africa	40.5	3040	-1.3	64

Source: *World Development Report, 1996,* pp. 118–119.

oped world and the developing world (all still used) and now also the South, are for all practical purposes the collection of countries whose governments, with the odd exception, demand and receive official aid from the West. The concept of the Third World or the South and the policy of official aid are inseparable. They are two sides of the same coin. The Third World is the creation of foreign aid: without foreign aid there is no Third World.

...From its inception, the unifying characteristic has been that the Third World is in practice the aggregate of countries whose governments demand and receive Western aid. In all other ways the unity or uniformity is pure fiction." [2]

From Optimism to Pessimism

Be that as it may, prevailing opinion in the West (or the North) concerning Third World prospects appears to have come full circle from a viewpoint of unbridled and rather naive optimism of the 1950's and the early 1960's to a much more negative and pessimistic assessment. Let me go off on a brief tangent to illustrate this point a bit more vividly.

The alert reader is probably aware that the "crème de la crème" of American economics departments is either Harvard or M.I.T., with the latter probably edging into first as economics becomes more technological. In any case, I have in mind a well-known book, which I'd like to discuss for a little bit, which epitomizes, typifies, represents the optimism of those early days. Let's do a bit of a treasure hunt. We're looking for the subtitle of a famous book. Clue No. 1— the author was a professor of economic history at the "crème de la crème" of American academic institutions (no, not Georgetown) in the 1950's (yes, fans, a full professor of economic history at M.I.T.!). As an aside, a bit of "fore-shadowing" for later on in this section, the alert reader is no doubt aware that academic respectability in the U.S. in largely, almost entirely, determined by geography —an academic institution's reputation and standing in its field are inversely related to the square (possibly the cube...) of its distance from Cambridge, Massachusetts 02139. The second clue for our treasure hunt is the author's initials — W. W., for Walt Whitman. Third, he was for a time LBJ's (for Lyndon B. Johnson) national security adviser and, fourth, his book was modestly sub-titled "A Non-Communist Manifesto." Finally, he is now at the University of Texas, which in itself is a comment on his current academic stature... (Well, it could have been San Diego State, I suppose...please, please, Texans and Californians, no hate mail — just a silly little joke on my part.)

In any case, the alert reader has already figured out that I am talking about W.W. Rostow, *The Stages of Economic Growth*, first published in 1960. While I am oversimplifying greatly, Rostow's basic message was that the economic growth experience historically was quite uniform and just about inevitable—all countries were essentially similar, and they all experienced his five growth stages. The first stage is that of the

---

[2] P.T. Bauer, *Equality, the Third World, and Economic Delusion* (Harvard University Press, 1981), p. 87.

"traditional society," where there was a definite ceiling on output per capita, due to a low level of saving and investment as well as the unavailability of modern science and technology. A high proportion of the labor force was of necessity engaged in agriculture, which led to the development of a "hierarchical social structure, with relatively narrow scope — but some scope — for vertical mobility." More importantly, the "value system of these societies was generally geared to what might be called a long-run fatalism; that is, the assumption that the range of possibilities open to one's grandchildren would be just about what it had been for one's grandparents."[3]

In the second stage, society begins to challenge this fatalism, as "pre-conditions for the take-off" begin to develop. These include social and political changes of the sort that we have discussed in the first chapter of this book — with particular emphasis on the development of an "effective centralized national state" and the emergence of an entrepreneurial class, emphasized by Schumpeter. The third stage, which Rostow terms "the great watershed in the life of modern societies" is, of course, "the take-off" — measured rather precisely by the rise of the ratio of national saving and/or investment from the old level of about 5% of national income to 10% or more. According to Rostow, Britain "took-off" during the early 1800's, France and the U.S. around 1850, Germany and Japan during the second half of the nineteenth century — while China and India "launched their respective take-offs" during the 1950's. This third stage involves the following changes:

> "...During the take-off new industries expand rapidly, yielding profits a large proportion of which are reinvested in new plant; and these new industries, in turn, stimulate, through their rapidly expanding requirement for factory workers, the services to support them, and for other manufactured goods, a further expansion in urban areas and in other modern industrial plants. The whole process of expansion in the modern sector yields an increase of income in the hands of those who not only save at high rates but place their savings at the disposal of those engaged in modern sector activities. The new class of entrepreneurs expands; and it directs the enlarging flows of investment in the private sector. The economy exploits hitherto unused natural resources and methods of production."[4]

The fourth stage in Rostow's scheme of things is called the "drive to economic maturity." For a period of about fifty years after the take-off has taken place, profits continue to be invested productively, science and technology advances, and compound interest takes over. Financial institutions are very important during this stage, facilitating both saving and investment. In many cases, natural resource exports have played a major role in the drive to maturity — Rostow mentions American, Russian and Canadian grain exports, Swedish timber and pulp, and Japanese silk in this connection, as well as agricultural exports of the People's Republic of China in the late 1950's. (Rostow notes

---

[3] W.W. Rostow, *The Stages of Economic Growth*, Second Edition (Cambridge University Press, 1971), p.5.
[4] *Ibid.*, pp. 8–9.

that these exports were being "...wrung at great administrative and human cost from the agricultural sector." He did not know at the time of his writing just how great this cost was—it is now estimated that "Mao's Famine" of the early 1960's involved more than thirty million deaths by starvation.) Still, "...it should be noted that the development of such export sectors has not in itself guaranteed accelerated capital formation. Enlarged foreign-exchange proceeds have been used in many familiar cases to finance hoards...or unproductive consumption outlays." Foreign capital can assist in the process of infra-structure development, but it can also be pointed out that Japan's drive to economic maturity was primarily based on the mobilization of internal sources of finance.[5]

The final stage is called "the high mass-consumption society," where the beauties of compound interest continue to generate increases in output, and demands of society concerning food, shelter, and clothing are all taken care of virtually automatically. The LDC's catch up with and duplicate American consumption patterns. One is tempted to think of Levittowns or Restons springing up in the suburbs of Bombay and Shanghai. Indian and Chinese families are living in identical pre-fab split-levels, driving Volvos or Hondas, and watching "Dallas" or "Dynasty" on a 23-inch Sony color TV. By the year 2000 or so, since Rostow claims that the "take-off" started around 1950, Indian and Chinese "yuppies" will be eating Brie and sipping Chablis every weekend. How to get there? Why, it's quite easy — just lift your capital formation ratio about 10% and allow compound interest to take over. If the private sector savings level has difficulties in achieving this "magic" ten percent level, why, the government can step in and extract higher taxes to finance investments through the public sector. Finally, we in the West, in the already successful mass-consumption societies, can help out by increasing foreign aid and transferring modern technology, in order to shorten the drive to maturity. Why, not only will we open up new markets for American exports, but we'll "win their hearts and minds" as well. (Remember Rostow's sub-title...)

I am being quite uncharitable to Professor Rostow in the above paragraph. He himself raised a number of interesting and subtle qualifications in the first edition of his book, and defended himself quite ably against his critics in an appendix to the second edition. Still, although I may have drawn a caricature of his approach a bit too simplistically, the prevalent approach to development problems in the 1950's and the 1960's was an optimistic, "can-do" attitude. Various simple growth models were developed in the early years of development economics, in part based upon the contributions of Keynesian macroeconomics. Many of these models relied centrally on the concept of the Incremental Capital-Output Ratio (the ICOR). The ICOR is the ratio of the previous year's investment, or capital formation, to this year's change in GNP, or national income. In most middle-income countries this number is around 3 — generally a bit lower in countries with a large agricultural sector, and a bit higher in resource-rich, but economically inefficient, nations. This number enables "the development economist" to link growth rate targets to "capital requirements" — as if capital were the only factor of production. Thus, for

---

[5] *Ibid.*, pp. 48–50. See also Michael T. Skully and George J. Viksnins, *Financing East Asia's Success* (Macmillan, 1987).

example, if ICOR = 3, then Faroffistan (a hypothetical LDC) would need to invest 15% of last year's GNP in order to attain a 5% growth rate this year, while an 8% growth rate would require 24% as the I/Y ratio, and so on. The use of a fixed ICOR and a target growth rate implies a rather crude theory of foreign aid — if Faroffistan can only manage a 9% I/Y ratio, foreign loans or grants (perhaps depending upon "strategic considerations" in the 1960's) can bring that ratio safely above the "take-off" level, enabling the target growth rate to rise above only 3% previously attained (which may only be enough to keep per capita GNP from falling). Thus, prevailing orthodoxy in the early years of development economics greatly oversimplified the growth process, linking all progress exclusively to capital formation, and implied that the "West" or the "Free World" could assist greatly through technical assistance and foreign aid.[6]

By the end of the decade of the 1960's, significant changes had taken place in American public opinion, academic "conventional wisdom," and acceptable approaches to the problem of underdevelopment. In Cambridge, Massachusetts, our most esteemed institution, the "crème de la crème" of American academia, produced yet another trend-setting volume. Ready for one more treasure hunt, fans? First clue—the book was published in 1972. Second clue — two of the four authors listed were a husband-and-wife team, Donella and Dennis Meadows. Third clue — this book was known as the first "Club of Rome" report. Surely, the alert reader will have already guessed the title: Limits to Growth.[7]

In clear juxtaposition to Rostow's optimistic message that growth was nearly inevitable, as long as his stages were permitted to develop "naturally," the message of this new book was starkly pessimistic: "growth is impossible." The basic structure of the Limits to Growth book is so seriously flawed, and the errors so obvious, as to deserve even less space than Rostow's model; still, the pessimistic seeds sown by the Club of Rome report have found fertile soil in American academia, in Western European media, and in many "green" adolescent minds. Why is this? Why is "doom and gloom" carrying the day? Why do our intellectuals instinctively "blame America first?" Combined with the teachings of the "dependencia" school, which teaches that incorporation into the world market economy is harmful for LDC's, we have a double dose of pessimism coloring the development economic field.

---

[6] For considerably more discussion of the early days of development economics, see G.M. Meier and Dudley Seers (eds.), Pioneers in Development (Oxford University Press for the World Bank, 1984) as well as a much more critical work, though still by a World Bank "insider," Deepak Lal, The Poverty of "Development Economics" (Harvard University Press, 1985). See also, however, Robert L. Ayres, Banking on the Poor (MIT Press, 1984) and Roger C. Riddell, Foreign Aid Reconsidered (The Johns Hopkins University Press, 1987)

[7] For bibliography fans, let us provide a full citation (since the authors' names have been somehow ignored by the media): Donella H. Meadows, Dennis L. Meadows, Jorgen Randers, and William W. Behrens, III, The Limits to Growth: A Report for the Club of Rome's Project on the Predicament of Mankind (Universe Books, in association with Potomac Associates, 1972).

The pre-cursor of *The Limits to Growth* was Jay Forrester's *World Dynamics,* which shows the world running out of natural resources, including arable land, generating pollution in ever-increasing amounts, and facing a dismal future. Except for the contemporary emphasis on pollution, the result is what Reverend Malthus would have come up with, if he had had access to the computers at M.I.T. Forrester's earlier work on "systems dynamics" dealt with urban areas, and he seems to see little difference between the planet and the city. As he concludes:

> *"... The population pressures and the economic forces in a city that was reaching equilibrium have in the past been relieved by escape of people to new land areas. But that escape is becoming less possible. Until now we have had, in effect, an inexhaustible supply of farm land and food-growing potential. But now we are reaching the critical point where, all at the same time, population is overrunning productive land, agricultural land is almost fully employed for the first time, the rise in population is putting more demand on the food supplies and urbanization is pushing agriculture out of the fertile areas into the marginal lands. For the first time demand is rising into a condition where supply will begin to fall while need increases. The crossover from plenty to shortage can occur abruptly."* [8]

As noted, the *Limits to Growth* volume has a message that is in sharp contrast to Rostow's "growth is easy and automatic" conclusion — and that basic finding of the latter M.I.T. volume can be summarized as "further growth is impossible as well as dangerous to the world as a whole." Basically, the resource base of the planet is exhausted and pollution worsens, while population continues to grow — I vividly recall seeing a graph reproduced in the national media, which shows "Gross Planetary Product" peaking in 2035 A.D. and turning down sharply thereafter. In re-reading the original volume, I do not find such a stark prediction — that "the world will end in 2035" — but the implications of a catastrophe are certainly there. In the words of the club of Rome report, their first conclusion is:

> *"...If the present growth trends in world population, pollution, food production, and resource depletion continue unchanged, the limits to growth on this planet will be reached sometime within the next one hundred years. The most probable result will be a rather sudden and uncontrollable decline in both population and industrial capacity."* [9]

After a series of simulations permitting a loosening of resource constraints and an improvement in pollution, the authors conclude, nevertheless, that the basic character of the world system being manipulated by their computer shows an "...exponential growth of population and capital, followed by collapse." (p. 142) The only way to avoid such a collapse is to slow population growth drastically, beginning as of 1975, hold down output

---

[8] Jay W. Forester, *World Dynamics,* Second Edition (Wright-Allen Press Inc., 1973), p. 113. It is interesting to note that a third edition has not appeared.

[9] Donella H. Meadows *et al, op. cit.,* p. 23.

gains in both industry and agriculture, and follow deliberate planet-wide policies for resource use and pollution control as soon as possible.

It is beyond our scope here to present a detailed analysis of the M.I.T. *Limits to Growth* model, and a summary of the most significant academic criticisms of it, which have been made to date. I would tend to agree that the systems dynamics methodology "...is an attempt to substitute mathematics for knowledge and computation for understanding" (these tendencies are present in other areas as well...). More specifically, it has been argued that the M.I.T. approach is inherently dangerous, "...since it encourages self-delusion in five ways:

■ By giving the spurious appearance of precise knowledge of quantities and relationships which are unknown and in many cases unknowable.

■ By encouraging the neglect of factors which are difficult to quantify such as policy changes or value changes.

■ By stimulating gross over-simplification, because of the problem of aggregation and the comparative simplicity of our computers and mathematical techniques.

■ By encouraging the tendency to treat some features of the model as rigid and immutable.

■ By making it difficult for the non-numerate or those who do not have access to computers to rebut what are essentially tendentious and rather naive political assumptions.[10]

Despite the fact that the assumptions of the *Limits* volume have been attacked by physical and social scientists alike, it appears to have struck a very responsive chord in the mass media and public opinion of the West. The themes of physical constraints to further growth and a pessimistic planetary outlook were certainly echoed by the Carter Administration's costly inter-agency assessment of the future, *Global 2000* (while Julian Simon and the late Herman Kahn ably rebutted the overall vision and the detailed analyses of the Carter volume in their book, *The Resourceful Earth*, the latter cost only a small fraction of the former, and was treated accordingly by the media).[11]

Be all that as it may, a simple factual assessment seems to be a good way to close this section of the chapter. If we take all of the countries comprising the so-called Third World and calculate an average annual growth rate in real GNP per capita, we find an overall advance of about three percent per year taking place over the past twenty years. Including all of the large but very poor countries shown in Table 8-1, also including all

[10] Again, a full bibliographical citation is probably in order — H.S.D. Cole, Christopher Freeman, Marie Jahoda, and K.L.R. Pavitt (eds.), *Models of Doom* (Universe Books, 1973), p. 12

[11] Cf. Council on Environmental Quality and the Department of State, *The Global 2000 Report to the President* (Goernment Printing Office, 1980), but see also Julian L. Simon and Herman Kahn (eds.), *The Resourceful Earth: A Response to Global 2000* (Basil Blackwell, 1984) as well as Charles Maurice and Charles W. Smithson, *The Doomsday Myth* (Hoover Institution Press, 1984).

of Africa (where numerous nations are showing negative growth on average), and including all of the debtors of Latin America as well, we still get a fairly large annual rate of increase in real output of the LDC's (corrected for inflation and population growth). While *three percent* may not seem very impressive, it should be pointed out that Japan's overall growth rate in the century or so since its "take-off" around 1880 has averaged only about *two percent,* but Western Europe's average compound growth rate from around 1780 to 1900 around *1.5 percent.* Therefore, even though the gap between the rich countries and the LDC's is very large (and growing in absolute terms), the prospects for Third World progress do not appear to be as pessimistic as often presented—and the world will not end in 2035 (it may well be that Rostow will retire from U.T./Austin, and take a part-time position somewhere in the Boston area in the not-too-distant future...). Still, as mentioned earlier, we have yet to present the main thesis of this chapter — so here we go.

The "World Economy" View

As noted in the first chapter of this book, the gulf between per capita GNP figures produced by the U.S. and Japan versus the Russian Federation and the rest of the FSU as well as China is quite large, in part due to systemic differences. On average, the industrialized countries of North America, Western Europe, and East Asia (recently) enjoy living standards many times higher than those of the Second or Third World taken as a group. Why is that the case? Is there a general model, a systematic approach or "paradigm," which can be used to explain the existence of this wide gulf in production, income and consumption? Indeed, as noted at the outset of this chapter, there are two principal approaches — the "world economy view," which focuses on historical and external constraints impeding growth and development, *versus* the "traditional society view," which identifies presently-existing internal bottlenecks as the principal reason for difficulties in kicking the engine of growth into a running position.

The world economy view owes a great deal to Karl Marx and his followers for an overall conception of the dynamics of capitalism. It is the Marxist position that capitalism provides a necessary historical stage in the world's evolution toward socialism, but also that doomed to fail, since it is suffering from internal contradictions. While the productive capacity of capitalism as a system grows by leaps and bounds, the proletariat becomes increasingly more and more miserable — certainly the unemployed ("the industrial reserve army") do not have the purchasing power to buy whatever is being produced. Greater concentration of economic power in the hands of fewer and fewer capitalists will lead to increasingly violent business cycles, forecasts Marx, resulting in an overthrow of the whole system — a violent international uprising of the proletariat, the working class. Though this is discussed rather briefly by Marx himself, the inevitable collapse of the capitalistic system can be partly delayed by *imperialism* carried out by the major industrial countries — sending the industrial reserve army off to conquer other areas is a most convenient way to reduce discontent at home. Furthermore, the colonies can serve as a convenient source of raw materials as well as a captive market for the "mother country's" finished goods, as we saw in our earlier discussion of mercantilism.

The concept of imperialism as a stage of capitalist development was further elaborated by Lenin in his often-noted pamphlet, *Imperialism — The Highest Stage of Capitalism,* and also a bit later by the so-called "Neo-Marxist school" (including authors like Paul Baran, Paul Sweezy, and Harry Magdoff, for example). The fundamental thesis of the neo-Marxists is that the world was irrevocably divided into the "haves" and the "have-nots" during the stage of imperialism — the rich countries of the *center* have benefitted from the exploitation of the poor countries of the *periphery.* The *center* (or the "core" or the "metropolis") needs the *periphery* in order for capitalism to survive a bit longer — the exploitation of the LDC's is the main explanation for the wealth of Western Europe and North America, while the historical integration of the LDC's into the world economy has been inimical to their growth and development. In the words of Michael P. Todaro:

> "...the early neo-Marxists saw imperialism as a system that created a necessary polarity between an extremely poor periphery and a prospering center. Poverty and wealth were thus seen as two faces of the same coin. This view, implying as it does the impossibility of capitalist development of the LDC's, is, in its resemblance to a zero-sum game, unrealistic, dogmatic, and subject to damaging criticism. Quite arbitrarily, the early neo-Marxists assumed: (1) that a very large part of the surplus is drained; and (2) that the part of the surplus not drained is not utilized in a way conducive to local development. Thus, for them, even if the proportion of drained to not-drained is low, there is no growth."[12]

To put it very crudely, in the United States, say most neo-Marxists, our wealth is the result of the exploitation of Third World countries, that the "North" is rich *because* they are poor. This is obviously a silly argument. Canada, for example, is a "First World" country enjoying a modern standard of living, but it has never had a colony — the same can be said of Australia and New Zealand. Possibly Denmark's exploitation of Greenland counts on this score, but the other Scandinavian countries have all grown rich on their own, as has Switzerland. The United States, at least for a while, held the Philippines in a colonial relationship (though it granted that country independence very quickly after World War II had ended) — and continues to keep Puerto Rico, Guam, and a handful of other "Southern" areas "in bondage." Still, in the 1950's, for example, the United States had attained the world's highest standard of living, but imported only 3-4% of its GNP. Regardless of how good a deal it was making in trading with Latin America, say, it seems quite unlikely that U.S. living standards were greatly influenced by keeping incomes low elsewhere. The second part of the neo-Marxist argument — that the countries of the periphery are poor because of unequal exchange with the rich — seems to have considerably more validity, and can be discussed at somewhat greater length.

---

[12] Michael T. Todaro, *Economic Development in the Third World,* Second Edition (Longman, Inc., 1981), pp. 79–80. See also L.S. Stavrianos, *Global Rift: The Third World Comes of Age* (William Morrow and Co., 1981).

We will be talking about three major arguments in the "world economy" model: (1) the legacy of colonialism; (2) the recent history of the international trading system; and, (3) the finance-investment-aid institutions of the world system. Let us note at the outset that we will be presenting a very brief and concise summary of the principal arguments; each of them has been treated at much greater length elsewhere.

One of the principal sub-themes of the "legacy of colonialism" argument is precisely the "center vs. periphery" analysis briefly discussed above. The mercantilistic system followed policies leading to the development of industrial activities in the "mother country" and forced the colonies into a specialized role as suppliers of raw material inputs. It has been estimated that British earnings on their investments in India amounted to about 2-3% of Indian national income in the inter-war period (1920-40, roughly). In those colonial areas exporting metals and other non-renewable resources, say, gold, silver, copper, tin, oil, gas, coal and so on, the most easily mined deposits were certainly exploited first by the colonial powers, leaving the newly independent countries a smaller stock of natural resources.

A closely-related argument concerning the colonial period is that of "unequal exchange." In many cases, the government of the colonial power granted monopoly and monopsony (single-buyer) rights to their chartered trading companies—or allocated banking licenses to their own banking firms—and were willing to enforce such rights by the force of arms. A trading company may have been the only buyer of labor or raw materials in a given port in the South Seas, and the only seller of medicine, textiles, mirrors, knives and other imported products. To quote Todaro again on this score:

> "...in the 'enclave' Third World economies, like those with substantial foreign-owned mining and plantation operations, foreigners pay very low rents for the rights to use land, bring in their own foreign capital and skilled labor, hire local unskilled workers at subsistence wages, and in general, leave a minimal impact on the rest of the economy even though they may generate significant export revenues. While such visible enclaves are gradually disappearing in the Third World, they are often being replaced by more subtle forms of foreign domination (i.e., the economic penetrations of multinational corporations).*[13]*

Although standard textbook discussions of international economics tend to stress the Theory of Comparative Advantage of David Ricardo, which shows how both "partners" will be better off as a result of trading, this theory tends to assume that the two trading countries (say, England and Portugal) are fairly even in terms of political power, are both close to or at full employment, and operate under purely competitive conditions for the two products being traded. In the colonial relationship between England, and, say, Burma, these standard assumptions fall apart quite quickly—especially the one about pure competition. As Hla Myint has pointed out:

---

[13] *Ibid.*, p. 357.

> "...the backward peoples have to contend with three types of monopolistic forces:
> in their role as unskilled labour they have to face the big foreign mining and plan-
> tation concerns who are monopolistic buyers of their labour; in their role as peas-
> ant producers they have to face a small group of exporting and processing firms
> who are monopolistic buyers of their crop; and in their role as consumers of im-
> ported commodities they have to face the same group of firms who are the monop-
> olistic sellers or distributors of these commodities."[14]

Another related aspect of the problem of unequal exchange is the development of an irreversible (or difficult to change, in any case) "bias in infrastructure." In Africa, the railroads all run from the interior to the ocean; they do not connect population centers. To make a telephone call from Thailand to Burma, right next door, in the past, it was necessary to ring up London first. The educational establishment in India and Burma was developed to serve the needs of the British—producing very few Burman graduates, for example, and emphasizing a liberal education "...to have a convenient supply of civil servants and clerks for the colonial administration (Myint, p. 224)." The banking system in most colonial areas, including the coastal provinces of much of China, was in the hands of foreigners, and were used primarily to finance export and import trade. In general, investments in infrastructure were made in order to assist the "export enclaves" rather than to assist in the development of the "country as a whole" (which, of course, did not exist at the time) or the "people."

Finally, as part of the "legacy of colonialism" argument, we can focus on the "gold standard itself" as a monetary regime of very uneven rewards, as a game with odds favoring established players. During the period of 1879 to 1931, for nearly a century and a half, our great-grandparents lived in a world very different from the reality of the 1990's. The monetary regime was characterized by one great constant, the price of gold was fixed at $20.67 per ounce. Furthermore, all major currencies, except for brief periods of inconvertibility (e.g., the "greenback" during the American Civil War), were defined in terms of a specific gold content. Thus, for example, as was pointed out in Chapter 2, the dollar price of a British pound was about $4.87 during this period.[15] An economic expansion in the U.S. would tend to raise the dollar price of pound sterling by a few cents, but the boom, leading to significant inflationary pressure, would eventually lead to an outflow of gold and a quasi-automatic tightening of monetary, the boom, leading to significant policy — as was pointed out in our earlier discussion of the "rules of the game" concept.

The so-called discipline of the balance of payments, on the whole, enforced rather conservative monetary and fiscal policies. If a country's money supply expanded faster

---

[14] Hla Myint, *Economic Theory and the Underdeveloped Countries* (Oxford University Press, 1971), p. 80.

[15] As noted by Friedman and Schwartz, the "mint par" was 109.45625 = 54*d*., which works out to $4.8647 a pound sterling. After 1874, the mint par is given at $4.8665, which would round up to $4.87. See Milton Friedman and Anna Jacobson Schwartz, *A Monetary History of the Unitd States, 1867–1960* (Princeton University Press, 1963) p. 59.

than money supplies in its major trading partners, inflationary pressure would lead to depreciation of its foreign exchange rate. Unless the central bank raised interest rates sufficiently, a continuation of an expansionary monetary policy would sooner or later cause a gold outflow — which would force a larger domestic contraction. In order to avoid such a "crash" or "panic," central banks always kept a careful eye on the foreign exchange rate, and would be thinking about higher interest rates at the first sign of a depreciation of the exchange rate below the mint par. Countries participating in the gold standard system gained considerable benefits from its operation. Stable exchange rates greatly facilitated foreign trade and investment. (I recall vaguely a character in one of Somerset Maugham's novels hanging about a bar in Singapore, living off the income from a rubber estate in Malaya, which brought in, say, 500 pounds sterling per year. Is that not an amazing statement? Can we think of any productive investment in 1996 which could be described in terms of its precise annual income or return? Since profit equals total revenue (PQ) minus total cost, think of the stability in prices, output and costs that such a statement would imply.)

Generally, exchange rate stability also contributed to a system of relatively low nominal interest rates, which facilitated long-term investments in what economists call "social overhead capital." British consols (pure debt instruments having no fixed maturity) yielded about 4.4 percent in 1820, about 3 percent in 1850, and as little as 2.45% in 1897. In the U.S., long-term railroad bonds fell from around 7% in 1870 to 3.8% in 1902. In this connection, when driving into New York City, it is instructive to think about how and when all those bridges and tunnels were financed by previous generations. To be sure, the D.C. subway system, "The Metro," was built some thirty years ago, and other real investments continue to be financed, but these kinds of long-term projects somehow seem to be more difficult and costly in today's environment than they were in the days of the international gold standard.

As we have argued, the gold standard system seemed to insure the participating countries against inflation. Central banks viewed the safeguarding of their exchange rates and currency convertability as their first priority — anyone even mentioning a possible devaluation or a change in the price of gold would have been regarded as "a dangerous Bolshevik," since such topics were not to be taken up in polite society. If anything, the gold standard system can be characterized as tending to create a "mild deflationary bias" — which can be easily understood by thinking in terms of the MV = PQ framework. As real output, Q, continued to expand by about 3-5% per year, and if velocity remained relatively constant, there would be a tendency for P to fall slightly unless the money supply rose. To be sure, gold discoveries in California, Alaska, and South Africa injected new M into the system from time to time, but the gold standard era saw a number of fairly lengthy periods (such as in the United States after the Civil War) when the general price level fell significantly. Quite clearly, a deflationary tendency hurts debtors and provides creditors with steady gains — the bankers of the silent movies, twirling their mustaches and tying farmers' daughters to the railroad tracks, were gaining purchasing power, while farmers/debtors were losing.[16]

Internationally, the farmers/debtors of the gold standard world were quite clearly the lands today termed the periphery. During periods of falling commodity prices such as after World War I, debtors found it very difficult to service their debt, and a number figuratively got tied to the railroad tracks. The gold standard system fell apart during the 1930's, as discussed earlier, but the countries of the periphery can argue, with considerable justification, that the gold standard itself was an integral part of the colonial legacy.

Thus, past penetration of the peripheral areas by the "mother countries" of the "core" has contributed to their continued economic subjugation, even after the colonial system ended, and most "Third World" countries achieved political independence. While I would certainly agree that there are some sound arguments in the overall view that present economic underdevelopment is rooted in the colonial legacy of the past, nevertheless, it is difficult to argue that their poverty in 1997 is mainly due to the colonial experience. There are quite a few countries in the Third World which have never been colonized, but which were and are equally poor as former colonies of about the same size and economic structure. For example, all of China was never colonized — and it is ridiculous to link the continuing poverty of the Chinese hinterland to a few coastal cities being ruled *de facto* by the European powers sixty or seventy years ago. Similarly, Thailand was never colonized, but its standard of living in the 1960's was somewhat lower than that of Malaysia, a former British colony, and the Philippines, first a Spanish and then an American possession, but a bit higher than in Burma (also a former British possession).

The World Trade System

Closely related to the colonial legacy thesis is the argument that the integration of poor countries into the capitalist world economy is harmful to their growth and development. Many of these arguments are associated with the so-called "dependencia" school of development analysis, which has its roots in a specifically Latin American view of history and politics. While it is beyond our scope to provide a careful discussion of the "dependencia" literature here, there seem to be three specific arguments that are usually made in this connection: (1) the commercial policy of the industrialized countries; (2) export-earnings instability; and (3) the Prebisch-Singer thesis that the terms of trade decline against primary producers.

---

[16] Richard N. Cooper has pointed out that "...the gold standard looks somewhat better to us than it did to contemporaries." Prices did fall in the last quarter of the 19th century, but rose in the first quarter of the 20th in the U.S. In the United Kingdom, the average annual change in wholesale prices during the 1870–1913 period was *minus* 0.7 perent. See Richard N. Cooper, "The Gold Standard: Historical Facts and Future Prospects," *Brookings Papers on Economic Activity*, 1982, pp. 1–45.

In the period right after World War II, as former colonies became independent nation-states, the economic environment appeared to be quite unfriendly to growth based upon export expansion. The U.S. dollar was the only convertible currency and all countries were experiencing severe dollar shortages. Government policies all over the world were designed to economize on the use of scarce foreign exchange, which then meant a lot of trade restrictions — multiple exchange rate systems, import licenses, outright prohibitions against luxury goods imports, quotas, tariffs, and other barriers. Tariff systems were often deliberately designed to keep out foreign manufactures, which would compete with rebuilding industries (in Europe and Japan) or emerging "infant industries" (in the richer developing countries). In the twenty years after the war, both China and the U.S.S.R. were not doing much trading with the rest of the world, deliberately minimizing the influence of foreign products and ideas, while their Communist rulers and parties consolidated their domestic position. This was certainly also true of the Eastern European satellites of the Soviet Union, as well as Yugoslavia. Thus, that left the American market for everyone to try to penetrate, and most foreign producers back then were quite pessimistic about ever being able to compete with very large and super-efficient U.S. companies on their home field. Detailed debates about how to deal with the dollar shortage and the economic hegemony of the U.S. dominated the literature of international economics during this period.

Even after the dollar shortage eased somewhat and other industrialized countries rebuilt their living standards, the structure of protectionist controls that had been developed during the Depression in the West and after the war elsewhere was dismantled rather slowly. Although the European Economic Community (EEC) was established in 1957, and major European currencies became convertible, the LDC's could not easily become exporters to either Europe, Japan, or their wealthier neighbors due to so-called "commercial policies" still in place. As a general rule, the structure of tariff rates varied directly with the stage of processing — the higher the "value-added" in the exporting country, the higher the import duty in the importing country. For raw materials, such as teak logs felled in northern Thailand, the tariff in most importing countries (say, Japan) would be very low, probably zero. If the logs were sawn up into boards, the "effective rate of protection" would become considerably higher, with a tariff at 20%, for example. Plywood and simple furniture might face a tariff of 50% while more finely processed wood products (office furnishings, souvenirs, and so on) be subject to still higher duties.

Since the 1960s, however, the United States has successfully led the way in liberalizing international trade in a multilateral framework. There have been several rounds (as in the Kennedy Round and the Tokyo Round) of general tariff reductions conducted under the auspices of the General Agreement on Tariffs and Trade (GATT). On the whole, tariff rates have fallen from more than 40% to less than 10% of import values. The recent Paraguay Round of multilateral negotiations was aimed at extending liberalization to trade in services (e.g., banking, insurance, and tourism) as well as at reducing other barriers. For the LDC's specifically, all of the OECD countries (OECD stands for the Organization for Economic Cooperation and Development, representing industrial aid-donor countries of the West) have had preferential GSP (Generalized System of Preferences) arrangements for almost all poorer countries, though these special tariff breaks have at times been hedged by exceptions. Thus, in the U.S., the Trade Reform Act of 1973 excluded textiles, footwear, watches, and some steel products. As far as the 1950's and 1960's are concerned, however, there was a period of general reductions in trade barriers and encouraging multilateral approaches to economic growth.

In recent years, however, liberalization appears to have slowed. Although "effective rates of protection" have been lowered in many areas, non-tariff barriers (NTB's) of various sorts have been erected instead. The agricultural policies of most OECD countries, in particular, are orchestrated by domestic political considerations — and "development altruism" has played a fairly small role. Knowledgeable observers have concluded that American (or Argentinean) wheat could not break into the EEC market, even if farmers outside the Common Market were willing to supply it free of charge. For another example, domestic sugar prices in the U.S. in recent years have been roughly three times as high as the world market price. We give economic assistance on a grant basis to a number of sugar producers (e.g., the Philippines), whose private sector economic activity would be assisted much more efficiently by freer trade instead. Agricultural pricing policies in Japan appear to be even further out of line with world markets for a number of commodities. The price of a kilo of rice in Tokyo is usually many times higher than the price in Bangkok, and the price of fresh fruit seems unbelievable ($3 for an apple?). Steak may cost as much as $40 per pound in Sapporo, about ten times its price in Omaha. While we're critizing the Japanese about food prices, let us also mention the fact that the Korean car-maker, Hyundai, has done very well in penetrating the Canadian and U.S. automobile markets during the past several years, but its sales in Japan amount to virtually nothing — despite the fact that Hyundai is partly owned by Mitsubishi.

Finally, concerning this first point in connection with the existing "international economic order," let us note the simple fact that a country's integration into the world economy carries with it the very substantial danger that the rules of play may change from time to time — and that the bigger players will seize the initiative in making such changes (old Asian proverb: "when elephants fight, the grass gets trampled..."). For example, though we have noted the successful ventures by Hyundai of Korea, first into Canada and then into the U.S. in 1980s, Hyundai was forced to fight a costly "dumping" case brought against it by a couple of big American car-makers. As a developing nation commits to develop a manufacturing sector aimed at exporting, it is potentially more vulnerable to external shocks of various sorts — such as recessions in its most important markets as well as a general wave of protectionist actions. As number of observers have noted a distinct change taking place in the international atmosphere on this score.

The general question of whether the commercial policies of the "First World" systematically discriminate against the exports of all "Third World" countries is ultimately an empirical question. However, as with many such questions in development economics, whether the answer is positive or negative appears to hinge upon the time period selected, the countries and commodities chosen for the study, and — in no small measure — the political/ideological credentials of the researcher. Since it is beyond our scope to present a careful and complete review of the relevant literature, let us end this section by citing the findings of one rather middle-of-the-road study. Michaely's main conclusions were:

> "...The existing structure of trade barriers does not imply, on the whole, any degree of discrimination either in favor of or against exports of low-income countries. This is true for barriers both in the United States and in the group of other major highly-developed countries — the original EEC members, the United Kingdom, Canada, and Japan — and it holds for the scales of nominal tariffs, of effective protection rates, and of non-tariff barriers.
>
> ...The structure of trade barriers does not reveal any distinction between major categories of goods; likewise no overall tendency is found towards either high or low barriers on imports of labor-intensive goods. A slight tendency appears to increase the level of barriers with the increase in intensity of unskilled labor in the production of goods.
>
> ...A clear tendency is revealed, on the other hand, for the level of trade barriers to increase with the extent to which a good is destined directly for final consumption...which may have a more substantial impact on the future expansion of exports by LDC's."[17]

A second crucial area of dissatisfaction with past institutional arrangements in international trade is the instability of the export earnings of the developing countries. Here too, a vast and technically complex literature exists — there must be a dozen different ways to measure export earnings instability, each with its own group of passionate adherents. Many less developed countries rely heavily on the export of a relatively few primary commodities, such as cocoa, sugar, tea, coffee and copper. Furthermore, the LDC's are generally more dependent upon foreign trade in terms of the export sector's share in national income than the industrial countries (or MDC's). While very large LDC's, such as Brazil, China, and India, show about the same degree of "export dependence" as the U.S. and the U.S.S.R., relatively small countries in Africa, Asia, and Latin America often earn between 20% and 40% of their GNP in the export sector. As Michael Todaro notes:

> "...the concentration of export production on relatively few major noncereal primary commodities such as cocoa, tea, sugar, and coffee renders certain LDCs very vulnerable to market fluctuations in specific products. For example, nearly half the Third World countries earn over 50 percent of their export receipts from a single primary commodity, such as coffee, cocoa, or bananas. Moreover, about 75 percent of these nations earn 60 percent or more of their foreign exchange receipts from no more than three primary products. Significant price variations,

---

[17] Michael Michaely. *Trade, Income Levels, and Dependence* (North-Holland, 1984), pp. 170–171. See also John T. Cuddington and Carlos M. Urzua, "Trends and Cycles in the Net Barter Terms of Trade: A New Approach," *The Economic Journal*, June 1989.

therefore, for these commodities can render development strategies highly uncertain. It is for this reason that international commodity agreements (such as those for coffee, cocoa, and sugar) among primary producing nations exporting the same commodity have come into being in recent years."[18]

It is certainly true that in many LDC's production structures are quite rigid (supply is quite inelastic), and factors of production relatively immobile. Capital investments are geared for the production of a specific product, and not easily liquidated, given an imperfect market for second-hand machinery as well as financial assets. There is also a significant time dimension to such investments — switching from coconuts to rubber, for example, will take nearly ten years. Even if rubber prices fall sharply, the plantation will keep on producing, as long as it is covering average variable cost — thus, increasing total supply even if all are tapping rubber at a loss. To cite Todaro once again:

"...In economies that have gradually become heavily dependent on their primary product exports, the whole economic and social infrastructure (roads, railways, communications, power locations, credit and marketing arrangements, etc.) may be geared to facilitate the movement of goods from production locations to shipping and storage depots for transfer to foreign markets. Cumulative investments of capital over time may have been sunk into these economic and infrastructure facilities and they cannot easily be transferred to different spatially located manufacturing activities. Thus, the more dependent less developed nations become on a few primary product exports, the more inflexible their economic structures become and the more vulnerable they are to the unpredictabilities of international markets."[19]

It is sometimes argued that the instability in primary product prices is the fault of "hoarders and speculators" in Western countries. For example, Paul Harrison has written:

"...Commodity dealers aggravate price instability. If the price of something is rising and they think it will go on rising, they buy up as much as they can get their hands on in the hope of selling it at a higher price later, and this buying activity pushes the price up even further — a self-fulfilling prophecy. Only when dealers feel a downturn is around the corner will they stop buying in as prices rise. A peak is reached; and after it, prices start to fall. And they fall rapidly, because merchants have garnered enough stocks to meet customers' needs for months ahead, and don't need to buy any more for a while. And when prices are falling, the speculators do not usually step in to buy up the bargain goods."[20]

---

[18] Michael P. Todaro, *Economic Development in the Third World*, Second Edition (Longman, 1981), p. 339.

[19] *Ibid.*, p. 353.

[20] Paul Harrison, *Inside the Third World*, Third Edition (Penguin Books, 1993), p. 351.

As journalists of a "progressive" bent sometimes suggest, there are "good" and "bad" market participants. How deliciously naive! As a conservative, I am delighted to hear that — because the bad market participants castigated by Mr. Paul Harrison in the above passage are certainly earning their own, very just punishment. By buying on the way up and selling on the way down, they are destabilizing commodity prices, but they must also be losing a hell of a lot of money in doing so!

While it can be established quite readily that the variation in primary product prices is substantially greater than in the prices of most manufactures whether this causes serious problems for the export-reliant LDC's is not an easy question to answer. To use a distinction formulated by Pan A. Yotopoulos and Jeffrey B. Nugent, there may be quite a big difference between "a priori theorizing" and "empirical evidence." On the basis of a priori theorizing, we would expect that most risk-averse decision-makers at the micro-economic level would shift out of risky export crops to other lines of economic activity — this would lead to lower growth in income and exports for those countries experiencing the greatest export price instability. Continuing our armchair theorizing, we would expect governments of such countries to be facing highly uncertain revenues. In many LDC's, a large portion of total taxes is collected from foreign trade transactions. A short-fall in export earnings may also force that LDC government to impose measures to restrict imports, which will then lead to lower revenues from both export taxes and import duties. Finally, an armchair theorist would probably forecast delays in investment projects during periods of export earnings shortfalls, making "rational planning" and "factor mobilization for developmental purposes" extremely difficult.

As can be seen from the preceding argument, a priori theorizing strongly condemns export earnings instability as a major barrier to economic growth and development in the less developed countries. Again, at the risk of being too brief and simplistic, the discussion can be reduced to a few empirical questions. First, is export earnings instability primarily caused by demand or supply? If it is primarily due to fluctuations in world demand, mainly in the industrialized countries, perhaps the only way to deal with the stabilization issue is by setting up "buffer stocks," or international commodity agreements. However, if output fluctuations are the primary explanation of variation in export earnings, a buffer stock scheme might conceivably be destabilizing — and it may well be that domestic efforts to stabilize the quantities exported would be more useful. There does exist some evidence that export prices and export volumes go up and down together, rather than offsetting each other, but the debate on this issue is likely to continue. (Economists are also likely to dream up buffer stock schemes for their favorite commodity, and hope that they will be appointed as its executive director — in a handsome office in London, Paris, possibly New York, and at an appropriate salary, of course).

A second, more fundamental, question is whether there exists any strong empirical evidence that export earnings instability is in fact harmful to economic growth. Does it appear to lead to the stop-and-go capital projects discussed during our a priori theorizing? That would imply lower savings and investment levels for countries experiencing high export earnings instability, and slower income growth as a result. While it is doubtful that there will ever be a definitive last word in researching this question, the empirical work carried out by Yotopoulos and Nugent suggests that the reverse may in fact be the case. They suggest that Milton Friedman's "permanent income hypothesis" may be very relevant to this question — if higher export earnings are viewed as transitory income and saved, the overall investment level in "boom-and-bust" economies could be considerably higher than in countries experiencing steady export earnings. [21]

The third, and final, issue to be discussed in this section is the so-called Prebisch Thesis argues that there is an inevitable, long-run tendency for the *terms of trade* to "turn against" primary product producers. Defining the terms of trade as the ratio of average export price (P_x) to the average import price index (P_m), Raul Prebisch, the famous late Argentine economist argued that P_x/P_m would decline *secularly* (meaning in the long run). This argument has taken on the nature of a strongly-held belief, almost a theological tenet, so that we will be oversimplifying a great deal in this section. The main reason for this decline in relative export prices, argued the "true believer," is that primary products (such as wheat, coffee, and copper) are traded in purely competitive markets, while LDC imports (such as radios, typewriters, and cameras) are priced by monopolists and/or oligopolists with a good deal of market power. In a recession, for example, while primary products experience falling prices, the manufactured goods imported by the developing countries do not decline at all — prices under imperfect competition are "rigid" or "sticky."

Prebisch's original statistical work focused on the United Kingdom's "net barter terms of trade" for the 1875-1914 period, which showed about a 30% increase in the real purchasing power of a unit of British exports. Prebisch's findings have been criticized on three main points: (a) quality improvements; (b) the transport cost issue; and (c) the general problem of "index number bias." Let us consider each of these in turn.

While the engineering characteristics of a ton of bauxite or a pound of copper are not likely to have changed at all from 1950 to 1990, say, it is nearly impossible to compare manufactured products, defined in the trade statistics as an "automobile," "television set," or "typewriter." A 1951 Chevrolet in its average or typical version had a manual transmission and brakes, an AM radio, and roll-down windows. Today's "Heartbeat of America" on average has an automatic transmission, air conditioning, power brakes, an on-board computer to monitor most electronic functions, a AM/FM radio with a tape deck, devices to control pollution, and possibly a few other (costly) technological improvements not even available in 1951. To say that "an average Chevrolet" has risen from $4000 in 1951 to $18,000 in 1996 is correct, but some sort of an adjustment of the "base price" is certainly needed to make the comparison meaningful. For instance, if the cost (not the price) of a more complex radio is $100, the pollution control devices cost $400, and everything else comes to an additional $500, then the price increase should be measured from $4000 to $17,000 — or perhaps from $5000 to $18,000. Clearly measurement problems are an area of considerable difficulty — adjusting base

---

[21] Pan A. Yotopoulos and Jeffrey B. Nugent, *Economics of Development* (Harper & Row, 1976), ch. 18.

prices upward by using the current costs of quality improvements would lower the percentage increase in the price of a car by more than subtracting such costs from the present price. One additional point deserves mention — there are quite a few new products available in 1996, which were simply not yet invented in 1950 (e.g., hand-held calculators and micro-wave ovens). Such goods are often introduced as very high-priced items — a hand-held Texas Instruments calculator initially sold for around $400, but a better version can be purchased today for $8.88 in any drug store. Enormous price reductions have also taken place in color TV sets and micro-wave ovens, which could not be included in a long-term comparison of LDC terms of trade.

While these kinds of quality improvements probably do not take place in primary products, there is undoubtedly some scope for making adjustments for change over time. It may well be that a ton of coffee or bananas actually is quite different in 1990 than these products were back in 1950 — agronomists no doubt have been working for new and improved varieties for the export market all along. For example, bananas are designed to be picked very green and to withstand long shipments today. Undoubtedly, the development costs of finding the appropriate varieties should be added to the base price or subtracted from the current price of the goods in question. Still, it seems unlikely that a ton of rice or wheat will be as different in 1996 from the 1950 product as an electric typewriter with a memory and a corrections feature is from its earlier manual version.

A second, rather more straightforward, issue in computing the terms of trade between LDC's and industrial countries involves the use of price indices of a significantly different definition. As is well known, import price indices are generally presented on a "c.i.f." basis — standing for "cost, insurance, and freight." Thus, Prebisch's series on U.K. imports from Argentina, collected on a c.i.f. basis, also included transportation costs. On the other hand, the index series for British exports to Argentina was calculated on an "f.o.b." ("free on board") basis, which does not. Since the period covered by Prebisch's analysis was characterized by significant technological improvements in shipping, which greatly lowered the unit costs of ocean transportation in particular, the export and import price indices should have both been presented on the same definitional basis. A good part of the improvement of the British terms of trade during the period right before World War I is, thus, due to the difference in c.i.f. and f.o.b. valuations. It was not so much a decline in the price received for Argentina's agricultural products raising Britain's terms of trade, just the cost of shipping them.

The third and final point to be raised in connection with Prebisch's contribution concerns a somewhat more messy technical issue, the question of "index-number bias." Since we are interested in measuring overall price changes over time, we essentially have two alternative price index definitions, which we could select — the Laspeyres Index (L) or the Paasche Index (P). As is well known, the Laspeyres Index will tend to overstate the amount of average price rise (it has an "upward bias"), while the latter will have a "downward bias." Around the turn of the century, Irving Fisher had already suggested using the "Ideal Index" (I), which would essentially be an average of the two (actually, the geometric mean, which is the square root of L times P), in order to resolve this problem.

In computing the terms of trade, Px/Pm, both the export and the import price indices generally will probably use the Laspeyres formula. Thus, *both* will tend to show greater price inflation than has "actually" taken place. However, the composition for LDC exports is likely to vary a good deal less than the composition of imports — thus, the problem of "index number bias" is likely to be greater for the denominator, Pm, than for the numerator of the terms of trade series. Those developing countries facing an exchange rate problem, and that includes probably the vast majority of LDC's, will no doubt restrict the imports of those products going up most in terms of price — but the import price index will continue to show a greater appreciation of import prices than has taken place, as long as fixed base-year weights continue to be used.

To recapitulate briefly the theme of the second section of this chapter, some development economists — and probably the majority of Third World "intellectuals" as well as policy-makers — tend to view LDC integration into the world economic system in rather negative terms. First, the commercial policies of industrialized countries have discriminated against LDC exports, or are likely to do so again in the near future. Second, export earnings instability will tend to hamper economic policies of those countries relying upon the exports of primary products, whose prices do fluctuate a great deal more than those of industrialized country exports. As an aside, this is widely perceived to be a serious problem, despite the ambiguity of evidence on this score. Thirdly, LDC primary product producers will suffer from an inevitable long-run deterioration in their terms of trade. To put it rather crudely, the Prebisch Thesis says that Faroffistan will have to trade more and more tons of cocoa and soybeans for its typewriter and Mercedes imports. All three of these themes or beliefs have contributed to a general attitude of profound "Trade Pessimism" on the part of the LDC's taken as a group — especially in the 1950's and 1960s. Even if Faroffistan was the world's lowest-cost cocoa producer — having an "absolute advantage" in that product — its economists might argue strongly in favor of export diversification, to get as far away as possible from single-crop dependence. Moreover, their arguments against primary product export dependence generally would be even stronger. "Self-reliance" and an "import-substitution-industriali-zation strategy" (ISIS) were the most popular key concepts of development planning thirty or even twenty years ago, as newly independent countries asserted their political and economic "rights." However, as we shall see in our discussion of Japan and the other "capitalist-roaders of Asia", such extreme views concerning the evils of the world trade system made increasingly little sense during a period of rapid trade expansion and general liberalization. Countries, such as Albania and Burma (now Myanmar), which carried the "self-reliance" concept as far as it can be carried, got left behind — and even a number of very large developing nations, which could logically become quite self-sufficient in most goods, such as China, India, and Brazil, recently have found out that somewhat greater openness to world trade had a number of generally positive aspects.

Financial Exploitation

To round out the "world economy view," the story would be incomplete without a serious castigation of past, present, and future arrangements in international investments and finance. Since topics such as the "global reach" of the predatory multi-national corporations (MNC's) and the "debt-trap" of other financial arrangements have been the subject of a plethora of books and articles, the financial exploitation argument will be presented very briefly here. The view of private finance being provided by the Western capitalist countries being exploitative fits well in the neo-Marxist thesis of "imperialism" constituting the highest (therefore, final) stage of capitalism. To put it a bit more colorfully, the only way that the "rotten old order" could survive a bit longer is to seize upon still more backward areas to conquer and exploit, perhaps not militarily, but certainly financially. In recent years, even official aid institutions, both bilateral and multilateral (such as the International Monetary Fund and the World Bank), have also been worked into the story as appendages of the exploitative international financial system.

The main villain of the tale, however, is the "dread MNC," the power-hungry octopus seeking world-wide control of resources and domination of markets, ruthlessly eliminating its competitors and corrupting LDC governments. The anti-MNC literature abounds with anecdotes and shocking case studies, and avoids factual information as a vampire shuns garlic. There is the maker of artificial formulas for baby bottles, sending sales-women in fake nurse uniforms into Third World villages, to convince women to forego breast-feeding — and mix inadequate amounts of the costly imported powder with contaminated water for nearly certain infant malnutrition and probably even death. Then one hears about the clever practices of "transfer pricing" — selling pharmaceutical materials at a very low price to subsidiaries in "tax havens," where the pills are simply put into bottles and instructions printed in Spanish — and the bottles are then resold at a very high price to Latin American affiliates of the U.S. pharmaceutical companies. This enables the MNC to pay very low taxes in the U.S., shelter its profits in Panama or the Bahamas, and declare a very modest profit in Colombia, say, when the final product is sold at only a 6-7% mark-up. Furthermore, there are also examples of gas leaks, oil spills, and other environmental disasters. These anecdotes are reinforced by the media — when we think of Chile, Liberia, or the Philippines, the names of particular American companies seem to pop into one's mind almost automatically.

A bit less impressionistically, there are a number of more specific charges that are often made against the operations of the MNC's. First, large global corporations tend to monopolize technical knowledge and dominate research and development. According to the authors of *Global Reach*, once poor countries decide to emulate Western patterns of consumption-oriented growth and development, they are going to be dominated the multinationals. The MNC's will soon own most of the patents, and the "nation's technology becomes subject to foreign control." A U.N. study is cited by Barnet and Mueller, showing foreign ownership of about 90% of all the patents in India, Pakistan, and several Middle East countries. In Chile, foreign patent ownership is alleged to have risen from about 65% before World War II to approximately 95% around 1970. In Colombia, 10% of all the firms in the drug, synthetic fiber, and chemical industries owned nearly two-thirds of the total patents in those fields, and that 10% consisted entirely of foreign-owned companies. Barnet and Mueller conclude:

> "...Concentrated control of technology is a classic device for eliminating effective competition and thereby establishing oligopolistic control of the marketplace. The result is, of course, high profits, which can then be used to further consolidate the firm's dominant position by massive investments in advertising." [22]

Although one of the arguments in favor of the MNC's is that foreign direct investment brings in needed capital, the critics of direct investment are quick to point out that MNC's often take over existing businesses, using funds raised locally. Monopoly/oligopoly power and concentration ratios would tend to increase as a result of foreign capital inflows. Further, it is argued that local affiliates of foreign firms have favored access to the local capital market — and for every dollar of new foreign investment actually brought in from the headquarters overseas, several more dollar-equivalents represent money raised in the host country. On balance, the main positive contribution that one would expect from foreign investment is to fill the gap between total desired investment and available domestic saving — or between probable export earnings and import requirements. However, critics of the MNC's have argued that the overall balance of payments effect may be negative (and that foreign investment may *replace* domestic saving rather than *supplement* it).

A third aspect of the impact of the MNC's on the underdeveloped world involves employment. Clearly, one would expect that job creation would be generally viewed as a positive contribution made by the foreign investors, even in the case of a pure export-processing zone, but the most virulent critics of the MNC's are not content to let the matter rest there.[23] They contend that the MNC's introduce both inappropriate products and techniques of production — seducing the population of LDC's away from (healthful) fruit juices to (nutritionally worthless) colas. The inappropriate products are likely to be produced by the MNC affiliates, using capital-intensive methods of production. Again, anecdotal evidence is often cited. One study noted that capital/labor ratios in Indonesia were generally much higher for foreign-owned operations than for foreign local firms. Many of these MNC activities, however, were in petroleum, nickel-mining and pulp-and-paper production, while the analysts did not bother to point out that more labor-intensive

---

[22] Richard J. Barnet and Ronald E. Mueller, *Global Reach: The Power of the Multinational Corporations* (Simon and Schuster, 1974), p. 140.
[23] Our export-processing zones and their costs and benefits, see F.A. Rabbani (ed.), *Economic and Social Impacts of Export Processing Zones in Asia* (Asian Productivity Organization, 1985) and Antoine Basile and Dimitri Germidis, *Investing in Free Export Processing Zones* (OECD, 1984). See Also Theodore H. Moran, *Multinational Corporations: The Political Economy of Foreign Direct Investment* (Lexington Books, 1985).

industries, such as food processing and textiles, were "off-limits" for foreign enterprises. In general, critics contend that production methods developed in the "First World" countries tend to be capital-intensive and labor-saving, which is generally true, and that such techniques are then transferred to labor-surplus "Third World" countries without much adaptation to local conditions, which may or may not be the case.

In this connection, let us go off on a brief but important tangent. Decision-makers in the LDC environment often face factor-price ratios, which signal to them that capital is cheap and labor is expensive. Many industrial investments are made by the managers of foreign-owned enterprises or so-called parastatals (firms owned entirely or partially by local governments). Such enterprises are highly visible, and are required to pay their workers the legal minimum wage and provide a full array of fringe benefits. A foreign enterprise, futhermore, may find it nearly impossible to lay off any of their local employees, once they are hired, since that would involve an intolerable "loss of face" for those being separated. On the other hand, capital may be readily available from special development finance institutions on very favorable terms. For example, there may be loans given by international aid agencies (e.g., the World Bank, A.I.D., or the regional development bank) carrying below-market interest rates, earmarked for industrial development projects in particular sectors of the economy. Even if capital is not available at subsidized interest rates for projects financed by foreign aid institutions, such funds will often be available on even more favorable terms under conditions of "financial repression." One simple way of defining financial repression is to say that it is a situation where an LDC experiences inflation rates above the market rate of interest, which in many cases will be kept constant by an administratively-imposed ceiling rate. Therefore, the real interest rate — defined as the nominal interest rate minus the expected rate of inflation — will be negative, and the "Third World" decision-makers will be encouraged to use as much capital as possible, and to economize on the use of labor.[24]

Except for this general macro problem of inappropriate signals being given regarding factor prices, there is little evidence that MNC's (or TNC's, for "transnational corporations," meaning basically the same thing) bias factor proportions in their LDC operations. Though considerations of brevity prohibit a detailed discussion of this interesting and important point, let us finish our consideration by citing a centrist writer on this score once again.

> "...The appropriateness debate has been conducted at a fairly high level of ab-
> straction, taking as a premise that TNC's in fact transfer unadapted technologies
> from developed to developing countries. At the micro-level, this premise is un-
> founded. Every new application of a technology involves considerable adaptive ef-
> fort. The core process may not be significantly altered, but changes in scale,

---

[24] For considerably more discussion on this point, see Michael T. Skully and George J. Viksnins, *Financing East Asia's Success* (Macmillan in association with the American Enterprise Institute, 1987), especially Ch. 1. See also Michael J. Fry, *Money, Interest and Banking in Economic Development,* Second Edition (The Johns Hopkins University Press, 1995).

inputs, outputs, automation etc., may constitute between 10-60 per cent of total project costs. Product ranges of TNC's in developing countries are very different from those in advanced countries, and new products are developed specifically for developing country conditions. There is no evidence that TNC's lag behind local firms in generating 'appropriate' technology in this limited sense." [25]

Finally, direct foreign investment is often blamed for political problems in recipient countries. Authoritarian regimes of a "right-wing" persuasion, in particular, are viewed as being "kept in power" by the U.S. establishment — large business firms are able to manipulate American foreign policy to serve their own interests, according to this point of view. A number of Asian countries are often mentioned as client-states of American interests in this connection, though a number of them have not received any foreign aid from the US in several decades. Furthermore, Japanese direct investment has outdistanced that of American firms in most cases during the past several years, and a number of Asian countries (e.g., India, Korea, and Malaysia) now are home countries of MNC's of their own.

Still, the critical literature continues to emphasize the doctrine of one-sided exploitation of mineral resources and cheap labor by firms headquartered in the industrial countries. The MNC's elicit the cooperation of non-representative elites in the periphery, by using bribery and corruption in most cases, and outright intimidation in others, it is alleged. Partly as a result of such "exposes," foreign direct investment in the LDC's was sharply curtailed in the 1970's. However, despite the decline in MNC activities in the Third World, the "theorists of the world economy view" have not changed the framework of their analysis very much. A good summary of the current situation is provided by Raymond Vernon:

"...In retrospect, it appears that the numerous threats to the multinationals that were launched in the 1970s — the spate of nationalizations, the codes of conduct, the U.S. legislation against bribery, the demands and resolutions of the General Assembly — were fueled by a number of different elements. One of these was a manifestation of a much larger phenomenon, namely a persuasive revulsion in much of the world against the effects of industrialization, against the symbols of entrenched authority, against the impersonal tyranny of big bureaucracies. Embodying all of these unfortunate attributes and burdened besides by the sin of being foreign, multinationals were inevitably a prime target of the period." [26]

---

[25] Sanjaya Lall, "Transnationals and the Third World: Changing Perceptions," in Toivo Miljan (ed.), *The Political Economy of North-South Relations* (Broadview Press, 1987), p. 260.

[26] Raymond Vernon, "Sovereignty at Bay: Ten Years After," in Theodore H. Moran (ed.), *Multinational Corporations: The Political Economy of Foreign Disrect Investment* (Lexington Books, 1985), p. 257.

Today, MNC's face a curious admixture of incentives and prohibitions in the developing countries. In many countries, special export-processing zones or industrial estates have been established to lure foreign investors. Host country governments often offer market research and feasibility studies, industrial sites with subsidized utilities, transport, and security, low interest loans, tax holidays and other fiscal-monetary inducements. At the same time, perhaps in order to appeal to local public opinion, foreign firms face various restrictions, or so-called "performance requirements." As already briefly noted, foreign investors are often deliberately excluded from certain sectors — e.g., it would be quite difficult to carry out agricultural activities, in countries where foreigners are barred from land ownership. In many countries, there are specific limits on the amount of dividends, interest and royalty fees, which an affiliate can legally remit to the home country headquarters, usually tied to the amount of invested capital. In other cases, foreign exchange is controlled by either the central bank or the finance ministry, making remittances to the head office a matter of negotiation. In some countries, quantitative limits have been established for the number of "ex-patriates," who can legally be employed by an MNC affiliate. In some other instances, the number of foreign workers is not controlled initially, but laws are established requiring specific targets for local employment to be met after a given number of years. In virtually all cases, foreign technicians and managers are expected to hold appropriate visas and work permits, making affiliate operations in practice quite costly and difficult. Finally, outright foreign ownership and total control of affiliates in developing countries will be encountered relatively seldom in the 1990's. Recipient countries almost uniformly require the establishment of joint ventures (probably good insurance against outright nationalization, anyway) and various indigenization laws are today the rule rather than the exception.

A good example of this principle is Malaysia's policy of deliberate "bumiputraization" (the word alone is worth a separate paragraph — I usually try to include something on this in an exam). Malaysia, a country of about 15 million people, is composed of about 50% ethnic Malays (called the "bumiputras", which means " sons of the soil"), 35-40% Chinese, with the remainder consisting of Indians, Pakistanis, and others. As a general rule, the Malays as a group have been historically a great deal poorer than the Chinese — and twenty years ago, most business equity in Malaysia's was in fact owned by foreigners. After a series of frightening and bloody riots with strongly racial overtones in May 1969, the Malaysian government has developed a New Economic Policy (NEP) of its own, with the overall goal of reducing and possibly eliminating "the identification of race with economic function." In addition to various "affirmative action" regulations in employment and education, the centerpiece of Malaysia's NEP is the gradual shifting of business ownership from foreign and Chinese hands to ethnic Malays. As Wu and Wu explain it:

> ..."The end result sought by 1990 is to have Malaysians in control of 70 percent of the country's economic activity and to reserve three sevenths of the 70 percent (that is 30 percent of the total) for Bumiputras. These targets are to be attained by gradually acquiring stock in foreign companies for redistribution to Malaysians and by reserving for the Bumiputras a share in newly formed foreign enter-

prises. These new enterprises will necessarily be joint ventures, therefore, in which foreign ownership will be limited to 30 percent, Bumiputras will have another 30 percent, and non-Bumiputra Malaysians will hold 40 percent." [27]

To put a reasonable end to all of this theoretical debate, a few facts are in order. A simple listing, without much editorializing, may suffice.

(1) In the 1970's, direct private investment in the LDCs averaged about *one-half* of total external financing. In 1980, direct investment was only about *one-seventh* of the total, while commercial bank lending had risen to more than half of the total.

(2) In 1986, direct private investment accounted for about one-third of the total; commercial bank lending had been more than cut in half, and was about at the same level as direct equity investment. (It can be pointed out that interest charges on foreign borrowing must be paid regardless of the profitability of the projects, but direct investment owners make a positive return only if the funds are invested productively. On could offer an editorial comment here, couldn't one?)

(3) If MNC investments are a major cause of Third World poverty and immiserization, one would expect Canada to be the poorest and most miserable country on earth. (Editiorializing? Yes, a bit.) Among the developing countries, foreign investments are not attracted either by low wages or cheap resources primarily, since most OECD investors have opted for Latin America or the higher-income countries of Asia, and not Bangladesh or Ethiopia.

(4) The "dread MNC" is often associated with American power and influence. In recent years, the relative share of U.S. based companies in LDC direct investments has been declining steadily, while European and Japanese investments have been expanding. As noted above, a number of third World countries have multinational firms of their own. Furthermore, with world-wide sourcing and sophisticated international financing for many products, it is becoming increasingly outdated to talk about economic policy in purely nationalistic terms.

(5) While the literature in this area cites a number of quite careful studies of transfer pricing and other sharp corporate practices, which lead to inordinately high profits being earned— but not reported or taxed—by affiliates in the LDC's, other studies of macro profit rates do not find significant differences between earnings in developing and developed country operations.

---

[27] Yuan-li Wu and Chun-hsi Wu, *Economic Development in Southeast Asia: The Chinese Dimension* (Hoover Institution Press, 1980), p. 58. See also Ruth McVey (ed.), *Southeast Asian Capitalists* (Cornell, 1992) and Sterling Seagrave, *Lords of the Rim* (G.P. Putnam, 1995).

Summary

To recapitulate very briefly the "world economy view" elucidated in this chapter, it is often argued that the poverty of Third World countries is *primarily* due to external factors. Growth and development of the LDC's were retarded by policies followed during the era of colonialism, which subdivided the world into an industrial core and a dependent periphery. The system of "unequal exchange" erected during the period of colonial domination has been perpetuated by commercial policies practiced by the industrial countries during recent decades. Some observers argue that "monopoly capitalism" in the industrial countries has survived as long as it has because of such imperialistic practices — take away Third World poverty, and the prosperity of the First World will disappear. The LDC's are poorly served by their integration into the world economy, it is alleged. As producers of primary products, they will always suffer from an extreme instability of export earnings and face an inevitable decline in their "terms of trade." The best remedy would be to withdraw from the "Old Economic Order" as rapidly as possible, perhaps through wars of national liberation to rid their countries of foreign domination. If that is not possible, a deliberate strategy of import-substitution-industrialization should be followed, while the countries of the "South" press politically for the establishment of a "New International Economic Order," which would repay them for past exploitation and establish a more equitable basis for exchange.   .

The "new order" would provide for more economic assistance, given automatically through multilateral agencies—as opposed to rather grudgingly by individual donor countries, with all sorts of strings attached as "tied aid." International institutions, such as the IMF, the World Bank, and the regional development banks would be administered more "democratically," rather than being dominated by the U.S. and a handful of other rich countries. In this connection, China and India would perhaps press for democratic voting on the basis of population size, while Vanuatu and Brunei might well favor the "one-country, one vote" principle, though they both might also be inclined to favor the inclusion of GNP-per-capita in the voting formula. The demand for guaranteed access to developed country markets for LDC industrial products may find stronger support in Singapore than in Indonesia, say, with Korea quite possibly favoring a special quota for cars manufactured in Third World countries. A "Common Fund," with $10 to $20 billion (in today's dollars) subscribed by OECD countries, to be used to stabilize (and "enhance") commodity prices seems quite appealing in principle, but problems do arise when we try to get a bit more specific. Thailand would certainly support higher rice prices, but Hong Kong might not — while a stabilized price for petroleum at about $40 per barrel would be helpful to Venezuela, but not to Brazil. ∎

SUGGESTED READINGS

Aldcroft, Derek H., and Ross E. Catterall (eds.), *Rich Nations — Poor Nations: The Long-Run Perspective* (Edward Elgar, 1996).

Ansari, Javed, *The Political Economy of International Economic Organizations* (Rienner Books, 1986).

Ayres, Robert L., *Banking on the Poor: The World Bank and World Poverty* (The MIT Press, 1983).

Bauer, Peter, *The Development Frontier: Essays in Applied Economics* (Harvard University Press, 1991).

Cole, H.S.D., *et al, Models of Doom* (Universe Books, 1973).

Council on Environmental Quality and the Department of State, *The Global 2000 Report to the President* (Government Printing Office, 1980).

Crane, George T. and Abla Amawi (eds.), *The Theoretical Evolution of International Political Economy* (Oxford University Press, 1991).

Danaher, Kevin (ed.), *50 Years is Enough: The Case Against the World Bank and the International Monetary Fund* (South End Press, 1994).

Deyo, Frederic C. (ed.), *The Political Economy of the New Asian Industrialism* (Ithaca, N.Y.: Cornell University Press, 1987).

Grimwade, Nigel, *International Trade Policy: A Contemporary Analysis* (Routledge, 1996).

Haggard, Stephan, *Pathways from the Periphery: The Politics of Growth in the Newly Industrializing Countries* (Cornell, 1990).

Harrison, Paul, *Inside the Third World*, Third Edition (Penguin Books, 1993).

Meadows, Donella H., *et al, The Limits to Growth* (Universe Books, 1972).

Michaely, Michael, *Trade, Income Levels, and Dependence* (North-Holland, 1984).

Packenham, Robert A., *The Dependency Movement: Scholarship and Politics in Development Studies* (Harvard University Press, 1992).

Padoan, Pier Carlo, *The Political Economy of International Financial Instability* (Croom Helm, 1986).

Preon, P.W. *Making Sense of Development* (Routledge & Kegan Paul, 1986).

Ranis, Gustav, and Syed Akhtar Mahmood, *The Political Economy of Development Policy Change* (Blackwell, 1992).

Swatuk, Larry A., and Timothy M. Shaw, *The South at the End of the Twentieth Century* (MacMillan, 1994).

The World Bank, *Structural and Sectoral Adjustment, World Bank Experience, 1980–1992* (World Bank, 1995).

Todaro, Michael P., *Economic Development in the Third World*, Fourth Edition (Longman, 1989).

Yotopoulos, Pan A., and Jeffrey B. Nugent, *Economics of Development: Empirical Investigations* (Harper & Row, 1976).

CHAPTER NINE

LESS DEVELOPED COUNTRIES: THE "TRADITIONAL SOCIETY" VIEW

*I*n his famous three-volume work, *Asian Drama,* Swedish economist (and Nobel economics laureate) Gunnar Myrdal points out that Western social scientists usually approach the complex problems of Third World underdevelopment with a number of inherent biases. We, Western social scientists, are taught to be polite, quantitatively-oriented, and optimistic, which may make it nearly impossible for us to contribute anything useful to solving the problems of underdevelopment and poverty — or even begin defining them reasonably precisely. Let us try to begin this chapter with a useful quote from Myrdal:

> "*Economic theorists, more than other social scientists, have long been disposed to arrive at general propositions and then postulate them as valid for every time, place and culture. There is a tendency in contemporary economic theory to follow this path to the extreme. For such confidence in the constructs of economic reasoning, there is no empirical justification. But even apart from this recent tendency, we have inherited from classical economics a treasury of theories that are regularly posited with more general claims than they warrant. The very concepts used in their construction aspire to a universal applicability that they do not in fact possess. As long as their use is restricted to our part of the world this pretense of generality may do little harm. But when theories and concepts designed to fit the special conditions of the Western world — and thus containing the implicit assumptions about social reality by which this fitting was accomplished — are used in the study of underdeveloped countries...., where they do not fit, the consequences are serious.*"[1]

The essence of the "traditional society" explanation of underdevelopment is to argue that Third World poverty is primarily due to internal bottlenecks and constraints, usually having very little to do with economic variables as such. It is generally assumed that

---

[1] Gunnar Myrdal, *Asian Drama: An Inquiry into the Poverty of Nations* (Pantheon, for the Twentieth Century Fund, 1968), pp. 16–17.

economists can exercise their influence through the manipulation of various macroeconomic magnitudes. Policy-makers in Faroffistan may be able to affect or even determine government spending and taxes, interest rates and the money supply. Furthermore, they may be able to control tariffs, quotas, exchange rates, and foreign exchange availability, at least in the short run. However, no matter how clever they are in following the dictates of the latest and most complex simulation model, they will not be able to overcome the very basic barriers to progress in the traditional societies of the Third World. Most of the factors obstructing economic progress can be grouped into the following five categories, though the list could probably be expanded even further:

(1)   physiological - demographic;

(2)   political - administrative;

(3)   sociological - psychological;

(4)   technological - educational;

(5)   environmental - climatic.

Physiological - Demographic Factors

When I first began teaching "development economics" in the early 1970's, I limited my discussion of the population problem to purely quantitative demographic magnitudes, and their impact on economic variables. Economists have become good at calculating GNP (even if there are severe data problems), looking up the population number, and then figuring out growth rates in "GNP per capita," the most basic indicator of a country's wellbeing from our point of view. Over the years, I have become a good deal more sensitive to the more difficult and qualitative aspects of the population of the Third World, although these kinds of problems usually are often not even mentioned by economists. Still, I will be very brief in this connection, but we should be aware that purely economic variables, such as "labor force" and "unemployment," "savings," "investment," and "income" may not have much meaning in very poor countries.

The "labor force" of Faroffistan does not consist of healthy, literate, and adult members of the population, ready and willing to work, registered with a Department of Labor or similar agency. The "human capital" there often consists of people who probably have suffered from malnutrition since birth. As a result, the average worker is often weak and ill, may not be able to read or write, and has generally been forced to live a hand-to-mouth existence on a daily basis since childhood. Many people in the "labor force" cannot work a full day, since their early malnutrition and perhaps disease has inhibited their full mental and physical development. They were obliged to abandon schooling at an early age, because they were needed to help out with the family's subsistence needs or perhaps because the distance to the next school was simply much too far. They may have intestinal parasites, or some other illness reducing their mobility and productivity. In some cases, it is much worse — they may be blind, deaf, mute, malarial, or suffer from some other debilitating handicap or disease. This means that they are being nursed through the day by other family members, who cannot really enter the permanent full-time labor force either. Not very long ago, many countries had rather large areas that could not be farmed because of malaria or other diseases — for example, for many decades in the recent past, the most fertile areas near the river in one African country were "off-limits" due to river-blindness. Finally, in many Third World countries life expectancy is quite low — they lose their most experienced, wisest, and wittiest professors well before my current age!

Most economists will probably be a good deal more knowledgeable about the "population problem" generally — often even called the "population bomb." Thomas Robert Malthus tried to formulate around 1800 a general theory of human population and resources — arguing that agricultural production tended only to increase arithmetically, while population grew geometrically. Looking at the "Malthusian warning" from the point of view of most European countries and the United States, he now seems to be very mistaken. Over the past two centuries, the industrialized countries of the "First World" have certainly not suffered from uniform population pressure. Most developed nations have generally all experienced the so-called "demographic transition" — over several centuries with greater urbanization and higher levels of education, birth rates in the richer developed countries have come down gradually and steadily. Over this same period of more than two hundred years, death rates also decreased very significantly. For all industrial countries taken as a group, annual population growth today is well below one percent. A number of countries are very close to "ZPG," zero population growth. This is certainly true of most of Western Europe, most of North America (but not Mexico) and the European part of the FSU as well.

On the other hand, there has been a veritable "population explosion" in Third World countries. Due to improvements in medical care, and overall infrastructure development as well, death rates have decreased drastically and life expectancy has risen considerably. However, over the past forty years, birth rates have fallen only slightly. In rural areas, throughout the world children are often viewed as an asset — they can be taught to do something useful around the family farm at quite an early age. In many cultures, the number of children that a man has is also viewed as a sign of potency, of good fortune, of success. The number of sons is often stressed especially, not only for their prestige value, but also as insurance policies as well — it being the son's duty to take care of his parents in their old age. In some countries, various "artificial" birth control methods go against religious teachings and interpretations, while in some others birth control information cannot be disseminated to women who are kept locked-up and are not allowed to talk to strangers. For all of these reasons, today Third World birth rates remain only slightly below historical levels — though, as we shall see in the chapter on China, the world's largest nation has recently implemented a very strong policy in order to stabilize its population in the next century.

Although the case of Hong Kong (where population has grown quite rapidly, as has income, on a rather small piece of real estate) suggests that population growth need not be viewed as an insurmountable barrier to progress, most developing countries find population pressure on balance to be a negative factor. In all those Third World countries already experiencing large-scale unemployment — as well as what economists call "disguised unemployment" — the problem of creating jobs is an immense one.[2] As an aside, Indonesia is a case in point. About half of Indonesia's population is under the age of twenty; also, a fifth of Indonesia's population is illiterate. About two-thirds of all Indonesians live on the island of Java, already very densely populated, and many are seeking jobs in urban areas. The capital, Jakarta, already very over-crowded, is by law a "closed city" — you must secure a special residence permit even to go there. Yet, even very marginal jobs in Jakarta allow one to earn wages three or four times as high as in rural areas and government services are much better (especially schools and hospitals). Also, of course, a lovely daughter might meet and marry a government official, or perhaps a foreign businessman. I recall vividly an Indonesian official reacting to a discussion of labor policies in Singapore at a conference I attended; "Singapore?" he said, "We have a Singapore arriving in Indonesia every year!" (Indeed, the number of births per year in Indonesia is approximately equal to the entire population of Singapore.)

Without deriving the formula below, let me hope that the so-called "Harrod-Domar Model" was briefly discussed in the Principles course you took. In the context of that model, we can recall that the growth rate in GNP (given certain assumptions) is at equilibrium equal to the MPS/ICOR. In terms of a simple example, if Faroffistan's "Marginal Propensity to Save" is equal to 0.15 or 15%, while the ICOR equals 3.0, the equilibrium growth rate will be .05 or 5%. ICOR is a simple "supply-side" variable — the acronym stands for "Incremental Capital/Output Ratio." Its formula is:

$$ICOR = \frac{I_{t-1}}{\Delta Y_t}$$

or the previous year's investment, either in currency units or as a percentage of national income or product, which will be "associated with" the current year's GNP in growth. The ICOR is a short-hand way of guessing the "capital requirements" of x percent growth in national output, in other words. In middle-income developing countries, the ICOR averages about 3.0, which enables a development planner to make a rough linkage between a target growth rate (say, 7% in real terms) and the "capital formation ratio." (The mathematically adept will already have seen that a 7%ΔY_t means a 21% investment rate in the previous year — or, in order to match Japan's "miracle" growth rate of the 1960's, which was ten percent, 30% of national income must be saved and/or invested.)

While we cannot indulge in a detailed discussion and critique of the "Harrod-Domar Formula," which implies that capital investment is the only determinant of GNP growth, we can carry our analysis on that same basis a little bit further. The ICOR figure of 3.0,

---

[2] "Disguised unemployment" refers to members of the labor force not actually classified as being out of work and actively looking for a job, but not really working on a full-time basis during the whole year. Many family members in rural areas, for example, go to work in other jobs without affecting the total output of the agricultural sector very much — their "marginal productivity" is very low.

obviously, is an average for the country as a whole, representing various industries — some likely to have a low ratio of capital to output (subsistence agriculture, textiles and beverages, or services) and others with a very high capital requirement (nuclear power, airplanes, automobiles, and petrochemicals). For the purpose of our analysis in this section, however, let us think very simply of all investment as being sub-divided into just two big categories: directly-productive activities (DPA), where the output of industries is sold, and social overhead capital (SOC), where the output is usually provided by the public sector without cost and consumed socially. Generally speaking, DPA investments will tend to have a lower ICOR (or a higher multiplier, to recall some basic Keynesian macroeconomics) than SOC projects. Making and selling shoes, shirts, and beer will result in a more rapid rise in next year's GNP than road, school, and hospital construction — though the latter may be even more important as determinants of Faroffistan's development from a longer-run point of view. To work through a simple example, let us assume that the country's total investment is split exactly "fifty-fifty" between DPA and SOC, and that DPA has an ICOR equal to 2.0, while the ICOR for SOC is exactly 4.0. This would then give us an average ICOR = .5(2.0) + .5(4.0) = 3.0, the "typical" level mentioned earlier.

At this point, we can link the "Harrod-Domar" equilibrium growth rate in GNP to population growth briefly. The Harrod-Domar formula is based on balanced growth in aggregate demand and supply. It can easily be seen that a rapid rise in a country's population will tend to make demand grow more rapidly than supply, as is pretty clear intuitively. In terms of the MPS/ICOR formula, population growth will put downward pressure on the country's marginal propensity to save (as the father of four children, I can certainly attest to that tendency personally). With more children, fewer families in Faroffistan will be above the subsistence-level income, which will tend to reduce voluntary saving as well as the government's capacity to extract tax revenue from its citizens. The second effect is to force the country to devote more of its investment funds to SOC-type investments. A larger population requires more hospitals for childbirths, more post offices for birth announcements, a greater supply of classrooms, and additional transportation and communications facilities. If, in our original example, Faroffistan was growing at 5%, with an MPS of 15% and an ICOR of 3.0 (with total investment split evenly as before between SOC and DPA) — ten or fifteen years later, the MPS might fall to 12% and the ICOR rise to 3.6 (with 20% in DPA and now 80% in SOC), which would cut the GNP growth rate to 3.3%. With a population growth rate of 3.3% as well, for example, Faroffistan would then remain in a "low-level equilibrium trap." The situation might be even worse if temporary increases in investment led to a slightly more rapid growth in GNP, which in turn might *raise* population growth as well, leading to a declining GNP per capita.[3]

---

[3]Further discussion of Richard Nelson's "low-evel equilibrium trap" concept can be found in the Todaro text (though he does not mention Nelson) — see Michael P. Todaro, *Economic Development in the Third World, op. cit.,* p. 184.

Political - Administrative Factors

An interesting way to begin a discussion of this issue may be to ask the reader to list the past and present best-known leaders of Third World countries. Such a list would probably include Mao, Marcos, Gandhi, Castro, the Shah of Iran, as well as the Ayatollah, Somoza, Nyerere, Nasser, Idi Amin, Khadaffi (however one currently spells the name), perhaps Sukarno and Suharto, and no doubt Saddam Hussein. I may have left out a few obvious choices, but it is rather clear that relatively few of the leaders listed can be easily identified as having pursued policies leading to development and modernization. Even in those relatively few cases, where the leader has steadfastly refused to accept personal enrichment as the reward of his position, and adopted a relatively ascetic life style, their policies were often grossly counter-productive from a development point of view (Mao's policies during the "Great Leap Forward" and the "Great Proletarian Cultural Revolution" of the late 1960's come to mind as the most obvious examples of egalitarian motivation and horrible results). However, in many other cases, personal enrichment of the charismatic leader won out over the goal of national development. The Swiss bank accounts and Miami-based money market funds of some relatively minor officials hold balances comparing favorably to LDC central bank reserves even today. I vividly recall visiting a small city in a very poor Southeast Asian country about ten years ago — after several hours of driving, chancing upon a white castle, in the midst of enormous formal gardens, with a herd of deer grazing on a beautiful lawn, surrounded by a wrought-iron fence, I asked, in amazement: "And, what is this mansion?" I was informed that it was the residence of one of the recently deposed dictator's "minor wives." Enough said.

In addition to the problems associated with high-level leadership, a second factor that needs to be mentioned is summarized by the term "prebendalism." This word harkens back to the Middle Ages, when various office-holders received "prebends," i.e., income in kind as the result of having a particular job. As an example, it might be simply to be expected as a matter of custom and tradition that the local priest and the head-master of the school would receive a chicken for Easter and a goose at Christmas. Thus, a special term should be used to denote low-level and culturally acceptable payments to government officials in Third World countries, rather than the more ordinary terms "graft" or "corruption," in order to indicate that such payments are usually regarded as perfectly acceptable and quite customary in many other cultures. As the mention of names such as Lockheed, IT&T, the "laundering of money" through Mexico City by the Republican National Committee, "pork-barrel," and "log-rolling" makes clear, Western countries are by no means exempt from such practices. However, it would be highly unusual for most Americans or Europeans to "slip a few bucks" to the customs inspector at the airport, or to offer a tip to the local policeman, or to bring a bottle to the telephone company to get a phone installed promptly. In many Third World countries, however, such extra-legal payments are viewed as an inescapable cost of doing business. The most important reason to bring up this point is to suggest that such costs tend to be highly variable, and that they greatly increase the risks of doing things in a new and different way. In other words, prebendalism as an institution tends to discourage innovation. For example, if your firm is hauling lumber from upcountry to the main port in an overloaded truck, but you have been doing so for years, the prebendal payments at each police check-point along the way are well known. Thus, you can include them as a permanent component of your total costs. Similarly, if you have a bank charter in Faroffistan, and two generals are needed to serve on your board of directors, their fees will tend to remain about the same from year to year, adjusted for inflation, of course. In the former case, if you are considering shipping copper ore instead of logs, the prebendal payments become rather more uncertain; in the latter, if you are thinking of opening an insurance company, you cannot be sure that two generals will be sufficient. In many "rent-seeking societies," (to use Anne Krueger's term) the existence of generally accepted prebendalism will tend to increase the riskiness of new ventures — the expected rate of return on new investment projects will be even harder to calculate than it usually is.

A third factor that needs to be mentioned, but which may in fact be the most important of all political considerations, is the issue of "national unity." If we look at a standard globe or a map of Africa or Asia, we can see quite a few large areas colored in pink, light green, yellow, or blue, called India, Indonesia, Nigeria or Kenya. If we were to provide a linguistic atlas of the world, however, these four countries (as an example) would be similar to a Van Gogh painting. Just in terms of major languages and religions, the following picture emerges:

Country	Languages	Religions
India	Hindi, English, Bihari, Telugu, Marathi, Bengali, Tamil, Gujarati, Rajastani, Kanarese, Malayalam, Oriya, Punjabi, Assamese, Kashmiri, Urdu	Hinduism, Islam, Christianity, Sikhism, Buddhism, Jainism, Zoroastrianism, Animism
Indonesia	Bahasa Indonesia, Indonesian and Papuan languages, English	Islam, Tribal religions, Christianity, Hinduism
Kenya	Kikuyu, Luo, Kavirondo, Kamba, Swahili, English	Tribal religions, Christianity, Hinduism, Islam
Nigeria	Hausa, Yoruba, Ibo, Ijaw, Fulani, Kiv, Kanuri, Ibibio, English, Edo	Islam, Christianity, Tribal religions

In the case of India, there exist more than a dozen major languages contending with Hindi and English for the accepted mode of communication in various local areas. In addition, there are nearly one-hundred major dialects and probably thousands of smaller tribal groups speaking their own languages. In Indonesia, the *Encyclopedia Brittanica* estimates "approximately 25 major languages and 250 dialects spoken." The tribal animosities of Africa have led to considerable political unrest, including full-scale insurrections. At the time of this writing, there are at least a half-a-dozen areas in Africa where armed conflicts are making economic progress just about impossible.

Focusing a bit more closely on Asia, which is my main academic interest, both India and Indonesia are quite heterogeneous nations, where loyalty to the central government is rather tenuous, even today. China's problems with Tibet have been in the news, but the "Middle Kingdom" could also potentially be faced with other regional rifts (Mandarin and Cantonese are as different as French and English). Sri Lanka is experiencing a continuing conflict between the Tamils and the Sinhalese. As mentioned above, Malaysia is currently living with an uneasy truce between the ethnic Malay plurality, and its Chinese and Indian populations. In the Philippines, there has been a Muslim insurgency in Mindanao, reputedly receiving some external support. In Indonesia, central government officials, mostly Javanese, are not kindly regarded in outlying areas. Even in Thailand, a relatively homogeneous country with great respect for the monarchy being shown even among minority groups, some border regions near the "Golden Triangle" are not really under the rule of law. Korea faces the issue of unification equally uneasily on both sides of the DMZ, and in Taiwan, one hears some noises from the "natives," who are gaining political participation rather slowly. Hong Kong and Singapore are Chinese city-states, which have achieved enormous economic gains, but remain rather vulnerable politically.

A couple of additional comments should serve to round out this section of the chapter. From the point of view of governmental administration, many LDC's devote sizeable budgetary resources to inefficient and/or unnecessary public sector expenditures. Many Third World countries maintain elaborate Foreign Affairs ministries, whose "national day" receptions in London and Washington rival the excesses of the Roman Empire in its final days. It may well be, however, that the same countries are negotiating for debt rollovers and reschedulings the very next day with the bankers sipping expensive whiskey and sampling caviar at the party that evening. (Some international officials in attendance may in fact be representing the International Development Association, IDA for short, which lends so-called "soft-loan" money from the World Bank to the "poorest of the poor" countries at a very modest "service charge" for periods as long as fifty years — with even a ten-year grace period.)

Probably even more objectionable than fancy parties in Washington and London are Third World military expenditures, often aided and abetted by the arms merchants. As Paul Harrison has pointed out, in the three decades following the end of World War II, "there were no less than 133 wars involving eighty states. On an average day twelve wars were being fought, and practically every one of them was in the Third World." Imports of armaments constitute a $10 billion trade flow annually with about three-quarters of the weapons going to the Third World. Furthermore, citing Harrison:

"Twelve out of the thirteen countries spending more than 10 percent of their gross national products on defence in 1975 were developing countries. Military spending in poor countries was often far higher than spending on key development sectors. In 1973, for example, India spent twice as much on arms and armies as on education, and four times as much as on health. Iran spent $73 per head on defence, but only $29 on education and $9 on health.[4]

One final concept worth discussing at some length in this section is the concept of "urban bias." Urban bias refers to the sum total of popular attitudes and government policies, which generally encourages economic activity in urban areas and discourages it in villages and small towns of the Third World. Since it is a very general, broad, and pervasive set of attitudes as well as policy actions, in part deliberate and in part almost accidental, we can only sketch a brief outline of urban bias. In this connection, attitudes may be even more important than deliberate policies. If we ask a student from a Third World country to provide a rough ranking of the prestige of various ministries and other government agencies — to mention the top three public sector agencies for his or her future employment — the institutions likely to be placed near the top of the list will probably include: the central bank, the ministries of foreign affairs, finance, foreign trade, and/or industry, the stock exchange, the investment-promotion board, or the economic planning agency. In general, all of these are government agencies supervising and regulating economic activity in Faroffistan's urban areas, mainly the capital city. If there is travel involved, it is likely to be to London, Paris, or New York (perhaps Bangkok or Manila), but certainly not up-country on a public bus or in second-class rail accommodations. On the other hand, what agencies are likely to have the lowest prestige rating — and probably the last call on budgetary resources? Yes, the ministry of agriculture, the department of vocational education, and the rural health service are all probably quite near the bottom of the list.

As is strongly implied by the previous paragraph, government expenditures are probably going to favor urban areas, especially the capital city itself. In many developing countries, government officials are likely to view assignments to provincial cities as "banishment" — even if they were asked to serve as the governor of a province, or the chief doctor of a regional health service unit. Their families may stay on in the capital, lest the education of the children or the wife's social contacts be interrupted significantly. Government spending on education will probably favor the most prestigious university in the capital city, the health ministry will look after the main research hospital first and foremost, and the armed forces will take care of the officers' training probably in the suburbs of the capital, as well as possibly overseas. The ministries of transportation and communications will be more interested in the links of their capital city to the outside world (e.g., the airport) than the infrastructure within the country itself, and so on. The felt needs of urban minorities — politically active, reasonably literate, and prone to riot — will generally take precedence over the desires of the rural majority in most cases.

---

[4] Paul Harrison, *Inside the Third World, op. cit.,* pp. 386–387.

While government spending programs in Third World countries tend to favor urban residents, tax collections often rely largely on rural economic activity — or, in any case, exempt the upper classes. LDC tax systems generally utilize so-called "indirect taxes," levied on sales, foreign trade, or certain kinds of production, while taxes on income and property (especially land holdings) are usually quite small. As a rule, indirect taxes tend to be "regressive," which means that taxes paid by poor consumers are a significantly larger proportion of their income than the tax payments made by the rich. While taxes on imported luxury goods for private use — for example, Rolls Royces and Mercedes — may be quite high in the typical developing country, the bulk of revenue collections often is derived from the country's principal agricultural export. If Faroffistan exports rice, for example, there may be an export duty on rice, which may account for 20 to 40 percent of total government revenue. This serves as a "double-edged sword" in keeping the cost of living low in urban areas, which facilitates urbanization and industrialization, while encouraging diversification in agriculture as well (if corn and tobacco are not taxed, farmers will switch from rice). A significantly higher tax on a country's principal export is often justified on the basis of the "Prebisch Thesis," discussed in the previous chapter. (As pointed out there, the downward trend in the terms of trade for rice, for example, has not easily established as a historical "law" — it may well be that Faroffistan is deliberately destroying its comparative advantage in rice quite unnecessarily.)

Finally, the government may be following pricing policies for agricultural and industrial products, in conjunction with government expenditures and tax collections, which lower the prices for the former and raise the prices for the latter category of goods. In large part, this relates to the problem of perceived factor prices, mentioned earlier. If the cost of capital is deliberately understated, while wages are perceived to be "high," virtually all industrial projects will generally appear to be more profitable than agricultural ventures. Generally speaking, regimes of "financial repression," which signal that real interest rates in Faroffistan are negative, will encourage over-borrowing and lead to higher capital/labor ratios. Distorted factor prices, favoring the use of capital, will often be reinforced by distorted product prices. As a result of negative real interest rates, as already noted, consumer products made with a greater capital-intensity (colas) are cheaper than labor-intensive products (fruit juices).

Furthermore, the use of interest rate ceilings and financial repression is usually associated with inflation — indeed, a negative real interest rate means that expected inflation exceeds the nominal return on financial assets. In an inflationary situation, there is a great deal of political pressure to exempt certain categories of expenditures from "the inflation tax." These usually include food staples, such as bread or rice, urban housing, and probably local transportation (such as bus fares in the capital city). The government tries to buy agricultural products as cheaply as possible — in a socialist state, forcing the farm sector to deliver certain quotas at very low prices — but the subsidies involved in selling staples below cost often consume a significant part of the government budget quite quickly. In such a setting, government employees and workers in parastatal enterprises will certainly press for an "indexation" of their wages and salaries — first on an annual, soon on a monthly, and then perhaps on a weekly or even daily basis. As a general rule, urban dwellers are able to make their wishes known to the policy-makers much more quickly and dramatically than people in rural areas — whose involuntary hunger strikes do not receive attention from the media.

In addition to government spending and taxation policies, as well as financial repression, the rural sector is often also squeezed by the foreign exchange policies adopted. As a rather obvious first point, there is a tendency for exchange rates to be "overvalued"—that is, for the local currency to be worth more in terms of foreign exchange than it really can buy locally in goods and services. As Michael Lipton, the originator of the concept of "urban bias," has put it, most poor countries manage their foreign-exchange rates by following a combination of two contradictory policies, making foreign exchange cheap, but also seldom readily available. Thus, their central banks are buying and selling foreign exchange at rates well below what would be suggested by the purchasing-power-parity concept.

In many instances, these domestic policies of the less developed countries were reinforced by the international measures adopted by the industrialized world. Foreign aid was often imbued with a strong urban bias — "let's help them air-condition this airport" and upgrading of central city communications/transport facilities would be the first ideas entering the mind of a foreign aid official upon visiting Faroffistan. While the World Bank has deliberately tried to emphasize rural development, its elite international bureaucrats are much more at home in manipulating and analyzing macroeconomic data on their desk-top computer than walking foot-paths in the rice paddies. Certainly the same can be said of aid technicians representing an individual aid donor country. Many of us have done "development tourism, " but the truly poor areas probably cannot be seen from a car. Furthermore, it is important to point out that OECD trade policy efforts to help the LDC's have generally emphasized lower tariffs and special provisions for the *manufactured* exports of the Third World (for example, the GSP), while their agricultural products often face competition from First World producers (e.g., U.S. rice) or highly protective barriers (e.g., the "common agricultural policy" of the Europeans).

To summarize this last point regarding the relationship between urban bias and foreign exchange policies briefly, we are not arguing that what is needed is simply reliance on the "invisible hand" of Adam Smith. To cite the intellectual godfather of this section, Michael Lipton:

> *"...The case against the foreign-exchange and trading policies of most poor countries' governments, then, is not that such policies have distorted a market that would otherwise have functioned beneficially, but that they have strengthened the aleady harmful market power of privileged groups of big monopolistic firms and their organised employers. That is natural, because 'the State' is not neutral, but is influenced by the powerful, the organised, the wealthy, and — under urban bias — the near. On relatively esoteric issues of foreign-exchange management, the voice of the villager is likely to be especially weak."[5]*

---

[5] Michael Lipton, *Why Poor People Stay Poor, Urban Bias in World Development* (Harvard University Press, 1977), pp. 322–323.

Sociological-Psychological Factors

In this section, we are venturing even further away from the safe world of measurement, quantification, and economic models to generalize in a dangerously loose way about Third World societies and even the personalities of people inhabiting those societies. While a few Western sociologists and psychologists have written about such matters, there exists a general paucity of "hard data" about them. Also, a few courses in sociology and psychology do not make one qualified to offer reliable generalizations about the varied and complex realities of more than one hundred countries covering about three-fourths of the world's population.

First, let us take up the fascinating issue of religion — man's attempt to define and understand the universe, and his place in it. We have already briefly mentioned the linkage between the so-called "Protestant Ethic" and "the spirit of capitalism" investigated by Max Weber nearly a century ago. Prior to the Reformation, the authorities of the Catholic Church in most instances occupied positions quite similar to the Ayatollah and his "mullahs" in Iran — they were "the judge and the jury" concerning what was politically correct and economically just. St. Thomas Aquinas and other medieval scholastics worked on the problems of "just price" and usury, among other economic issues. There was a great deal of emphasis on *communal* want-satisfaction, tithing to the church by the wealthy to finance cathedrals, education, and poor relief. In sharp contrast, later on, as capitalism grew, various Protestant denominations in the West put great emphasis on *individual* achievement. As we mentioned in the first chapter, the amassing of personal fortunes became identified with salvation, the wealthy also viewed themselves as "the elect" or "the saved". The "Protestant Ethic" became a suitable philosophy for the emerging capitalist class, glorifying hard work, abstaining from consumption, and the plowing-back of profits into the family business. For someone strongly imbued with these values, the greatest sin of all became wasting precious time — embodied in the phrase, "time is money."

This is in sharp contrast to many Third World religions. Some teach that the surest way to salvation is to die in battle fought as part of a holy war — and not through asset accumulation at all. Other religions emphasize various rituals as ways to influence economic activity — in other words, business success is granted by various deities or spirits. It is viewed primarily as a matter of good luck, with personal ability and effort being put in a rather distant second place. In Latin America, Catholicism appears to have been strongly influenced by the shamanistic practices of the local populations — rural churches often seem to be more akin to the temples of the Far East than houses of worship in North America or Western Europe. In such a setting, poor people pray for progress, but do not act to bring it about. In some primitive cultures, personal wealth is periodically destroyed by orgiastic rituals, perhaps also distributed to other members of the group through dowry payments, or "invested" in non-productive ceremonial objects. Although a number of countries nominally Buddhist, such as Japan, Korea, and Taiwan, have achieved considerable economic success, the concept of "Nirvana" seems to be as anti-capitalist as possible. The so-called Middle Way to Nirvana is the knowledge of the "Four Truths." In passing, the third truth is defined as the cessation of pain, "the remainderless cessation of craving, its abandonment and rejection, emancipation, and freedom from support." The enlightened disciple moves toward Nirvana throughout many lives, each reincarnation moving one a little closer, until... Well, in southern California in the 1990's, one could define this state as being "totally laid-back" or "radically mellowed-out." Probably not the right attitude for trading "junk bonds" or doing M&A.

The role of religion in some Third World societies is also quite negative in relation to a range of production and consumption activities. In some religions, a specific period of time is set aside for ritualistic fasting and praying (e.g., the month of Ramadan). In many others, religious obligations are a part of every person's passage to adulthood (in a number of Southeast Asian countries, you're expected to shave your head, don the robes of a monk, and spend the day chanting and begging, which will probably defer your finishing the MBA). Dietary restrictions of various sorts inhibit the modernization of diets — "prejudice against the pig" in a number of countries has certainly slowed down the development of the bacon industry. In India, the "sacred cow" contributes virtually nothing to output, while continuing to consume resources which might have better alternative uses. Finally, in quite a few Third World societies the "best and the brightest" of the young are encouraged to devote their lives to religious vocations permanently, which may impede economic progress and the development of entrepreneurial skills (though, as a professor at Georgetown I would hardly be able to conclude that the Jesuits are not contributing to progress or lacking in entrepreneurship...).

To continue this "pop sociology" a bit more, let us contrast the role of the family in the "Third World" with that familiar to most of us. The basic decision-making unit in the United States, and most other industrialized countries, is the so-called "nuclear family," consisting of husband, wife, and minor children. If we think about it functionally, the nuclear family is very well suited to the demands of an industrial civilization. The adults must become disciplined members of the labor force, earning enough to sustain and educate the children first, and then continue working to take care of most of their own needs in old age (because by then the children will be raising their own offspring). The nuclear family needs to be self-reliant, hard-working, mobile geographically, and savings-oriented. While the nuclear family is also the basic unit of many Third World societies, the extended family or the tribal unit plays a more significant role than in the United States, say. On a very personal level, if our brother's or sister's family comes for a visit, they could probably stay with us for a while, perhaps a week or so, without any hard economic questions concerning rent or food costs being asked. A cousin might be invited to stay with us for a day or two, as would an aunt or an uncle. However, in our culture, longer-term claims are somewhat doubtful. Even parents or grandparents are more likely to turn to government agencies or church groups for help with permanent living arrangements than to their family. In many other societies, such attitudes would be unthinkable — if you have a good job or have inherited some assets, a much larger group of people will expect to share your good fortune, or will feel that they have a legitimate claim to do so. In a tribal situation, and to some extent in the extended family as well, decision-making power does not rest with you, or you and your spouse, but with the elders of the group. Your father, grandfather, or even an uncle can be the one to decide where you will go to school or where you will work.

Another aspect of "Third World" societies is closely related to the differing concept of the family, and has both political and sociological implications. Many traditional societies are subject to quite rigid social stratification, which tends to impede modernization and economic progress. An extreme case of stratification, of course, is the "caste system" of India — which reached its zenith (or nadir) during the time of British control of "the jewel in the crown." J.H. Hutton has reported on elaborate distance tables "...laying down the limits of approach within which the mere presence of the low-born was held sufficient to pollute their betters." To cite an extreme example of such rules:

> "...a Nayar might safely approach a Brahman within a few feet, but could not touch him without defiling him. The presence of a Tiyan toddy-drawer was enough to pollute a Brahman at a distance of 36 paces, and that of a Pulayan at no less than 96 paces. As late as 1932 an Indian newspaper reported...the presence of a caste group, called the Purada-Vannan, so degraded by its occupation — that of washing the clothes of untouchables — that it was classed as unseeable and compelled to live a nocturnal existence."[6]

Even today, it is estimated that the so-called "untouchables" constitute about 15 percent of India's population—more than 100 million people viewed as "unclean." To quote a couple of European geographers on their status:

> "...Untouchables have always been the innocent victims of extreme discrimination. To give some examples: they were not allowed to walk on certain streets and roads unless they removed their footprints with a broom; on some streets and paths they had to warn other pedestrians in order to enable them to avoid their unclean shadow; even the sound of their voice was considered unclean; in many parts of India they were not allowed to have an umbrella, walk on shoes, milk cows, posses pet animals, or wear bracelets, earrings, necklaces and other ornaments."[7]

While the Indian caste system is an extreme example of formal social stratification, other Third World cultures also employ rather rigid "us versus them" classifications, where members of hill tribe groups (in Southeast Asia) or Indians (in Latin America) are viewed as only marginal members of the larger society. Tribal animosities in Africa

---

[6] *Encyclopedia Britannica*, Vol. 4 (William Benton, 1959), p. 978.

[7] H.A. Reitsma and J.M.G. Kleinpennig, *The Third World in Perspective* (Rowman and Allanheld, 1985), p. 323.

continue to provide major barriers to the integration of national societies and economic systems, and separatist sentiments survive in many modern nations.

Though there exists a strong temptation to do a bit more "pop psychology" as well, many writers have already tackled this interesting topic, and we can be very brief in commenting on the psyche of Faroffistan. In sharp contrast to the individualistic and scientific world-view held by ourselves (ahem!), a Faroffistan citizen is usually fatalistic, often superstitious, and risk-averse. A well-known Harvard social-psychologist, David McClelland has, in fact, attempted to quantify the extent of the achievement motivation of various societies.[8] By investigating such sources of early childhood values as nursery rhymes and fairy tales, McClelland developed a "Need for Achievement" index called an "*n-ach*" scale. Generally speaking, the psychological make-up of most industrialized country citizens stresses individual responsibility for one's own actions, and seeks rational/scientific explanations for observable events. For example, physical or mental illness is viewed as a temporary state to be analyzed, explained, and cured — not the result of a witch's curse, evil spirits, or punishment for past transgressions. Even today, most Americans can explain the physical causes of thunder and lightning, at least rather vaguely, but people in rural areas of the Third World continue to rely on various traditional/magical explanations of such phenomena. One charming story from Asia explains thunder as the curses and roars of a demon chasing a princess across the sky, and finally throwing his axe at her— which the princess wards off by holding up a magic gem-stone. (The sparks flying off the gem are the cause of lightning, of course.)

Technological-Educational Factors

As a fourth set of constraints to economic growth and development in the Third World, we can mention problems of technology and education. To put it very crudely, there isn't very much of either readily available — and what is being made available may not be very relevant or appropriate. I know that I shouldn't start this section with a bad joke, but I will anyway (I do want the reader to realize that this was written by an actual human being, not an editorial committee or a computer...). The setting is Ireland in the Depression of the 1930's, plagued by unemployment and falling incomes — and we have Pat and Mike walking by the only construction site in town. There is a big yellow bull-dozer moving huge mounds of earth around down in the hole. Says Pat: "Say, lad, see that infernal machine there, taking the jobs away from a hundred men with shovels." Mike: "Ay, mate, so true — or a thousand men with tea-spoons..." Think about that one — it is a rather relevant "appropriate technology" story.

As mentioned earlier, there are a number of reasons why decision-makers in the less developed countries will tend to select capital-intensive technologies for most industrial projects. First, we can mention what might be termed the "engineering-man" bias — the unwritten rule that the latest, "state-of-the-art" technology is simply the best one to use,

---

[8] Cf. David McClelland, *The Achieving Society* (Van Nostrand, 1961).

regardless of local economic conditions. Again, may I be permitted a brief, anecdotal story to illustrate this point? When I arrived in Thailand in 1968 as an employee of the U.S. Agency for International Development, I was a bit of a "computer freak" — and rather soon made my way to a computer lab at one of the local universities, where one of my former graduate students was teaching, to see what was going on. I was delighted to find a machine identical to the one that I had learned to use in the early 1960's at the Federal Reserve, and eventually wrote a couple of simple programs for some of the local economists. Generally, the machine was used about three days a week, mostly for accounting and grade reporting, with a little bit of statistics lab-work as well. When I was ready to return to the States in 1970, the usage was up to four days a week, but it was still only turned on during the business day. On my last visit to the facility, the director greeted me: "Khun George, I have good news to tell you — next month we'll be getting an IBM 360!" I simply asked: "Why?" His answer: "Because it's so much faster..." (It would save a couple of nano-seconds of calculating time!)

Most technological advances in Western countries have tended to focus on large-scale, standardized production in a labor-scarcity environment. Thus, since wages were relatively high, technical improvements in most industrial countries were usually of a labor-saving variety. If LDC's follow along the same technological road, the results can be very disappointing. As E.F. Schumacher has put it:

> "...Far more serious is the dependence created when a poor country falls for the production and consumption patterns of the rich. A textile mill I recently visited in Africa provides a telling example. The manager showed me with considerable pride that his factory was at the highest technological level to be found anywhere in the world... Even the raw materials had to be imported because the locally grown cotton was too short for top quality yarn and the postulated standards demanded the use of a high percentage of man-made fibers. This is not an atypical case. Anyone who has actually taken the trouble to look systematically at actual 'development' projects — instead of merely studying development plans and econometric models — knows of countless such cases: soap factories producing luxury soap by such sensitive processes that only highly refined materials can be used, which must be imported at high prices while the local raw materials are exported at low prices; food-processing plants; packing stations; motorisation, and so on — all on the rich man's pattern. In many cases, local fruit goes to waste because the consumer allegedly demands quality standards which relate solely to eye-appeal and can be met only by fruit imported from Australia and California, where the application of an immense science and a fantastic technology ensures that every apple is of the same size and without the slightest visible blemish. The examples could be multiplied without end. Poor countries slip — and are pushed — into the adoption of production methods and consumption standards which destroy the possibilities of self-reliance and self-help. The results are unintentional neo-colonialism and hopelessness for the poor."[9]

---

[9] E.F. Schumacher, *Small is Beautiful: Economics as if People Mattered* (Harper & Row, 1973), pp. 194–195.

This passage from the "Guru" of "intermediate technology," E.F. Schumacher, reminded me of a visit I made to a large banana plantation in the Philippines in 1979, where I naively asked to taste a local banana — apparently all the bananas are picked very green and the only few potentially edible yellow bananas were being thrown away in a garbage heap in the back of the plant, to be fed to pigs.

In the context of many Third World countries, the educational system often suffers in terms of both quantity and quality. The budgetary claims of the Ministry of Education in Faroffistan, as already mentioned, may tend to have a lower priority than many other sectors — for example, the industrial promotion board, the tourism agency, the foreign affairs establishment, and (almost certainly) defense and police. Public school teachers, especially in rural areas, are likely to be among the lowest-paid government workers — and budgetary allocations to the best university in the capital city will probably be considerably more generous than those going to vocational education (or the agricultural faculty). Urban bias is very relevant here as well — the chances of a bright student in a small town or a village of even completing eight grades of formal schooling are small, of his/her going to on to high school, college, or university truly miniscule. I remember being briefed by the local U.S./A.I.D. representative in Nakorn Phanom, way up in the northeast corner of Thailand near the Laotian capital, Vientiane, who had developed some local statistics on the probabilies of a student in his district ever finishing high school — or going on to the university in the capital city, very roughly one in a million. In many countries, the school system lacks resources for educational materials — old textbooks with missing pages are used from year to year — and the emphasis is on rote memorization rather than discussion and analysis, even at the university level.

Hla Myint has discussed the difficulties facing post-independence Southeast Asian universities in his native Burma and other countries at some length. The university authorities were facing considerable political pressure to make university education much more democratic and egalitarian, reminiscient of the United States in the late 1960's and China during the Cultural Revolution. In particular, the sheer number of students clamoring for admission to post-secondary education greatly lowered its value very quickly. To cite Professor Myint:

> *"...The result is that university education in non-professional courses in all these countries has degenerated into giving lectures to huge overcrowded classes with hundreds of students, lectures being frequently given at 'dictation speed' so that students can get complete lecture notes which they learn by heart to be reproduced in the examinations. The overworked professors can do little else and, owing to shortages of textbooks and to students' difficulties in understanding them, few students read anything beyond their lecture notes. There is very little outside reading for general education, and the meagrely stocked libraries are used merely as places where students can memorize their lecture notes. The professional courses, such as medicine and engineering, still try to impose a restrictive selection on their numbers, but this seems to be a losing battle and their*

standards also have suffered in varying degrees from the pressure on limited laboratory facilities."[10]

If anything, during the nearly twenty years since the above passage was written, the higher education situation in the typical Third World country has probably worsened somewhat. Overworked professors with good credentials are stretched very thin—being courted as consultants by aid agencies and private firms, being asked to write for local and international mass media, being invited to overseas conferences and symposia, and forever being visited by well-meaning friends and colleagues out on lecture tours and/or sabbaticals (including yours truly, of course). Many competent Third World professionals find the living standards of First World appointments with the World Bank, U.N. organizations, and universities hard to resist, contributing to the well-known "Brain Drain." (As an aside, this phenomenon has affected the countries of the "Second World" to some extent as well. Scientists and mathematicians, not to mention athletes and performers in the former Soviet Union and Eastern Europe, know that their skills could command incomes ten, twenty, perhaps even a hundred times higher in the outside world.)

One final comment seems to be in order to finish up this section. Just as production processes are often capital-intensive, reflecting reliance on Western models and "inappropriate external prototypes," Third World educational systems were often constructed by the colonial powers — and subsequently "inherited" by newly-independent governments in the developing world. Faculty members had been recruited to duplicate the curriculum of "home universities" in England, France, and so on, with European literature, history, and philosophy being emphasized. Law, medicine, and engineering were taught just the same as "back home," assuming that all of the assumptions that held in these professions in their European context could be made to hold true elsewhere as well. As a result of the high status associated with academic success in the "First World," many LDC students pursue courses of study leaving them virtually unemployable in their own countries. As the Gillis development economics text notes:

"...the employment exchange in Calcutta is daily thronged with college graduates (some of them 'firsts' — recipients of top academic honors) in mathematics, English, and physics. Yet employers who approach the same office seeking workers skilled in air conditioning, silk-screen printing, or plumbing, come away disappointed. In these circumstances, graduates must eventually accept work to which their education bears little relevance. Graduate taxi drivers are said to be common in Manila, as they are in some American cities. Employers then have to use on-the-job training to obtain the skills they need."[11]

---

[10] Hla Myint, *Economic Theory and the Underdeveloped Countries* (Oxford University Press, 1971), p. 228.

[11] Malcolm Gillis *et al, Economics of Development,* Fourth Edition (W.W. Norton & Company, 1996), p. 258.

Environmental-Climatic Factors

In many Third World countries, economic activity is also inhibited by climate, terrain, and other geographic constraints. In part due to the vagaries of nature, but also as the result of firewood collection and overgrazing, quite a few developing countries face problems of deforestation and desertification. Deforestation in many tropical countries is associated with so-called "slash-and-burn agriculture," where the forest is cut down and burned, planted with crops (like opium poppies in the "Golden Triangle" of Southeast Asia) for a few years, and then the process is repeated in another area. While the population engaged in such nomadic agriculture was relatively small, forests were able to renew themselves, but in recent years more serious consequences have become apparent. For example, Haiti, now essentially deforested, suffers from long-term drought, there is persistent flooding of lowland areas in a number of Asian countries, and the incidence of major forest fires has increased. The problem is exacerbated by over-logging of forests — as Gillis *et al* have pointed out, an area equal in size to Belgium was burned in Indonesia in 1983, along with an almost equally large area in neighboring East Malaysia. Sometimes the problem crosses national boundaries in terms of negative externalities — the cutting down of trees in Nepal has led to serious silting problems in the major rivers of India.

An important point that can be made is that *timber* may be a renewable resource, tropical *forests* may not be. As has been pointed out, the lush tropical rain forest seen in Tarzan movies does not really reflect rich, fertile soil, but in an ingenious adaptation of nature to a soil type too poor to support most food crops, or even other kinds of trees other than the ones Tarzan used for his swinging. Without delving into the biology of all of this very deeply, the very tall trees are apparently necessary to cool the forest floor sufficiently to produce compost from falling leaves and other biodegradable stuff. If you chop down the trees and try to plant something else, it won't work — as an American billionaire found out in trying to set up a mammoth pulp-and-paper operation in Brazil. As Gillis *et al* note, certain kinds of tropical timber (e.g., teak) really cannot be thought of as a renewable resource, since they have a very long growing cycle (40 to 150 years) and are part of a complex ecology not very well understood even today. Furthermore, tropical forests, produce medicinial herbs (e.g., cinchona bark for malaria control), oils and fats, barks, flowers, and various chemicals, which can only be produced without cutting down the forest.[12]

Ethiopia, one of the poorest countries in the world, suffers from famine periodically — and relies on foreign aid, grudgingly distributed to the people by its government due to tribal animosities. Yet, it has the largest livestock resources in Africa, because a herd of animals is a social asset rather than an economic investment. However, livestock breeding is more influenced "by ritual and taboos than by profitability considerations." Indeed, it is estimated that the country could feed several times its present population, if some land were to be switched from grazing to crop production.

---

[12] *Ibid,* p. 523 ff.

Generally speaking, the climate of many Third World areas is not conducive to economic activity. As anyone who has spent a couple of years in Bangkok (or stayed in Washington, D.C. during all of the month of August) knows, heat and humidity make sustained physical labor almost impossible even for people in top-notch physical condition, and even mental effort quite difficult. (I haven't even yet mentioned scorpions, spiders, or poisonous snakes as integral parts of the ecosystem...). In many tropical countries, water is also a central problem — often there isn't any, but when it finally rains, there's much too much. In recent years, Bangkok has suffered from severe flooding — the "klongs" (canals) have been paved over by real estate speculators, and an above-average rainy season results in a couple of feet of water in many "sois" (lanes or streets), making automobile travel virtually impossible and greatly affecting the decorum of business attire (think about a three-piece suit soaked to the waist...).

Finally, the risks of living in Third World countries seem to be simply much greater than in Northern temperate areas. Earthquakes, volcanic eruptions, tidal waves, hurricanes and typhoons seem to visit the South much more regularly than the North. Still, roughly nine out of ten disaster-related deaths take place in Third World countries. On average, life expectancy is much lower as well, which means that the opportunity to transfer useful knowledge from one generation to the next is greatly reduced — and since even officially-reported literacy rates are quite low, making such transfers of knowledge relatively permanent, establishing a written record, is a difficult matter.

Conclusion

While the "world economy view," is discussed in the previous chapter, argued that economic interaction with the rest of the world contributed to a continuation of economic backwardness — indeed, was the *primary cause* of underdevelopment — the main thrust of this chapter is quite different. Without even really taking up the question of whether foreign trade and capital flows are of a benign nature or not (and there may not be a satisfactory general answer to that question), the "traditional society view" focuses on internal constraints. As we have enumerated these constraints above, they consist of demographic pressure, political problems, sociological and religious barriers, technological and educational issues, and unfavorable environment/climate situations. If one accepts the world economy view as being essentially correct, the policy implications are quite significant. Then the key solution to underdevelopment involves a general change in the international economic order — more generous foreign aid to compensate the LDC's for past depradations, more favorable terms for foreign trade, and probably international monitoring of capital flows. As far as LDC governments are concerned, the best strategy is to minimize foreign economic contacts in the sphere of private sector dealings, while pressing for more favorable treatment collectively. On the other hand, if the traditional society view is more nearly "right," the basic approach has to emphasize "self-help" efforts to modernize the society and the political system, to control population growth, to improve government policies, and to mobilize domestic resources — perhaps, to overcome excessive trade pessimism and reliance on foreign aid or capital flows in the process. Clearly, for many real-world situations, a combination of both explanations of historical underdevelopment makes sense, but, as we shall see in the next three chapters, the world economy view of exploitation leading to underdevelopment makes less and less sense with every passing year. As the two largest and most-self-reliant socialist countries, the FSU and the P.R.C. today eagerly open up to foreign "penetration," it seems quite silly for Burma, say, to argue that its poverty today is still due to the past colonial policies of the British. ■

SUGGESTED READINGS

Bauer, P.T., *Equality, the Third World, and Economic Delusion* (Harvard University Press, 1981).

Bigsten, Arne, *Income Distribution and Development: Theory, Evidence and Policy* (Heinemann, 1983).

Colman, David, and Frederick Nixson, *Economics of Change in Less Developed Countries*, Second Edition (Barnes and Noble, 1986).

Gillis, Malcolm *et al*, *Economics of Development*, Fourth Edition (W.W. Norton & Company, 1996).

Grabowski, Richard, and Michael P. Shields, *Development Economics* (Blackwell Business, 1996).

Ito, Takatoshi, and Anne O. Krueger (eds.), *Growth Theories in Light of the East Asian Experience* (University of Chicago Press, 1995).

Lal, Deepak, *The Poverty of "Development Economics"* (Harvard University Press, 1985).

Lau, Lawrence J. (ed.), *Models of Development* (Institute for Contemporary Studies, 1986).

Lipton, Michael, *Why Poor People Stay Poor: Urban Bias in World Development* (Temple Smith, 1977).

Little, I.M.D. *et al*, *Boom, Crisis and Adjustment: The Macroeconomic Experience for Developing Countries* (Oxford University Press for the World Bank, 1993).

MacDonald, Scott B., Jane E. Hughes, David Leith Crum, *New Tigers and Old Elephants* (Transaction Publishers, 1995).

Maurice, Charles, and Charles W. Smithson, *The Doomsday Myth* (Hoover Institution Press, 1984).

Meier, Gerald M., and Dudley Seers (eds.), *Pioneers in Development* (Oxford University Press for the World Bank, 1984).

Moran, Theodore H. (ed.), *Multinational Corporations: The Political Economy of Foreign Direct Investment* (Lexington Books, 1985).

Morrisey, Oliver, and Frances Stewart (eds.), *Economic and Political Reform in Developing Countries* (St. Martin's Press, 1995).

Myint, Hla, *Economic Theory and the Underdeveloped Countries* (Oxford University Press, 1971).

Rangel, Carlos, *Third World Ideology and Western Reality* (Transaction Books, 1986).

Reitsma, H.A., and J.M.G. Kleinpennig, *The Third World in Perspective* (Van Gorcum & Company, 1985).

Riddell, Roger C., *Foreign Aid Reconsidered* (The Johns Hopkins University Press, 1987).

Salomon, Jean-Jacques, and André Lebeau, *Mirages of Development: Science and Technology for the Third World* (Lynne Rienner, 1993).

Seligoon, Mitchell A., and John T. Passe-Smith (eds.), *Development and Underdevelopment* (L. Rienner Publishers, 1993).

Simon, Julian, and Herman Kahn (eds.), *The Resourceful Earth: A Response to Global 2000* (B. Blackwell, 1984).

Syrquin, Moshe, Lance Taylor, and Larry E. Westphal (eds.), *Economic Structure and Performance: Essays in Honor of Hollis B. Chenery* (Academic Press Inc., 1984).

CHAPTER TEN

CHINA: ONE NATION, TWO SYSTEMS

*A*s the focus of world trade and economic growth shifts from the Atlantic to the Pacific in the next century, a most interesting role will be played by the world's largest nation, China. In this chapter, we will provide a very brief overview of the economic history of China, with particular emphasis on its experience with the socialist model adopted after 1949, and its future prospects. But, before we begin our bird's eye view of the recent economic history of China, let us devote a paragraph or two to something called the "Moulder thesis," after the Marxist sociologist, Frances Moulder, who wrote a book called *Japan, China, and the Modern World Economy* about twenty years ago. Subsequently, she appears to have left academic social science, but at the time that this book came out,[1] I recall a bit of a stir among younger scholars of the "political economy" frame of mind.

The world economy view was outlined in Chapter 8 above — its basic theme being that the roots of underdevelopment are to be found in past and present exploitation of the LDC's by the metropolitan countries. The world was inevitably and permanently divided into the core and the periphery during the colonial era, according to this view. As a result of being forced into a subordinate position, the LDC's could not ever hope to carve out a niche for themselves in the modern world by trading with the metropolitan nations. In other words, by participating in existing economic arrangements and following a market-oriented development path, peripheral nations would forever be doomed to a specialized role as suppliers of primary products, penetrated at will by international financial capital. Japan has always been a major embarrassment to this view of the world, as have a handful of other Asian nations following a "capitalistic road", but China's deliberate closing itself to foreign contacts during the 1950s and 1960s at that time had provided significant support to this approach. China's resolute independence implied

---

[1] Frances V. Moulder, *Japan, China, and the Modern World Economy:* (Cambridge University Press, 1977). Here the term "political economy" is used in its "modern" version to refer to the neo-Marxist or "radical" views, rather than to the faithful followers of Alfred Marshall, whose definitive economics text was called that — just as the term "liberal" in its current definition means quite the opposite to its 19th century conception.

that autarchy and socialism were the better answer. Therefore, adherents of the world economy view were delighted by the appearance of Moulder's book, which argued that: (1) *internal* conditions in China and Japan were essentially the same around the turn of the century, while (2) China's subsequent backwardness was due to its greater *external* economic contacts during the 19th century, primarily considerably more extensive trade with Great Britain. While we shall comment a bit more on Japan's modernization efforts in the next chapter, a few general observations are in order here.

In the period before World War II, China provides a classic example of the "traditional society view" of the causes of underdevelopment, suffering from demographic pressure and a lack of national unity, having a feudal society structure as well as an illiterate and superstitious populace, and facing serious environmental and ecological problems in many provinces. Dr. Sun Yat-sen (1866-1925), whose bust graces the foyer of the Intercultural Center at Georgetown, is generally regarded as the father of the Chinese republic, but even he failed to establish a unified government in all of China in the 1920's and the 1930's, despite early help from the Communist Party and the USSR. The Nationalist Party leader, Chiang Kai-shek, came closer to establishing a modern and unified government later in the 1930's, but his break with the Communists and Japanese aggression, with the outbreak of an undeclared war in 1937, prevented his success. It is very tempting to delve much more deeply into the fascinating and incredibly complex details of Chinese economic and political history in the first half of the 20th century, but that is much beyond our scope here.

At the very outset of our brief discussion of China in this chapter, we ought to be on guard against over-simplification. While the love affair of Western assistant professors and sophomore students with the thoughts of Mao has decreased somewhat, as we learn more about the realities of China, there is still a rather strong tendency to treat it as:

> "... a myth , an abstract ideal projection, a utopia which allows them to denounce everything that is bad in the West without taking the trouble to think for themselves. We stifle in the miasma of industrial civilization, our cities rot, our roads are blocked by the insane proliferation of cars, et cetera. So they hurry to celebrate the People's Republic, where pollution, delinquency, and traffic problems are non-existent. One might as well praise an amputee because his feet aren't dirty."

Leys continues to point out that:

> "... China confronted the modern world blind and paralyzed, with the worst possible political heritage. A fair evaluation of the Maoist regime should take into account the heavy burden of the past. The totalitarian cancer, the organized cretinization, the dictatorship of illiterates, the crass ignorance of the external world together with a pathetic inferiority complex toward it — those traits are not the natural features of the most civilized people on earth. To understand how Maoism could temporarily lead them into a rut so unworthy of their calling and

their genius, it would no doubt be necessary to retrace the historical events by which the nation was so incredibly derailed." [2]

After the Tiananmen Square massacre in 1989, the romantic fascination with China has been in decline — but quite a few professional Sinologists are ready to forgive and forget remarkably easily and very, very quickly.

Twenty-Five Years with the Little Red Book

Since the fall of 1949, when the Nationalists withdrew to Formosa (now Taiwan), to the incapacitation and death of Mao Zedong in 1976 (earlier spelling, Mao Tse-tung), China's development strategy was shaped by the beliefs and whims of this one man, the author of hundreds of wise sayings included in the "Little Red Book," of which 740 million copies had been printed by the end of the 1960's. As we mentioned at the very outset, there are generally three organizing principles that can be used to govern economic activity in any society — coercive (command), normative (similar to tradition), and renumerative (as in the market). While the Maoists certainly did not seem to have any qualms about using coercion, a distinguishing feature of the Maoist control system in the 1950s and 1960s seemed to be its emphasis on *normative* organizing principles, and a very deliberate de-emphasis of *renumerative* signals. It is an amazingly bold concept — to organize nearly a billion people on the basis of everyone saying to each other "you really ought to...", to create a traditional control system in a couple of decades, and to capture the essence of this system in the "Little Red Book" of Chairman Mao. Everyone was to be encouraged to behave as a member of an extended family, contributing his/her efforts to the overall improvement of the community without a very specific linkage of reward to effort — every worker was theoretically held responsible for overall enterprise management. The "Thoughts of Chairman Mao" substituted a Chinese version of the Protestant Ethic for the individualistic, profit-maximizing worldview of the Western capitalists. Instead of stressing the importance of individual success and a higher income, the Chinese were emphasizing the virtues of hard work, abstinence, and communal benefits. While criminal acts were punished swiftly and brutally, a lot of effort was put into "re-education" activities in the school and the work-place. If Comrade X was caught fondling Comrade Y behind a lathe at the "East is Red" Commune, poor X would have to undergo some serious communal re-education — "exactly what were you thinking when you did this?" "Did you feel Chairman Mao would approve of this?" A meeting of several hundred members of the work unit, lasting for several hours, and probably repeated several evenings, would soon convince Comrade X (and all potentially like him) to leave his/her comrades alone.

Following Alexander Eckstein, Maoist China in its first few decades had to wrestle with the following four decisions:

---

[2] Simon Leys (Pierre Ryckmans), *Chinese Shadows* (Penguin Books, 1978), pp. 201–211.

(1)   Population policy;

(2)   Rate and pattern of investment;

(3)   Role of material incentives;

(4)   Role of professionalism and technology.

To be very brief about all of these, Mao himself initially favored a pro-natalist population policy. To put it very simply, the motto seemed to be "the more the merrier," possibly a perverse extension of the labor theory of value, since Mao felt that China's greatest strength probably was associated with the sheer size of its population. Initially, any expression of concern about population growth, according to Mao,

> "...was regarded as Malthusianism and as such was viewed as a manifestation of imperialism. However, beginning in 1954 one can detect a subtle change in official attitudes. Circumstantial evidence suggests that the Chinese leadership may have been surprised at the results of the 1953 census, revealing a considerably larger population than officially estimated... (However, the initial anti-births campaign)... was called off quite suddenly in late 1957 and 1958. This was coupled with leadership pronouncements that population was to be treated as an asset rather than a liability..." [3]

More recently, however, as is well known, China has emphasized late marriage, a ban on premarital sex, and a "one-couple, one-child" policy — a rather cruel policy graphically examined by the Western media in recent years. There was a television special on "Sixty Minutes" about this question a while back — a young woman carrying her second child was repeatedly visited by "aunties" from her place of employment, and was eventually cajoled into having a very late abortion. It is also said that the one-child policy has led to considerable female infanticide. The longer-term future for a society peopled mostly by "one-and-only" sons, having received enormous attention from both parents and two sets of grandparents, is rather frightening to contemplate. Furthermore, demographers have recently pointed out that the one-child policy would produce a population with 40% of the people over age 65 by the year 2050.

The second broad issue raised by Eckstein concern investment. During the "Ten Great Years," from 1949 to 1959, China received considerable assistance from the Soviet Union, and followed the "Stalinist Model" of growth very explicitly. As mentioned earlier, this model emphasizes a high rate of saving and investment, mostly in heavy industry and infrastructure, tends to treat agriculture as an "internal colony," and follows a policy of minimizing contacts with the rest of the world, especially with market-oriented countries. During the First Five-Year Plan period (1953-1957), the ratio of investment to GNP was raised to about 25% (an extraordinary level for a country near subsistence income), and

---

[3] Alexander Eckstein, *China's Economic Revolution* (Cambridge University Press, 1977), p. 49.

"... great emphasis was placed on industrial development on a wide front. That is, the growth of all branches of mining and manufacturing were to be pressed. However, highest priority was assigned to the development of basic materials-producing and investment- goods branches. This meant that greatest attention was paid to the development of the iron and steel, cement, electric power, petroleum, chemical, and engineering industries. This is illustrated by the fact that during the First-Five Year Plan period close to 90 percent of the investment funds earmarked for industrial construction were channeled into the expansion of these industries." [4]

During the first decade of Communist power, agriculture was very definitely treated as an internal colony in China. Following the Stalinist model, landlords as a class — just like the "kulaks" in the Soviet Union — were to be eliminated in the early 1950's. In the latter half of the "Ten Great Years," the organization of gigantic collectives was emphasized and compulsory deliveries of grain and other agricultural products were instituted. As in Ukraine in the 1930's, this led to a serious famine in China in the 1959-61 period — estimates of starvation deaths during this period range from 15 to 35 million people. As Carl Riskin notes:

"... Excessive procurement of grain was a prime contributor to shortages in the countryside...Under the mistaken belief that harvests had miraculously broken all records, the government in 1958, 1959, and 1960 procured, respectively, 22, 40, and 6 per cent more grain than in 1957... In 1957 gross procurement had come to 24.6 per cent of the harvest; by 1959 it had gone up to 39.7 per cent, and in the year of highest mortality, 1960, it was 35.6 per cent. Even after resales to deficit rural areas, it remained a full 10 percentage points higher in 1959, and 4 points higher in 1960, than in 1957. Rural areas were the chief sufferers:.. in fact, rural per capita supplies remained lower than urban thenceforth until the 1980's... Substantial grain imports, designed to supply the coastal cities and relieve pressure on the countryside, finally began in 1961, two years late." [5]

This same period of time coincides with Chairman Mao's strategy of the "Great Leap Forward," which was part of the Second Five-Year Plan begun in 1958, with a planned investment level above 40% of GNP! Around this time, the close partnership between the Soviet Union and China came to an end, apparently due to the criticisms of Stalin being voiced, however carefully, in the USSR. Mao sought to implement a "walking on both legs" policy — the simultaneous development of capital-intensive investments in industry and infrastructure, coupled with experimental labor-intensive industrial development. There are heroic tales about roads and dams built without using bulldozers, using pig

---

[4] *Ibid.*, p. 120.

[5] Carl Riskin, *China's Political Economy: The Quest for Development Since 1949* (Oxford University Press, 1987), p. 138. It is interesting/shocking to note that Eckstein says, in a book written only ten years earlier, "that the Chinese were finally forced to begin large-scale imports of grain in early 1961 as a means of averting a serious famine" — implying that it was in fact averted. Cf. *ibid.*, p. 59.

excrement to generate electricity, and the famous Maoist policy to smelt steel by using the "backyard steel furnace." As Alexander Eckstein put it:

> "...The Great Leap bore particularly the stamp of an evolving Maoist vision—much more so than the Stalinist strategy preceding it. Mao saw in the Great Leap an opportunity to fully emancipate China from reliance on the Soviet Union, and more importantly, to break out of the vicious circle of backwardness through a discrete leap, through a supreme effort, through a once-and-for-all mobilization effort designed to tap all the energies and latent capacities of the Chinese people. The hope was that one vast supreme effort could push China significantly upward in terms of its stage of development and thus launch the country on a path of more or less automatic and self-sustaining growth."[6]

The third issue, with which Chinese leadership continues to wrestle to this day, is the role to be accorded to material incentives. As mentioned before, generally speaking, an economic system can choose among coercive-command, normative-traditional, and market-material incentives — usually, some combination of all three will be used — in organizing economic activity. While the Chinese Communists did not hesitate to use harsh command methods in the agricultural collectivization drive, some income differences were always tolerated — in most factories, for instance, formal pay scales and wage differentials were established already in the 1950's. In industrial jobs, the Chinese policy-makers even then set up an eight-grade classification system, with each grade being associated primarily with seniority and responsibility. As a general rule, however, senior workers did not earn much more than three times the entry-level wage, while in the U.S., a skilled worker might earn ten times or even more than the minimum wage. For example, Riskin cites a Grade 1 monthly wage of 104 yuan being paid in the Shenzhen Special Economic Zone about ten years ago, while the wage received by a Grade 8 worker stood at 260 yuan per month.[7] In general, urban workers' incomes have usually been a good deal higher than those in rural areas. In particular, large-scale industrial enterprises usually treat their workers quite well, relatively speaking, providing them with residence permits in favored urban areas, housing, ration cards, and other benefits — and an aristocratic, hereditary urban proletariat appears to have emerged. For example, rice in official shops was distributed at a price that is only about a third of what it cost the government to procure it.

The fourth issue discussed by Eckstein concerns the related "Red vs. expert" debate. In industry, just noted, differences in monthly wages have been allowed to exist in China, but money often is a less important indicator of personal success and status than other things, such as power and influence. In most societies, both money and power tend to accrue to individuals possessing technical skills and formal training. For example, doctors, scientists, engineers and technicians usually tend to have high status, in large part because of their personal abilities which are in short supply in the population as a whole

---

[6] Alexander Eckstein, *op. cit.*, p. 58. It is ironic that Mao, viewed as the "Great Protector" of the peasantry, followed policies which mainly brutalized the countryside.

[7] Carl Riskin, *op. cit.*, p. 328.

(intelligence, discipline, dedication and so on). Concerning the balance between professional competence and party loyalty, Deng Xiaoping allegedly said: "It does not matter what color the cat is, as long as it catches mice..." In the mid 1950s, Mao himself also supported the pragmatic view, encouraging relatively free expression of ideas and opinions: "Let a hundred flowers bloom." (This freedom withered quite abruptly in 1957.) The situation then even permitted the growth of a meritocracy — to be sure, the son or daughter of a capitalist or a rich landlord would find advancement most difficult, but even some people with American university degrees were able to function relatively normally in the early days. Middle-class families in most cities continued to live in their old compounds quite comfortably.

In part as a reaction to the failure of the Great Leap, Mao felt the need to re-emphasize the egalitarian character of the Chinese revolution, and unleashed the leftists in the mid-1960's, especially urban youth (the "Red Guards"). The Cultural Revolution challenged every notion of elitism and privilege. Each work-place was encouraged to ferret out individuals with capitalist and/or feudal ideas and to re-educate them, usually by brutal punishment. Former employees of foreign companies were an obvious target (see Nien Cheng's book mentioned in the Bibliography). The "Red Guards," mainly vocational and high-school students, were turned loose to teach the elite a strong lesson — attacking "capitalist roaders" in party, academic, and government institutions, and seeking to banish all traces of the "Four Olds" (old ideas, old culture, old customs, and old habits). Clearly, anyone having rare old books or art objects in his or her residence was not sufficiently "Red" — all professors, especially those with foreign degrees, were automatically suspect. As Gregory Chow has pointed out:

> "...From September 1966 to February 1972, all universities were closed in China. From February 1972 to the autumn of 1976, universities were open again, but admission was decided by political considerations rather than by scholastic qualifications. Youths from workers' and peasants' families having insufficient academic qualifications were assigned by their units to go to universities. The quality of instruction was below standard, and the preparation of the students was generally inadequate. Therefore, for ten years from September 1966, college education in China practically stopped. The disruptive effect on the formation of human capital was tremendous."[8]

Brain surgeons and physics professors were forced to "hsia fang" — literally translated as to go "down to the farm" — to transplant rice, live with the peasants, and be cured of their high-faluting ways. Once the Red Guards were turned loose, it was not easy for the authorities to bring them under control again. It seems that a few years later approximately 17 million youths had to follow their teachers into "hsia fang," i.e., to be forcibly "rusticated." As an interesting aside, Deng Xiaoping himself was stripped of all of his party posts in 1976, branded as an "unrepentant-capitalist-roader," and sent off

---

[8] Gregory C. Chow, *The Chinese Economy* (Harper & Row, 1985), p. 262. See also Andrew G. Walder, *Communist Neo-Traditionalism: Work and Authority in Chinese Industry* (University of California Press, 1986).

to do penance in a rural area. The so-called "Gang of Four" — Jiang Qing (Mrs. Mao), Wang Hongwen, Zhang Chungqiao, and Yao Wenyuan — reigned supreme. During this period, Lin Biao died in a mysterious plane crash in Outer Mongolia, while Zhou Enlai died of cancer toward the very end of the Cultural Revolution. Deng was eventually reinstated as a member of the inner ruler circle, somewhat miraculously.

Quite remarkably, during the past two decades, the Chinese have been following policies dictated by Deng's pragmatism. Thousands of Chinese students have been sent to study in the West, and professionals once again seem to be held in high esteem. Foreign investment, in the form of joint ventures, has exploded in recent years, totalling more than $100 billion as of 1995. There has even been some discussion of requiring university students in China to pay tuition, and to compete for jobs upon graduation, rather than being assigned to positions by the state. However, memories of the Cultural Revolution may well inhibit some of the most able people seeking higher education, especially in the West — after all, the line between wholesome modernization and decadent "bourgeois liberalization" is not easily drawn. Quite a few of the Chinese students in the U.S., in particular, are deciding not to return, since they may have become permanently infected with the very dangerous diseases of democracy and rationality, but remarkably many do go back — which will probably help the development of a civic society at some point.

The Decade After Mao

After the death of Mao in 1976 and the purge of the Gang of Four shortly thereafter, "...the real patron saint of the post-Mao policies was Chou En-lai, and the real prime mover pushing for their rapid implementation was Teng (Deng), who, after his second purge by Mao and the radicals in early 1976, was rehabilitated a second time in 1977 and again assumed a key position in the leadership." [9]

The philosophical framework was drawn from a speech by Chou En-lai (now generally spelled Zhou) in 1975, possibly also earlier, where he mentioned the need for the "Four Modernizations" — policies to move China to the forefront of modern, major world nations in agriculture, industry, defense, as well as science and technology by the year 2000. Visitors to China in the mid-1970s reported seeing many colorful posters, emphasizing positive colors, such as red (of course), yellow, and light blue, with a rider on a white steed galloping toward a glorious future described by various Chinese characters and featuring the number "2000." Currently one seldom hears grandiose claims about being at the "forefront among major nations" by the end of the century. Statistically, the official target appears to have been scaled down to a per capita GNP of US$800 to $1000 by 2000. Even the $800 level is still rather optimistic, compared to the most recent World Bank estimate of 1994 GNP per capita for China equal to approximately US$530, but output has been growing quite rapidly in the past decade.

---

[9] A. Doak Barnett, *China's Economy in Global Perspective* (The Brookings Institution, 1981) pp. 14–15.

Any discussion of China's economic prospects must, first and foremost, focus on the agricultural sector — more than 80 percent of its population is classified as primarily employed in agriculture. Despite relatively low prices paid for farm products, agricultural production accounted for more than 40% of GNP in the early 1980s in part also as a result of the emphasis on industrialization (value added in agriculture fell from 58% of GNP in 1952 to 42% in 1981). During the decade of the 1950's the Stalinist strategy of forced collectivization and treatment of agriculture as an "internal colony" was followed. As Chow has put it:

> "...The transformation of Chinese agriculture through the land reform of 1949-1952, the formation of mutual aid teams and cooperatives in 1951-1957, and the introduction of the commune system in 1958 are a fascinating chapter of political, social, and economic history. ...It is a testament to the political power and organizational skill of the leadership of the Chinese communist party that within about five months, between April and September 1958, 98.2 percent of the total number of peasant households had been organized into 26,425 communes." [10]

Initially, private plots were still permitted in the communes — while they were strictly limited to less than 5% of the cultivated land area per capita in any village, more than 80% of all hogs raised in China could be found on private plots in 1956, and it has been estimated that 20 to 30% of total household income for peasants on average was derived from private farming even in the late 1950s. During the period of the Great Leap Forward, 1958-1960, however, private plots were abolished and rural markets were not allowed to function. Virtually all grain was subject to mandatory delivery to the government at very low prices. At the same time, in many areas, peasants were mobilized to build roads, dams, bridges, and other macro infrastructure projects favored by the central authorities. The massive drive of the Great Leap to nearly double the capital formation rate from the First Five-Year Plan period (from 24% to 44%!) withdrew labor in rural areas from repair and maintenance tasks during the "off-season," while government investment in agriculture at that time amounted to less than 10% of total budgetary outlays. The result of these policies was the Great Crisis, the famine of 1959-61, which has already been mentioned, with about 35 million famine deaths.

Even under Mao, an "Agriculture First" policy was quickly instituted in the early 1960's, though the Cultural Revolution was later aimed at those with excessive enthusiasm for the free market in the countryside as well. Still, private plots were reinstated once again in 1962, though initially limited to vegetables and poultry in most areas. From 1960 to the mid-1970's, farm procurement prices rose by about 30%, while the prices of industrial goods bought by farmers rose by only 13%—thus, the "parity" or purchasing power position of farmers rose by about one-fifth. Furthermore, in 1971 the price of chemical fertilizers was decreased by about 10% and the prices of farm equipment by about 15%.[11] Such modern agricultural inputs, as well as high-yielding seed varieties,

---

[10] Gregory C. Chow, *op. cit.*, p. 97.
[11] Alexander Eckstein, *op. cit.*, p. 119.

Agriculture first

were initially made available to the most productive areas of the South and Central "rice belt," evidently placing efficiency considerations ahead of egalitarian concerns. Industrial investments were designed according to the "Five Small Industries" concept — emphasizing those industries having the closest direct linkage to increases in agricultural output. As Barnett has put it:

> "...In the 1960's, also, special emphasis was placed on rural small-scale industries. This time the program was more rational and viable than the one pushed during the Great Leap. Small plants began producing increased quantities of fertilizer, agricultural tools, machinery (including irrigation pumps), cement, and other inputs for agriculture and the rural economy in general. In the early 1970s this policy received even greater emphasis, and the regime also called for accelerated efforts to mechanize agriculture."[12]

In recent years, the emphasis on agricultural productivity has increased even further, and it is possible to talk today about the decollectivization of agriculture in China. During 1978-1980, the limits on the size of private plots — under pressure not to exceed 5 to 7 percent of cultivated land during the decade of the Cultural Revolution — were raised, diversification of production to crops other than food-grains (as well as "side-line activities" such as handicrafts) was encouraged, and the output of private plots could be marketed. Instead of limiting themselves to a small flock of chickens and/or ducks, enterprising peasants soon developed fairly large herds of individually-owned livestock as well — although raising a couple hundred chickens seemed to be the surest way to wealth. Various "Household Responsibility Systems" became standard in the countryside by the early 1980's, with contracting output to an individual household ("baogan daohu") becoming especially popular.

It is quite likely that greater reliance on the market system in agriculture will increase existing income differentials, which are already quite substantial. Chow reports considerable dispersion in the distribution of agricultural output per capita for China's various provinces and municipalities in 1981. At the head of the list, we find Shanghai with a value of 762.4 yuan, then 507.3 yuan for Tianjin, and 485.4 for Beijing (an average of 585 yuan for the top three). At the end of the ranking, we find Guizhou (164.0 yuan), Gansu (169.8 yuan), and Yunnan (207.3 yuan). The average for the bottom three provinces stands at 180 yuan, which means as range of about 3.25-to-1.0 from the top to the bottom in agricultural output. While the rise in agricultural incomes will probably lower the Gini coefficient for the country as a whole — as incomes on average become more equal — the individual Gini coefficients for both rural and urban incomes are likely to rise in the near future, with potential political risks associated with that.

It can be pointed out that China's income distribution data are not significantly different from those of a number of large, poor, and agricultural Asian countries, such as Bangladesh, Pakistan, and Sri Lanka. The share of the poorest 40% is about the same as of the above-mentioned three countries as well as India (which has a Gini coefficient

---

[12] A. Doak Barnett, *op. cit.*, p. 303.

slightly higher than that of the United States). Still, on the basis of most socioeconomic indicators, such as infant mortality, life expectancy, and literacy, the standard of living for the bottom 40% in China compares favorably with that of other Asian countries.

The other three modernizations also involve the basic tradeoff between economic efficiency and egalitarian concerns, but also raise the question of international trade and other foreign contacts. Moving China's science and technology toward the forefront among other major nations by the beginning of the next century probably implies considerable expenditure for overseas training of scientists and technicians. The upgrading of its defense capabilities seems to suggest arms purchases and training abroad to some extent as well, while industrial advances are likely to be closely linked to the availability of foreign capital and technology. One striking feature of Chinese industrial development before its opening up to the rest of the world was its "extraordinary dispersion of industrial production," with each locality trying to come as close to self-sufficiency as possible. As John B. Sheahan says,"...it would be difficult to find anywhere a more through-going contradiction of the principles of specialization and comparative advantage. All of Adam Smith's themes about the gains of efficiency through division of labor and trade were explicitly repudiated."[13]

The concept of the "Iron Rice Bowl" — guaranteed employment at a level of income somewhat above subsistence — is being challenged. The *Far Eastern Economic Review* notes that labor productivity in China's industry averages less than 10% of that in Japan, that as much as 30% of the workers in urban enterprises are "redundant", and that more than 150 million workers in rural areas can be considered as "surplus". Instead of the system of lifetime employment, since 1980, many public-sector enterprises have experimented with a labor-contract system (with 80% of all new hires being contract labor by 1986).

As mentioned above, a key constraint to overall modernization for China is likely to be the availability of foreign exchange — for both consumption and investment. During the 1950s, China's foreign trade was mainly carried on with other communist countries, and expanded relatively modestly — rising from total trade per capita (exports plus imports divided by population) of 4.03 yuan in 1952 to 6.52 yuan in 1959. During the decade of the 1960s, after the Soviet advisors had been withdrawn (or, depending upon whom you ask, been asked to leave), the Chinese followed a policy of deliberate and conscious autarky (self-reliance or self-sufficiency) — indeed, its per capita total trade declined to 5.53 yuan by 1970. Even before Mao's death, while the Cultural Revolution was still going on, the "opening-up of China" to the rest of the world in the early 1970's involved more than a tripling of foreign trade by the second half of the 1970's (per capita total trade reached 21.44 yuan by 1978). The slogan in the early 1970's (going back to Mao's 1956 speech on "Ten Great Relationships," which was not published in China until

---

[13] John B. Sheahan, *Alternative International Economic Strategies and Their Relevance for China* (World Bank Staff Working Paper No. 759, 1986), pp. 45–51. Today this is changing rapidly, of course — not only the Special Economic Zones, but the whole of coastal China is experiencing rapid economic development.

1978) was "making foreign things serve China." After the death of Mao in 1976, central control over overall economic policies has been a good deal less firm, and foreign trade has not been very well disciplined. The 1978-80 period, in particular, has been characterized as the "Great Leap Outward," with import volume rising be about 50 percent in 1978 and 20 percent more in 1979. Beginning in 1978, China experienced three successive years of trade deficits, drawing down its foreign exchange reserves to a dangerously low level.[14] In the mid-1980s the *real* growth of trade was quite rapid, although the dollar amounts of both exports and imports then decreased somewhat — in part due to the lower price for oil and other primary commodity exports, and in part due to the devaluation of the Chinese yuan relative to the U.S. dollar. While most of the mid-1980s also showed a deficit in China's balance of trade, more recently its foreign trade balance has moved into a large surplus position, surprising quite a few experts.

A very interesting point of view on China's foreign trade is provided by looking at it from the perspective of the Japanese, now by far its most important trading partner. Japan managed to expand its trade with China even during the period of extreme Chinese autarky, in the mid-1960s, though such trade declined significantly in the latter half of the 1960s. As Chae-Jin Lee has put it:

> "...The political environment of Sino-Japanese economic relations markedly deteriorated during the Chinese Cultural Revolution. Radical Red Guards paralyzed the Ministries of Foreign Affairs and Foreign Trade in 1967 and purged the key personnel of these and other central bureaucracies. ...the number of Japanese trade personnel in Beijing had dwindled from 100 to 20 by mid-1968. ...Japanese trade negotiators were required to praise the Cultural Revolution, to study the little red book of Chairman Mao's quotations, and to listen to prolonged political lectures delivered by their Chinese counterparts."[15]

A key determinant of China's future development strategy is likely to be the availability of energy resources. One of the main reasons for Japanese and American interest in China during the past decade is the size of its known reserves of oil, natural gas, and coal — though its probable reserves of energy supplies, especially offshore oil, may be an even more important consideration. Some energy experts have suggested that its offshore oil reserves could potentially rival those of Saudi Arabia, while others have been less optimistic. It might also be pointed out that various offshore areas may well involve conflicts with Japan, Korea, Taiwan, and Vietnam, just to name a few of the major potential contenders. While oil and gas are probably the most significant sources of export earnings, it is also true that China's modernization efforts during the next several decades are likely to increase its domestic demand for energy quite considerably. Some

---

[14] For further details, cf. Carl Riskin, *op. cit.*, pp. 316–320. However, it might be noted that China's foreign exchange reserves in the fall of 1996 were second only to those of Japan, and are larger than those of either Taiwan or the U.S..

[15] Chae-Jin Lee, *Japan and China: New Economic Diplomacy* (Hoover Institution Press, 1984), p. 7.

estimates of China's internal energy requirements for the rest of the century have projected a probable quadrupling of the demand for oil, for every doubling of real GNP per capita. However, the search for oil has been rather disappointing to date and China seems to be turning more to coal as well as nuclear power. The future development of China's energy sector is likely to involve both economic and political considerations of some complexity.

While the development of China's energy industry, especially offshore drilling, is going to require considerable foreign investment in deep-sea drilling and recovery, with relatively weak bargaining prospects for China itself, the overall foreign investment posture of China still continues being formulated. As John B. Sheahan has written in a World Bank study, China has a range of options to choose among: (1) the Japanese model, with almost complete exclusion of foreign ownership and control of domestic manufacturing operations; (2) the Korean approach of permitting foreign investment in the past, often by Japanese trading companies, "... while stipulating export requirements for most foreign firms; " and, (3) the Brazilian case of a "wide-open welcome," which probably has greater short-term benefits, but "... involves a high share of foreign influence in the modern industrial sector and may involve retarding effects on domestic entrepreneurship as well." Professor Sheahan suggests that it would probably be a mistake for China to barter its very large internal market for temporary gains brought about by foreign investment and transfer of technology, which would probably have negative longer-run consequences:

> "...For countries in weak bargaining positions, or with indecisive governments, there is always the danger that the foreign firm can exert pressure to distort policy decisions in its favor on such issues as taxation and protection. Another problem which has been common in Brazil and Mexico is that foreign firms may initiate or expand their role by buying control of the best local firms, downgrading domestic entrepreneurs to secondary management levels and reducing the scope for independent growth. China would seem to be relatively safe from such problems: its bargaining power is high, it should not need to give excessive concessions to attract foreign investors, and it should not be subject to takeovers of independent domestic firms. The varied methods already in use to improve access to new technology without direct foreign ownership provide promising options which should serve to minimize difficulties in dealing with foreign investment." [16]

In general, the reform of Chinese industrial policies has proven to be considerably more difficult than the decollectivization of agriculture. Gregory C. Chow has noted four reasons why the rationalization of the farm sector has been much easier to accomplish than industrial reform. First, "true believers" in the Chinese leadership are understandably quite reluctant to "... surrender the control of large state enterprises to

---

[16] John B. Sheahan, *Alternative International Economic Strategies and Their Relevance for China* (Washington D.C.: World Bank Staff Working Paper No. 759, 1986), pp. 67–68.

nongovernment individuals and allow them to keep substantial profits for themselves..." The potential earnings from the sales of large volumes of consumer goods probably greatly exceed those from a hundred or even a thousand chickens or ducks. Second, government bureaucrats in the various ministries and the bureau of material supplies are unwilling to give up their power and vested interests. Third, large industrial enterprises are objectively more dependent on factors outside their control than individual farms — the whole system "... of pricing and distribution of industrial products and material inputs has to be changed to provide more autonomy to the state enterprises." As Chow points out, if enterprises are encouraged to maximize profits and have access to inputs priced below their opportunity costs, while at the same time their output can be restricted to extract monopoly profits, the end result could be quite undesirable. Fourth, Chinese enterprise managers "... often do not have sufficient knowledge and experience to run a modern enterprise as an independent entity." Recognizing these problems, the Chinese leadership has sought to develop further reforms of industrial decision-making, pursuant to the "Third Plenary Session" of the "Twelfth Central Committee of the Chinese Communist Party" (October 20, 1984) — which were to be carried out during the Seventh Five-Year Plan period, 1986 to 1990. The often-quoted slogan of these changes was: "Invigorate the microeconomic units. Control by macroeconomic means."[17]

While that sounds eminently sensible in principle, the Chinese authorities do not have much practical experience in carrying out monetary and macroeconomic policies. Even though Professor Chow himself has been most helpful to the Chinese leadership in training younger economists in "post-Marxian, modern economics" in United States graduate programs (where, unfortunately, presently they learn mostly useless mathematical modeling) as well as by running workshops of a more practical nature in China, monetary policy can probably be characterized as being a bit "out of control" in recent years.

Generally, the Chinese authorities have insisted that the fundamental nature of their planned economy is not being changed — that it will become "socialism with Chinese characters," whatever that may ultimately mean. In an influential article "Planning and the Market" (*Beijing Review*, July 1986), Chen Yun said "...that the planned economy is fundamental and predominant; the market-regulated economy, though supplementary and secondary in nature, is indispensable." (While the plan comes first, I find it difficult to judge which adjective — "predominant" or "indispensable" — is stronger. Perhaps something was lost in the translation ...) The concept of market-determined prices in all areas of economic activity is rather dangerous for Chinese planners to contemplate.

To conclude our discussion of recent economic trends in the People's Republic of China, a couple of paragraphs on the trends in its overall balance-of-payments and the near-term outlook seem to be in order. As mentioned above, China's opening-up to the

---

[17] Cf. Gregory C. Chow, "Development of a More Market-Oriented Economy in China," *Science*, January 16, 1987, pp. 296–297.

rest of the world, especially the market-oriented economies, has been quite impressive. In sharp contrast to the self-sufficient policies followed during the Cultural Revolution decade ending in 1976, the last twenty years have witnessed a significant — though not a very smooth or steady — rise in the overall trade-to-output ratio. However, as in the case of the transition economies in the former CMEA, the demand for imports at times has been tending to outstrip the capacity to earn foreign exchange through exports, tourism, and other invisible earnings. On the import side, the demand for consumer goods has been growing quite rapidly. There are also reports of rapid growth contributing to corruption, as in the case of the "Hainan Island scam," where party cadres used their favored access to foreign exchange to import (tax-free) "... an astonishing 2.86 million color television sets, 252,000 video cassette recorders, 122,000 motorcycles, and 10,000 cars and minibuses, most of which were resold throughout the country at double or triple the original prices. A large part of the population of Hainan Island seems to have been involved in this activity..."[18] In addition to the rising demand for imports of consumer goods — which will undoubtedly be bolstered by returning students and Chinese officials having had overseas travel or assignments in the West — higher levels of foreign investment also imply a greater need for foreign exchange. There was a significant decline in foreign investment right after the Tiananmen Square massacre in 1989, but by 1995 the coastal areas of south China were growing even faster than Taiwan or Hong Kong, mainly on the basis of investments made by businessmen from the latter two areas.

On the export side, during the past several years, earnings have been growing quite rapidly. About a third of export earnings comes from crude oil, mainly shipped to Japan under a long-term trade agreement. At the present time, China faces a double problem on this score — oil prices have been a bit weak, while its export earnings denominated in dollars have been losing ground to the Japanese yen (which has more than doubled in value, from about 260 yen to the dollar a couple of years ago to about 100-110 yen in the fall of 1996). Japan, of course, remains China's most important trading partner, with about a third of all imports coming from Japan, and China has a significant deficit in its trade with Japan. Generally, China usually has experienced a significant surplus in its trade with Hong Kong and Macau, with exports nearly twice the value of imports from those two principalities and currently has a huge surplus with the U.S.. In order to improve its overall balance of payments situation, China has devalued the "renminbi" (the foreign exchange equivalent to the yuan, with the rate controlled by the Bank of China) from Rmb. 2.80 to one U.S. dollar, which had been quite unrealistic and under some "black market" pressure, to Rmb. 3.70 in 1988, and now about 8.3 (mid-1996). The "black market" existed, but was generally not very significant in the past ten years. Most Chinese prices for "tradeables" have not been as far out of line with world prices than those in the FSU — and possibly that penalties for foreign exchange speculation differ (there are still executions for "economic crimes" in China).

---

[18] Carl Riskin, *op. cit.*, pp. 336.

The scope of the Dengian reforms during the past decade has been nothing short of astounding. The decollectivization of agriculture, considerable decentralization and greater emphasis on profitability in industry, as well as a rapid expansion in foreign trade and investment are all very significant developments — and there are even a couple of stock exchanges in operation now. Economic liberalization now co-exists with political repression. That raises the issue, if capitalism is re-established, can democracy (the "fifth modernization") be far behind? To conclude that, I fear, would be much too optimistic by far. To cite the dean of American Sinologists, Harvard historian, John King Fairbank, on this score:

> "...However, before we Americans idealize the PRC, let us keep in mind that it re- mains a party dictatorship. Most of us have difficulty imagining what totalitarian life is really like. Marriage and family, work and play look to the tourist not so dif- ferent from an open society. The difference comes in interpersonal relations, where a hierarchy of authorities gives some people power over others. Your work unit keeps your secret dossier as a massive kind of report card. In your work unit (danwei) or its equivalent, your superiors control your work assignment, housing, rations, education, travel, entertainment, and even marriage and child bearing. Both thought and conduct are under constant scrutiny. Despotism was an old Chi- nese custom. We may feel totalitarianism is trying to become a new Chinese cus- tom. But what if we look back to the way the Chinese family used to dominate its members? Isn't today's all-providing, all-controlling work unit an updated form of the old family system? This raises a disturbing question: how far from outside a foreign culture can one reach large conclusions without jumping to them?[19]

China and Russia

In any course on comparative economic systems being taught in the latter half of the 1990s, an obvious final exam question stares us in the face: "Compare and contrast economic reform efforts in China and Russia in recent years." Where to begin? An obvious starting point seems to be a brief mention of the ethnic issue, which we discussed earlier. The USSR was a "prison of nations," and Moscow dictated the policies of its Comecon neighbors, while China is much more homogeneous. Although it is true that there are significant differences among the major dialects, and Tibet remains very unhappy, there is a unifying influence of Mandarin and thousands of years of the history of the "Middle Kingdom" dutifully learned by students in Beijing, Shanghai, and Hong Kong. With hindsight, we can see how Moscow's effort to create a Russian-speaking "Homo Sovie- ticus" was doomed to fail, while Beijing did not need to work at creating "Chineseness" at all. As we noted above, Gorbachev felt that political liberalization ("glasnost") was a precondition for economic reform ("perestroika") and technical progress. In China, economic progress has been encouraged, but political pluralism has not yet developed

---

[19] John King Fairbank, *The Great Chinese Revolution, 1800–1985* (Harper & Row, 1986), p. 358.

— prison labor camps continue to function, and dissidents are dealt with brutally. The slaughter of the "best and brightest" of China's youth in 1989 has sent a strong signal to the society at large.

One area of significant difference is agriculture — China has decollectivized, while in Russia private ownership of land is moving forward very slowly. While the land in China is still not fully privately-owned, there are 15-year contracts and legal provisions for renting land to others. Land is tilled in "tiny garden-like strips, typically 8-12 plots per household, each a fraction of an acre," and producing, already by the beginning of the 1980s, yields per acre that were well above Asian average yields and not very far behind Japan's (China's 4200 vs. Japan's 5100). As the collectives disintegrated, heretical ideas about efficiency and distribution began to surface in other areas as well. As Mark Selden says:

> "... The countryside was in the forefront of a comprehensive economic and social reform whose dimensions eventually included opening to foreign capital, dramatic growth of foreign and domestic trade, expansion of the private sector, partial lifting of restrictions on population mobility, decentralized control of industry, and price reform. These institutional changes, sustained and deepened over more than a decade in rural China, far exceeded anything that has yet to occur in the Russian countryside." [20]

In Russia, a long list of impediments to private farming can be drawn up — starting with the lack of experience in ever doing so historically. A survey carried out by Goskomtat in 1992 gives the following listing, with the percentage of respondents in parentheses:

(1) High cost of equipment and building materials (80%);

(2) Shortage of material-technical resources, including seeds and fertilizer (66%);

(3) High interest rates on credit (52%);

(4) Uncertainty about long-term land and agrarian laws (46%);

(5) Difficulties in obtaining credit (45%);

(6) Lack of legal protection (42%);

(7) Lack of transport and other utilities-connections (41%);

(8) Local leadership obstacles (23%);

(9) Difficulties in getting land (21%);

---

[20] "Post-Collective Agrarian Alternatives in Russia and China," in Barrett L. McCormick and Jonathan Unger (eds.), *China After Socialism* (M.E. Sharpe, 1996), p. 24

(10) Rural population's negative attitude toward those on private farms (15%); ___

(11) Lack of knowledge (15%); ___

(12) Problems with health and education access, lack of stores, and so on. [21] ___

It is estimated that a mere 8% of the land in Russia was privately owned, and the output of agricultural inputs (fertilizer) and outputs fell. Indeed, there were large declines in "superior foodstuffs," such as milk, eggs, meat, and fish, while there was a small increase in the production of some grains and of potatoes in 1992.

In China, by way of contrast, all physical indicators of material well-being showed significant gains in the 1978-1992 period, as shown in Table 10-1. As can be seen, real per capita consumption increased by more than 150% over this period. While there was an increase in the per capita consumption of grain, from 196 kg to 236 kg in 1992, much larger relative gains were shown by pork, eggs, and fish. Nolan also notes that the incidence of poverty in China fell from 270 million people (28% of the total population) to 98 million (or 8.6% of the total) by 1990, citing a World Bank study. Gains are also being made in other Basic Human Needs indicators (BHN), such as life expectancy, where China is now well ahead of Russia (the latest *World Development Report*, 1996, lists China at 69, and Russia at 65, but the gap for male life expectancy is larger). Thus, in agricultural production and consumption statistics, China is improving, while Russia has experienced negative rates of change (though we should keep in mind that China's GNP per capita stood at $530, and Russia's at $2650 in 1994).

A second area of very substantial contrast has to do with foreign trade and investment. Earlier in this chapter, the "Great Leap Outward" in China was discussed, with its enormous rise in imports, the setting up of Special Economic Zones, and an "opening up" to foreign direct investment. There were, to be sure, elements of risk associated with the rapid growth of such contacts with the outside world — not the least of which was "bourgeois spiritual pollution" of Coca-Cola, rock music, and worse. The growth in appetite for imports at times led to a rapid fall in the foreign exchange reserves and to episodes of large-scale corruption, such as the already-mentioned "Hainan Island Scam." As China moved from being the world's 30th largest trader to the 10th largest, inflationary pressure threatened economic stability from time to time. Indeed, the student demonstrations at Tiananmen Square were protests against corruption, economic injustices and inflation as much as they were a call for greater democracy. While foreign investment flows slowed down for about a year after the massacre of the students, they have accelerated in recent years — and China's foreign exchange reserves, at $88.6 billion in the fall of 1996, are second only to Japan's, at $211 billion (Taiwan has $85 billion, Germany $84 billion, and the U.S., $74 billion, excluding gold). With Hong Kong's $60 billion in reserves, coming under the control of the Bank of China in July 1997, its

---

[21] Peter Nolan, *China's Rise, Russia's Fall* (St. Martin's Press, 1995), p. 272.

Table 10-1: Changes in the material standard of living in China, 1978–92.*

	1978	1992
Index of real per capita consumption	100	252
Consumption per capita of:		
grain (kgs)	196	236
edible oil (kgs)	1.6	6.3
pork (kgs)	7.7	18.2
fresh eggs (kgs)	2.0	7.8
sugar (kgs)	3.4	5.4
aquatic products (kgs)	3.5	7.3
cloth (metres)	8.0	10.7
Ownership of consumer durables (no./100 people)		
washing machines	-	10.0
refrigerators	-	3.4
tape recorders	0.2	12.2
cameras	0.5	2.3
TVs	0.3	19.5
sewing machine	3.5	12.8
bicycles	7.7	38.5
radios	7.8	18.4
watches	8.5	51.6 (1990)
Retail outlets and food and drink establishments (per 10,000 people):		
establishments	12	101
personnel	57	249
Health provision (no. per 10,000 people)		
hospital beds	19.3	23.4
physicians	10.7	15.4
Housing space per capita (sq. m.)		
cities	3.6	7.5
villages	8.1	20.8

*Peter Nolan, *op. cit.,* p. 13.

position will be even stronger. Investment inflows appear to be continuing, even accelerating. To quote Barrett L. McCormick,

> *"...Arguably China's single most important step toward prosperity has been to join the international Asia Pacific economy. While the East European states have had to adjust to the collapse of their formerly most important markets in the Soviet Union and to cope with a European recession, China has been able to exploit cultural affinities...and geographic proximity to the world's fastest growing regional economy."* [22]

China's inflation rate, which had at times exceeded 20% per year, has been brought down to only 8% (in August 1996, compared to a year earlier) versus 37% in Russia. In many ways, the bottom line on foreign dealings is the exchange rate — over the past year, the exchange rate for the Chinese yuan has been stable, at 8.3 to one U.S. dollar, while the Russian ruble has fallen from around 4500 to about 5400 to the dollar over the same period. Over a longer period, the picture favors China even more — the yuan was around four to one in 1991, when the dollar was equal to about 100 rubles.

A third area for our question covers macroeconomics — monetary and fiscal policy. As the exchange rate numbers just cited strongly suggest, China has been much more successful in bringing inflation under control than Russia. Without going into a lot of statistical detail, both central governments have been facing an eroding revenue base. The fastest-growing provinces in China, notably Guangdong, have been quite reluctant to collect taxes to remit them to Beijing. Many of the enterprises under the control of the central government have generated demands for subsidies from the budget rather than tax revenues. The most rapidly growing category of industrial firms has been the "township and village enterprises," which divide their profits along partnership lines, and probably avoid taxes entirely. Tax avoidance has also become an "art form" in Russia, where there has been a massive redistribution of income in favor of the top decile or so, and away from the bottom deciles of the income distribution. In both countries, the financial system is evolving slowly — with considerable problems in the collection systems, the growth in moral hazard, and the proliferation of bad debts. Russia's system has been more inflation-prone to date, but private banks have started to operate more significantly. The scope for private finance in China has been more limited, despite the opening of a couple of stock exchanges.

A number of development experts have posed an interesting question — is China's relatively better performance due to its willingness to ignore the advice of the IMF and other donor agencies? Did the "Big Bang" approach of Jeff Sachs and other Western advisers damage Russia and the other former Comecon member countries permanently and unnecessarily? Is the "Washington orthodoxy" of balanced budgets, low money growth, realistic exchange rates, privatization, and a movement to world market prices

---

[22] "Concluding Thoughts," in Barrett L. McCormick and Jonathan Unger (eds.), *op. cit.,* p. 207

the wrong medicine for the transition countries? As White and Bowles have argued, the World Bank and the IMF have both been arguing that:

> *"...the thrust of financial reform in developing countries should be to restrict the role of government as an active promoter of development and promote its role as the regulator of a market-led development process supported by a market-based financial system. This involves supporting competition within the financial system between banks and other financial institutions, the privatization of financial institutions and the encouragement of money and capital markets, especially equity markets."* [23]

The Other China(s)

To conclude this chapter on "China: One Nation, Two Systems," a few remarks seems to be in order about the economic success of those Chinese lucky enough to have escaped the totalitarian experiments of Chairman Mao. In particular, there is the enormous contrast between the standard of living on the Chinese mainland and Taiwan, but Hong Kong, Singapore, and some "Overseas Chinese" communities elsewhere in Asia come into the picture as well. Since we will be discussing a number of these countries in further detail in Chapter 13, let us focus our attention specifically on Taiwan and Hong Kong, since both of these Chinese entities can be compared to the mainland most directly — and since both face at least a theoretical prospect of political reunification at some future date. As Hofheinz and Calder put it:

> *"...Taiwan and Hong Kong are part of the larger political sphere of the People's Republic of China, whether they like it or not. Hong Kong is regarded by China as a part of Guangdong Province presently under British administration. The question is not whether China will take over the colony but when. The treaty which leased a large part of Hong Kong — the New Territories — to the British crown expires in 1997, a date which some regard as the doomsday for foreign enterprise. ...(However) that China does not intend to dismantle and destroy foreign investment in Hong Kong as it did in Shanghai after 1949 is suggested by the growing Communist official presence — in personnel and investment alike — in the colony. Were China's intention to plunder the colony in 1997, it would hardly be prudent to build expensive factories and high-rise buildings now, as China is doing."* [24]

While China's GNP per capita in 1994 is officially estimated by the World Bank at about $530, Taiwan's level is about twenty-five times that figure (although it has been kicked out of the World Bank, but not out of the Asian Development Bank — which

---

[23] "The Political Economy of Late Development in East Asia," in *ibid.*, p. 153.

[24] Roy Hofheinz, Jr., and Kent E. Calder, *The Eastasia Edge* (Basic Books, Inc., 1982), p. 225. Of course, the basic law formulated by the U.K.-China agreement provides for a continuation of capitalism for a fifty-year period.

continues to provide comparable statistics) and that of Hong Kong is currently more than forty times higher in per capita income terms than on the mainland. In general, even though Hong Kong's economic success might conceivably be explained in terms of British influence, foreign capital, and imported technology — though, in fact, the linkage to Great Britain is by no means the most important point of the Hong Kong story (Hong Kong's GNP per capita is about $3000 higher than in the UK!) — Taiwan's reliance on foreign investment has been quite modest. The case study of Taiwan, in particular, demonstrates the potential for success that exists in many less developed countries today, which could be translated into actual progress rather quickly and successfully, if only... (feel free to fill in the remainder of the sentence). To be sure, in some respects, Taiwan is a special case, responding to a clear danger from "an enemy," — as I put it in my book with Michael T. Skully:

> "...the enemy had succeeded in nearly obliterating it (Taiwan) from the diplomatic map of the world. The enemy country, mainland China, is also the ancestral homeland of most of Taiwan's ruling elite. Though one should resist the temptation to indulge in psychological musings about mother-son relationships here, one can still imagine the best-seller prospects on an Oedipal play. In this play the gifted and dutiful son (the Chinese nationalists) is thrown out into the street by a beautiful young mother, temporarily insane because of drugs administered by an evil witch (Marxism). The son then makes his way in the world to become a great prince and hero, eventually to return to save her, and live happily ever after at the end of the tale. For the actors in such a play, economic success becomes a patriotic duty, and anything less than superhuman effort is to be regarded as a failure." [25]

While it is beyond our scope here to provide a complete answer to the question of whether Taiwan's success story is a unique tale, and to what extent it could reasonably be replicated elsewhere, a few of the most important factors in the recent history of Taiwan need to be mentioned.

When the Kuo-min-tang (KMT) reconstituted the nationalist government of the Republic of China at Taipei in December 1949, they found themselves in control of a large, fertile island farmed by a rather docile population, which had been under Japanese rule since 1895. Virtually all of the Japanese, numbering nearly half a million people, were repatriated after the war, leaving behind a relatively well-developed infrastructure, but few concentrations of local political or economic power. As Thomas Gold has put it:

> "... the KMT began, in effect, as a colonial power occupying and restructuring a conquered and leaderless society. Comprising little more than a bureaucracy and army, the KMT had no social base on Taiwan with demands to constrain its actions. Taiwan was also devoid of foreign economic interests that might have

---

[25] Michael T. Skully and George J. Viksnins, *Financing East Asia's Success* (Macmillan in association with the American Enterprise Institute for Public Policy Research, 1987), pp. 97–98.

hindered the KMT's efforts at control. The mainlander regime confiscated industrial and financial assets, carried out a land reform, and remolded social groups from an unassailable position of strength virtually without parallel in the Third World." [26]

In the early 1950s, along with virtually all other developing countries, Taiwan experimented with import-substitution policies and a multiple exchange rate system. The export earnings derived from sugar, rice, and salt were converted into local currency at a lower-than-average rate, while domestic textile producers benefited from a dramatic increase in tariff protection. Still, even during this period, the overall wage share rose somewhat and the structure of production emphasized relatively labor-intensive industries. Also, partly as a result of pressure from the U.S. aid mission (which declared Taiwan a success, and left in the early 1960's), land reform and education received serious attention early in the development process. The percentage of students continuing on to junior high school rose from 32% in 1951 to more than 50% in 1961 and 80% in 1971. As Shirley W.Y. Kuo, Gustav Ranis, and John C.H. Fei have pointed out:

"... The labor-intensive bias of manufacturing, the good distribution of industrial assets, the pattern of growth and spatial dispersion of the more labor-intensive industries, the relatively mild price distortions — all these factors served to improve the overall distribution of nonagricultural income or at least to prevent its worsening. This performance, together with the rapidly improving rural income distribution, paved the way for the substantial decline observed in overall income inequality during the 1950s." [27]

During the 1960's, economic policies in Taiwan shifted toward more outward-looking export-oriented growth as well as financial reform. The multiple exchange rate system, with its customary tendency to discriminate against agricultural exports, was replaced by a unified exchange rate regime, pegging the N.T. (New Taiwan) dollar to the U.S. currency at the rate of N.T. $40 to U.S. $1. The exchange rate subsequently remained quite stable at around that level for more than twenty years. In the latter half of the 1980's, when the U.S. dollar depreciated sharply relative to the Japanese yen, the N.T. dollar was also allowed to appreciate (to about 28 N.T. to one U.S. dollar), but by a good deal less than the yen. Another key aspect of the liberalization of economic policies in the early 1960s involved interest rate reform — while interest rates have at times been temporarily below the inflation rate, the real rate of return on bank deposits averaged nearly ten percent during the decade of the 1960s. The ratio of the narrowly-defined money (M1, which includes currency and have checking accounts) rose from about 14

---

[26] Thomas Gold, *State and Society in the Taiwan Miracle* (M.E. Sharpe, 1985). p. 123.

[27] Shirley W.Y. Kuo, Gustav Ranis, and John C.H. Fei, *The Taiwan Success Story: Rapid Growth with Improved Distribution in the Republic of China, 1952–1979* (Westview Press, 1981), p. 71. See also the articles by John C.H. Fei and Li-li Chang and Tzong-shian Yu in Chung-Hua Institution for Economic Research, *Conference on Inflation in East Asian Countries*, May 20–22, 1983.

percent of GNP in the early 1960's to more than 20 percent in 1980; the broader definition of the money stock (M2, which also includes savings accounts and time deposits), which is probably a better indicator of overall confidence in the monetary system of a country, expanded from 30% in 1980 and to more than 100% today. Over this same period, net private national saving roughly doubled.[28]

Since the early 1960s, Taiwan's overall economic performance has been remarkable. Probably the most obvious driving force behind Taiwan's growth, averaging nearly ten percent per year during the 1960-85 period, is the expansion of the export sector. Indeed, much has been written about the "export-led growth" of the Asian NIC's (Newly Industrialized Countries) generally as well as about Taiwan specifically. Along with South Korea and the two Chinese city-states of Hong Kong and Singapore, Taiwan emerged as an important exporting entity already by the early 1970s. Despite generally prevalent "trade pessimism" among LDC's during that period, Taiwan diversified its agricultural exports (emphasizing some rather unusual products, such as mushrooms and asparagus), but moved into manufactured exports even more decisively. This trend was accelerated somewhat by Japanese direct investment in its former colony, where the language barrier was less of a problem, but investments made by "overseas Chinese" from other countries, including the United States, have also made a significant contribution. Still, foreign direct investment in Taiwan has been vastly less important than domestic resource mobilization. A large part of total investment is financed by the government institutions, such as the banks, with foreign funds generally accounting for less than ten percent of total investment. In recent years, foreign investment is relatively even less important, and Taiwan has become a very significant capital exporter on a net basis, with foreign exchange reserves of more than $80 billion (third in the world, after Japan and the PRC in 1996).

It is quite true that American economic and military aid played an important role in Taiwan's early development efforts — for example, by helping to design and finance the port complex at Kao-hsuing, the world's first "export-processing zone." But it would be a serious mistake to overestimate its importance; as Hofheinz and Calder point out:

"... this does not mean that American aid was indispensable, or that Taiwan was incapable of developing on its own. American assistance was used largely to off-set the enormous military expenditures required to defend the island against the Communist Chinese. Certainly after the termination of aid in 1964 the picture suggests a vital native economy, able to repay international loans and build up current account surpluses. The share of domestic savings in gross capital formation rose from 65 percent in 1961 to 96 percent in 1969, with foreign capital accounting for only 5 percent. Indeed, Taiwan was the first U.S. aid recipient in the non-Western world to become self-sufficient enough to 'graduate'. Within ten years it was dispensing aid of its own." [29]

---

[28] See Michael T. Skully and George J. Viksnins, *op. cit.,* p. 116. It can also be noted that the number of commercial bank branches increased three-fold from 1960 to 1980.

[29] Roy Hofheinz, Jr., and Kent E. Calder, *The Eastasia Edge, op., cit.,* p. 124.

The capacity of Taiwan to generate domestic saving has been even more impressive than that of Japan, and may be as important (or even more so!) as export-led growth in explaining its very admirable economic accomplishments. *Domestic saving*

It is quite important to point out that most Asian countries have corrected their tendencies toward "urban bias" in government policies a bit earlier and with a good deal more determination than other nations in the developing Third World. In Taiwan, land reform was carefully designed and carried out with the assistance of American aid authorities, putting a rather modest limit on the size of individual land holdings and land rents. An important role in agricultural modernization was played by the Joint Commission on Rural Reconstruction, established by the U.S. Congress in 1948 — to allocate aid and provide technical assistance.

In general, the improvements in agricultural productivity were taxed rather lightly, so as not to destroy incentives, and the proceeds invested in labor-intensive and export-orientated industries. Initially, most industrial projects involved agricultural processing and the use of local raw materials. One of the chief lessons from Taiwan's development experience is its maintenance of a reasonably balanced relationship between agriculture and industry — this point has been aptly summarized by Hla Myint:
balanced development

> "... the savings extracted from the agricultural sector can be used either wastefully in supporting import substitution policies or productively in promoting efficient export industries. ... In this connection it is well recognized that some developing countries with abundant natural resources can afford to prolong their inefficient import-substitution policies because they are cushioned by the rent from the natural resources. For the purpose of subsidizing inefficient industries, gains from improvements in agricultural productivity are no different from rent from abundant land. The cynic may also go to say that one reason why the city states of Hong Kong and Singapore have been so successful is that, having no agricultural sectors to batten upon, they were obliged to choose efficient types of manufacturing industries right from the start!"* [30]

Conclusion

The economic accomplishments of Taiwan, Hong Kong, and other Chinese communities outside the mainland are well known all over the world. As restrictions on the flow of information have also been eased in China itself, these facts have also become recognized there as well. Foreign travel undertaken by Chinese officials and study overseas by tens of thousands of students has injected personal testimony by these people into a closed society to an unprecedented extent during the past decade. Market-oriented reforms, especially in agriculture, have led to great improvements in

---

[30] Hla Miyant, "Comparative Analysis of Taiwan's Economic Development with Other Countries," in Kwo-ting Li and Tzong-shian Yu (eds.), *Experiences and lessons of Economic Development in Taiwan* (Academia Sinica, 1982), p. 68. Also cited in Skully and Viksnins, *op. cit.,* p. 100.

productivity. Today, it is possible to assert that there has been a general decollectivization of China's agriculture. Shortages and the ever-present threat of another famine have been replaced by surpluses, sometimes so large that the government has encountered serious problems of finding enough storage capacity. Instead of thinking about a radio, a bicycle, and a sewing machine as the three basic consumer goods to be purchased eventually, most Chinese are probably thinking about a TV, a refrigerator, and even a car today — their relatives and friends elsewhere all have them, after all. While the government of Taiwan has been reluctant to endorse economic contacts, its policy of the "Three No's" (no negotiation, no compromise, and no contact) may well change in the near future. Lee Teng-hui, the current leader in Taiwan, was born there, and has been much more flexible in permitting travel (both ways?) and normalizing trade relations (estimated at more than $5 billion per year even now, mostly through Hong Kong). It certainly seems obvious that the virus of economic rationality is likely to spread quite rapidly on the mainland, especially in the coastal areas being set up as Special Economic Zones (e.g., Shenzhen, next to Hong Kong) — which will also inevitably lead to pressures for political freedom and overall modernization. As the Chinese nation moves toward a unified economic system in the near future, there is little doubt that capitalistic ideas and practices will tend to be dominant.

This point has also been discussed at some length by Harry Harding, who links the success of the economic reforms carried out during Deng's "Second Revolution" to the prospects for eventual reunification quite explicitly:

> "...If the present reforms are sustained, and particularly if the radical reforms dis-
> cussed since 1986 are adopted, the differences in economic system, social struc-
> ture, and even political institutions between Hong Kong and Taiwan, on the one
> hand, and the rest of China, on the other, should be narrowed, although not elimi-
> nated. The standard of living and the style of life in certain parts of China, par-
> ticularly Shanghai and the southern coast, should increasingly come to resemble
> those in Hong Kong and Taiwan. Under such circumstances, the citizens of Tai-
> wan and Hong Kong would find greater appeal in extensive economic and cul-
> tural interaction with the mainland. And future generations of leaders in Peking
> would become even more flexible in their treatment of Taiwan and Hong Kong —
> more accommodating toward the former and less interventionist toward the lat-
> ter. Together, all these developments would make the concept of 'one country,
> two systems' more feasible, credible, and workable and would therefore increase
> the possibilities for a creative resolution of the Taiwan question at some point in
> the next century." [31]

Still, we need to end this brief overview of China on a cautionary note — Deng Xiaoping will not live forever, and the second revolution has been largely his doing. The sudden and striking dismissal of Hu Yaobang, the man Deng appeared to be grooming

---

[31] Harry Harding, *China's Second Revolution: Reform After Mao* (The Brookings Institution, 1987), p. 263..

as his most important successor, in January 1987 sent a strong signal to all those thinking about pushing for even more radical reform. The Communist Party may be ready for more individual initiative in agriculture and retail trade, a few discos and some foreign investment, but student demonstrations and open challenges to Marxism were not to be tolerated. If I were a Chinese graduate student returning to a job with the Bank of China, I am not at all sure whether I would bring back many books by Milton Friedman for my bookshelf. For the longer run, a resumption of economic progress is sure to lead to pressures for privatization and political reforms as well. The contrast of the former USSR and the PRC is a most interesting one — there have been tremendous political changes in the former, but the economy is disintegrating. In China, human rights do not mean much, but inflation has been brought under control and exports are growing rapidly. Chinese agriculture has been decollectivized, but not so in the Soviet Union. U.S. trade with China is at least ten times larger than with the USSR, and the difference in foreign investment is the same order of magnitude. ∎

SUGGESTED READINGS

Cheng, Nien, *Life and Death in Shanghai* (Grove Press, 1987).

Chen, Feng, *Economic Transition and Political Legitimacy in Post-Mao China: Ideology and Reform* (State University of New York Press, 1995).

Chow, Gregory C., *The Chinese Economy* (Harper & Row, 1985).

Eckstein, Alexander, *China's Economic Revolution* (Cambridge University Press, 1977).

Fairbank, John King, *The Great Chinese Revolution, 1800-1895* (Harper & Row, 1985).

Gao, Shangquan, *China's Economic Reform* (Macmillan, 1996).

Griffin, Keith (ed.), *Institutional Reform and Economic Development in the Chinese Countryside* (Macmillan, 1985).

Lardy, Nicholas P., *China in the World Economy* (Institute for International Economics, 1994).

Lyons, Thomas P., *Economic Integration and Planning in Maoist China* (Columbia University Press, 1987).

McCormick, Barrett L., and Jonathan Unger (eds.), *China After Socialism: In the Footsteps of Eastern Europe or East Asia?* (M.E. Sharpe, 1996).

Naughton, Barry, *Growing Out of the Plan* (Cambridge University Press, 1994).

Nolan, Peter, *China's Rise, Russia's Fall: Politics, Economics, and Planning in the Transition from Stalinism* (St. Martin's Press, 1995).

Perry, Elizabeth J., and Christine Wong, *The Political Economy of Reform in Post-Mao China* (Harvard University Press, 1985).

Rawski, Thomas G., and Lillian M. Li (eds.), *Chinese History in Economic Perspective* (University of California Press, 1992).

Riskin, Carl, *China's Political Economy: The Quest for Development Since 1949* (Oxford University Press, 1987).

Shaw, Yu-ming (ed.), *Mainland China: Politics, Economics, and Reform* (Westview Press, 1986).

Sheahan, John B., *Alternative International Economic Strategies and Their Relevance for China* (The World Bank, Staff Working Paper No. 759, 1986).

White, Gordon, and Paul Bowles, *The Political Economy of China's Financial Reforms: Finance in Late Development* (Westview Press, 1993).

Wong, Kwan-yiu and David K.Y. Chu (eds.), *Modernization in China: The Case of the Shenzhen Special Economic Zone* (Oxford University Press, 1985).

CHAPTER ELEVEN

JAPAN: CAN IT SERVE AS A MODEL?

*L*et us begin with a very brief overview of Japanese history, beginning in the period around 1900. You will recall our earlier mention of the so-called "Moulder Thesis," which argued that China and Japan were essentially very similar societies around the turn of the century — and that China's backwardness until the Communist take-over was primarily due to foreign exploitation during the 19th century. In particular, most of this claim was supported by a table of mid-19th century statistics showing that British trade with China exceeded its trade with Japan. While one would certainly expect two relatively resource-poor island countries, such as England and Japan, to trade more with a large continental entity (China) than with each other, let us compare and contrast China and Japan briefly in terms of the "traditional society" model. Without going into a lot of detail, in the latter half of the 19th century, Japan moved very quickly to limit population growth, improve health and education, establish a unified nation-state, and to understand and adapt Western science and technology, while China did not.

Before the opening-up of Japan by Commodore Perry in 1853, it was very much a closed feudal society. Quite a few readers will probably be familiar with James Clavell's novel, *Shogun*, either in book or TV movie form, which portrays the Tokugawa Shogunate in the 17th century (Tokugawa is the family name — the "shogun" was the chief of all the nobles, called the "daimyo"). Earlier contacts with the West had not gone well, apparently especially with the Jesuits (as shown in Clavell's novel), and by the early half of the 19th century, Japan was leading a consciously and deliberately isolated existence. Shipbuilders were not permitted to build vessels of ocean-going size, the export of various commodities (such as rice, silk, and copper) was prohibited, and trade with Europeans was kept to an absolute minimum. The Dutch were permitted to operate a strange little factory at Deshima, and to make an annual pilgrimage to the shogun's court in Yedo (Edo), where they were obliged "...to dance, jump, pretend to be drunk, and perform other antics supposed to be illustrative of European life." In the early part of the 17th century, Christianity was vigorously suppressed — in some areas, the practice of "Efumi," the trampling of the pictures of Christ or the Virgin and Child, was continued in the first month of each year until the middle of the 19th century. The isolation of Japan from the rest of the world during the period of the Tokugawa Shogunate is best summarized by the relative prices of gold and silver. In Japan, the ratio was at about five ounces of silver to one of gold, while in the rest of the world at this time, it was approximately fifteen-to-one. Right after Japan's opening, it was immensely profitable to sail in a ship loaded with silver, buy gold, and make a three-fold profit by buying silver in the cities on the coast of China, and then repeat the voyage.

Domestically, Japan's economic and commercial development had been greatly affected by nearly three centuries of the practice of *sankin kotai*, the clever system of double residence set up by the Shogun to keep the other feudal nobles (the *daimyo*) under control. These nobles, numbering nearly three hundred and each with a hereditary claim to a particular part of the country, kept their households at the imperial capital, sort of as hostages, and were expected to reside there themselves in alternate years. This system led to the development of a relatively well-established infrastructure and some very early capitalistic institutions in Japan. The requirement to transport retinues of relatives and retainers (including personal armies of *samurai*) led to the development of relatively sophisticated system of transportation and communications linkages throughout much of Japan. The reliance of a rather sizable class of nobles and professional warriors on their landed estates (*han*) was possible only if a significant surplus was being generated by agriculture, which required the development of a system of irrigation and other improvements in productivity. A rather well-developed system of cash as well as futures markets for agricultural products developed as a result, along with some banking and financial institutions. Literacy rose steadily, approaching the levels of Western Europe, and it is estimated that Edo, later Tokyo, was the largest city in the world around 1900, with a population of more than a million people. After Japan's opening-up to the West, science and technology quite quickly became *the* ruling religion of its populace, however, with Shintoist and Buddhist ideas remaining in the background. Rapid urbanization contributed greatly to a permanent decline in the birth rate (assisted by female infanticide, so it is said).

Monetary and fiscal policy practices in Japan greatly assisted the modernization process in the second half of the nineteenth century. The Meiji Restoration (in 1869) put the teen-aged emperor officially in command of the central government with the Shogun becoming just one of the nobles (soon to lose power anyway) — in order to contend with Western influences. The central government soon abolished dress restrictions and export prohibitions, and removed the power of the *daimyo* to tax commercial travelers passing through their lands (this move was the equivalent of the German "Zollverein," or customs union, which was an important step in the formation of a unified Germany). The state also began to play an important role in the economic life of the nation. As the central government grew in importance, the *daimyo* and the *samurai* were granted government pensions, which were soon turned into government bonds. These lost purchasing power due to inflation quite quickly — and the status and power of these old ruling strata diminished accordingly. As Maddison says, "the large scope of Japanese government activity and the heavy fiscal burden of supporting it were perhaps due to some degree simply to the need to find an outlet for the vast class of samurai." A very important aspect of Japan's modernization around the turn of the century was the careful attention paid to the educational system, which is probably even more significant than the emphasis on export-led growth associated with the so-called "East Asian Model." To cite Maddison:

> "...Japan redesigned its educational system to produce modern skills... The Ministry of Education was established in 1871 and the school system law was passed in 1872. The education system was standardized throughout Japan, and in 1886 four years of schooling were made compulsory, and in 1907 this was extended to six years. In 1868, school enrollments...were about 10 per cent of children aged 5 to 19. By the end of the Meiji period almost two-thirds of children in this age group were getting elementary schooling, and a fifth went to secondary schools...mass education was effective in producing literacy in the pupils who received education, and this helped considerably in diffusing new techniques, particularly in agriculture. Vocational schooling was stressed and modern university faculties were established as well as agricultural colleges." [1]

It is interesting to note that the literacy rate for many Third World countries in 1980 was only slightly above 50%, a level which Japan reached around the turn of the century. Japan's primary school enrollment rate rose from less than one-third of the eligible population to approximately 100% by 1911. As Nafziger has pointed out:

> "...Starting with a common language, the Meiji government developed a relatively uniform primary education that fostered national unity as well as speeding up acquiring Western ideas and technologies. ...(However,) while the Meiji Japanese experience reinforces studies indicating a high rate of return to LDC investment in primary, science, and vocational education, it provides no model for countries using the educational system to promote democracy, human rights, and female equality." [2]

It can also be pointed out that the development of a modern financial structure is another key element of the Japanese model often ignored by those exclusively stressing Japan's export-led growth policies. By 1872 (along with educational reforms, and just a few years after the Meiji Restoration), the Japanese government adopted a national banking law along the lines of the legislation passed in the U.S. at the end of our Civil War, which gave banks chartered by the central government a monopoly power in note issue. In the period between 1876 and 1880, more than a hundred new commercial banks were created, often by daimyo and samurai groups using their government compensation bonds as initial capital. By 1882, after inflation had been brought under control, the Bank of Japan was established as a central bank — more than three decades before the United States established the Federal Reserve System. Several other financial

---

[1] Angus Maddison, *Economic Growth in Japan and the USSR* (W.W. Norton & Company, 1969), p. 16.

[2] E. Wayne Nafziger, "The Japanese Development Model," in Howard F. Didsbury, Jr. (ed.), *The Global Economy: Today, Tomorrow, and the Transition* (The World Future Society, 1985), p. 116.

institutions were set up by 1900, with specific economic development responsibilities. In particular, the Industrial Development Bank of Japan (*Nippon Kogyo Ginko*) deserves mention, since it represents the central government's commitment to guiding the country's industrial development. It quickly established branch offices in Japan's 46 prefectures (roughly the same as our state capitals), and began to serve as a conduit for economic and commercial intelligence on behalf of the government. This is in rather sharp contrast to our economic history — in the United States, the Federal Reserve was established as a rather passive "lender of last resort," and any suggestions that the twelve district banks play an active development role would have probably been viewed as "creeping socialism" by politicians in the beginning decades of this century. (As a slight tangent on this score, it is interesting to compare and contrast the different roles played by the market and the central government in reducing regional disparities in incomes, living standards, and economic conditions in Japan and the U.S. While the government has been active in this respect in both countries, in the U.S., government spending in the 1920's, for example, was less than 5% of GNP, while in Japan it was close to 20%).

The latter part of the 19th century was a period of remarkable financial development and monetization in Japan, as the number of commercial banks rose from only four institutions in 1872 to over 2000 by the turn of the century. Initially, banks were quite heavily reliant on government credit (about half of total financial resources in the mid-1870's), but quickly because self-sufficient (by 1900, such public sector support was only about one-tenth of total resources). As Teranishi says:

> "...Meiji banking is a story of the creation of a self-sustaining banking system through manipulation of government credit. A more important factor in the development of deposit banking, however, was the growth of the corporate business sector and the development of a close relationship between banks and businesses... The financial intermediation role of banking became substantial only after 1895, when the larger part of bank liabilities had become private deposits."[3]

A key point to recognize is that the Japanese government moved decisively to establish its control over money and credit, joining the international gold standard system by the end of the 19th century, and gaining access to the London money market. As an example, the Yokohama Specie Bank quickly established itself as the most important foreign exchange dealer, edging out the Hong Kong and Shanghai Bank, which had played an important role in that regard after Japan's opening. By way of contrast, a generally acceptable monetary unit in China was never established (*viz*, the Mexican "trade dollar")

---

[3] Juro Teranishi, "Government Credit to the Banking Systems: Rural Banks in 19th century Japan and the Postwar Philippines," in Kazushi Ohkawa and Gustav Ranis (eds.), *Japan and the Developing Countries: A Comparative Analysis* (Basil Blackwell, 1985), p. 306. See also Hugh Patrick, "Japanese Financial Development in Historical Perspective, 1868–1980," in Gustav Ranis *et al*, *Comparative Development Perspectives* (Westwood, 1984).

and banking system remained largely in the hands of foreign institutions until the Communist take-over in 1949.

The Japanese government quickly moved to establish itself as a positive economic development force in a number of other areas as well. Around 1900 central government expenditures amounted to about 10% of GNP, and about 40% of capital formation at that time was financed by the public sector. The transportation and communications infrastructure was modernized quite rapidly after the Meiji Restoration — as G.C. Allen has pointed out:

> "...In 1871 a postal and telegraph system was introduced, and six years later Japan joined the Postal Union. In 1869 a steamship line between Osaka and Tokyo was formed, and shortly afterwards the first railway was built — it connected Tokyo and Yokohama — on the proceeds of a Government loan raised in England. What is more, the State took the initiative in establishing a large number of manufacturing establishments equipped with Western machinery for producing new products or goods hitherto manufactured by traditional methods.

> ...(For example,) from 1858 onwards exports of raw silk had grown rapidly, but even so the development of this trade was handicapped by the lack of suitable equipment. For instance, the Japanese type of reeling machine, driven by manual or water power, was incapable of producing the standardized qualities of silk demanded abroad. So, in 1870 the Government established at Maebashi and Tomioka factories on French and Italian models. Other model factories built during the seventies with the object of encouraging the importation of Western technique, were the Shirakawa White Tile Works, the Fukugawa Cement Works, the Senji Woollen Web Factory, and a sodium sulphate and bleaching powder works. Certain factories were established for the specific purpose of stimulating the development of particular localities; for instance, the Development Commission of Hokkaido set up at Sapporo a brewery and a sugar factory." [4]

Japan's government supported both foreign technicians as advisors to ministries and enterprises as well as a system of extensive study overseas for promising Japanese youths. Japan also quickly developed a modern merchant marine; by 1919 about 80% of its trade was carried by Japanese ships (the role of Mitsubishi was quite important in this connection).

In general, Japan's foreign trade growth after its "opening-up" to the West, and the Meiji reforms, was quite spectacular. Export growth averaging more than 8 percent per year was attained during the 1880-1913 period, compared to about 5 percent for Thailand, about 4 percent for Indonesia and Malaya, and about 3 percent per year for the United States and the United Kingdom. (It is interesting to note that this period is usually greatly praised in American high school history texts as one of export-led growth,

---

[4] G.C. Allen, *A Short Economic History of Modern Japan* (Macmillan, 1981), p. 35.

when the U.S. became an international creditor country.) The main reasons cited by Maddison for this favorable economic performance included:

(1) the government's commitment to economic growth and technological modernization, as well as the willingness to use "drastic" fiscal policy and monetary measures. In general, the paternalistic role played by the Japanese government was seldom second-guessed by its populace, which might be due, in part, to the "Confucian ethic."

(2) the opening of a previously closed country to the benefits of international trade and transfers of technology led to the development of various economies of specialization. For example, the textile industry expanded rapidly, accounting for about a quarter of the industrial labor force by 1930, and the average plant grew larger and more integrated. The development of large firms in Japan at this time was blocked neither by anti-trust laws nor strong labor unions.

(3) the Japanese population demonstrated great discipline and loyalty as workers, on the one hand, and a tremendous capacity to abstain from consumption as individual spending units, on the other. It is tempting to speculate that these traits derive partly from a "Samurai Ethic" of sorts — as the military caste became integrated into government service and the business sector, some of their qualities of self-sacrifice and unquestioning deference to command and authority probably carried over, and may have infected other workers as well. The Japanese financial system was able to mobilize funds for investment projects quite effectively in the pre-war era, and this has certainly continued in more recent times.

The Recovery and Reconstruction Period

After World War II, few countries faced bleaker economic prospects than Japan. Japan had been at war more or less continuously during the 1931-45 period — thus, much of her industry and infrastructure had been geared to the needs of the military. During the last days of the war, Japan's cities suffered extensive damage from the bombing — it is estimated that about a quarter of all buildings and structures was destroyed. Much of Japan's trade before the war had been with China, now being taken over by Communists. Also, Japan's former colonies, Korea and Formosa, were not in any position to do much trading in the late 1940's. Furthermore, much of Japan's merchant marine had been sunk. The occupation authorities carried out a purge of more than 200,000 former leaders of the establishment in the period after the war — the purge list included all persons who had held commissioned rank in the army and the navy since 1930, members of ultranationalist organizations, and all high government officials who had remained in office under the militarists. The purge list eventually also included those holding positions of responsibility during the war period in major industrial, commercial and financial corporations. Those on the list were barred from political positions, and were also forced to resign from the corporations with which they had been associated. The Supreme Commander of the Allied Powers (S.C.A.P.), General Douglas MacArthur, was also committed to breaking up the "zaibatsu," the family-owned large-scale conglomerates, and distributing their shares to others as part of a general "decentralization program." While the ambitious goals of this program of eliminating oligopoly power were never fully met, since corporate names such as Mitsubishi, Mitsui, and Sumitomo seem to be very much around today still, the threat of their disbanding slowed Japan's recovery considerably. As Maddison has pointed out:

> *"...The dismemberment of Japan's powerful trading organizations by the occupation authorities struck a heavy blow at her commercial efficiency, as Japanese manufacturers had relied almost exclusively on these firms for foreign sales. Restrictive trade and payments policies by European countries hindered Japanese exports in the early post-war years and she was not admitted to G.A.T.T. until 1955. In the immediate post-war period Japan had to assimilate 5 million returned soldiers and expatriates from the old colonies."* [5]

Finally, the Allied powers expected Japan to make reparations payments to China and several countries in Southeast Asia for war damages, even if this involved the wholesale dismantling of industrial plants in some instances.

In general, it appeared that the "six small islands, poor in natural resources, but housing a large population" — as the Japanese often describe their country in trade negotiations — would have a difficult time in feeding and clothing themselves, to say nothing of exports or reparation payments. In the latter part of the S.C.A.P. rule, many influential American economists were espousing a system of comprehensive national planning as the only way to deal with the crippling shortage of foreign exchange and to allocate scarce resources to priority sectors. It was thought that Keynesian economics could be used to stabilize aggregate demand, and input-output analysis would provide the basis of aggregate supply management.[6] Fortunately for Japan, the debate was eventually won by those favoring the market system over comprehensive planning. The Dodge Mission, in particular, recommended reliance on conservative fiscal and monetary policies, a devaluation of the yen and its subsequent stabilization at 360 yen to the dollar, but the overall organization of the Japanese economy to be based upon a market-oriented system of decision-making and resource allocation. Of course, as we shall see below, the Japanese government today plays an important role in the economy, as it did historically, but it is one of general guidance rather than one of centralized decision-making. The

---

[5] Angus Maddison, *op. cit.*, p. 45.

[6] Input-output tables, developed by Nobel Laureate Wassily Leontief, provide an inter-industry matrix of the entire economy — showing that an x percent rise in beer brewing produces a z percent increase in the demand for barley, y percent for hops, and so on. These linkages are similar to those used in "material balances" planning in the U.S.S.R.; the main problem is that one has to assume that z and y, for example, remain the same over time.

hierarchy in resource allocations depends upon market-determined profitability and not the wishes of government bureaucrats.

On the whole, the contribution of the American occupation to Japan's subsequent development was a positive one, as is the special bilateral relationship that has emerged over the years, but it should not be exaggerated. As is noted elsewhere in this book, U.S. economic assistance also played an important, but not a determining, role in the successes fashioned by Korea and Taiwan. In all three cases, U.S. aid contributed by insisting upon the redistribution of land and other institutional reforms, as well as some initial development funding, but it is downright silly to continue regarding these Asian "success stories" as American "client-states" (silly for us as well as for our critics and enemies). The positive aspects of the U.S. contribution are aptly summarized by G.C. Allen:

> "...It may be that in the first years of SCAP preoccupation with reform impeded recovery. Yet without the 'aid' furnished so lavishly by the Americans at that time Japan might have plunged further into ruin, and the foundations of recovery could certainly not have been laid. Similarly, in the early and middle 1950s the large, 'special procurement' expenditure kept Japan supplied with dollars which enabled her to re-equip her industries at a time when the export trade was still very small. Even the reforms themselves cannot be lightly dismissed as agents of economic progress. Some of them were out of time with Japan's purposes and did not long survive. But others endured and contributed not merely to social stability but also to economic efficiency. For instance, the Land Reform initially made some contribution to agricultural productivity as well as to social stability, even though in later years the legal restraints imposed on the alienation of peasant properties may have impeded the transition to large-scale farming. The breaking up of the zaibatsu and the 'purging' of the industrial leaders for a time brought confusion to the economy, but in the end they probably helped to stimulate development by opening the way for new men and new methods."[7]

This last point is closely related to the "Olson Thesis," identified with Professor Mancur Olson of the University of Maryland, who argues that the main causes of economic growth and decline of nations tend to be political. As an overly brief summary of a thought-provoking argument, excessive political stability may be an impediment to economic progress, because increasingly powerful interest groups form coalitions and guilds to bid for a larger share in the political distribution process and then to protect the "status quo," denying newcomers the chance to make their contribution and discouraging entrepreneurship. Thus, paradoxically, being defeated in a war and/or suffering a revolutionary upheaval is good for a society, as long as it is fundamentally stable (he seems to include this last proviso in order to deal with the case of Latin American countries, which otherwise would not fit into his story very well). The decline of Great Britain is in large part due to the development of such powerful interest groups

---

[7] G.C. Allen, *A Short Economic History of Modern Japan*, Fourth Edition, *op. cit.*, p. 230.

over several centuries, while the failure of China and India to develop is rooted in the role of various guilds in the former (for a while, for example, all Chinese foreign trade was controlled by a guild of merchants in Canton) and the caste system in the latter. Japan, thus, was doubly fortunate. The power of the *daimyo* and the existing commercial guilds was greatly diluted by the Meiji Restoration—few of the early capitalist entrepreneurs of the latter half of the 19th century came from established merchant families. Japan's weakness at that time forced it to accept free trade and a low revenue tariff, not to exceed 5 percent (1866-1899), which Japanese historians have described as a "humiliation." However, as Olson says:

> *"...Lo and behold, the Japanese were humiliated all the way to the bank. Trade immediately expanded and economic growth apparently picked up speed, particularly in the 1880s and 1890s, and just after the turn of the century a new Japan was able to triumph in the Russo-Japanese War. Once again, multiple causation must be emphasized. For example, the government subsidized industries that were deemed important for military purposes and also promoted education effectively. Quantitatively speaking, however, the overwhelmingly important source of Japanese growth in the nineteenth century was the progress of small-scale private industry and agriculture, such as exports of silk and tea. Interestingly, most of the important Japanese entrepreneurs in this period do not trace to the merchant houses belonging to the guilds of the pre-Meiji period; but rather, they came disproportionately from the ranks of impoverished lesser samurai (who, by the precepts of traditional Japanese culture, were not supposed to engage in commerce at all) or from rising farm and trading families in rural areas that were more likely to be beyond control by guilds or officials. It is said that when markets opened up, many of the houses that had belonged to guilds were disoriented and at a loss what to do."* [8]

Similarly, the destruction of at least some zaibatsu power and the wholesale management turnover of the later 1940's probably contributed a great deal to Japan's dynamic advance in the period to follow. *[investment saving ↑]*

The period from 1955-70 has been called the High Economic Growth Period, with an annual real GNP growth of about ten percent. The growth rate actually rose as the period progressed, investment and personal saving rose sharply, but even more impressive progress was made in overall efficiency. In other words, after real output is linked statistically to measured growth in both man-hours worked and capital investment, the "unexplained residual" grew larger, suggesting that all factors of production were being employed more effectively. In addition, the high-growth period was characterized by very moderate inflation (with wholesale prices essentially constant), a conservative fiscal policy (with the central government's budget usually close to a balance), a more equal *[fiscal conservatism]*

---

[8] *Mancur Olson, The Rise and Decline of Nations: Economic Growth, Stagflation, and Social Rigidities* (Yale University Press, 1982), p. 152. This upheaval of privilege and group power was duplicated in the period after World War II, as it was in West Germany and a few other countries as well.

distribution of income, and a steadily improving balance-of-payments. The investment to GNP ratio rose from 0.25 in 1955 to 0.39 in 1970 — while the personal savings rate increased from 13 percent to 20 percent over the same period, and corporate saving, in the form of retained earnings and depreciation allowances, rose even more quickly.[9]

Following Maddison's outline of potential explanatory factors, let us discuss eight significant reasons that would tend to account for Japan's superior economic performance during its post-war recovery period. These are not listed in any particular order of significance — the list could probably be expanded or contracted somewhat, but an appreciation of these manifold factors is necessary for a reasonably thorough understanding of Japan's experience.

First, it can be pointed out that Japan's planning agencies tend to be more influential than those in any other MTE, or market-type economy (except perhaps in France, said Maddison in 1969). A distinction needs to be made between hierarchical and indicative planning in this connection — the former refers to the central authorities determining the priorities of resource allocation for a formal planning period, such as the five-year-plan of the CPE, the centrally-planned economies.[10] A good deal of uninformed discussion of "the way Japan works" tends to suggest that this is in fact the case. The image behind "Japan, Inc." and its superior "industrial policy" portrays the country as a single-minded business entity, cleverly picking out firms and industries to subsidize — a fiendishly single-minded organization designed to drive all U.S. firms out of business.

In fact, the Japanese government carries out only indicative planning, providing the broad outline of where the economy has been in the recent past, where it now stands, and approximately where it ought to be heading. It sets out some rather general macroeconomic goals, but allocative details are left to the forces of the market. It is also true that the forecasts of Japanese planners have been subject to a rather wide range of error — though usually it has been a mistake of underestimating plan results (as in the "Income-Doubling Plan" of the 1960s), while in the United States official forecasts are generally overly optimistic. In this overall framework, it is important to stress, however, that government-business relationships in Japan tend to stress cooperation, while in the U.S. government agencies are supposed to confront business firms to safeguard the interests of "people." Liberals are wont to say something like, for us, "people are more important than profits" (on the assumption that the two are always antagonistic, and that omniscient and objective government officials represent the general public good rather than pursuing their own ends). One very interesting practice in Japan is that of *amakudari* (translated as "descent from heaven"), which means that senior government

---

[9] A good overview of these statistics is provided by Yutaka Kosai and Yoshitaro Ogino (translated by Ralph Thompson), *The Contemporary Japanese Economy* (M.E. Sharpe, Inc., 1984).

[10] While planning agencies, such as MITI, have played an important role in Japan, the market works — prices can change at any time, private property exists and financial institutions are not directed by the state. See Chalmers Johnson, *Japan: Who Governs?* (W.W. Norton, 1995), but also Daniel Okimoto, *Between MITI and the Market* (Stanford University Press, 1989).

[handwritten margin note: Japan's planning agencies]

officials — from agencies such as MITI (the Ministry of International Trade and Industry), MoF (the Ministry of Finance), and BoJ (the Bank of Japan) — take retirement from their jobs at age 55 in order to join business firms or financial institutions as directors or consultants. In the Japanese context, this is not perceived as an anti-social "conflict of interests" at all. The role of the *Keidanren* (the Japanese counterpart of our National Association of Manufacturers, or perhaps the Chamber of Commerce) in supporting the Liberal Democratic Party (LDP) is also very important, and generally accepted — facilitating the interchange of information and easing the negotiation of policy changes very considerably.

Secondly, for a number of reasons, macroeconomic policy instruments in Japan tend to be more effective and less influenced by short-term political considerations than in many other countries, including the United States. Monetary policy, for example, is able to influence total spending quite directly. Why this is so takes a bit of explaining. The key words here are "overborrowing" and "overloan" — the first refers to the fact that Japan's commercial banks (there are today fewer than a dozen nation-wide "city banks" and another 50-60 major "regional banks") rely heavily on central bank credit, while the concept of "overloan" signifies that Japanese corporations historically have always been relatively much more dependent on commercial bank credit than on any other sources of corporate finance. By way of contrast, in the United States, we still have more than 10,000 individual commercial banks (as well as a couple of thousand mutual savings banks and savings and loan associations), which typically borrow only 2-3 percent of their total reserves at the discount window of the Federal Reserve. In Japan, the ratio of borrowed reserves is often as high as 30-40 percent. In turn, American corporations use the bond and stock markets relatively much more than Japanese *keiretsu* (business groupings, the re-incarnations of the *zaibatsu* in a number of cases). The keiretsu borrow heavily from city banks (known as the "main Bank" system), in which they often also have a significant equity stake. Moreover, Japanese consumers seldom use consumer credit to make major purchases; until recently, even credit cards were rarely used, and many people would save the full purchase price of a car, an apartment, or a house. Thus, a relatively small change in interest rates by the central bank in Japan would have a much more significant impact on aggregate demand than it probably would have in the U.S. — most corporations were heavily dependent on bank borrowing, which in turn used central bank credit extensively, while consumers hardly ever used access to credit.[11] Finally, fiscal policy in Japan has generally been rather conservative, and less subject to political pressure than elsewhere. With a *de facto* one-party system, the so-called "political business cycle" — a nearly certain increase in government spending in an election year plus a virtual ban on tax increases at that time — appears to be less influential in Japan than in the U.S..

---

[11] Further discussion of this point can be found in George J. Viksnins and Michael T. Skully, "Asian Financial Development: A Comparative Perspective of Eight Countries," *Asian Survey,* May 1987, as well as James Horne, *Japan's Financial Markets* (George Allen & Urwin, 1985) and Robert F. Emery, *The Japanese Money Market* (D.C. Heath, 1984).

Thirdly, labor unions in Japan appear to be "more responsible" and conscious of their dependence on their company's well-being, which is closely tied to their remaining competitive in the export market. A number of Japanese economists have focused almost exclusively on the difference in institutional arrangements concerning unions in Japan and the U.S. as the reason for the former outperforming the latter in several key industries, notably automobiles, electronics, ship-building, and steel. In the U.S., there is industry-wide collective bargaining, with the union often concentrating on the one company having the highest profits in the recent past to strike a "key bargain." The wage gains extracted from that firm are then used as the basis for further negotiation with the others. In the past, at least, union leaders probably felt that the oligopolistic industry will then be able to simply pass the wage increases on to the consumers in the form of higher administered prices. (In more recent years, however, the powerful United Auto-mobile Workers has actually accepted some "roll-backs" in average wage levels.) In Japan, on the other hand, only about 30 percent of the employees of even large companies are members of unions, and unions bargain with individual firms. Thus, there is a single union for Toyota, but another for Nissan. Moreover, because of the system of life-time employment and basing wages more on seniority than on skills (and the job classification as such):

> "... employees have a very strong sense of belonging to the company. Unions carefully consider the condition of the company when making wage demands, and employees are not merely extremely cooperative — for example in imple-menting quality control measures — but also very positive in such areas as sug-gesting possible improvements in production methods. This 'company spirit', this view states, contributed greatly to improvements in energy conservation methods and reduction of costs." [12]

It can also be argued that in the U.S., wages are relatively inflexible, but the volume of employment adjusts to demand changes, in Japan the emphasis is on the adjustment of wages to overall economic conditions. Wage settlements in Japan have a bit of a ritualistic nature — all unions negotiate during the so-called "Spring Offensive" (*shunto* in Japanese), when union members can picket, demonstrate, carry insulting placards, and even strike briefly. However, in a day or two they are all back at work (perhaps wearing black armbands as the final protest against an inadequate wage settlement!), and the number of days lost to strikes in Japan is very small. Labor-management relations in Japan are characterized by Edward J. Lincoln as follows:

> "...Although the union movement was militant in some industries and strikes were frequent in the early postwar years, by the late 1950s and early 1960s most of the radical unions had been crushed and replaced by more moderate ones. This was a divisive period for labor, but the fact that the radical unions could not

---

[12] Yutaka Kosai and Yoshitaro Aquino, *The Contemporary Japanese Economy, op. cit.,* p. 79. It is sometimes said that there are "Three Sacred Treasures" in Japanese labor relations: the company union, seniority wages, and lifetime employment.

command sufficient loyalty among workers to stay in power confirms the broad nature of the social consensus on rapid growth and hard work. Japanese workers accepted a system of enterprise-based unions with very weak national organizations, moderate strike activity (in which strikes are of limited, preannounced duration), transfers between jobs or factories within a company as technological change eliminated old functions, and moderation in wage demands when corporate profits fell. In general, unions have been flexible on wages and work rules." [13]

A fourth factor that needs to be mentioned is the role of the Japanese government in the control of the balance of trade and payments — not necessarily an entirely positive contribution from the point of view of a free-market economist, but an integral part of the Japanese development model historically. During the 1950s and the 1960s, foreign exchange availability was carefully monitored by the Ministry of Finance and the Bank of Japan. Even Japanese businessmen going overseas to sell Japanese products and establish affiliates, first in Taiwan and Korea and later elsewhere, were subjects to quite stringent limitations on their daily expenditures — the limits that faced tourists were considerably lower, of course. The Japanese government worked very hard to limit "non-essential imports" by using both tariff barriers and other controls — such as very rigid safety and engineering specification standards — as well as promoting a general "Buy Japanese" campaign. Investment flows were also subject to a complex system of reviews, approvals, and regulations. This was the case for both outgoing and incoming investments — of course, during the period of serious foreign exchange shortages (e.g., the 1950s and the early part of the 1960s), there was not much of a prospect for significant outflows, in any case. Concerning foreign investment in Japan, Edward J. Lincoln says:

restrictions in non-essential imports.

Buy Japanese.

"...The strict control of imports and capital flow was also strongly influenced by economic xenophobia. Since it began to develop as a modern economy in the late nineteenth century, Japan has striven for an economy owned, operated, and supplied by Japanese firms. Policies to that effect proliferated in the 1930s and, postwar policies continued and strengthened the tendency. Xenophobia was given additional impetus in the 1950s by the fear that in the absence of strict controls war-weakened Japanese companies would be quickly over-run by foreign competition." [14]

A fifth factor facilitating Japan's rapid recovery during the High Economic Growth period is the fact that its statistical indicators and "economic intelligence" are superior to those of many other countries. While the governments of most OECD countries also produce volumes of detailed statistical information about economic performance, Japanese data seem to set the standard for promptness and precision. For example, among

---

[13] Edward J. Lincoln, *Japan: Facing Economic Maturity* (The Brookings Institution, 1988), p. 20.
[14] *Ibid.*, pp. 74–75.

academic economists, there has been considerable criticism of the use of GNP as a measure of economic welfare for at least twenty years. (We mentioned some of these in connection with the Tobin-Nordhaus "Measure of Economic Welfare" in the first chapter.) Yet, in the United States, the Department of Commerce has continued to grind out GNP numbers using the same old methodology, turning a deaf ear to suggestions that alternative measures could also be compiled and presented. In Japan, for quite a few years there have been estimates made of more utility-oriented measures, such as "Net National Welfare." Also, in the late 1960s, slogans such as "Welfare before Growth" and even "To Hell with GNP" ("Kutabare GNP") were being bandied about, demonstrating a good deal of public interest in such matters. Perhaps even more important is the concept of "economic intelligence" — the production and distribution of information about the Japanese as well as the world economy. Japanese businessmen and students are far more likely to know the numbers giving the GNP per capita of Japan and the U.S., the level of exports and imports of both countries, and the current prices of gold, oil, and rice than their counterparts in the U.S. Language competence is also symptom of this aspect of Japanese competitiveness — while I now encounter fairly large numbers of Georgetown students studying Chinese and Japanese at quite an advanced level, up from just a handful ten years ago, I would guess that no more than a hundred American businessmen dealing primarily with Japan can read a daily Tokyo newspaper, while the number of Japanese businessmen stationed in the U.S. and reasonably fluent in English is probably in the hundreds of thousands. Regarding economic intelligence as such, Angus Maddison has pointed out that:

> "...Most Japanese government departments have large research units, usually much bigger than in European countries. The Bank of Japan and the Economic Planning Agency both have rooms the size of department stores packed with economists and statisticians. As a result economic (and other) policy decisions are informed by a good deal more statistical and analytic information than is at the disposal of West European governments.
>
> In 1963, about 210,000 abstracts of foreign scientific papers were made by the Japan Information Center for Science and Technology. Japanese businessmen and government officials are constantly visiting foreign countries to pick up new ideas. Some of this is considered a form of industrial espionage by Western countries, but the prewar Japanese practice of gross copying and abuse of foreign trade marks has been substantially abated. Japan also translates into English a very large body of her own material which is not fully exploited abroad." [15]

A sixth related factor, worthy of much more space than we are able to allocate here, is the Japanese educational system — educational efforts tend to be functional and growth-promoting. The system emphasizes the development of a "meritocracy" in upper-level managerial positions, with a relatively small role played by an aristocracy, of either hereditary status or wealth. To be sure, wealthy families can send their children

---

[15]   Angus Maddison, *Economic Growth in Japan and the U.S.S.R.*, op. cit., p. 61.

to private universities (such as Keio) or even abroad to study, but admission to the "creme de le creme" of Japan, the University of Tokyo, is based upon a national examination. The nationwide examination for places in public universities, both less expensive and more prestigious, is "ferociously competitive." Generally speaking, a university degree brings with it high levels of prestige. Indeed, in Japan, relative status in society is often the highest for graduates in technical fields, such as accounting, economics, engineering, and the sciences. Japan graduates more engineers than the United States from a college-age population of only one-fifth as large as ours. (By way of contrast, can you yourself imagine encountering an "accountant," who is willing to admit it and had somehow been invited, at a fashionable cocktail party in Georgetown or Greenwich Village? Surely you'd mumble an excuse, go fix another drink, and look for someone more interesting — perhaps an artist, a journalist, or a poet...). As a closely related point, the salaries and status of teachers — and university professors especially (he said rather pointedly...) — in Japan are both quite high in comparison with the U.S. (popular attitudes here are well captured by: "if you're so smart, why aren't you rich?").

At lower levels of training, especially in the vocational high schools, competition and discipline in Japan appear to be exemplary. Anecdotal examples along these lines abound — most taxi drivers in Tokyo wear white gloves, and Toyota mechanics (not only graduate engineers) often get overseas assignments. The system of life-time employment has forced Japanese firms to be very selective in their hiring practices at all levels. Professor Bronfenbrenner has discussed this at some length in his essay on the Japanese practice of the "negative screening" of undesirable workers:

> *"...Screening can be usefully sub-divided into positive screening (the search for maximum scores in a few key traits or attributes) and negative screening (weeding out applicants with low scores on a wider range of traits or attributes).*
>
> *Among the attributes particularly sought to be screened out negatively are militance and the multifarious varieties of 'trouble-making.' (yakkaimono)*
>
> *Negative screening has also played a greater part in Japanese personnel performance than is generally recognized. Its effects are both direct — on the prospective employment candidate himself or herself — and indirect — on parents and teachers who preside over the socialization of the prospective candidate."* [16]

A seventh and eighth factor in Japan's recovery can probably be mentioned in the same breath, so to speak — research and development (R & D) expenditures and government investment. Regarding the former, Japan's R & D tends to be very commercially oriented and directed toward tangible results. That is to say, Japan has been able to rely on the American "defense umbrella," and has not needed to "waste" its scientific manpower and research funds on military applications of technology, which may or may

R & D expenditures

---

[16] Martin Bronfenbrenner, "An Essay on Negative Screening," in Toshio Shishido and Ryuzo Sato (eds.), *Economic Policy and Development: New Perspectives* (Auburn House Publishing Company, 1985), p. 187.

not have some civilian applications in the longer run. In a similar vein, many U.S. universities, think tanks, and even corporate laboratories (e.g., "Bell labs") devote a good part of their budget to basic research of a rather general theoretical nature, while Japanese efforts are usually devoted to practical applications. (Actually, this may be a somewhat outdated generalization, and students reading this in the 1990s should take it with the proverbial "grain of salt." Many of my Japanese colleagues in economics, at least, are as proud of being totally out of touch with the "real world" as most modern economists anywhere else.) In any case, Japan's R & D spending is high and growing — as is government investment relative to GNP. Having visited Japan four times during the past twenty years, I can report at least a tourist's impression — Japan's transport and communications system works very well, and is being improved steadily. In sharp contrast to other countries in Asia, when one picks up the phone or turns on the light, the result is predictable. Also, in contrast to New York or Washington the "bullet-train" (*Shinkansen*) is much more often on time than the Metroliner, and the road between the Narita airport and Tokyo compares favorably with both the road from Washington to Dulles as well as that from Wall Street to LaGuardia (indeed, in the latter case, the comparison favors Japan by a very large margin...).

U.S. - Japan Trade Issues

A relatively productive method for gaining a pretty good understanding of the comparison of the U.S. and Japan can be a case study of our trade imbalance, which will conclude this chapter. In the next chapter, we will examine some longer-term trends in the Japanese economy, which raise some fundamental questions about "Japan As Number One." Still, at the present time, despite the collapse of the "bubble economy," Japan's positive attributes seem to outweigh the negatives — and this is also reflected by the current imbalance of the trade between the two economic super powers.

Table 11-1 is adapted from Bergsten and Cline's monograph on this same topic published more than ten years ago. It provides a very useful four-way classification of the underlying reasons for the existence of the large bilateral deficit, which accounted for about one-third of the total deficit in U.S. current account (the total has been averaging approximately $150 billion over the past three years).

It should be pointed out that official balance of trade statistics are becoming less and less meaningful, as economic activity becomes integrated on a global basis. A hefty share of Asian exports to the United States comes from the Asian operations of American multinationals, which may produce components in Bangkok and Seoul, then assemble them in Hong Kong, and then ship them to the U.S. Some of the component parts may also have come from the U.S. itself in the first place, be shipped in American-owned ships under Liberian or Panamanian registry, and insured by a U.S. company, but the full c.i.f. (cost, insurance, and freight, as you remember) is included in our imports from Hong Kong. In the case of Japan, as has been argued by Kenichi Ohmae, the overall picture is quite complicated:

Table 11-1: Major Influences in the U.S.–Japan Trade Deficit

U.S.		Japan	
Structural	**Policy**	**Structural**	**Policy**
Macro Low saving ("poor discipline")	Growing deficits in the government budget; "high" interest rates	High savings ("catch up to the West")	Falling deficits in the government budget; low interest rates
Micro U.S. firms "can't sell," especially in Asia	Various export controls, actual as well as potential	Japanese firms "won't buy," especially from American suppliers	Non-tariff barriers and a general attitude against "non-essential" imports

Source: Adapted from C. Fred Bergsten and William R. Cline, *The U.S.–Japan Trade Problem* (Institute for International Economics, 1985), pp. 4–5.

> "...Our markets may be protected in some cases (e.g., rice, financial services), but we are buying a large amount of American goods. These purchases are hidden, however, because goods manufactured by American companies in Japan and shipped to the United States count as Japanese exports to the United States, whereas those sold to users in Japan by the same U.S. companies count as neither exports nor imports and do not show up on the trade statistics on either side." [17]

The amounts involved are quite significant. In 1984, production and sales of American affiliates in Japan represented more than $40 billion, while those of Japanese affiliates in the U.S. were about $13 billion. Ohmae points out that the average Japanese spends about 6% of his income on American products, while we spend only about 2% of our income on their goods, on average. Still, the trade imbalance is a sensitive political issue — and we need to spend some time analyzing it carefully.

Let us begin with a discussion of the main structural macroeconomic problem — the fact that the United States tends to be a low-savings country, while the Japanese save a lot. A few of the reasons for the low savings rate in the United States were mentioned in Chapter 4, but bear some elaborating here. As a general proposition, the policy of the American government in the post-war period has subsidized consumption and penalized saving — certainly in comparison to Japan, but also relatively to most Western European countries as well. Moreover, as the federal government became more generous in its

---

[17] Kenichi Ohmae, *Beyond National Borders* (Dow Jones-Irwin, 1987), p. 26.

transfer programs aimed at senior citizens (who certainly do *vote* faithfully), a general attitudinal change took place — suggesting that governments rather than families should accept primary responsibility for the elderly. In fact, during the seventies, it became obvious that borrowing to consume was a rather painless way to lift one's standard of living — and that saving was usually a foolish thing to do. Consumer interest payments could be deducted from income without limit; as noted earlier, this often meant that the after-tax interest rate faced by American borrowers was only 2-3%. This made "overinvestment" in residential structures very attractive, developing an entire tax-shelter industry of limited partnerships for highly-taxed professionals (Whitewater comes to mind). The purchases of new homes and condos would still generally be included in both national saving and investment, but existing housing would not be. Furthermore, the deductibility of interest payments also made new cars (many of them imported) and other consumer durables much more affordable — thus, tax policy tended to subsidize consumption. On the other side of the coin, in the latter half of the 1970s, American savers were subject to a double penalty (even a triple one, in real terms). Interest rates that could be earned on passbook savings accounts in banks and other financial institutions were regulated by the Fed's Regulation Q, yielding a maximum of 5.25% at commercial banks and slightly higher 5.50% at savings and loans. For many savers, in the 1970s, interest income received was taxed at more than 50% (when the top marginal tax rate was 70%). Then, finally, in quite a few years, the Reg. Q interest return was well below the inflation rate! In the early 1980s, the situation changed substantially— the Reg. Q ceiling was gradually phased out, marginal tax rates were cut in several steps, a few tax-exempt vehicles were created (although the IRA, the completely tax-free "Individual Retirement Account," seems to have been only a short-lived experiment), and the rate of expected inflation came down sharply. Furthermore, the deductibility of interest payments was curtailed somewhat, but overinvestment in housing was left largely untouched. Even today, we, the American taxpayers, continue to subsidize hefty interest payments for vacation homes for the wealthy in Aspen, Laguna Beach, and Orlando. (After the change in tax rules, U.S. financial institutions quickly came up with the innovation known as the "home equity credit line," which in effect can keep interest payments for most other purchases fully deductible!)

It may be that the general acceptance of Keynesian economics, which views savings as a negative act, has something to do with the low U.S. savings rate. It can be argued that the Depression decade was indeed associated with inadequate aggregate demand, and that the world-wide recovery after World War II was largely fueled by rising American consumption and stimulative government policies. In Japan, however, the bias in policies has been just the reverse. Generally speaking, institutional arrangements and attitudes have favored abstaining from consumption — and government policies have generally promoted saving. Japanese households, on the average, saved more than four times as much as their American counterparts, and business and government saving tended to be positive and rising. (One is tempted to mention that the Japanese were following "supply-side economics" even before that term was invented.) A number of observations concerning the high Japanese savings rate can be made. But, before we get started, I often like to spring a "surprise-quiz," asking the following multiple-choice question:

"The largest financial institution in the world is:"

(a)   the World Bank;

(b)   Daichi-Kangyo Bank;

(c)   Bank of America;

(d)   the Federal Reserve System;

(e)   the International Monetary Fund;

(f)   Citicorp;

(g)   None of the above.

The correct answer, of course, is (g) — it is the Japanese Postal Savings System, with total assets of more than $1 trillion, overshadowing the Fed, with assets in excess of $400 billion, which is, in turn, nearly twice the size of both the IMF and the World Bank. Among private commercial banks, in terms of total assets, Dai-Ichi Kangyo is now the largest, with Citicorp no longer in the top ten, not to speak of the Bank of America, which indeed once was the world's largest private commercial bank.

There are at least five or six reasons for why the Japanese personal savings rate is relatively so much higher than that of the United States, though possibly we could come up with even more. First, the formal pension system, both government and private, is relatively undeveloped — and, second, Japanese workers usually retire at a much earlier age (historically, at age 55). While some workers retiring from responsible business groups could expect lucrative "amakudari" (descent from heaven) director-ships or consultantcy arrangements, others would receive a retirement bonus of several years' salary, most of which would be then saved. With rising life expectancy rates, retired workers usually had to look for additional post-retirement incomes, as the time to leave their "life-time jobs" approached, which meant that many households did not draw down their savings very much. Third, a significant portion of a Japanese "salary man's" income comes in the form of an annual or a twice-yearly bonus and/or profit-sharing payments, of which a significant portion is generally saved (as suggested by Milton Friedman's "permanent income hypothesis" and related theories of consumption behavior). Fourth, as mentioned before, the Japanese consumer credit system differs greatly from our "plastic-payment" society. American Express and other credit cards are still usually limited to official expense-account entertaining; even relatively well-paid "salary-men" turn over their paychecks to their wives, who in turn grant them a small weekly allowance for necessary expenditures (perhaps enough for a couple of beers on Friday after basic necessities, such as a daily paper and commuting costs—surveys report that the size of this allowance is a major source of marital tensions and arguments). For most Japanese families, it is customary to save up the full purchase price for a new condominium apartment, a car, or a consumer durable good. Saving for expenditures associated with getting married or sending children to a really good university (now sometimes in the U.S.) is yet another factor. It might also be noted that the purchase price of a house or a "flat" in densely-populated Japan (particularly within commuting distance of downtown Tokyo) is so high that property values in Honolulu, Los Angeles, and Georgetown seem quite reasonable by comparison. Finally, we might mention the general psychological attitude of "saving for a rainy day," virtually a national phobia having to do with potential shortages of food, fuel, and other resources (coupled with the need to "catch-up"), which leads to risk-averse behavior on the part of the Japanese.

It might also be noted that the accumulation of financial assets in Japan is treated very kindly by the tax authorities, especially in the case of deposits with the Postal Savings System, though this has changed recently. For all of these reasons, as we have noted, the Postal Savings System of Japan is the largest financial intermediary in the world, and Japanese commercial banks are rapidly becoming much more important than their American and European competitors.

It can be pointed out that the first half of the 1980s, the federal budget deficit in the U.S. was stimulating aggregate demand, while, at the same time, it was making supply-side improvements much more difficult, by "crowding-out" private investment by pushing up interest rates to record levels. To be sure, marginal tax rates were cut, but real interest rates remained very high. In Japan, the size of the government's budget deficit was being reduced significantly over this same period, permitting a lowering of interest rates. Toward the end of the 1980s, for example, corporate bond yields in Japan averaged only 4.61 percent, while in the United States they were roughly twice as high, at 9.31 percent. The discount rate at that time in Japan was only 2.5 percent, while the Federal Reserve discount rate stood at 6 percent). On the whole, the overall policy of the U.S. authorities combined a rather "easy" fiscal policy with relatively "tight" money, which tends to boost private consumption, but discourages investment, as a general proposition. In the mid-1990s, U.S. interest rates are again significantly higher than rates in Japan.

At a microeconomic level, American firms can be characterized as encountering structural problems ("can't sell") in the Asian market, especially in Japan — while Japanese companies seem to have a strong preference ("won't buy") for developing a reliable network of domestic suppliers. Historically, American companies were not very interested in international trade. In the post-war period, many of the areas with which American firms had earlier traded when they had colonial or semi-colonial status (e.g., China trade), had become independent. These countries tended to follow very national-istic economic policies, influenced in part by the emergence and popular acceptance of the "world-economy view," which we have already discussed. Even though the United States was often sympathetic to independence movements, granting full autonomy to the Philippines right after the war, for example, there was a tendency on the part of the newly independent countries to regard all trade and investment contacts with the "North", broadly speaking, in general, as exploitative. There was little sentiment for an expansion of economic ties on both sides. In the 1950s, the huge American market was expanding quite nicely, and our total imports were only about 3 percent of the U.S. GNP. Many American firms probably regarded their sales in the Seattle district as more important than all of their business in Asia. It is said, for example, that American automobile companies simply did not want to bother making right-hand drive vehicles, regarding

Britain, Japan, India, Thailand, and even Australia and New Zealand as very small markets. Even in Europe, currency convertability was not restored until around 1960. There was not much attraction to earning additional pounds in Great Britain, for example, in order to have them sit there in so-called "blocked sterling accounts," which could only be spent there and not be brought back to the U.S..

After the formation of the European Economic Community (EEC) and the restoration of currency convertability in most European countries, U.S. investment in and trade with Europe grew quite rapidly — facilitated in part by historical ties, of course. Furthermore, if a U.S. firm was thinking about additional international marketing, there was Canada (where there was no language barrier) and relatively familiar Latin America — which in the 1950s was considerably more prosperous and friendly than mysterious Asia. Travel time was much shorter, cultural differences were relatively slight (and quite a few Americans could at least order a meal in Spanish), and government officials were relatively easy to deal with.

On the whole, American firms in 1950s and the 1960s were not very interested in Asia generally. Mainland China and much of Indo-China (Burma, Cambodia, Laos, and North Vietnam) was essentially closed to American travel although the large American military presence in Southeast Asia during the 1965-75 period provided very lucrative business opportunities. Also, it was difficult to do business in South Asia, especially in India and Sri Lanka, both of which were following socialistic policies, while Indonesia effectively closed itself off to American businessmen until the late 1960s. That left a relatively small number of countries — probably too few to establish a regional office with a permanent staff in the Far East. Most firms would send out a traveling salesman with a couple of catalogs to set up licensing and representative arrangements in Tokyo, Hong Kong, Singapore, and perhaps Bangkok, but probably marked up their products considerably for sale in such unimportant markets and were generally rather lax in service and follow-up. It might also be noted that an aggressive, brash, and hurried American business representative, having ten days to make calls in Tokyo, Taipei, Hong Kong, and Singapore, would often offend the sensibilities of people trained in the subtleties of Asian business rituals.

On the Japanese side, a great deal has been written about their structure of industrial organization, which makes it very difficult for foreign suppliers to break into the Japanese market — in other words, the large business conglomerates (*keiretsu*) "won't buy," preferring to be as self-sufficient as possible. In part, this may harken back to the *zaibatsu* system of the 1930's, when the "quasi-war-time economy" (*Junsenji Keizai*) was in operation. As free trade ground to a halt during the Depression decade, Japan began to emphasize self-sufficiency in industrial products important to its military build-up, reliance on her colonies and other "trustworthy" suppliers ("the Greater East Asia Co-Prosperity Sphere"), and bilateral arrangements in trade with most countries.

This involved the creation of a so-called "yen bloc" in Asia, and greatly strengthened the position of extreme nationalists and the military.[18]

Conclusion

To end this chapter, let me borrow a few ideas from a thoughtful (Sept. 1987) article by James Fallows in *The Atlantic* (I know that an academic shouldn't be reading such popular media, and I do apologize...) The free-trade approach to economic issues is based on three important assumptions: (1) economic imbalances will always be redressed by more trade, with goods flowing from lowest cost countries to higher cost ones; (2) free trade will be based upon consumers maximizing their utility; and (3) "... competition is always good, because it offers people more, and a free world trading system is best, because it offers people most."

Over the past decade, the followers of free trade ideas have been hoping that the market mechanism would begin to restore a balance of sorts to the United States trade with Japan, but the deficit just seems to be growing larger — almost regardless of income growth, prices, interest, and exchange rates. As Fallows says, this is in part based upon our children not learning enough math and science, our "smartest people...planning hostile takeovers or designing attack submarines," as well as not naturally thinking of export markets, but even if our attitudes were to change, the problem would persist. As Fallows has put it:

> *"... The reason is that the free-trade solution — everyone buying more from every-one else — runs counter to a deeper value in Japanese life: the non-capitalist de-sire to preserve every Japanese person's place in the Japanese productive system. In the United States and in most of the world Adam Smith described, peo-ple suffer indignities as producers — through layoff, job changes, shifts into new businesses — in order to improve the welfare of the society's consumers. In Ja-pan, it's the other way around. The Japanese consumer's interest comes last — and therefore so does the motivation for buying from overseas."[19]*

A number of illustrations can be provided — "food is the classic illustration," says Fallows. A coalition of consumer groups recently protested plans to import more cheap food (!), arguing that Japanese rice should never be exposed to foreign competition. Clearly, Japanese taxpayers would save by buying military aircraft from American producers — "although our own military budget may make this hard to believe, it is cheaper to buy the next F-15 off the production line than to set up a production line of your own." Still, even though its cost may turn out to be twice as high as buying them from us, the Japanese seem almost certain to begin building their own fighter aircraft.

---

[18] Further discussion can be found in G.C. Allen, *A Short Economic History of Japan, op. cit.,* pp. 160–165.

[19] James Fallows, "Japan: Playing by Different Rules," *Atlantic,* September 1987, p. 24. See also his more recent *Looking At the Sun* (Pantheon, 1994).

One final illustration is soda-ash, used in glass, chemicals, and detergents — which the American trade association claims can be imported at a significantly lower price than the made-in Japan product. In 1983, Japan's own Fair Trade Commission found that collusion had kept the Americans out.

> *"... American suppliers quickly expanded their share of the market from three to 15 percent, but then got very little more. The yen has gone up, dollar prices have plummeted, but the market share has barely budged. An executive of Asahi Glass, a major purchaser, recently announced that he'd never leave his high-cost Japanese supplier — they'd been friends in school."* [20]

The Japanese view of the trade surplus is that it reflects their society's "inborn frugality, moderation, and unsurpassed skill," while also mirroring the laziness and general lack of discipline of most Americans. The opinion prevalent in the United States, as reflected by the August *The New York Times* is to "... badger them relentlessly for more access to their markets..." As Fallows says, and I agree, "... threats not backed up by action annoy the Japanese, make America look weak and nervous, and leave the bothersome trade patterns unchanged." Certainly, even the United States has restricted trade, when completely free trade has threatened other values. For instance, as Fallows says, "child labor would make household help affordable again," and unlimited immigration would probably reduce the cost of restaurant meals. On the whole, the bilateral trade imbalance is mainly a Japanese problem — as long as they are willing to accept these funny pieces of green paper with George Washington's picture on them for their high-quality cars, electronic gadgets, and other products, should we worry? Perhaps we should — as choice real estate in New York and Honolulu, the equity of major banks and corporation shares, and a significant part of our Treasury bonds wind up in Japanese hands... Still, in a world system predominantly disposed toward inflation, in the long run, I would worry more about being a lender than a borrower. Somewhat cynically, then, is it not a good idea for the U.S. to become a net debtor country, joining Mexico and Brazil? Or is it? ■

SUGGESTED READINGS

Abegglen, James C. and George Stalk, Jr., *Kaisha: The Japanese Corporation* (Basic Books, 1988).

Allen, G.C., *A Short Economic History of Modern Japan* (The Macmillan Press, Ltd., 1981).

Bergsten, C. Fred, and William R. Cline, *U.S.-Japan Economic Problem* (Institute for International Economics, 1985).

Callon, Scott, *Divided Sun: MITI and the Breakdown of Japanese High-Tech Industrial Policy, 1975-1993* (Stanford University Press, 1995).

Dore, Ronald, *Flexible Rigidities: Industrial Policy and Structural Adjustment in the Japanese Economy, 1970-80* (Stanford University Press, 1986).

Fallows, James, *Looking At the Sun* (Pantheon, 1994).

Johnson, Chalmers, *MITI and the Japanese Miracle* (Stanford University Press, 1982).

---

[20] *Ibid.*, p 26.

Kosai, Yutaka, and Yoshitaro Aquino, *The Contemporary Japanese Economy* (M.E. Sharpe, Inc., 1984).

Lincoln, Edward J., *Japan: Facing Economic Maturity* (The Brookings Institution, 1988).

Maddison, Angus, *Economic Growth in Japan and the USSR* (W.W. Norton, 1969).

Nafziger, E. Wayne, *Learning from the Japanese: Japan's Pre-War Development and the Third World* (M.W. Sharpe, 1995).

Nakamura, Takafusa, *The Postwar Japanese Economy*, Second Edition (University of Tokyo Press, 1995).

Ohmae, Kenichi, *Beyond National Borders* (Dow Jones-Irwin, 1987).

Pilot, Dirk, *The Economics of Rapid Growth: The Experience of Japan and Korea* (Edward Elgar, 1994).

Sato, Ryuzo, *The Chrysantemum and the Eagle: The Future of U.S.-Japan Relations* (New York University Press, 1994).

Schmiegelow, Michele (ed.), *Japan's Response to Crisis and Change in the World Economy* (M.E. Sharpe, Inc., 1986).

Smith, Dennis B., *Japan Since 1945: The Rise of an Economic Superpower* (St. Martin's Press, 1995).

Suzuki, Yoshio, *Money, Finance and Macroeconomic Performance in Japan* (Yale University Press, 1986).

Takamiya, Susumu, and Keith Thurley (eds.), *Japan's Emerging Multinationals* (University of Tokyo Press, 1985).

CHAPTER TWELVE

JAPAN: AS NUMBER ONE?

*I*n the previous chapter, we have discussed some important aspects of the economic history of Japan, the main explanatory factors of its rapid recovery from the dislocations of the Pacific war (as World War II is generally called in Japan), and the manifold sources of the U.S. — Japan trade problem. On the whole, the approach of the discussion to this point has been positive, indeed admiring of Japan as a superior system. Of course, there is a lot to admire, and perhaps to imitate, in the Japanese "development model" — the benefits of the road taken by them seem to outweigh the costs, at least at first glance. Some of the discussion of this chapter may seem to be excessively negative and critical, probably especially so to my Japanese friends and colleagues. But, I do mean to be critical, when such criticism seems to be warranted objectively, in the hope that it will turn out to be constructive and helpful. Over the past twenty years of my professional interest in Asian economic development, the overall attitude of the Japanese seems to have shifted from one that was quite timid and apologetic to a very self-righteous and self-congratulatory one — and there is a strong temptation to bring them down a peg, so to speak. Over this same time period, the number of books and articles on the Japanese model has also grown exponentially, with many suggesting that developing countries have an opportunity to learn from the Japanese example — and that we Americans would probably benefit by doing so as well. We shall return to these two issues at the conclusion of this chapter: first, can and should the developing countries seek to follow Japan's example, and, second, how relevant is the Japanese model to the United States today? Quite a few authors treat the "Eastasia Edge" as a challenge to be met, argue that only one country can be "Number One," and view economic growth as a horse race, where only one horse can win, with all others coming in to place, show, or finish out of the money. In the early 1990s, Japan's GNP per capita, measured in U.S. dollars, became slightly higher there than in the U.S., but I have no temptation whatsoever to learn Japanese and to move to Sapporo permanently. If Japan's or even China's total GNP eventually surpasses that of the United States, which may indeed happen at some point early on in the 21st century, the importance of such an event would be relatively minor. The overall tone for this chapter can be well summarized by the following citation from Kahn and Pepper:

"...Some Americans are concerned that Japan's economic strength might eventually be used against U.S. interests, but as long as world economic growth continues, the prospect that a strong Japanese economy would amount, on balance, to a threat to American economic interests is extremely small. It is only when growth is limited that economic activity becomes, in the language of mathematicians, a zero-sum game. As long as economic development proceeds, and can thereby be seen as a non-zero-sum game, the gains can continue to be positive for all players, even if the rate of each player's gain varies from time to time.

Nevertheless, Japan does present a challenge to the United States. Its success creates pressure on the United States to seek, and then to achieve, even greater success than in the past. If Americans take up this challenge, they would indeed achieve the gains available from such an effort. In any event, an attempt to 'keep Japan down' would probably not work. The United States need not fear that Japan can continue to 'hoard' the benefits of trade indefinitely, since, as we have argued earlier, the Japanese economy is likely to have to open itself up simply because of internal and external market pressures if not for broader political reasons." [1]

The End of High-Speed Growth

Even though Japan's growth rates for the decade of the 1990s may compare quite favorably to those attained in the United States and elsewhere, the early 1970s appeared to mark a distinct end to the "growth-at-all-costs" attitude of the 1955-1970 period. As Yutaka Kosai has put it, an analogy can be drawn to the French Revolution — the "rebuilding-the-archipelago" boom may be thought of as the Jacobian Reign of Terror, while the suppression of aggregate demand in the first half of the 1970s corresponds to the reaction of Thermidor. While I may be taxing your knowledge (and mine!) of French history, Kosai notes that growth was decreased by:

"...(1) the limits that external dependence placed on economic growth, as attested to by the oil crisis, trade frictions, and fluctuations in the yen exchange rate; and (2) internal limits to economic growth as well, in the form of environmental problems, price increases, labor shortages, and so on. In the midst of all this, growth was no longer a simple consensual goal, and growthmanship itself was on the decline in Japan's already affluent middle-class society. When accelerating growth became impossible, the long-term expected rate of growth declined, the decelerated growth became a reality instead. The ideology of modernization that had sustained growth lost its power, its popularity displaced in the final phases of rapid growth by Japanese social theories such as the vertical society and the society of familism..." [2]

---

[1] Herman Kahn and Thomas Pepper, *The Japanese Challenge: The Success and Failure of Economic Success* (Thomas Y. Crowell, 1979), p. 152.

[2] Yutaka Kosai, *The Era of High-Speed Growth* (translated by Jacqueline Kaminski) (University of Tokyo Press, 1986), p. 200.

In the early 1970s, a number of unexpected shocks hit the Japanese economy — a number of them caused by the United States. During 1971-73, President Nixon opened relations with mainland China, without even notifying the Japanese, announced an embargo of soybean exports (for which Japan was the principal customer), put in place a short-lived import surcharge, devalued the dollar twice (after the U.S. government had steadfastly promised not to do this), and finally closed the gold window at the U.S. Treasury. The previous organizing principle of international finance under the Bretton Woods system, 1944-1971, was that the U.S. dollar "was as good a gold" at a fixed price of $35 to the troy ounce of gold — and now it suddenly was no longer valid. The Bretton Woods system, organized in 1944 with the establishment of the World Bank and the International Monetary Fund, which the Japanese had worked so hard to join and support, was now defunct. This was tantamount to finding out that your honored "elder brother" was secretly playing the horses, and in debt up to his ears, and that his promises to pay for your college education were worthless. After more than a decade of convincing the Japanese monetary authorities to hold U.S. dollars and not to convert their reserve assets to gold, the Nixon administration raised the official price of gold — first to $38.50 (a 10% devaluation of the U.S. dollar), then to $42.22, and then severed the tie to gold entirely. By the end of the decade of the 1970s, the price of gold approached $900 per ounce, and the credibility of the United States (the "elder brother" in the eyes of many Japanese) fell dramatically. This series of shocks (*shokku*) associated with the Nixon administration was further intensified by the 1973-74 oil crisis — which, in the opinion of many knowledgeable observers, could have been better "handled" by Western governments than it was.

Japan, almost completely dependent on imported energy and raw materials, was especially hard hit by the quadrupling of oil prices in the 1973-74 period. It might also be noted that various other important commodity prices rose sharply at this time, and that it was then quite trendy to write about the problems of "world hunger," "the food crisis," and "resource shortages" generally. The *Limits to Growth* volume had just been published, with a good deal of publicity in the media, and pessimistic soothsayers of all kinds were the rage of the talk shows. In this overall atmosphere, even Japan's traditional economic stability was threatened — in the first quarter of 1974, wholesale prices in Japan soared at an annual rate of about 50%, while consumer prices in 1974 rose by nearly 30% for the year as a whole. It was a period of "crazy prices," as Kosai says. Furthermore, even in Japan, "...as adverse criticism of business firms continued during the classical inflation, symptoms of social dissolution were evident." However, the determination of the Japanese authorities to bring an end to inflationary pressure eventually won out — calling into question both Keynesian and Marxian orthodoxy. An important role in this episode was played by the company labor unions, which exercised a great deal of self-restraint in their wage demands.

In addition to all these changes in external conditions facing the Japanese, the internal consensus had shifted a great deal by the early 1970s. When I first visited Japan in 1968, I was struck by the high degree of pollution and congestion — since that visit, I have read quite a few thoroughly-documented horror stories having to do with ecological issues, which have finally forced the Japanese authorities to confront the problem. In the early 1950s, strange things began happening in Minamata, a small city of the west cost of Kyushu, which was dominated by the industrial facilities of the Japan Fertilizer Company (Chisso). Birds seemed to be disoriented, falling from their perches and flying into buildings. Cats were walking with a rolling gait, as if intoxicated, and then suddenly going mad — running in circles and foaming at the mouth. The "disease of the dancing cats," as the local fishermen called it, soon spread to humans:

> "...Robust men and women who had formerly enjoyed good health suddenly found their hands trembling so violently that they could no longer strike a match. They soon had difficulty thinking clearly, and it became increasingly difficult for them to operate their boats. Numbness that began in the lips and limbs was followed by disturbances in vision, movement, and speech. As the disease progressed, control over all bodily functions diminished. The victims became bedridden, then fell into unconsciousness. Wild fits of thrashing and senseless shouting comprised a later stage, during which many victims' families, to keep the afflicted from injuring themselves or others, resorted to securing them with heavy rope." [3]

It took nearly twenty years for the mercury poisoning cause of the "Miramata disease" to be identified and for Chisso eventually to clean up its operation and to begin paying compensation — which did little good to those who had died from the disease.

As the Japanese industry developed into a mass-production giant during the high-speed growth era, consumption followed — it quickly became more economical to buy a new product than to repair and restore an old one. Before long, even goods in perfectly acceptable working order were being discarded as outmoded and old-fashioned. As Huddle and Reich point out:

> "...Frugality was also abandoned by the owners and managers of Japanese industry. When the nation entered its period of rapid growth, imported resources were available and relatively inexpensive; industrial users had little incentive to recycle materials or re-use their wastes. Industry made few moves to develop treatment facilities for factory effluents, much less to channel precious capital into research and development of recycling techniques. The aluminum industry, for example, extracted usable ore from imported bauxite, then dumped the remainder — about three-fourths of the initial volume — into the ocean, the wastes coming to be known as 'red mud.' Sludge generated by the plating industry and containing chrome, lead, copper, and zinc was also discarded, with no thought given to retrieving the metals. In their drive to produce goods at the lowest cost, Japanese industrialists, like those elsewhere, assumed air and water to be 'free commodities' to be used and contaminated at will; wastes were disposed of with maximum cost-efficiency, given the technology then available." [4]

---

[3] Norie Huddle and Michael Reich, *Island of Dreams: Environmental Crisis in Japan* (Schenkman Books, Inc. 1987), p. 107.

[4] *Ibid.*, p. 213.

In the 1970s, both the external and internal conditions favoring rapid growth in the Japanese economy had changed. During the period of "high economic growth," four rules had to be obeyed, according to Kosai and Ogino:

(1) The fixed exchange rate of 360 yen to the U.S. dollar had to be maintained;

(2) Monetary policy was dictated by changes in the balance of payments (which is, in a sense, implicit in the first rule);

(3) The central government budget should be kept as close to balance as possible; and,

(4) The tax burden should not exceed 20% of national income.

Currently, these four rules have been largely abandoned, in part due to the fact that Japan's role in the world economy has changed — it is no longer a "small country." At the same time, internal conditions have also changed considerably — as noted in the previous chapter, the government's industrial policy favoring economic growth has been modified quite significantly. Indeed, outsider views concerning the omnipotence of the planning authorities in Japan (e.g., MITI *et al*) have always been a bit simplistic. To cite Kosai and Ogino:

> "...Industrial policy is not of course confined to actual dealings with industry. It is also connected with land policies, the preservation of the environment, protection of consumers and social welfare. Thus, before industrial policies can be accepted by the public, they are inevitably subject to a great deal of criticism and amendment. An excellent example of this has been the government plan to introduce nuclear power as a substitute for oil in the nation's power stations. These plans have been greatly delayed because of public protest, and what has in fact contributed most to solving Japan's energy problems has been the economies of oil consumption by companies and ordinary households. This episode has demonstrated clearly that the image of a powerful elite of government officials guiding Japan's industries is a far cry from reality..." [5]

In aggregate terms, the era of high speed growth ended in the early 1970s, as real output growth was cut in half from its previous ten percent per year. As a result, private domestic demand in Japan declined, while government spending for infrastructure improvements, pollution control (an environmental protection agency was finally established), and social security programs expanded. During the high-growth era, tax revenues rose sufficiently quickly to permit the budget to be balanced in most years, but by the late 1970s government deficits as large as 4-6% of GNP were encountered. However, by

---

[5] Yutaka Kosai and Yoshitaro Ogino (translated by Ralph Thompson), *The Contemporary Japanese Economy* (M.E. Sharpe, Inc., 1984), p. 128. For a more up-to-date discussion, see Scott Callon, *Divided Sun: MITI and the Breakdown of Japan's High-Tech Industrial Policy, 1973–1993* (Stanford University Press, 1995).

this time, Japan had essentially "caught up with the West." As Patrick and Rosovsky say:

> "...'Catching up with the West' — the other era that has ended — is not an entirely rigorous concept, but nearly all indicators support the proposition that Japan has reached that goal. We are definitely dealing with an affluent society. Today, Japan is on a level with the United States and Western Europe: in some areas slightly behind, in others, ahead. It has better health care than most other nations but still lags behind in housing and some areas of social infrastructure (reflecting in part the extremely high value of land). Japan's educational system turns out literate and well-trained high school and college graduates with good vocational skills for a modern industrial society. In the mass consumption of consumer durables (automobiles, household appliances, and the like) and of information (newspapers, telephones, and television), Japan seems at least as advanced as every other industrial society."[6]

To recapitulate the argument of this section, economic growth in Japan slowed in the early 1970s, due to both external and internal factors. In terms of *external* influences, the following points can be mentioned:

(1)   Resource problems — various commodity prices, especially that of crude oil and its derivatives, rose sharply in the early 1970s. In part, this was due to bad luck, deliberate attempts on the part of some commodity producers to restrict supply by setting up cartel-like arrangements, and also the result of rather short-sighted policies followed by the industrial countries (possibly influenced by the climate of public opinion, associated with popular predictions of various "doomsday scenarios," such as *Limits to Growth*);

(2)   Competition from the NIC's in Asia and elsewhere, as well as other countries bidding to become more industrialized;

(3)   Growing protectionism and a general slowing of demand in Japan's traditional markets — for example, the United States began negotiating "trade frictions" with Japan and pressured Japan to adopt a policy of formal voluntary export restraints in automobiles (in part, the perception of probable protectionist responses contributed to a slowdown in Japanese export expansion in other goods as well); and

(4)   The appreciation of the yen, which had been "pegged" at 360 yen to the U.S. dollar during the years of the Bretton Woods system, produced a lessening of the international competitiveness of Japanese exports (by the end of the decade of the 1970s, the U.S. dollar bought only about 180 yen — this was followed

---

[6] Hugh Patrick and Henry Rosovsky, "The Japanese Economy in Transition," in Toshio Shishido and Ryuzo Sato (eds.), *Economic Policy and Development: New Perspectives* (Auburn House Publishing Company, 1985), p. 161.

by the significantly stronger "Reagan dollar" during the early 1980s). Today (1996), the yen/dollar rate is only slightly above 100.

Among *internal* factors contributing to the super-growth slowdown, the following can be mentioned:

(1) Various changes in the labor force structure, such as labor shortages in some areas, greater female participation rates, a more rapid aging of workers, and possibly some "bottlenecks" in the educational system;

(2) Greater sensitivity to pollution and "quality-of-life" issues, which led to a rapid rise in outward foreign investment flows for some industries (thus, "exporting pollution"); and

(3) The objective fact, just noted above, that Japan had essentially "caught up with the West" in terms of GNP per capita, and could afford to modify its emphasis on "growthmanship." (One would also imagine that the younger generation of Japanese became increasingly subject to American "spiritual pollution," with its emphasis on consumerism, rebellion, greater leisure and less discipline, and so on.)

Japanese Groupism

While the Japanese economy is primarily a capitalistic one, with individual entrepreneurs, private property rights, a good deal of competition, and organized financial markets, it is important to recognize and appreciate the "village survival mentality" that still permeates modern Japan. In sharp contrast to the individualistic ideology of the United States, Japanese society is characterized by the requirement that individual interests remain subordinate to those of social groups. The historic roots of such attitudes may be a going back to the "*gonin gumi*" (group of five) principle, which required a group of five families to be jointly responsible for the payment of their annual rice tax to the local feudal lord. There has generally also existed a sense of larger group cooperation to deal with emergencies in a resource-poor and harsh environment. As Haitani says:

"...in order to survive, individuals must stick together as a group; their survival and prosperity depend largely on their group's survival and prosperity. The group in this context may be a family, a village, a corporation, or the nation. A group, then, must establish priorities and channel resources and members' efforts into high-priority tasks, or else the whole group may fail to survive. The setting of priorities, choice of objective, and their implementation are naturally carried out in the vertical organization of the Japanese group. The authority of those higher up

must be respected by those below them, and everyone must sacrifice his or her personal interests for the sake of the group." [7]

Many Japanese factories and offices usually begin their workday with a singing of the company song, take brief coffee breaks with group calisthenics, and often go on group vacation outings. In many Japanese companies, there are at least two company-sponsored trips every year, e.g., all the workers go together for a weekend in the countryside to view cherry blossoms, or some such. At middle management or higher levels, virtually all entertainment activities are expected to be job-related, often exclusively financed by a company expense account (the use of personal credit cards ten years ago was virtually unheard of in Japan — if you saw an American Express card being used, it would be virtually certain that the workplace was paying).

As mentioned in the previous chapter, there is great emphasis on harmony, group participation and consensus in Japanese decision-making, which is said to maintain a high morale for the company as a whole. In theory, *all* employees participate in corporate policy decisions through the so-called *"ringi system"* (ringi = requesting a decision), which dates back at least to the seventeenth century Tokugawa period. The actual writing of a *ringi* is preceded by informal discussions among all the people involved — this process is called *nemawashi* (digging around the roots before transplanting). After this spade-work is completed, the *ringi* is written by a relatively low-level employee and passed upwards for approvals. Thus, if anyone on the way up has any objections, it is returned to the writer, who must overcome these or do a rewrite. Before the action outlined in the *ringi* becomes policy, it must bear the personal seals (be literally rubber-stamped by) of everyone concerned. A good summary is provided by Keitaro Hasegawa:

> *"...I have had occasion to examine numerous ringi. One was prepared by the chief of the public relations office of Sanyo, proposing that the former president...meet me for an interview. The contents of the ringi were as follows. First, my personal history was given in detail. Next came a list of people whom I had interviewed in the past and the magazines in which the interviews appeared, followed by a description of public reaction to the interviews. Then came a statement on the advantages to the company of such an interview, and finally an estimate of expenses.*
>
> *On the document were impressed the seals of a number of officers of the company. And, last, there was the president's seal. The ringi had made the rounds, opinions had been sounded out, and official approval had been obtained. The interview took place."* [8]

---

[7] Kanji Haitani, *Comparative Economic Systems: Organizational and Managerial Perspectives* (Prentice-Hall, 1986), p. 283. The Japanese term "kokutai" is an interesting one — it seems to have a nuance of "group cooperation," but also a sense of "submission to a higher authority.

[8] Keitaro Hasegawa, *Japanese-Style Management: An Insider's Analysis* (Kodansha International, Ltd., 1986), p. 29.

Another couple of very important points discussed by Hasegawa focus on the relatively small spread between the incomes of the management and the average experienced worker and, second, the personal stake that executive management has in the economic success of their firm. There is virtually no difference in starting salary for blue-collar and white-collar workers — a senior high school graduate after four years with the same company makes essentially the same salary as a newly-recruited university graduate. To be sure, the opportunities for advancement are much greater for the most successful white-collar managers. However, their pay-off generally comes only after twenty or twenty-five years with the company, when they make section chief (*bucho*) or director. Thus, Japanese managers stress long-term results much more than "quick deals" of short-term profitability. Still, Hasegawa cites a fairly recent survey, which shows that the average annual income of directors without line responsibilities in Japan was approximately $77,500 and that of other directors, $50,000. These figures are generally only *five* times as much as those for the average employee of large firms, and a good deal less than that after taxes. In other countries, the spreads tend to be much greater — in Great Britain, the chairman of the British Oil Corporation made *seventy* times the income of a bus-driver, and that is the sort of spread between union labor and CEO's in most American firms. The second point made by Hasegawa is probably much more important:

> "...*corporate managers* personally *guarantee the loans made to their companies. For instance, a newly appointed president's first duty is to affix his seal to such a personal guarantee. In the admittedly rare event of bankruptcy, he immediately forfeits all his private assets to the creditors of the company.*
>
> ...*The personal fate of the corporate manager is thus irrevocably tied to the fate of his company. Low salary or not, there is no alternative but to expend every effort to forward the development of the company. It is fair to say that the fear of bankruptcy constantly spurs Japanese top management into feverish activity to ensure the company's continued good health."* [9]

Much more could be said about Japanese industrial relations, already briefly discussed in the previous chapter. Quite a few Japanese scholars and Western Japanophiles (those of the "fawning twaddle," as Jon Woronoff calls them) talk admiringly of the "Three Sacred Treasures" of Japanese industrial relations: lifetime employment, the length-of-service reward system, and enterprise unionism. As Haruo Shimada, a professor of economics at Keio University, has pointed out, these ideas are attaining the status of "myths," which probably need exploding. The concept of lifetime employment covers only 30-40% of the Japanese labor force, the "labor aristocracy" working for the largest *keiretsu*, while the remainder of workers may be doing piece-work for pitifully low hourly or daily wages. Some of the most dirty and dangerous work may be done by the two

---

[9] *Ibid.*, pp. 4–5. See also Martin L. Weitzman, *The Share Economy: Conquering Stagflation* (Harvard University Press, 1984) for a further discussion of the importance of equity participation by management as well as workers.

groups of people treated about the same, or even worse, than blacks in the U.S. forty years ago — the Koreans (about one million, without citizenship rights) and the so-called *eta*. The latter group, also known as the *burakumin* — or village people, a more polite term (*eta* means animals, and they are sometimes privately signified by pointing four fingers downward, i.e., suggesting "walking on all fours...") — are physically indistinguishable and ethnically Japanese people, but they are considered as constituting an "unclean caste." They are the descendants of those working at special jobs regarded as unfit for the fastidious Japanese people, such as butchers, leather-tanners, or garbage collectors. Historically, these outcasts, whose descendants number two to three million people today, lived in special villages, so as not to contaminate the rest of society. While the Japanese pride themselves as being modern in every possible way, the old prejudice against the *eta* appears to be still as strong as ever. Today, many have become gangsters with special ties to the beef industry, it is said. Japanese families spend thousands of dollars on a name-checking service provided by specialized private detective agencies to make sure that a prospective bride or groom is not descended from one of "them," the animal caste.

The role of women in the labor force of Japan is worthy of a separate section, but suffice it to say that this area of labor relations is one where "groupism" and "consensus" do not apply at all. On the whole, women generally do not enjoy the benefits of the life-time employment system. They are expected to depart gracefully after four or five years of serving tea to their male colleagues before getting married, and then remain at home, in order to raise children on a full-time basis. I have taught a handful of Japanese women at Georgetown over the past thirty years, who had hoped to short-circuit the Japanese system by getting a foreign degree, but generally they have not been successful in doing so. They can make a good living by working for foreign organizations in Japan, or free-lancing, but they do not join the labor aristocracies of the keiretsu as equals, at least not yet. Over the years, I have lectured to many Japanese groups, always 100% male, and have asked how many had wives that worked outside the home — in very recent years a few hands have begun to go up, but still only about one in twenty or thirty. Aggregate statistics suggest that female participation in the labor force is a good deal higher than that, so that it may be that Japanese men are reluctant to admit to having working wives to a *gaijin* (foreigner) in front of their colleagues. As an aside, both labor force participation of women and divorce in Japan show strongly rising trends, but are still well below U.S. levels. It is interesting to point out that getting a divorce would greatly reduce your chances of advancement in your company (the prevalent attitude being: "if you can't manage your wife, what *can* you manage?"). In a normal case, the woman can rejoin the labor force after the children are grown, but generally that will be in a peripheral job of some sort, exempt from the lifetime employment system perquisites.

Even for the most privileged workers in the keiretsu groups, the concept of total employment security is a bit of a myth. The typical Japanese worker is forced to retire at a relatively early age — fifty-five used to be the standard retirement age, but now it is between 55 and 60. At the same time, life expectancy for Japanese men has risen from about 65 in 1960 to nearly 80 today, and will probably continue to go up, while the governmental pension system is inadequate. In many cases, after official retirement, both husband and wife have to go to work for smaller firms, retail outlets, or in the service industry. Wages are often very low, piece-work is pretty exploitative, and when there were reductions in force during recessions, these older workers were likely to be dismissed first. The concept of harmonious labor-management relations as the key to Japanese successes, to a considerable extent, is a myth perpetuated by foreign observers:

> "...Most foreigners visited Japan after it had entered its era of miraculous economic growth. They studied mostly successful large business corporations in the private sector. They ignored Japanese experiences in the difficult and painstaking period preceding the era of rapid economic growth, when the crucial conditions and ground for the remarkable growth were in fact prepared. By overlooking this critical period, they failed to understand the causes responsible for triggering Japan's dynamic and successful development in the subsequent period.
>
> Also, by visiting only successful large firms, they ignored a large number of unsuccessful, unstable small firms and problematic public corporations. This bias deprived foreign observers of opportunities to investigate critical elements that generated successful cases and differentiate them from unsuccessful ones. These omissions distorted foreigners' evaluation of Japanese industries by imposing an illusion that Japanese firms are successful because they all enjoy a uniquely Japanese cultural inheritance." [10]

According to Shimada, about 10 to 20% of all employees actually leave their firm every year — with considerably higher turnover rates for females and the workers of smaller firms, suggesting that the life-time employment system does not cover everyone. Roughly one-half of newly-hired people have occupational experience somewhere else, and recent graduates account for only about one-third of new recruits. The second "Sacred Treasure," the length-of-service wage system (*nenko*), turns out to be about in line with other industrial countries and not at all uniquely a Japanese institution— "...age-wage profiles are affected significantly by technological and organizational factors regardless of national differences." Third, collective bargaining at the firm level also often takes place in the United States and other industrial countries —

> "...What is unique is a system of joint consultation by which management and worker representatives, usually union officials, exchange information on various matters relating to management policies, fringe benefits, and the like.
>
> This system is formally distinguished from collective bargaining. It is the place for consultation and information sharing and not for bargaining or making collective agreements." [11]

---

[10] Haruo Shimada, "The Perceptions and the Reality of Japanese Industrial Relations," in Lester C. Thurow (ed.), *The Management Challenge: Japanese Views* (The MIT Press, 1985), pp. 46–47.

[11] *Ibid.*, pp. 47–52. See also Keitaro Hasegawa, *Japanese-Style Management*, op. cit., Chs. 4–5.

The Japanese management system, celebrated in countless books and articles, has also quite a few negative aspects. Without providing a detailed critique, it is a bit stultifying to think about lifetime employment, at least to age 55, as the *only* alternative. Even though I currently plan to remain at Georgetown until retirement (probably to the consternation of many of my colleagues and some students), the idea that I could not ever "test the market" for a better offer somewhere else would be quite frightening. In the U.S. and Western Europe, there is considerable movement of workers between firms in a single industry, between industries, and also in and out of the private sector. In recent decades, in the U.S. many specialized firms, known as "the headhunters," have been established to match up positions and management skills at higher levels, and private employment agencies have been in the business of providing information about jobs for a long time. In recent years, temporary employment agencies have also grown very rapidly — seemingly filling an important need. It seems perfectly natural to me that an economist might start on an academic career, go to work for the Fed or the Treasury, serve in the private sector for a while, and then perhaps return to teaching. On the whole, a more flexible labor market is probably a good thing — labor mobility assists our economy in adjusting to changing supply and demand conditions.

In addition to making labor mobility quite difficult, the Japanese system appears to go too far in demanding individual loyalty to the company. The prospect of limiting my social life to visiting other members of the economics department at Georgetown is pretty frightening...as is the idea of submitting any ideas about doing things differently to a *ringi* system. Although I have no plans to divorce my wife of many, many years at this time, the very idea that this would interfere with my performance on the job is simply unacceptable. The kind of institutional loyalty required by the Japanese *keiretsu* comes very close to the old Soviet system of bureaucratic control over all aspects of one's personal life, which eventually stifles individual initiative and innovation. It may well be that the Japanese management system maximizes the performance of a group, but does this not inhibit the individual excessively?

The Japanese Standard of Living

While Japan's GNP per capita on an official exchange rate basis in the mid 1990s was well above that of the United States — and it is also quite possible that Japan's total GNP will be larger than that of the U.S. at some point in the not-too-distant future — it should be pointed out that both of these accomplishments may not be as significant as they might seem. As pointed out in the previous chapter, Japan is a society with a very high savings rate, with a particularly large share of total net savings being contributed by households, and the other side of that coin means a low level of consumption. Let us recapitulate briefly some of the main reasons for the high Japanese savings rate:

- Early retirement, a high life expectancy, and a relatively underdeveloped structure of pensions, both public and private;

- Housing prices continue to be very high, while long-term mortgages are still not very common;

- While consumer credit instruments, such as credit cards, revolving charge accounts, and automobile loans, are growing rapidly, many Japanese families still prefer to pay in full at time of purchase;

- Getting engaged and married, including a fashionable "honey-moon" week overseas, is a very costly business;

- Saving for the education of children is an important motive — private pre-schools and kindergartens are surprisingly costly as are private universities; and

- Other factors, such as a well-developed and competitive banking system, the tax aspects of saving (especially in the Postal Savings System, though this has now been changed), and a culture that tends to stress prudence, frugality, and being ready for emergencies.

In connection with this last point, it is interesting to note that the savings rate actually rose during the 1973-74 episode of "crazy prices" — Japanese households reacted to the brief outbreak of inflation *not* by borrowing and anticipatory buying *but* by saving more! While, on the whole, a high national savings rate is probably a good thing, contributing to lower interest rates and a higher level of capital formation, it needs to be recognized that the average household in Japan has considerably lower consumption. Indeed, if a Martian economics professor visited Earth to observe the goings-on, it would be difficult to explain the situation. On one side of the Pacific Ocean, there are these hard-working, disciplined Japanese (and other Asian) people making cars, motorcycles, television sets, and all sorts of marvelous gadgets, which are shipped in huge ships at great expense to the other side of the ocean. Some products, mostly agricultural goods and raw materials, are shipped across the other way, but the Asians are mainly piling up bank accounts of something called "dollars." After his return, our Martian colleague was teaching his Inter-planetary Economics class about the economy of Earth. A comely Martian coed interrupted the professor's story: "Revered master, could you tell us — just what is this thing called a dollar?" The professor pulled a piece of paper from his ear —"why, dear, this is a dollar I picked up near Las Vegas — it is a piece of paper with the picture of a dead American president..." On the back, it does say: "In God We Trust..."

Ultimately, the test of the success of any economic system needs to be related to the welfare of its consumers, at least if you accept the view of economics espoused by Adam Smith. To be sure, there may be a trade-off between the short-run and long-run welfare of individuals — and the individual's welfare is probably affected somewhat by the well-being of "the group" or "the community." It may well be that the American economy is excessively concerned with short-run utility-maximization, and that "consumer sovereignty" almost always takes precedence over longer-run "group interests," while the Japanese system tends to lean the other way. On the whole, I would argue that greater balance is needed in both cases — we now turn to a somewhat impressionistic overview of the Japanese consumer, implicitly assuming that the household too will benefit eventually.

While Japan has overtaken the United States in GNP per capita (as officially measured by the World Bank), with $34,630 in 1994, compared to only $25,880 in the U.S., the average Japanese may be having some misgivings about whether her living standard is, in fact, nearing that of the U.S. Ten years ago, the hourly wage was well below the U.S., Canada, and Western Europe, while the work week was longer. The GNP per capita, using international dollar purchasing power estimates, stood at only $21,140 (and some would argue that GNP is not well related to consumption at all), some four thousand dollars below the American average.

The average "salary-man" in the greater Tokyo area lives more than an hour's commute from his place of employment. The daily crush of people must be seen to be believed — there are special ushers acting as "pushers" to maximize the number of people being hauled by each subway car. The number of hours actually spent at the office in one of the big *keiretsu* is staggering; to cite Jon Woronoff:

> *"... We all know that Japanese work very long hours, coming in before the official opening time and staying long after the closing time. That is a manifestation of 'loyalty,' if you will, but also of social pressures at work. The young employees arrive early and leave late because their boss does the same, and to do anything else, in a highly conformist society, would mean to stand out as different and perhaps also unreliable. Whereas once these long hours could be justified by work, they now often become ludicrous in a recession when employees sometimes have nothing better to do than read newspapers, chat with colleagues, drink tea or play chess. Yet, they would not dream of leaving the office on time."* [12]

Social pressure also plays a large role in maximizing the number of days worked in the year, as well as the number of hours in the day.

Most workers do not take the annual vacation time to which they are entitled, since the boss does not do so either. Sick leave is also under-utilized— because the foreman or someone else would have to take your place. It is generally recognized that increased leisure time would improve the quality of life in Japan. Virtually every government report in recent years has endorsed the idea of increased leisure, arguing also that most households have a high savings rate because they have so little time to spend what they make. According to Edward J. Lincoln, the government could do more than just promote this idea in its reports:

> *"...While use of vacation time and choices about Saturday work are a matter for companies and their employees, government policy could provide a powerful stimulus to increase leisure time. In 1987 it was doing just that by considering legislation to establish a forty-hour workweek instead of the present forty-eight*

---

[12] Jon Woronoff, *The Japan Syndrome: Symptoms, Ailments, and Remedies* (Transaction Books, 1986), p. 69.

hours. This would promote Saturday holidays by necessitating overtime pay on Saturday for anyone already working Monday through Friday. In addition, the government could counter the vacation problem by mandating more national holidays, and especially by expanding the 'golden week', the period at the end of April and beginning of May that now contains three holidays.

...The principal obstacle to implementing these changes comes from an attitude, mostly among older Japanese, that improving the quality of life is simply synonymous with encouraging laziness." [13]

In recent years, rising incomes and living standards in Japan have reduced the relative share of consumer expenditures for food very rapidly. Nevertheless, the average Japanese consumer spends roughly 50% more of his income on food, in relative terms, than his American counterpart. While official Japanese statistics (provided by the Keizai Koho Center) show the consumer prices of beef and pork in Japan to be only two to three times their U.S. level, my own impression is that ordering steak in a restaurant in Tokyo costs five times more than Washington, D.C., and ten times what it would be in the Midwest. The price of rice, in particular, is also vastly higher than in the U.S. — or, what is even more relevant, other Asian countries, which could be suppliers of rice to Japan in a free-trade world. The producer price of rice in Japan is approximately five times as high as in the United States in 1984, while the consumer price was roughly twice as high. Furthermore, the wholesale price of rice in Tokyo has at times been more than ten times as high as in Bangkok or Rangoon. In a free-market world, some clever Yankee traders (or Chinese middlemen, for that matter) would surely be able to buy rice in New Orleans or Southeast Asia, pay transportation costs, and still pocket a tidy profit. However, for various reasons, having to do with export taxes and other impediments to trade in Southeast Asia, as well as Japanese policies, this cannot take place. Of course, such policies are very silly from an economic point of view, but not from a political one — "Americans cannot imagine that the Japanese feel as strongly about rice as they do." As mentioned in the previous chapter, producer price supports are strongly backed by Japanese *consumer* groups, despite the fact that farmers are paid more than twice as much as the retail price of rice in Japan. It is also true that the percentage of household consumption expenditure for housing has more than doubled in the thirty years from 1950 to 1980, rising from 8.8 percent of consumption spending to 22.8 percent over this period. It is sometimes said that the Japanese live in "rabbit hutches" — a somewhat unkind, but rather accurate, observation. It should be pointed out, however, that many Japanese seem to prefer small, closed-in areas that require physical proximity and intimate conversation, which may be a cultural attitude incomprehensible to Americans accustomed to wide-open spaces ("give me room, lots of room, don't fence me in...," in the words of a popular American song of long ago). Housing space in Japan is expressed in terms of the number of *tatamis* per room or per dwelling — a *tatami* is a woven-straw floor mat equal to about 1.6 square meters (about 6 feet by 3 feet, enough to sleep one person). The average Japanese dwelling is less than 30 *tatamis*, or about 85 square

---

[13] Edward J. Lincoln, *Japan: Facing Economic Maturity, op. cit.*, pp. 272–273.

meters, a small living space by U.S. standards. In addition to the very high price of land in Japan, particularly in the Tokyo-Osaka megalopolis, home ownership is inhibited by the relatively underdeveloped mortgage market and the fact that mortgage interest payments are not deductible from income in computing income taxes. As Edward J. Lincoln says:

> "...The largest consumer durable, of course, is housing, and one hypothesis is that Japanese savings behavior is motivated by the large down payments required. Even if mortgages were as available in Japan as they are in the United States, the size of down payments relative to income would be larger because of the higher average cost of housing in Japan and, until recently, the lower incomes — a prudent bank extends credit only up to a certain multiple of a borrower's annual income. As a result, Japanese households must save more than American households before purchasing a house.

> ...One way to reduce such savings would be to devise policies that subsidize or lower down payment requirements. However, no such policy could be pursued without a major commitment of funds by the central government. These could be provided through tax expenditures — mortgage interest payments could be made deductible on individual income tax returns. Such a change would increase the maximum size of the mortgage a bank would be willing to provide to a household with any given level of income, thereby reducing the proportion of the total price that would have to be met through a down payment." [14]

In addition to being well-fed and suitably housed, most of us probably attach considerable importance to having a really nice "set of wheels" as well. It is somewhat ironic that the Japanese, who are bidding to become the one automobile supplier to the whole world, themselves do not seem to be able to afford to own private cars to the same extent as it the case in the United States. About ten years ago, only about 30% of all Japanese households owned automobiles — today that percentage has more than doubled, but the incidence of families having several cars is very small. The costs of owning a car in Japan are much higher than in the United States, as are the costs of operation, leading us to suggest that the utility of having an automobile (and, hence, the overall standard of living) is considerably lower. Even getting a driver's license, something that an American teenager has come to consider an inalienable right (probably guaranteed by the Constitution...), is a costly and difficult business. One is expected to take driving lessons with one of a handful of companies having a monopoly for providing them, at the cost of a thousand dollars or more. Then, there are road-user fees, annual inspections, sales taxes, and so on — making car ownership an expensive proposition. Taxes on automobiles generate about 10% of the government budget — taxes on Japanese cars are about five times the U.S. level. Actually *using* the car becomes even more unpleasant — gasoline costs about twice as much as it does in Europe and about four times its price in the United States — and parking is an unbelievable headache. Many

---

[14] Edward J. Lincoln, *Japan: Facing Economic Maturity, op. cit.*, pp. 272–273.

streets and lanes in Tokyo are so narrow that two full-sized American cars could not pass each other, even if there were no parked cars on either side (although big off-the-road vehicles from the U.S. sell well!).

Some other aspects of the lower Japanese standard of living have already been mentioned, such as the high cost of education — particularly if we include the so-called "cram schools" in which Japanese teenagers prepare for standardized university examinations during evenings and weekends. Other items of leisure and recreation appear to be much more expensive than they are in the U.S. — hotel rooms and restaurant meals have seemed to me much more expensive in Japan, even though I have always used rather modest accommodations in so-called "business hotels" in most Japanese cities (costing more than $200 per night, with bathrooms not well-suited for a 200-pound-plus *gaijin*...). The high price of land has made golf-club reservations and tennis court fees prohibitively expensive, but even nominally "free" items of leisure are often hard to attain.

Japan in the 21st Century

The alert reader will already know that I greatly admire Joseph Schumpeter, whose view of capitalistic progress was a very positive and even romantic one; furthermore, I also think that there are valuable lessons to be learned from Japanese economic history, though its blueprint may have limited applicability for other countries. Thus, I found Michele Schmiegelow's linkage of Japanese economic development and Schumpeterian economics a most interesting one. It will be recalled that Schumpeter's overall assessment concerning the survival of capitalism as a system was quite a gloomy one. As was pointed out of Chapter 5, Schumpeter forecast that capitalism would be a great economic success. He predicted that the market power of large businesses would be held in check by "The Gale of Creative Destruction," living standards of the masses would continue to improve, and poverty in market economies would essentially disappear. However, these economic accomplishments of the capitalistic system would sow the seeds of its sociopolitical demise, hastened by the hostility of the intellectuals. They would agitate for "reform" and government regulation, eventually taking over the production and pricing decisions of the entrepreneur. In a tantalizingly brief note, Schmiegelow has suggested that the recent experience of Japan may provide a way out of this dilemma:

> "...The heavy evidence of policy involvement in the Japanese economy does not imply the demise of the capitalist system, as Schumpeter might have anticipated. On the contrary, evidence suggests that it is instrumental in the continued development of a capitalist economy beyond maturity: it supports entrepreneurs ready to share, but unable to bear alone, the risks of Schumpeterian innovation.
>
> ...Schumpeter did not conceive of supply-side-oriented government policies. He acknowledged the increasing role of government in the economy. The policies he had in mind, however, were of the distributive type and therefore effective for the demise rather than the promotion of capitalist development... On the other hand, from Schumpeter's leniency with less-than-perfect competiton it is only

a relatively small step to envisaging that pragmatic supply-oriented government policy." [15]

It is beyond our scope here to pursue this fascinating argument much further. Can the United States and other capitalistic countries learn from Japan — in labor-management relations, in banking and finance, and government policies? The answer is probably in the affirmative — and such lessons may be learned more easily as Japanese overseas investments (including many branches and affiliates in the U.S.) continue to grow. The citation from Schmiegelow implies that there is greater "socialization of risk" in Japan — if a company has a really bad year, it is not only the stockholders being affected. Management at the highest levels has pledged personal assets, workers depend on bonus payments, and banks are heavily exposed — everyone has a stake in a positive outcome. In the U.S., by way of contrast, a tax loss for a "corporate shell" may be viewed as a "good thing," and the courts may be asked to decide (many years later) who was ultimately at fault in the matter. On the other hand, it is also likely that the Japanese could learn a few things from us, and are probably doing so quite quickly. I certainly wish them good luck in dealing with the generation gap and the feminist revolution that they will soon face. We now conclude this chapter by focusing on some important medium-term trends in the Japanese economy and society.

Conclusion

It is time to return briefly to the two broad questions posed earlier — what are the "lessons from Japan" to be utilized by other countries wishing to "catch up?" Second, now that the Japanese have caught up with the U.S., and have surpassed Western Europe, are there certain aspects of the Japanese system that we should be trying to copy? I am very reluctant to provide neat, pat "answers" (suitable for memorization...) to these interesting and complex questions, but we can discuss them a bit.

Concerning the first issue, a number of Asian nations, discussed a bit further in the next chapter, appear to be following the Japanese model rather closely. Both Korea and Taiwan, as former Japanese colonies, would probably be reluctant to say that is in fact the case — but the leaders of a number of other countries have suggested a "Look East" development strategy quite explicitly. What are the most essential elements? First, a sense of national unity, a common purpose and a patriotic attitude, seem to me to be very important. Japan's homogeneous society (with a few exceptions) is also duplicated in a number of other Asian countries, but by itself this sense of national togetherness does not seem to provide the only answer. As a second important factor, control over population growth needs to be mentioned — as well as improvements in education, probably a close third. In a number of developing countries in Asia, population growth continues at 2-3% per year, while Japan brought its population pressure down to only

---

[15] Michele Schmiegelow (ed.), *Japan's Response to Crisis and Change in the World Economy* (Armonk, N.Y.: M.E. Sharpe, Inc., 1986), pp. 304–305.

about one percent per year very quickly already around 1900. In part, this was due to the fact that Japan was already a relatively urban society by the turn of the century, and that industrial employment grew quite rapidly thereafter. There is a big problem in sorting out cause and effect here — as both urbanization and industrialization contributed to falling birth rates in Japan over time.

As we have been saying, Japan's educational system has played a significant role in its development. This has also been the case in a number of other countries, with Korea being a good example of a tremendous push to achieve universal literacy and reward merit. While students in Korea and a number of other countries, such as Thailand and the Philippines, have been quite active in political protests and debates, a fundamental respect for scholarship and technical accomplishments seems to persist through thick and thin. This is so in Asia, in contrast to many African and Latin American countries, where universities often provide a forum for left-wing posturing, and little else. In Japan, as also noted earlier, competent technicians and vocational school graduates are not automatically downgraded in their status in the society at large — in other words, physical labor is not viewed as being suitable only for some sort of a permanent lower-class caste (as seems to be the case among some American "yuppies" these days, not to mention Europe, Latin America, and quite a few other regions). In higher education, the rigorous system of national entrance examinations has assured the development of a screening process mainly based on merit, rather than family position and income. In sharp contrast, in some of the newly independent countries after World War II, universities were viewed as institutions designed primarily to promote equality and nationalism, with their educational mission becoming only a distant third goal.

In terms of economic policy "lessons," the Japanese model seems to emphasize the importance of conservative fiscal, monetary, and foreign exchange policies. The period of inflation following the Meiji Restoration was relatively brief, brought under control by higher consumption taxes under Prince Matsukata — Japan was able to join the international gold standard system as a full member right around the turn of the century. In more recent years, the yen was kept absolutely stable at 360 yen to the dollar over the 1949-1971 period. Despite Japan's reliance on imported raw materials, when the Bretton Woods system of pegged exchange rates ended, the yen appreciated to nearly twice its former value by the end of the decade of the 1970s. In large part, this was due to the determination of the Bank of Japan to deal expeditiously and promptly with the resource-price inflation of the early 1970s. In general, the Japanese government historically has also played an important role in creating and regulating financial institutions. These included several financial intermediaries owned by the government, such as the Postal Savings System of Japan and several development banks created even earlier, with the explicit function of mobilizing and allocating funds for economic development, as well as a system of private banks closely supervised by the Bank of Japan. During the era of severe "dollar shortage," after World War II, the monetary authorities (mainly the Ministry of Finance and MITI) carefully monitored access to foreign exchange and regulated foreign investment — policies difficult to admire for a market-oriented economist, but which have seemed quite wise in retrospect. Finally, in terms of economic policies, the Japanese approach of using international competition and "market-clearing exchange rates" to spur technological improvements and efficiency holds a significant lesson for most of today's LDC's.

Finally, what about the United States? Should we worry about the "Eastasia Edge," the "Japanese Challenge," and "Japan as Number One?" At a very simplistic level, we can note that a number of other countries have already passed the U.S. in GNP per capita during the past decade, but very few Americans have opted for permanent residence in Brunei, Kuwait, Switzerland, or the United Arab Emirates. As noted earlier, economic growth is not a horse race or a "zero-sum-game" like poker — so that Japan passing us in GNP per capita would mean their gain and our loss. Of course, it is true that a stronger yen and a weaker dollar will make us Americans feel poor when we visit Japan, will enable Japanese firms to buy U.S. real estate, stocks and other assets more cheaply, and make imported Japanese consumer goods much more expensive. In sharp contrast to the situation even five years ago, Japan has become the world's leading creditor and we have become the largest debtor, today owing much more than Brazil and Mexico combined, on a net basis.

Should the U.S. be learning from Japan, trying to copy its cultural traits and emulating its government policies? These are not easy questions to answer. Let me bring up a few points to ponder, but avoid a straightforward response. First, our private sector has been learning — for example, the automobile industry is now producing smaller, more efficient and higher quality cars. Our labor unions are more conscious of larger-term goals, and Japanese investments in the U.S. are transferring some "learning-by-doing" examples. Second, not all Japanese cultural traits are very attractive — they could probably learn from us in a number of key areas, such as individual expression and innovation, the treatment of women, minorities, and the handicapped, and policies regarding immigration. Third, the Japanese system of emphasizing community values over short-run individual gain probably contains some valuable lessons for us — the concept of "socialization of risk" is worth much more thought and discussion than we can afford here.

Very briefly, business failures in the U.S. may be accepted too readily — many managers and directors seem to take the view of "let's have the courts figure out who owes how much to whom." In the Japanese context, a bankruptcy would involve a great loss of "face" (personal prestige), for all leading executives as well as their bankers, as well as personal financial liability. In the case of a poor earnings performance, the bonus receipts of many more people would be affected. Fourth, and closely related to the last point, greater business-government cooperation rather than confrontation is to be desired, but I myself would be very wary about establishing an American DITI (a Department of International Trade and Industry) to have the federal government coordinate American trade and industrial investment in some way. With the American political system composed of two major parties, powerful interest groups, and a regional system of funds allocation, the transfer of a Japanese-style industrial policy to American soil seems to invite a large-scale disaster.

SUGGESTED READINGS

Abegglen, James C., *Sea Change: Pacific Asia as the New World Industrial Center* (Free Press, 1994).

Feldman, Robert A., *Japanese Financial Markets: Deficits, Dilemmas, and Deregulation* (The MIT Press, 1986).

Hasegawa, Keitaro, *Japanese-Style Management* (Kodansha International, Ltd., 1986).

Huddle, Norie, and Michael Reich, *Island of Dreams: Environmental Crisis in Japan* (Schenkman Books, Inc., 1987).

Ito, Takatoshi, and Anne O. Krueger (eds.), *Financial Deregulation and Integration in East Asia* (University of Chicago Press, 1996).

Johnson, Chalmers, *Japan, Who Governs? The Rise of the Developmental State* (Norton, 1995).

Krugman, Paul (eds.), *Trade with Japan: Has the Door Opened Wider?* (University of Chicago Press, 1991).

Lawrence, Robert Z., Albert Bress and Takatoshi Ito, *A Vision for the World Economy: Openness, Diversity, and Cohesion* (The Brookings Institution, 1996).

Minami, Ryoshin, *The Economic Development of Japan: A Quantitative Study*, Second Edition (St. Martin's Press, 1994).

Ohkawa, Kazushi, and Gustav Ranis (eds.), *Japan and the Developing Countries: A Comparative Analysis* (Basil Blackwell, 1985).

Ohmae, Kenichi, *The End of the Nation State: The Rise of Regional Economies* (Free Press, 1995).

Shishido, Toshio, and Ryuzo Sato (eds.), *Economic Policy and Development: New Perspectives* (Auburn House Publishing Company, 1985).

Suzuki, Yoshio, and Hiroshi Yomo (eds.), *Financial Policy: Asia and the West* (University of Tokyo Press, 1986).

Solomon, Robert, *The Transformation of the World Economy, 1980-93* (St. Martin's Press, 1994).

Thurow, Lester C., *Head to Head: The Coming Economic Battle among Japan, Europe, and America* (Morrow, 1992).

CHAPTER THIRTEEN

THE CAPITALIST-ROADERS OF ASIA

*I*n Maoist China, one of the worst possible insults was to call your enemy or rival a "capitalist-roader" — during the Cultural Revolution, for example, Deng Xiao-ping himself was branded an "unrepentant capitalist-roader" by the Red Guards. Today, this term could be used to describe those Asian countries, which have adopted a market-oriented development model of export-led growth. Most of them can be characterized as being on the capitalistic road today — they are generally emphasizing economic contacts with market-oriented systems, safeguarding private property rights, and relying mainly on market signals in resource allocation. While the public sector plays an important role in most of these countries, they have avoided comprehensive central planning. In addition to Japan, this grouping includes the five original members of the Association of Southeast Asian Nations (ASEAN — Indonesia, Malaysia, the Philippines, Singapore, and Thailand) as well as Hong Kong, South Korea, and Taiwan. Some other countries in Asia have also been experimenting with greater reliance on free-market allocation principles and greater openness, but lessons to be learned from the "Asian Eight" will be the focus of this chapter.

not laissez faire

All in all, none of these eight countries can be thought of as following or espousing *laissez-faire* capitalism of the sort idealized by Adam Smith and the "classical school," except possibly Hong Kong. The assumptions of the purely competitive model are certainly violated by the large concentrations of economic power in the hands of important business groups in most of these countries, aided and abetted by substantial governmental influence in trade, banking and finance. The size of the government sector itself also does not seem to be significantly smaller in the "Asian capitalist-roaders," although state role in taxing, regulating, and inhibiting private sector initiatives seems to be. While many Western development economists view these Asian "success stories" as being primarily examples of "export-led growth," our main theme will be that there is more to their tale than that. Indeed, it may be that rapid growth in exports was the result of other policies that were being followed by these countries, rather than the other way around, with successful exporting leading in turn to their other favorable results.

more than just export led growth

As Chalmers Johnson has said, the Japanese model (which he calls the "developmental state") is, generally speaking, "a challenge to the main political and economic doctrines that currently dominate global thinking about human social organization." It is certainly a challenge to the Leninists-socialists, who tend to argue that a capitalistic development strategy inevitably leads to class conflicts, greater inequality of wealth and income, and eventually to political instability and an overthrow of the exploitative system. It also calls into question the faith of the most extreme Anglo-American "free-enterprisers," who would usually tend to argue that "governmental intervention in the economy is inevitably inefficient and distorting." However, the emergence of a number of new cases of capitalist-type "developmental states" may make the positive linkage between authoritarianism and capitalism in a number of Asian countries a bit too obvious to ignore. Johnson focuses on Korea and Taiwan, but his arguments appear to be quite relevant to a number of other Asian countries as well:

> "... These new cases of absolutist states and capitalist economies suggest that there may indeed be a Japanese 'model' that the Koreans and Taiwanese have been refining and perfecting. In fact, the study of the new cases may reveal to us what is intrinsic and what is superficial in the older, Japanese example, particularly because the Japanese always prefer to stress the superficial in their own case, shielding the intrinsic from foreign gaze. Thus, for example, it may turn out that the real Japanese contribution lies in the method of operating the soft authoritarian side of the capitalist developmental state — the Japanese have been much more effective on this score than either the Koreans and Taiwanese — whereas Japan's 'unique' labor relations and innovative managerial techniques, staples of Western journalism on the Japanese economy, may actually be insignificant or even counterproductive because they are missing from Korea and Taiwan with no noticeable effect on economic performance." [1]

As I have also argued elsewhere, the main (and certainly not the only) lesson from the experience of these Asian countries is not the success of export-led growth, although their export performance has been remarkable. U.S. trade with the countries of the Pacific Rim surpassed our trade with Europe more than a decade back, and it is growing even more rapidly today. Table 13-1 provides some interesting comparative statistics for the past ten years or so. It is quite clear that the "Asian Eight" still have living standards well below those attained in the United States and Japan, but well above much of the rest of the so-called "Third World." Both Hong Kong and Singapore have already reached equality with most of the so-called "First World." Except for the Philippines, in many ways a special case, all of the other Asian countries in Table 13-1 (including mainland China) have experienced a higher annual rate of growth than Japan and other industrialized countries, and this trend appears to be continuing.

---

[1] Chalmers Johnson, "Political Institutions and Economic Performance: The Government-Business Relationship in Japan, South Korea, and Taiwan," in Frederic C. Deyo (ed.), *The Political Economy of the New Asian Industrialism* (Cornell University Press, 1987), pp. 137–138.

Table 13-1: Economic and Financial Indicators,
Selected East Asian Countries, 1996 Data

	GNP per capita, 1994	Growth rate, 1985-94	Exchange rate, USD		Money		Annual money growth	Inflation rate 1989	Oct. 1996
			1989	1995	1989	1995			
China	530	7.8	4.7	8.3	583	1424[2]	25%	18.3	7.5
Indonesia	880	6.0	1797	2308	20,559	28,801[1]	12%	3.7*	7.0
Philippines	950	1.7	22.4	26.2	81.3	159.9[3]	14%	14.0*	4.4
Thailand	2,410	8.6	25.7	25.1	174.7	346.4[3]	15%	5.9*	4.6
Malaysia	3,480	5.6	2.7	2.5	22.0	56.2[3]	20%	2.7*	3.5
Korea	8,260	7.8	680	775	14.3	32.5[3]	18%	8.6*	4.7
Taiwan	11,550**	9.9	26.2	26.2	2068	3151[3]	9%	3.3*	3.8
Hong Kong	21,650	5.3	7.8	7.7	95	185[3]	14%	10.1	5.1
Singapore	22,500	6.1	1.89	1.41	13.7	23.4[3]	11%	3.4	1.4
Japan	34,930	3.2	143	103	114	152[3]	6%	3.1	0.2

* 1990 growth in CPI.
** Estimate

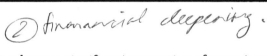
② financial deepening.

While there certainly has been a significant expansion of exports, which may or not still be an option for other developing countries, there are a number of other trends that can be noted in these Asian countries. "Financial deepening," defined as a sustained increase in real financial assets per capita, appears to have been at least equally important. Let us recap very briefly some of the discussion on the role of money and finance in the process of economic development. First of all, the use of money greatly facilitates economic growth by lowering transaction costs. Most of us, in the United States and other capitalistic countries, generally tend to take the use of money for granted. When we sell assets or labor services, we are quite happy to accept little pieces of paper with various magical symbols and pictures on them, since we know, generally speaking, that these little pieces of paper can be readily converted a little bit later into real goods or services of roughly equivalent value. The use of money greatly lowers "search and information costs," in contrast to a barter economy. In addition, money also serves as a unit of account, a standard for deferred payments, and a store of value. When we accept money for goods that we have produced or services that we render, we are implicitly giving a vote of confidence for the issuers of those little pieces of paper — that in the future we will be able to exchange this money for comparable assets or services.[2] We are usually quite willing to hold bank deposits and other financial instruments rather than hoard precious metals and other commodities, knowing that our financial assets can readily be converted into "real wealth."

In many developing countries of the "Third World," that assumption does not hold. In the very poorest countries, production is limited to the family's subsistence needs — there people live in "pre-monetization" societies, where the use of paper money and bank deposits is not yet generally accepted; people prefer to store their wealth in commodity form, e.g., cattle, sea shells, and perhaps coins or gold and silver jewelry. In other countries, many in Latin America (and in much of the former Soviet Union), a process of "de-monetization" has recently set in. For many complicated reasons, monetary standards, which worked reasonably well ten or twenty years ago (e.g., in Mexico and Belorus), have become suspect. As a result, most people are no longer willing to accept and hold little pieces of paper with magical symbols printed on them, and long-term financial instruments are even less desirable. They have lost their magic, their "moneyness," which is based on confidence and expectations. Many of these countries are reverting to barter, or experiencing "dollarization" (the U.S. dollar is emerging as the basic unit of account) — people are opting for "gold or goods," to put it bluntly. The exporting of capital from Latin America was one of the main explanations for the unusually strong "Reagan dollar" in the early 1980s. Most of these Latin American countries have also experienced what development economists call "financial repression" in the recent past, where nominal interest rates were kept at constant levels by legislation, while the rate of expected inflation rose sharply. As a result, "real" interest rates — the rate earned by bank deposits or government bonds minus the expected inflation rate — became negative, signalling holders of money and other financial assets that holding such pieces of paper was very dangerous. Indeed, perhaps governments should be required to warn their citizens, as cigarette packages do in the U.S., by printing on bonds that holding such pieces of paper is probably quite hazardous to their net worth.[3] Financial repression causes real money holdings per capita to shrink rapidly.

In sharp contrast, all of the Asian countries discussed in this chapter have experienced a significant rise in overall monetization statistics and other financial indicators in recent years. On the whole, money in these countries has not rapidly lost its purchasing power over time, and the holders of financial assets have usually been able to earn positive real returns on their domestic investments. A number of these Asian countries (e.g., Indonesia in the 1960s) have sometimes had episodes of financial repression and

---

[2] For some further discussion, see George J. Viksnins, *Financial Deepening in the ASEAN Countries* (University of Hawaii Press, 1980), Ch. 1.

[3] This is discussed at greater length in George J. Viksnins and Michael T. Skully, "Asian Financial Development: A Comparative Perspective of Eight Countries," Asian Survey, May 1987, as well as in Michael T. Skully and George J. Viksnins, *Financing East Asia's Success* (Macmillan in association with the American Enterprise Institute for Public Policy Research, 1987), Ch. 7.

periods of negative real interest rates, but the very real fear of "losing it all and quickly" has been absent — generally this has been the result of comparative economic and political stability. In large part, the credibility of Asian monetary and financial policies has been strengthened by a positive "demonstration effect" — the appreciation of the Japanese yen and a number of other Asian currency units has suggested that it is indeed possible to gain by shifting out of U.S. dollars. Table 13-1 provides information about recent exchange rate movements. Most Asian countries have been encouraged to study the Japanese example (the "look East" model, as Malaysia's Prime Minister Dr. Mahathir called it) and to seek to emulate it, while in much of Latin America, the situation has been exactly the reverse. There, this demonstration effect has been negative, leading to a certain "contagion," as Maxwell J. Fry calls it (this concept is also repeated in the World Bank project on East Asia discussed further below). Macroeconomic stability is closely linked to the credibility of policy-makers, especially that of the monetary authorities. Establishing high real interest rates, and doing away with government controls over credit allocation, is clearly not the simple answer to ending a regime of financial repression, as Chile and a number of other Latin American governments found out. As the late Carlos Diaz-Alejandro pointed out ten years ago, such policies of "goodbye, financial repression" can quickly lead, as happened in Chile, to "hello, financial crash!" — where the Chilean authorities devised yet another way to arrive at a mostly-nationalized commercial banking system. As Fry says:

> "...Political will, political stability, and consistent macroeconomic policies are all needed for policy credibility. Fixing the exchange rate without fixing the fiscal deficit is a recipe for disruptive capital flight. Chile's experience shows that even the most radical financial liberalization followed by inordinately high domestic real interest rates can not deter capital flight when the domestic currency becomes seriously overvalued.

> ...Credibility can rarely be induced over-night. One currency reform per generation may be swallowed, but hardly more. There is also the problem of contagion. If the Cruzado Plan fails, then even the soundest Austral Plan is thrown into suspicion. For some countries, macroeconomic stability may be wishful thinking." [4]

Other Factors

Increases in saving, investment, and domestic resource mobilization by utilizing the financial sector has been at least as significant in the Asian success stories as export growth. It is important to point out that only a relatively small part of total investment has been financed by foreign funds generally, and foreign official funds specifically—

---

[4] Maxwell J. Fry, *Money, Interest, and Banking in Economic Development*, Second edition, (The Johns Hopkins University Press, 1995), pp. 457–458. On capital flight, see also John T. Cuddington, *Capital Flight: Issues, Estimates, and Explanations*, Princeton Studies in International Finance, December 1986.

though the development literature is strongly influenced by articles written under World Bank, IMF, USAID, or other donor agency auspices. Having been an employee of USAID, and a consultant with the World Bank, I am aware of the implicit pressure on development economists writing about policy to magnify the role played by donors. Still, in macro terms, the role of "official development assistance" (ODA) is not all that important, even for countries especially favored by the givers of foreign aid, and private direct capital flows to many countries have also been declining, in terms of their relative overall significance.

Other factors which should be noted in analyzing the causes of successful modernization in Asia include at least two other significant developments. An entire volume could be devoted to the role played by education or "human investment" in the "success-story" cases. Korea provides a very good example. Right after World War II, the percentage of Koreans with university degrees was miniscule, and the literacy rate was very low indeed (whereas today it is highest in the region, except for Japan). More generally, much more so than Western countries,

> "...Eastasian states tend to see technology as part of a larger, integrated economic and social whole. To create and adopt technology, a nation needs scientific researchers; to apply it, a nation needs engineers. Eastasian educational policy is therefore closely coordinated with technological objectives to ensure a strong mix of specialists and lay people educated in general science. The science and especially the mathematics curricula in Eastasian high schools tend to be extremely rigorous by international standards. Japanese students sixteen and seventeen years of age regularly place at the top of their peer group on standardized international mathematics tests.
>
> Rigorous secondary school training creates a high general level of scientific knowledge among the work forces of Japan and the newly industrializing countries (NICs) of Eastasia. Eastasian educational policies at the university level vary in their emphasis on the basic sciences, but they all target engineering, a discipline vital for follower nations seeking to apply technology developed elsewhere. During the 1970s the number of accredited engineers in Japan, South Korea, and Taiwan more than doubled; by 1980, Japan was annually graduating as many engineers of all types as the United States, although its population was only half as large. China, after losing a generation of students during the Cultural Revolution, has begun breeding engineers as rapidly as it did in the 1950s, when 100 percent annual growth in engineering manpower was typical." [5]

In addition to the emphasis on education, most Asian countries have shown remarkable progress in terms of other, related socioeconomic indicators, such as life expectancy and health statistics (see Table 13-2). As is well known, for example, China's literacy and life expectancy statistics are today relatively much higher than its GNP per capita, which has

---

[5] Roy Hofheinz, Jr., and Kent E. Calder, *The Eastasia Edge* (Basic Books, Inc., 1982), pp. 149–150.

been growing quite rapidly as well. As a tentative general observation, taking better care of the so-called "Basic Human Needs" of a country's population tends to support overall economic growth — and not hinder it. In other words, BHN expenditures tend to complement economic progress and not to be a substitute or a "trade-off" for economic growth.

Table 13-2: Human Development Index and Other Indicators,
Selected Asian Countries, 1995

	HDI	Life expectancy at birth	Adult literacy	Real GNP per capita (PPP)
Japan	.937	79.5	99.0	$20,520
Hong Kong	.905	78.6	91.2	20,340
Korea	.882	71.1	97.4	9,250
Thailand	.827	69.0	93.5	5,950
Malaysia	.882	70.8	81.5	7,790
Philippines	.677	66.3	94.0	2,550
Indonesia	.637	62.7	82.5	2,950
China	.594	68.5	79.3	1,950

Source: *Human Development Report, 1995* (New York: Oxford University Press for the UNDP, 1995).

Another lesson from Asia concerns the balanced growth of industry and agriculture — in sharp contrast to other LDC's, in recent years, a more balanced and symbiotic relationship has emerged among the primary sectors and the other areas of the economy.[6]

Somewhat surprisingly, the existence of abundant natural resources (oil or gas, for example, in the concept of the "Dutch disease") may be more of a curse than a blessing. Both Hong Kong and Singapore are not very far behind Japan in their current living standards and overall modernization; yet, they are piles of rock, (to cite Lal's book), jutting out above the surrounding ocean, able to support only a little bit of vegetation, but having to import even most of the water that they use. Taiwan and South Korea are

---

[6] For further discussion, see the chapter by Hla Myint in Li, Kwoh-ting, and Tzong-shiam Yu (eds.), *Experiences and Lessons of Economic Development in Taiwan* (Aademia Sinica, 1982).This argument is also echoed by Deepak Lal, *The Poverty of 'Development Economics'* (Harvard University Press, 1985).

a bit better off in terms of land availability and natural resources, but only very slightly so. A key aspect of their post-World-War-II development, along with the case of Japan as well, is their American-assisted land reform program, based on the "land-to-the-tiller" principles and limits on farm size. Both Malaysia and Thailand are a good deal better off in terms of their resource base, but both are today also characterized by a relatively mild "urban bias," with the vast majority of the population consisting of subsistence farmers farming their own land. In Indonesia and the Philippines, where the rents from land and resource ownership have tended to be higher, there exist relatively more plantation-type operations, and there is somewhat greater landlessness. Land reform attempts have been a bit less successful — Marcos tried, but the temptation to exempt his cronies was great (as in "crony capitalism") and the land holdings of influential family groups in Indonesia have generally not been touched either. Still, in comparison to the distribution of land ownership in Latin America, and the exploitative taxation of agriculture in Africa, the efforts of all four of the latter-named countries should receive a strong passing grade (a B+ at least) in the eyes of most fair-minded observers. While most of these "Asian Eight" nations followed rather inward-looking policies of import-substitution industrialization (ISIS) in the 1950s and the early 1960s, a gradual shift toward a more open economy has taken place by now — by fits and starts, "urban bias" has lessened. Today most of these countries have relatively dynamic agricultural sectors; the "Green Revolution," associated with high-yielding rice varieties ("miracle seeds") has come to most of these Asian countries, and the standard of living in rural areas is today significantly higher than it was just twenty years ago.

The Glittering City-States

The compact city-states of Hong Kong and Singapore are a pair of show-pieces for "law-and-order" and private enterprise, which may serve as more specific models for smaller developing countries. The larger of the two, Hong Kong, has a population of nearly 6 million, many of whom arrived as penniless migrants from mainland China right after the Communist take-over, or have managed to make their way there since then. Hong Kong's GNP per capita is slightly lower than that of Singapore, and it stands to be "re-united" with China in 1997, but its vigor and free enterprise atmosphere are immensely appealing. The Bank of China has built an enormous skyscraper in Hong Kong, right across the street from the Hilton, which appears to be deliberately designed to dwarf the ornate headquarters building of the Hong Kong and Shanghai Banking Corporation ("the Pearl of the Orient"). Hong Kong's economic success in itself challenges many myths of development economics having to do with population, resources, planning and foreign aid. As Thomas Sowell has succinctly put it, some forty years ago its situation must have looked really hopeless:

> "...How would you rate the economic prospects of an Asian country which has very little land (and only eroded hillsides at that), and which is indeed the most densely populated country in the world; whose population has grown rapidly, both through natural increase and large-scale immigration; which imports all its

*oil and raw materials, and even most of its water; whose government is not en-
gaged in development planning and operates no exchange controls or restrictions
on capital exports or imports; and which is the only remaining Western colony of
any significance? You would think that this country must be doomed, unless it received large external donations."* [7]

Hong Kong

As has been suggested in the earlier discussion of China, Hong Kong is worth much
more to the mainland "alive" rather than "dead." Indeed, the Sino-British agreement
seems to promise that private property rights will be respected for a period of fifty years
in what has been termed the "one country, two systems" approach. It now seems very
likely that the germ of money-making will spread along the entire coast of China very
rapidly — most of the "red" Chinese seem every bit as interested in the maximizing of
rates of return as their compatriots ("green" Chinese?) elsewhere. After a brief sinking
spell at the time of the "1997 negotiations," the Hong Kong dollar has stabilized at HK
$7.80 to US $1, signifying fundamental confidence in the economic future of the "Happy
Kingdom" (to use Robushka's term). The peg to the U.S. dollar, by the way, has also given
Hong Kong producers a competitive edge relatively to the Japanese, the Koreans, the
Chinese on Taiwan, and in Singapore — and any suggestions that the exchange rate might
change (in either direction!) will probably result in your being treated as "a dangerous
Bolshevik" in Hong Kong. In recent years, there has developed a significant two-way flow
of investment funds between China and Hong Kong — China has invested in Hong Kong's
finance and trade sectors, while Hong Kong funds have been a leading source of
development money for China's "special economic zones," notably nearby Shenzhen SEZ.
It is interesting to note that after unification, Hong Kong's $60 billion in foreign exchange
reserves will be added to China's $90 billion, outstripping most other countries.

Singapore, with a population of only about one-third of that of Hong Kong, is also a
former British colony. While Hong Kong was the trading center for the products of
mainland South China, Singapore served as an "entrepot" for Indonesia and Malaysia,
and the rest of "Nan-yang" (the Chinese term for the "south seas"). Its GNP per capita is
slightly higher than that of Hong Kong, and it has recently celebrated its twenty-year
anniversary as an independent country. About three-quarters of its population is Chinese
(whereas Hong Kong's is 98%), with the remainder being Malay, Indian, and "other." Unity
has been carefully promoted by the "moderate and pragmatic" People's Action Party,
headed by Prime Minister Lee Kuan Yew. In 1986-87, Singapore weathered its first
recession ever, and the future seems very bright — despite spats between the government
of Singapore and international media, such as the *Far Eastern Economic Review*, and
the occasional spanking. Singapore is the home of the Asian dollar market, while Hong
Kong does a good deal of the lending of these funds. Both provide a "safe-haven" function
for the Chinese business groups all around the region, and their literacy and life
expectancy rates are about equal or better than those in other developed and industrialized countries.

Singapore

---

[7] Thomas Sowell, "Second Thoughts about the Third World," *Harper's*, Nov. 1983, pp. 40–41.

The people of Singapore are taxed and regulated somewhat more heavily than the inhabitants of Hong Kong. This has both positive and negative aspects. Singapore's government has provided superior health and education facilities, developed an excellent transport and communications infrastructure, built a good deal of subsidized public housing, and helped develop a sound and safe monetary system. Indeed, as Linda Lim has argued, the "free market" economy of Singapore is a bit of a myth.[8] On the other hand, the government of Singapore is a bit heavy-handed in its censorship of the media and treatment of dissident opinions as well as its rather detailed regulation of banking and finance. Still, both are doing just fine — and are wonderful alternatives to living in Beijing, Hanoi, Pyongyang, and Phnom-Pen.

Both South Korea and Taiwan, as former Japanese colonies, share many of Japan's sociological and political features. Indeed, their economic success and political stability may be due to a special "Eastasian edge," as argued by Hofheinz and Calder:

> *"(Most of the people of these Eastasian countries), far from being mere 'economic animals,' may be the most politically sophisticated people on earth. No people builds authority structures more elaborately, or respects them, once clearly established, with as much commitment. No people so consistently subordinates individual interests to those of the group. And no people remains as loyal to the nation or the state, even in times of deep trouble. In many respects, the miracle of Eastasian economic performance is squarely based on an even more remarkable phenomenon of political coherence."* [9]

In the case of South Korea and Taiwan, a special impetus to their growth-oriented development strategies is provided by the "other side." It is important to demonstrate to countrymen on the other side of the 38th Parallel and the Formosa Straits, respectively, that they had chosen the wrong road in adopting Marxism/Leninism/Maoism and Marxism/Leninism/Kim Il Sungism as their state religions.

On a macroeconomic level, there are many similarities between Korea (at more than 40 million people, more than twice as large as Taiwan) and Taiwan, while the per capita GNP of "green China," is about one-quarter higher than that of Korea, both countries have relatively homogeneous populations and a fairly meager resource endowment. As noted, both feel threatened by a totalitarian enemy, which may explain their unusually positive performance on economic growth and distributional equity grounds. In the case of Taiwan, the enemy has nearly succeeded in obliterating it entirely from the diplomatic map of the world — for example, in getting Taiwan kicked out from both the IMF and the World Bank. The contrast between a market economy and central planning is more pronounced, if we compare Taiwan and the mainland — with GNP per capita in the former being roughly twenty times as great, while their distribution of income statistics

---

[8] Linda Y.C. Lim, "Singapore's Success: The Myth of the Free Market Economy," *Asian Survey,* June 1983.

[9] Roy Hofheinz, Jr., and Kent E. Calder, *The Eastasia Edge, op. cit.,* p. 217.

are roughly comparable. Nevertheless, of course, it can be argued that the comparison is a bit unfair. The Chinese nationalists (the KMT) who came to Taiwan after the Communist take-over were mostly government leaders, intellectuals, and military officers — in other words, "the best and the brightest." Furthermore, they received generous amounts of American aid, including technical assistance (many of Taiwan's top technocrats have American degrees financed by U.S. aid programs), and were able to carry out a comprehensive land reform program, which weakened concentrations of local economic power in the existing polity. Thus, a comparison of mainland China and Taiwan really does not "hold culture constant." The comparison of the two Koreas might be fairer therefore.

The division of Korea after World War II left the northern part with most of the country's industrial base and energy resources as well as its most effective political leadership. Few countries in the early 1950s had more dismal prospects than South Korea — a costly war had just ended in an uneasy truce, requiring vast sums to be spent on national defense, the labor force was uneducated and the capital stock very primitive. Furthermore many of the political leaders in the South were viewed as "traitors" by the Korean nation (having collaborated with the Japanese during World War II). Quite a few governmental leaders had essentially switched their loyalty from one set of foreign occupation forces (the Japanese) to another (the Americans). The desperate economic situation during the early years of independence is aptly described by McDonald:

> "...security and social-economic demands took precedence over anything else. Food, clothing, shelter, education for children, economic opportunity, and equitable distribution of wealth were the primary wants. (The annual 'spring hunger,' when considerable numbers of Koreans ate grass and tree bark for want of grain, did not end until the mid-1960s.)"[10]

Following his seizure of political power in 1961, General Park Chung Hee placed primary emphasis on economic growth. Exports have grown from $30 million in 1960 to nearly $100 billion in 1995 — despite two serious oil shocks, a world recession in the early 1980s, and growing protectionist sentiments. Over this same period, per capita GNP has grown enormously — exceeding $8200 per year in 1994. At the same time, the distribution of income has continued to improve. Although the Gini coefficient rose somewhat in the latter half of the 1970s — still today Korea's income distribution is not very different from that of the United States. Professor McDonald cites a "comprehensive Harvard University study" in listing the following explanatory factors contributing to the "Korean miracle:"

---

[10] Donald S. McDonald, *The Koreans: Contemporary Politics and Society* (Westview Press, 1988), p. 121.

Korean miracle

- A Confucian work ethic, comparable to the "Protestant Ethic" of Western Europe and the United States;

- The positive "residue" associated with Japan's colonization of Korea, with emphasis technological and managerial skills;

- Social mobility, accelerated by the unsettled political situation after the war;

- Cultural homogeneity and an improving educational system;

- Foreign financial, technical, and military assistance.

McDonald also cites basic political stability and the shift in government policies from "inward-looking import substitution to outward-looking export orientation."[11]

The ASEAN Example

It may be argued that the "Gang of Four" countries just discussed constitute a special case without very much relevance to the rest of the Third World. Both Hong Kong and Singapore are small city-states, whose trading success has been based on an excellent infrastructure for trade, finance, and shipping built by the British. In the former case, the basic framework maintaining law and order, providing utilities and education, and carrying out appropriate macroeconomic policies was provided by the British until 1997. Taiwan and Korea have benefitted from very significant amounts of American aid in the past — and Korea continues to receive injections of foreign exchange even today from the U.S. troops stationed there. As noted above, both countries have been strongly motivated by the fact that the rest of their countrymen are governed by a totalitarian government — an ideology that teaches that capitalistic arrangements are but a historically necessary "lower" stage of development before the establishment of "advanced" socialism. Thus, the rest of the Third World may view comparisons to the above four countries as either unfair or irrelevant, possibly both.

The other four ASEAN countries, on the whole, are a good deal more representative — ranging from Indonesia, with a population rapidly approaching 190 million and a per capita GNP of only a little more than $700 per year, to about 19 million in Malaysia, with a per capita GNP of more than $3000. In between, we have the Philippines with a population of about 15 million and a per capita income marginally above that of Indonesia and Thailand with a slightly smaller population and a somewhat higher GNP per person. Except for the Philippines, where the overall growth rate averages to a small positive number for 1980-94, the other three countries have shown very significant economic progress during the past 15-20 years, with real growth in per capita income of more than three percent per year (compared to only about 1.5 percent for what the

---

[11] *Ibid.*, p. 189. The citation referring to a Harvard study is Edward S. Mason *et al, The Economic and Social Modernization of the Republic of Korea* (Council on East Asian Studies Monograph 92, Harvard University, 1980).

World Bank calls the "middle-income economies"). These four countries can be considered quite typical representatives of all developing countries — they are primarily agricultural societies, slowly overcoming the growth constraints associated with the traditional society view (discussed in Chapter 9). Let us discuss the main elements of that view, using this group of countries as case studies.

The first category of factors discussed as part of the traditional society view concerns "demographic-physiological" influences — in other words, the quantity and quality of a country's population. The World Bank reports that population growth in all middle-income countries has decreased from 2.5 percent per year in the 1965-73 period to a projected 2.1 percent for the 1980-2000 time span. Thailand, which was the above the mean for all middle-income countries, has been most successful in reducing population growth — from 2.9% in 1965-73 to a projected 1.4% per year until the end of the century. Malaysia has brought down its annual population increase from 2.6 to 2.2 percent over the same period, while the Philippines has managed a reduction from 2.9 to 1.9 percent. Indonesia's population growth actually rose from 2.1 percent to 2.3 percent from 1965-73 to the 1973-84 time span, but World Bank projects the rate of growth at only 1.4% for 1991-2000. These reductions in population growth have been achieved at the same time as infant mortality has declined sharply, and life expectancy has risen significantly. Life expectancy is probably a rather good general proxy for overall health and nutrition standards. The UNDP has recently developed a "Human Development Index," shown in Table 13-2, along with life expectancy and literacy indicators. Similar gains have been made in other socioeconomic statistics reflecting improved "basic human needs" (BHN) satisfaction in the ASEAN countries. As pointed out by Wong and Cheung:

> "...economic growth in ASEAN has been accomplished by remarkable social transformations signifying considerable social progress in the region. Demographic changes over the past two decades have lengthened life expectancy, reduced average family size, and brought down population growth. Expansion of educational opportunities has raised the average level of educational attainment and improved the life chances of the poor. The social structure has become more open, and there has been a broadening of the middle class."[12]

The second broad category of factors retarding economic progress, according to the traditional society approach, includes "political-administrative" constraints. One of the sub-themes mentioned under this heading was the quality of political leadership, with particular emphasis on the personal enrichment of developing country rulers. Obviously, Marcos of the Philippines comes quickly to mind as a possible example — the term "crony capitalism" appears to have been coined especially for him and his friends. Their personal enrichment via government intervention during the 1970s may be the main reason for the fact that the Philippines lagged so far behind its other three neighbors during the past twenty years. As S.K. Jayasuriya has put it:

[12] Aline K. Wong and Paul P.L. Cheung, in Linda G. Martin (ed.), *The ASEAN Success Story, op. cit.*, p. 34.

"...The link between the extension of state intervention in the financial markets and the growth of crony capitalism was close. The Central Bank ceased to be an independent institution in any sense, and its policies in relation to the commercial banking sector was directly influenced by the needs of crony capitalists. But the government also extended its influence directly through the state-owned banks — The Philippine National Bank, the Development Bank of the Philippines and other state financial institutions...

These financial institutions were the source of funds for the commercial empires that were being built by the cronies. Literally billions of dollars were lent to the major crony firms by these banks. Major sections of the Philippine capitalist class, which had supported Marcos as the savior of the country from communism and anarchy, now found that their very survival was at stake. In the 'New Democracy,' only the cronies could flourish."[13]

On a less grand and comprehensive scale, various military leaders in Thailand also accumulated major personal fortunes in the 1950s and the 1960s. It is probably fair to say that even today a high-level government position in any of these countries is associated with economic perquisites far exceeding the official salary. The practices of "rent-seeking" and prebandalism still exist, to a greater extent in Indonesia than in Malaysia, say, but their role in economic decision-making seems to be less significant than it was in the past. Such an assertion is very difficult to prove, since data on corruption are not regularly collected by anyone, but there are a number of reasons explaining a probable decline in rents now collected by government officials. First, there has been considerable expansion in the technocratic governmental superstructure, with emphasis on merit, foreign degrees, and so on, which has supplanted the traditional patron-client relationships in Asian bureaucracies — or, at least, modified them significantly. Only somewhat tongue-in-cheek, quite a few of the MBA's returning from the States probably still have their "Business Ethics 101" courses fresh in their minds. Second, governments in these countries carry out quite a few contracts and projects involving foreign finance. One would surmise that such projects employ fairly strict accounting standards, making large bribes and payoffs less likely — though the experience of Westinghouse in Indonesia can make one question that assumption. Third, most of these Asian countries are moving slowly toward greater democratization and openness in government. There exists considerable freedom of expression in the press domestically — then, there is also the *Far Eastern Economic Review* and the *Asian Wall Street Journal*, to name but two, poking around as well. Fourth, we can again mention a positive "demonstration effect" in Asia. Since the governments of Singapore and Malaysia appear to be relatively "clean," with these countries doing well economically, the ruling circles of the other ASEAN countries have tended to lessen their "rent-seeking" activities.

---

[13] S.K. Jayasuriya, "The Politics of Economic Policy in the Philippines during the Marcos Era," in Richard Robison, Kevin Hewison, and Richard Higgott (eds.), *Southeast Asia in the 1980s: The Politics of Economic Crisis* (Allen & Unwin, 1987), p. 106. See also Yoshihara Kimio, *The Nation and Economic Growth: The Philippines and Thailand* (Oxford University Press, 1994).

Another important aspect of this political-administrative category is their issue of national unity. While this is difficult to quantify, Korean pride and patriotism are important factors in explaining its economic success. On Taiwan, the rule of the "mainland mandarins" has become much less authoritarian over the past four decades, and contacts with the mainland have expanded enormously. It is now the "red" Chinese who are the villains, even in the eyes of the notoriously liberal Western media, when they harrass shipping in the Straits. Thailand's treatment of its "overseas Chinese," estimated at about 10% of the population, has been very positive, on the whole. Most Chinese have taken Thai names, learned the language, and intermarried quite freely. Today most of the Thai-Chinese youths regard themselves as Thais first, and probably have the same reverent respect for the royal family and the Buddhist hierarchy as the ethnic Thais themselves. In the other ASEAN countries, the Chinese have been integrated a good deal less successfully.

In the Philippines, the Chinese constitute a relatively small minority — a bit more than 100,000 in a country of about 60 million people. There, the main problems of national unity are the communist insurgency (the New People's Army, which has still not disappeared), and the Muslim separatists on Mindanao, reported to be receiving considerable support from outside sources, such as Libya. Other regional rivalries continue to fester as well — the northerners against the southerners on Luzon itself, the inhabitants of Luzon versus other islands (e.g., the Viscayas), and so on. The "Chinese problem" is more serious, however, in Indonesia and Malaysia, which have both had serious outbreaks of racial violence. In Indonesia, the abortive coup by the Communists in the late 1960s resulted in a wave of anti-Chinese violence, leading to massacres of Chinese estimated to range from "hundreds" to "hundreds of thousands," depending upon whom one believes in this.[14] In Indonesia, there are the so-called "peranakan Chinese," people of mixed ancestry and Indonesian-born, who usually do not even speak Chinese, and the "totok Chinese," who are the China-born Chinese, but both tend to remain quite separate from the Indonesians. The situation there is greatly complicated by the fact that the Dutch colonizers encouraged a separation to develop between native Indonesians and the "Vreem Oosterlingen" (foreign orientals). The Chinese had their own schools and fraternal organizations, a higher standard of living, and came close to being treated as Europeans under the law. Many Chinese had Indonesian servants, but not the other way around, and married Indonesian women — although it was unthinkable for a Chinese girl to wed an Indonesian man. It is reported that many Chinese organizations were decidedly lukewarm about the Indonesian quest for independence from the Dutch. All of these factors undoubtedly contributed to the anti-Chinese violence during the "The Year of Living Dangerously" — and continue to make the lives of successful Chinese businessmen in Indonesia quite stressful even today. The relative peace of the New Order accommodation with the Chinese was also shaken by the anti-Japanese riots of January

---

[14] For further discussion see Charles A. Coppel, *Indonesian Chinese in Crisis* (Oxford University Press, 1983), pp. 58–59. Further information is found in R. A. Brown (ed.), *Chinese Business Enterprise in Asia* (Routledge, 1995) and Ruth McVey (ed.), *Southeast Asian Capitalists* (SEAP, 1992).

1974, and a number of other incidents since then, and the attempts to assimilate the pork-eating Chinese to Islam are encountering difficulties. As Coppel has put it:

> *"...As a small ethnic minority, the Indonesian Chinese have little choice but to try to come to terms with the government of the day. So long as anti-Chinese preju-dice and conflicting interests persist, however, there is the perennial dilemma that too great an identification with the powers that be at a given time may spell disaster for the minority as a whole if those powers are overthrown."*[15]

In Malaysia, the Chinese minority is much larger, constituting about one-third of the total population. Serious racial riots broke out in Malaysia in May 1969, resulting in the government's adopting a New Economic Policy (NEP), also often called a policy of "bumiputraization." As formulated in the Second Malaysia Plan (1971-1975), this policy adopted a two-pronged approach: (1) the eradication of poverty among all Malaysians, and (2) "the restructuring of Malayan society in order to reduce and ultimately eliminate the identification of race with economic function and geographical location." Along these lines, two explicit quota goals were set for 1990 — employment on a sector-by-sector basis should "approximate more the racial composition of the population, which is 54 percent Malay, 35 percent Chinese, 10 percent Indians and 1 percent others." The second goal, to be achieved through economic growth and not through redistribu-tional measures, was that "bumiputras," meaning "sons of the soil" — i.e., indigenous Malays) "should own and manage at least 30 percent of the share capital of the corporate sector, as compared to the 2.4 percent share in 1970." While the proportion of Chinese and Indian equity ownership would be permitted to rise slightly, foreign ownership in Malaysian enterprises was scheduled to fall from a bit more than 60% to only 30%.[16]

By 1990, the equity ratios had changed to 18% in the hands of the bumiputras, 55% was in the hands of other Malaysians (mostly Chinese), while the foreign share declined to 27%. More recently, there has been a rise in foreign investment, with Taiwan a major investor. It is said that a good bit of that money is controlled by the Chinese from Malaysia. Since the end of the NEP, Malaysia has been following the goals of the New Development Policy (NDP), "to enable Malaysia to become a fully developed nation by the year 2020." This "20/20 Vision" seeks to eradicate hard-core poverty, consolidate the preferential option for the bumiputras, and rely more on private sector involvement. Nevertheless,

> *"...the two communities have not mixed and still stand apart despite their com-mon economic interest. As long as Malaysia's economy continues to grow as it has, the tension will remain just that. But it is important that the government*

---

[15] *Ibid.*, p. 176.

[16] David Lim, "The Political Economy of the New Economic Policy in Malaysia," in David Lim (ed.), *Further Readings on Malaysian Economic Development* (Oxford University Press, 1983), p. 3. See also Ahmad Idris, *Malaysia's New Economic Policy* (Pelanduk Publishers 1990) and Harold Brookfield (ed.), *Transformation with Industrialization in Peninsular Malaysia* (Oxford University Press, 1994).

continue to forge ahead strongly on this count (and be seen doing it) to keep these domestic forces at bay."[17]

Despite these serious remaining problems, especially the "Chinese issue," these four ASEAN countries have made significant progress in establishing national unity and political stability. Twenty years ago, there was a lot of discussion of the so-called "Domino Theory" — if Vietnam fell to the communists, the rest of Southeast Asia would surely follow, it was argued. At that time, Indonesia had barely escaped a communist coup attempt, in which Sukarno (the previous ruler to Suharto) appears to have been implicated. In Malaysia and the Philippines, serious communist insurgencies had been defeated — though not eliminated entirely in the latter country — the New People's Army as well as the Muslim separatists on the island of Mindanao are a continuing threat even today. In Thailand, various insurgent groups caused concern about twenty years ago — ranging from a separatist movement in the south to disaffected hill tribes in the north and pockets of communist supporters receiving Chinese support in the northeast. Today, the government controls the country quite effectively — except for the small armies of the drug lords in the far north. For various reasons, in part due to what happened in Vietnam and Kampuchea after communist victories there, the ASEAN region today is well on its way to becoming a Zone of Peace, Freedom, and Neutrality (the so-called ZOPFAN concept). While ASEAN intellectuals are often quite critical of government policies in all of their countries, and the students are always dissatisfied, there is little sentiment for an overthrow of the existing system, in order to start over with a centrally-planned economy.

A third general category of developmental constraints includes a very broad grouping of cultural-religious factors. One could talk at some length about the treatment of women,[18] for example, and the persistence of traditional psychological attitudes toward individual decision-making and risk-bearing. However, this chapter is getting a bit too long as it is, and the subject of generalizing about cultural and religious differences seems to be a rather dangerous topic. Indonesia and Malaysia are Muslim countries: Islam is a religion that teaches that the surest way to heaven is to die in battle in a holy war, fighting infidels. This seems to be a far cry from the view of 19th century Protestantism, which taught that economic success is probably a sign from the Deity that you have also been selected as one of the pre-destined for salvation. Islamic dietary restrictions also affect the full development of the food and beverage sector (e.g., bacon and booze), while the month of Ramadan and other holidays and practices (the pilgrimage to Mecca) tend to lower production and savings. As a professor at Jesuit Georgetown, I do not wish to dwell on the Catholic faith of the Philippines for very long, but there are obvious problems in that country in implementing population control measures — and a tendency to

---

[17] L.D. Howell and R.D.F. Palmer, "Malaysia: The Anxieties of Success," in Young C. Kim (ed.), *The Southeast Asian Economic Miracle* (Transaction Publishers, 1995), pp. 36–43.

[18] For further discussion of the role of women, dealing mainly with Taiwan, see Susan Greenhalgh, *Sexual Stratification: The Other Side of "Growth with Equity" in East Asia* (The Population Council, 1984).

substitute religious rituals for an individualistic, problem-solving approach. Thailand is predominantly Buddhist — a very tolerant religion, but one which certainly does not emphasize profit-maximizing behavior. Indeed, as noted earlier, the concept of salvation, after many reincarnations, is to achieve "nirvana," a state denoted by a cessation of striving and an absence of passion — hardly the attitude necessary to trade "junk bonds" or to strike the "Really Big Real Estate Deal." Religious rituals, such as entering the monkshood for several months (to spend the first half of the day begging for food) and soliciting economic success by making offerings to temples and statues, tends to lower productivity and suggest that advancement is primarily a matter of good fortune, not hard work.

As a gross generalization, many rural societies tend to regard economic failure and success as almost equally undesirable, and relegate trading and financial activities to a special group of outsiders (Jews in Eastern Europe, Indians in East Africa, and Chinese in Southeast Asia). As Parkinson has put it, in discussing Malay values, but which could be applied to most village societies in the region:

> "...Islamic Messianism may well have had a profound effect on the Malays' economic ambition and aspiration. To the persons who believe in the likelihood of the coming of a 'golden age,' into which they would be led and in which all problems would be solved, there is the tendency to sit and wait passively for change to occur rather than to become active vehicles of change. In short, there is a tendency to adopt an attitude of resignation rather than of innovation. And it must be remembered that the golden age for which the Malays yearn and which they expect is essentially an extension (albeit a perfect one) of their existing way of life. It does not seem to envisage a change in their pursuits, their customs, their religion or their ambitions, but merely the removal of all imperfections and evils. In other words, it does not seem to envisage a commercial or industrial community with all the trappings of material wealth, and any economic changes that merely promise to lead towards this end are therefore not accepted with quite the same exuberance as they might be in the West."[19]

In many traditional societies, in addition to an attitude of resignation and/or fatalism as discussed above, individual decision-making is strongly discouraged by customs and mores. Instead of the nuclear family: husband, wife, and minor children being "free to choose," decisions about economic activity are in the hands of the elders of the tribe or the village, and the whole tribe, or at least the extended family, stands to benefit from individual success. If there is a very good harvest, or high prices for your output, higher income for the individual or the family is to be shared by a large group of people rather than saved or invested by the nuclear family itself. While this principle provides a useful "safety net" or insurance function, it also tends to lessen the attractiveness of profit-maximizing activities for the individual. As another gross generalization, these traditional and

---

[19] Brian K. Parkinson, "Non-Economic Factors in the Economic Retardation of the Rural Malays," in David Lim (ed.), *Readings on Malaysian Economic Development* (Kuala Lumpur: Oxford University Press, 1975), p. 336.

religious constraints to profit-maximizing behavior are decreasing in importance in most of these countries of southeast Asia. Modern, secular values are finding their way even into rural areas; farmers have switched from traditional subsistence agriculture to profitable cash crops (e.g., maize in Thailand), and multiple cropping has spread rapidly during the past twenty years — despite its impact on the traditional annual cycle of religious observances and rituals.

The fourth area mentioned earlier includes educational and technological barriers to growth and development. As discussed above, technological progress is often synonymous with moving toward more capital-intensive technologies — in most Western countries, innovations have tended to be of the labor saving variety. This tendency to choose an "inappropriate technology" is reinforced by the practices of foreign-aid donors and foreign investors, the prestige value of using "state-of-the-art" techniques, and distorted factor-price signals. Regimes of financial repression, leading to negative real rates of interest, in particular, signal decision-makers that the use of additional capital instead of labor is the rational choice. *inappropriate technology from developed*

Educational systems in most developing countries tend to be pale carbon copies of those found in the countries of former colonial masters. For example, in many countries, the popularity of law degrees and the low status associated with vocational-technical training are both a clearcut "legacy of pre-independence days." From the point of view of education policy-makers, technical training tends to be more expensive, in part because of equipment costs and also because qualified instructors can receive considerably higher salaries in other branches of government or in the private sector. As Gunnar Myrdal said: *technical training regarded as low status*

> "...Underlying all this, and inherited from colonial times, are the traditional ideas of higher education, which serve as brakes to governmental intentions and plans for reform. It is perhaps natural that a very large number of girls should prefer the humanities and liberal arts, following the path of least resistance in choosing the least job-oriented studies, since marriage is, for them and their families, the eventual goal. But boys follow the same pattern. The low economic and social status of teachers is probably one of the chief obstacles to recruiting students for training in teaching careers at the secondary school level; in the Philippines, Thailand, and Malaya, where teachers enjoy better conditions, education is chosen as a career by larger numbers of the enrolled students."[20]

While the citation from Myrdal is from a volume written nearly thirty years ago, it is echoed by Gustav Papanek in a somewhat recent source:

> "...Colonial heritage and current political pressures in South Asia have resulted in an educational system which is in large part poorly adopted to the needs of a modern society. It primarily has trained clerks at the secondary level, and lawyers,

---

[20] Gunnar Myrdal, *Asian Drama: An Inquiry into the Poverty of Nations* (New York: Pantheon Press, 1968), p. 1781.

administrators, and liberal arts graduates at the higher level, rather than techni-cians, engineers, businessmen, and agriculturalists. In the first few decades after independence at least, many of the best students prepared for government serv-ice. A large proportion of the products of the educational system, especially in In-dia, could not find suitable employment and formed a disaffected elite that contributed to social and political tensions rather than to economic productivity.

Partly as a result of more effective market pressures, and partly as a result of a more authoritarian approach to education in others, the system in East Asia was more appropriate to the needs of the economy as a whole. In Korea, for instance, admissions to higher education were adjusted by government fiat to produce the skills that were deemed to be needed; to the extent that it was designed to assure that there were neither surpluses nor shortages in any skill or profession."[21]

In Southeast Asia, too, the educational system has tended to move closer to those of East Asian countries, placing somewhat greater emphasis on utilitarian technical training. In general, there has been considerable investment in human capital in all fields. For example, when I lived in Thailand from 1968 to 1970, there were perhaps half-a-dozen Thai economists with the Ph.D. in the entire country; today there are several hundred, many with degrees from the most prestigious Western universities. Although this is difficult to document, the choice-of-technique issue appears well handled in a number of areas. Rather than buying expensive American-built tractors, which destroy the irrigation systems of Southeast Asian rice paddies in the plowing process, most countries now manufacture inexpensive "walk-behind" tillers. In the north of Thailand, a former student of mine owns a factory that produces such machines. In fact, everything, except ball-bearings, is machined locally. As of ten years ago, each unit could be built and sold profitably for less than a thousand dollars. The policy shifts in most of these countries, which took place more than twenty years ago, from import substitution (ISIS) to export promotion have also facilitated more labor-extensive production, contributing to an expansion of employment opportunities. For most of these countries, greater openness has also meant a distinctly lower "urban bias" in government policies. As Bruce Glassburner has put it:

"...Expanded international trade is not a cure-all. To be effective, increased eco-nomic openness must be supported by appropriate economic policies on a broad front, including those that stimulate agricultural growth, avoid serious price dis-tortions, maintain reasonable price stability, expand the supply and variety of fi-nancial services, strengthen and improve the equity and revenue-generating capability of the tax system, and expand employment opportunities. Few govern-ments manage to perform superlatively in all these areas. However, steady pro-gress across this spectrum is essential, and liberal international trade policy is

---

[21] Gustav Papanek, "The New Asian Capitalism: An Economic Portrait," in Peter L. Berger and Hsin-Huang Michael Hsiao (eds.), *In Search of an East Asian Development Model* (New Brunswick, NJ: Transaction Books, 1988), p. 67.

both supportive of and supported by good domestic economic management, as the experience of the trade-oriented Asian economies has shown."[22]

The fifth and final area discussed in connection with the traditional society explanation of underdevelopment included environmental and climatic factors. Some of the most important problems faced by the people of these ASEAN countries include problems of irrigation and water control, the practices of shifting cultivation ("slash-and-burn" agriculture), and the pressure of population on land resources. The hill-tribes of northern Thailand, for example, practice slash-and-burn agriculture to grow opium and other crops. While the population of such cultivators was quite small thirty or forty years ago, the damage done to the ecosystem was also minimal. Today there is serious concern about the run-off problem in a number of major watersheds, and the government is hard at work to get villages to stay put, switch to other crops, and use different techniques.

All of these countries have benefitted greatly from the Green Revolution. Over the past twenty years, considerable progress has been made in the development of the so-called "miracle seeds," hybrid rice varieties with a shorter growing period initially developed at the International Rice Research Institute in the Philippines. Theoretically, this enables the users of these varieties (HYV's, for high-yielding varieties) to increase their total output during the year by a multiple of two or even more — and to increase employment opportunities as well, since this kind of rice must be carefully transplanted in straight rows, fertilized, and weeded. However, as Paul Harrison has pointed out:

> *"...In theory, the technology of HYVs is scale neutral, that is, it can be put to just as good effect on tiny farms as on huge ones. In practice, a farmer who wants to grow these needs extra cash for fertilizer, insecticides, small irrigation improvements and wages for the additional labor he needs to take on. He will more than recoup these costs from the extra harvest yielded; but in the meantime he needs credit to tide him over till then. The big landowners invariably get precedence for credit from official sources. They are more 'credit-worthy' because they have a bigger collateral to offer, but equally important, their economic power gives them political and social pull with local government and bank officials. At the other end of the scale, the smaller a man's land, the less likely he is to get credit. Tenants and sharecroppers, with no title to their land to offer as collateral for a loan, have serious problems getting any credit at all. They are dependent on their landlord to provide the extra inputs needed. As his part of the bargain he will often insist on increasing the rent for tenants and for sharecroppers or pushing up his share of the crop or converting it to cash. As for landless laborers the only benefits they can hope to gain are through the additional employment available. But there*

---

[22] Bruce Glassburner, "Asean's 'Other Four,' Economic Policy and Economic Performance since 1970," in Robert A. Scalapino, Seizaburo Sato, and Jusuf Wanandi (eds.), *Asian Economic Development — Present and Future* (Berkeley: Institute of East Asian Studies, 1985), p. 182. See also *The World Bank, The East Asian Miracle: Economic Growth and Public Policy* (IBRD, 1993) and Albert Fishlow *et. al.*, *Miracle or Design?* (Washington, D.C.: Overseas Development Council, 1994).

may be such a surplus of them that wages do not increase as a result. And as we shall see, the mechanization that has often accompanied the Green Revolution may wipe out as many jobs as the new seeds create, or more. Access to the advice and help of government extension workers, and even to supplies of the new seeds and fertilizer, may be just as unevenly distributed as credit. Government programs in the early phases often concentrated quite deliberately on the best-endowed areas, believing they would produce the greatest quantity of extra food, and on the richest farmers, believing they would be more adaptable to new methods, and more influential in persuading other farmers to adopt them."[23]

While it is beyond our scope to offer a definitive assessment of the Green Revolution in Asia at this point, there has been a tendency for "the rich to get richer" in most of these four countries. The HYV's require irrigation and good water control — if there is too much water, the plants will drown. Thus, the Central Plains region of Thailand, consisting of the richest provinces, could switch to multiple cropping quite readily, which was not the case in much poorer Northeast Thailand. Nevertheless, agricultural progress has been quite rapid, large agricultural estates and absentee landlords are the exception rather than the rule, and there has been some lessening of urban bias in all of these over the past twenty years.

Another aspect of the ecology nexus involves the forestry sector. In a number of countries in the region, the combination of slash and burn agriculture and logging operations have destroyed large areas of precious tropical forests. While the situation in the ASEAN countries is not as serious as in Nepal and many parts of Africa, Thailand allegedly now imports teak. Forest management plans in both Indonesia and the Philippines, on the books since the early 1960s, are reportedly not being implemented. As Malcolm Gillis *et.al.* point out:

> "*Indonesia grants logging concessions for only 20 years, which encourages wasteful logging practices because regeneration times are 70 years; charges no fees for the concessions; discourages transfers of the concessions; imposes inadequate taxes and fees that do not encourage conservation; and is ineffective in policing the regulations aimed at conservation. Thailand's policies were so wanton that its rainforest has all but disappeared, and the Philippines is on the same path.*"[24]

In passing, it is interesting to note that relatively little ecological damage is attributable to the "dread MNCs." Most logging operations in Indonesia and Malaysia, two of the world's leading exporters of wood products, are undertaken by local entrepreneurs, who often do not reseed the areas harvested. I have heard a story about an LDC government official objecting to the "needless costs" of a replanting program carried out by an American MNC, which was operating on a profit-sharing basis — on the grounds that

---

[23] Paul Harrison, *Inside the Third World* (Middlesex: Penguin Books, 1981), pp. 97–98.
[24] Malcolm Gillis *et. al.*, *Economics of Development*, Fourth Edition (W.W. Norton & Company, 1996), p. 173.

the country still had plenty of trees! This point was made quite forcefully by Hla Myint twenty years ago:

> "...In this connection, Southeast Asian experience in the timber industry is particularly interesting. During the pre-Second World War period, private foreign investment was freely admitted into the timber industries of Burma and Thailand. But the economic value of the teak forests was fully recognized, and through proper regulations and conservation it was the standard practice to extract timber on a permanent basis. In the postwar period, in spite of her laws prohibiting foreign investment to work her natural resources, the Philippines suffered a notable depletion of her timber resources. The reason for this was the lack of proper regulations and controls over the timber cutting by the Filipino entrepreneurs and also by peasants clearing the land for food production. Thus, there is no connection between free entry of foreign investment into the timber industry and the depletion of forest resources. The maintenance of the forest resources depends on proper regulations and conservation, and on the economic terms on which these resources are permitted to be exploited, whether by the foreigners or by the indigenous people. One of the social purposes of charging the 'economic rent' on the natural resources is to regulate their rate of exploitation over time. Thus where there is no owner (public or private) to charge a rent for the rights of fishing, hunting, firewood cutting, etc., these natural resources are soon depleted. They are free for everyone and they will be wastefully used. When this is understood, it will be seen that the free entry of private foreign investment to exploit the natural resources need not lead to an uneconomic depletion of these resources. If anything, private foreign investment, by bringing out the true market value of the natural resources, will emphasize the economic importance of conserving and developing the natural resources." [25]

Conclusion

The relatively successful record of the "Asian Eight" is associated with their overcoming, or at least lessening, the non-economic constraints to growth identified by the traditional society model. Since all of these countries have experienced very significant growth in export earnings, one is also tempted to question the validity of the world economy explanation of the causes of underdevelopment. However, as we have argued above, exports have not been the whole story of East Asian success — good economic management, broadly speaking, has had a lot more to do with it. In all of these countries, domestic resource mobilization has been considerably more important than foreign investment — and foreign aid. While it is beyond our scope to provide a detailed discussion of the East Asian political model, the three main themes outlined by Lucian W. Pye seem to be relevant:

---

[25] Hla Myint, *Southeast Asia's Economy: Development Policies in the 1970s* (New York: Praeger Publishers, 1972), p. 94.

*"...First, there is the strong ethical-moral basis of government in the Confucian tra-
dition that both sets limits on the pragmatic uses of power and requires that
authority act with compassion for the people. ...At one time such interventions
tended to be detrimental to economic growth, but that is no longer the case now
that government officials know more about how economies grow. In short, the
Confucian tradition had to be coupled with advances in economics as an intellectual discipline in order to produce the economic miracles of East Asia.*

*Second, and closely related, is an elitist view of the sociopolitical order... In recent
times the idea of rule by an educated elite has meant the legitimization of technocrats in government...*

*The third quality is the Confucian stress on harmony... Rulers are expected to pre-
serve order, prevent social confusion, and thus keep in check any and all who are
likely to disrupt the smooth flow of economic and social life. This valuing of harmony in Confucian political cultures places obstacles in the way of political critics, labor agitators, student rebels, and other challengers of the status quo."*[26]

Pye also warns, however, that East Asian governments may be quite vulnerable, if
economic progress in these countries falters. Willingness to defer to authority "...can
become an angry explosive force when authority has failed to provide the expected
benefits." An interesting point that seems to be raised here — authoritarian regimes need
economic success to establish their legitimacy, but other regimes apparently do not.

The "Development Economics Vice Presidency" of the World Bank was given the task
of conducting "a comparative study of economic growth and public policy in East Asia"
at the Bangkok meeting in 1991. Two years later, a large team led by my colleague John
Page produced a volume titled *The East Asian Miracle: Economic Growth and Public
Policy*, which has led to the publication of a large number of derivative works. The central
question of "market vs. state" can probably never be resolved, and will undoubtedly
continue to be debated. A brief summary of the four competing theories of "The Miracle"
is provided by a World Bank paper by Peter A. Petri, *The Lessons of East Asia: Common
Foundations of East Asian Success* (The World Bank, 1993).

The first of these, called "The Right Fundamentals," would be adopted by most
neoclassical economists, who would stress the importance of incentives and reliance on
market forces. First, these countries have fostered strong linkages to world markets and
technological progress — although policies have ranged from nearly total liberalization
to significant government management of price signals. Second, this school would
emphasize the key role played by conservative macroeconomic policies. Both budget and
trade deficits have been kept within reasonable bounds, most countries have been
cautious about foreign borrowing, and both inflation and exchange rates have been
relatively stable. As can be seen in Table 13-1, money growth in most countries has been
in the low double-digit range, usually less than 20% per year, but inflation rates have

---

[26] Lucian W. Pye, "The New Asian Capitalism: A Political Portrait," in Peter L. Berger and
Hsin-Huang Michael Hsiao, *op. cit.*, pp. 86–87.

generally turned out to be single-digit numbers. Thirdly, these nations have invested vigorously in "human capital," to develop an educated and technically competent labor force. Of course, the government played a role in this regard, but most of this human investment was privately financed and generated by market forces. Finally, relatively competitive markets were maintained (though not by antitrust laws) to facilitate the structural transformation from primary production to manufacturing and eventually to knowledge-intensive industries.

The second school, generally called the structuralists, are termed by Petri, the "Wrong Prices" group. Petri cites Alice Amsden on this score: "economic expansion depends on state intervention to create price distortions that direct economic activity toward greater investment." I rather doubt that this was done in such a deliberate way, but let me continue with the summary of the argument. The governments of East Asia created elite and autonomous bureaucracies that could design and implement sectoral policies without becoming the agents of special interests. The Confucian tradition mentioned by Pye concerning a meritocratic government service would apply in a number of cases here. These bureaucracies were able to target sectors offering the best opportunities for growth and productivity improvements. They directed resources to such sectors by distorting prices with selective trade restrictions, preferential access to credit and other important inputs, and provided governmental investments in infrastructure. The special economic zone established at Kaohsiung by the government of Taiwan is a good example. Fourthly and finally, governments avoided policy errors — they provided support and subsidies for only a limited period of time and tied such benefits to performance-oriented criteria. In other words, "infant industries" were forced to grow up quite quickly, and compete internationally. This school of thought is accepted by many political scientists, and is a slight restatement of the "developmental state" model by Chalmers Johnson discussed at the beginning of this chapter.

A third school, "Conducive Culture," is also identified by Petri. It is argued that Confucian cultures have an especially high propensity to undertake saving and educational investments. East Asian cultures emphasize group values, as opposed to "rugged individualism," giving rise to cohesive forms of political and business organization (e.g., the "keiretsu" in Japan and the "chaebols" in Korea). These cultures emphasize the role of merit in distributional decisions — it is possible to speak of the marriage of Confucian ethics and modern macroeconomics as also pointed out by Pye and others. Third, mutual obligations have been created between the government and the state, yielding relatively public-oriented policy making. Finally, economic success has led to a legitimization of authoritarian rule, leading to long-lived regimes (e.g., Indonesia, Taiwan) and stable, consistent policies. An optimist might also add that such regimes over time may gravitate slowly toward pluralism and democracy.

A fourth and final school may simply be called "contagion," though it probably exists only if one or more of the other three are present. In East Asia, geographic proximity may have encouraged the imitation of successful policies in neighboring countries — or, as noted earlier, limited at least the grossest forms of rent-seeking. Such proximity may have promoted the imitation of technology and business strategies, expedited trade and direct investment. The literature about the ASEAN as a relatively successful regional organization presents a rather mixed picture — it is quite a success story from a political point of view, but less so from an economic one. ■

SUGGESTED READINGS

Berger, Peter L., and Hsin-Huang Michael Hsiao (eds.), *In Search of an East Asian Development Model* (Transaction Books, 1988).

Bergsten, C. Fred, and Marcus Neiland (eds.), *Pacific Dynamism and the International Economic System* (Institute for International Finance, 1993).

Calder, Kent E., *Strategic Capitalism*, (Princeton University Press, 1993).

Fishlow, Albert *et al*, *Miracle or Design?* (Overseas Development Council, 1994).

Glick, Reuben, and Michael M. Hutchison (eds.), *Exchange Rate Policy and Interdependence: Perspectives from the Pacific Basin* (Cambridge University Press, 1994).

Gold, Thomas B., *State and Society in the Taiwan Miracle* (M.E. Sharpe, 1986).

Hofheinz, Roy, Jr., and Kent E. Calder, *The Eastasia Edge* (Basic Books, Inc., 1982).

Jackson, Karl D., Sukhumbhand Paribatra, and J. Soedjati Djiwandono (eds.), *ASEAN in Regional and Global Context* (Institute of East Asian Studies, 1986).

Kim, Young C. (ed.), *The Southeast Asian Miracle* (Transaction, 1995).

Kunio, Yoshihara, *The Nation and Economic Growth: The Philippines and Thailand* (Oxford University Press, 1994).

Leipziger, Danny, *Korea's Industrial Policy* (World Bank, 1993).

Martin, Linda G. (ed.), *The ASEAN Success Story: Social, Economic, and Political Dimensions* (The East-West Center, 1987).

McDonald, Donald S., *The Koreans: Contemporary Politics and Society* (Westview Press, 1988).

McVey, Ruth (ed.), *Southeast Asian Capitalists* (SEAP, 1992).

Morley, James W. (ed.), *Driven by Growth* (M.E. Sharpe, 1993).

Ohkawa, Kazushi, and Gustav Ranis (eds.), *Japan and the Developing Countries: A Comparative Analysis* (Basil Blackwell, 1985).

Palmer, Ronald D., and Thomas J. Reckford, *Building ASEAN: 20 Years of Southeast Asian Cooperation* (Praeger, in association with the Center for Strategic and International Studies, 1987).

Robison, Richard, Kevin Hewison, and Richard Higgott (eds.), *Southeast Asia in the 1980s: The Politics of Economic Crisis* (Allen & Unwin, 1987).

Scalapino, Robert, *et al* (eds.), *Asian Economic Development: Present and Future* (University of California Press, 1985).

Seagrave, Sterling, *Lords of the Rim: The Invisible Empire of the Overseas Chinese* (Putnam's, 1995).

Skully, Michael T., and George J. Viksnins, *Financing East Asia's Success*, (Macmillan in association with the American Enterprise Institute, 1987).

Somjee, A.H., and Geeta Somjee, *Development Success in Asia Pacific* (St. Martin's, 1995).

Tan, Augustine H.H., and Basant Kapur (eds.), *Pacific Growth and Financial Interdependence* (Allen and Unwin, 1986).

Toye, John, *Dilemmas of Development: Reflections on the Counter-Revolution in Development Theory and Policy* (Basil Blackwell, 1987).

Wade, Robert, *Governing the Market* (Princeton University Press, 1990).

Warr, Peter G. (ed.), *The Thai Economy in Transition* (Cambridge University Press, 1993).

World Bank, *East Asian Miracle: Economic Growth and Public Policy* (World Bank, 1993).

CHAPTER FOURTEEN

THE FUTURE OF SYSTEMS

*I*t is a challenging task to try to peer into the future of economic systems. As we observed in the first chapter, all countries use some elements of tradition, command, and the market in answering the basic questions of what to produce, how to produce it, and for whom this production is to be destined. As a very broad generalization, market-type economies have done vastly better in terms of resource allocation — GNP per capita in the U.S., Western Europe, and Japan is generally a five-digit number, while the formerly communist bloc was stuck in the lower end of a four digit range, and the "capitalist-road-ers" are doing much better than those on the other road in Asia. On the other hand, the distribution of income tended to be somewhat more equal in centrally planned econo-mies, but whether the distribution is more equitable is a point that could be debated at some length. After all, income differences in a market economy generally reflect effort by the participants, while under socialism such differences are generally due to political power. (We have also noted that the Gini coefficient for mainland China appears to be about the same as for Taiwan, suggesting that a capitalistic country need not necessarily have a more unequal distribution.) It is also true that centrally planned economies historically came out ahead in terms of full employment and price stability. However, in a changing world, fixed prices quickly become irrational prices — leading to practices such as feeding government-subsidized bread to pigs in the Soviet Union not very long ago, while the abolition of unemployment created significant problems of labor discipline under socialism.

In the Stalinist growth model, enterprise managers were judged primarily on the basis of fulfillment of output targets specified by the central planning authorities. In addition, the notions of "socialist competition" emphasized the periodic "storming of targets" — plan over-fulfillment by, say, 10% to celebrate Lenin's birthday, the 50th anniversary of the October Revolution, and the like. In addition, enterprise managers in the Soviet Union, China, Eastern Europe, and in other "people's democracies" histori-cally operated under what Hungarian economist Kornai has called a "soft budget constraint," meaning that they, the managers, did not need to worry very much about the relationship between their enterprise revenues and total costs. To be sure, various reform attempts in the Soviet Union and Eastern Europe, beginning about thirty years ago, led to some decentralization in decision-making about enterprise earnings, such as "profit" reinvestment in capital funds of the firm and/or paying bonuses, but still, enterprises were never allowed to fail. While it is reported that this situation is now changing in China, up to now, there have not been any reports of any large-scale closing of uneconomic state enterprises, in the FSU, or even Hungary or Yugoslavia, who embarked upon reform much earlier. Historically, therefore, managers in the CPE's tended to hoard inputs, including labor, to pay little attention to externalities, such as pollution, and to emphasize output growth at the expense of quality.

Furthermore, a couple of other considerations can be mentioned. First, many enterprise managers in the CPE's undoubtedly were convinced and dedicated party members, who regarded continuing employment and income equality as important social goals. Second, there is also the natural bureaucratic urge to maximize the number of workers that they, the managers, control — in other words, even if they do not or cannot maximize profits of the enterprise or their own personal income, they can maximize their power over people's lives by running a *large* and *important* enterprise, as measured by total output, revenue, or number of workers. The continued operation of large public sector enterprises (producing "negative value added" in some cases) continues to drain budgetary revenues in nearly all of the countries experiencing the transition from socialism. The managers of partly privatized enterprises may be hoping for (or fearing) a return to central planning and/or more generous governmental procurement of their output. As a result, such enterprises keep unproductive and redundant workers on the books, because there are some positive benefits to doing so, while the costs of such practices are minimal or non-existent. Economic efficiency relies on private property rights, which take a long time to establish and protect.

Two Cheers for Capitalism

In a book of essays bearing that title, Irving Kristol suggests that the system under which the OECD economies operate is deserving of two, but not three, cheers. First, market capitalism delivers the goods, so to speak, in terms of a significantly higher standard of living. We are all aware of the fact that the average monthly wage in FSU factories very recently was about $200. This generally means that a typical family has an income of a bit less than $400. For the average American family, monthly income is a bit above $2000 today. In comparison with other ages of history and other economic systems, our standard of living is a wondrous accomplishment. Even a poverty-level income, currently estimated at approximately $1000 per month for a family of four, enables a poor American family to consume at a level that would be greatly envied by more than two-thirds of the world's people. The historical dimension should also be kept in mind, for some of the comforts enjoyed by people living in the worst of our slums (clean water, electricity, telephones and TVs) also compare very well with the rigors of daily life of the pioneers in the Wild West only a hundred years ago.

The second rousing cheer earned by capitalism echoes the earlier discussion associated with Milton Friedman. This is the argument that political and economic democracy tend to be associated with each other. Socialism implies, first and foremost, government ownership of the major means of production. Generally speaking, in practice, this has meant single-party political systems. State ownership of land and capital seems to rule out any possible challenges to the legitimacy of "The Party" in principle, at least in all Marxist-Leninist states to date. As was pointed out earlier, groups wishing to criticize and dissent from government policy would need to get permission from that same government to hold meetings, hire office space, buy paper and duplicating machines, secure media time, and so on. One can imagine permission being granted to religious and cultural groups, some "single-issue" political gatherings (e.g., environmentalists), and other miscellaneous activities, but it seems unthinkable for the Communist Party in China or Cuba to countenance organized political activity by an opposition "Free Market Party" of some sort. That would be a frontal challenge to Marxist-Leninist theology — after all, a capitalistic system should be regarded as a historically inevitable stage in mankind's evolution to advanced socialism, on its way to full communism, which only awaits a further development of the consciousness of the people. Still, this situation has changed dramatically in the FSU and Eastern Europe these days. In opting for a market-oriented system, communist ideology has been completely discarded by most of the intelligentsia of these countries — interestingly, most economists tend to be familiar with Hayek and Friedman, and are learning about Schumpeter, but are not really interested in Keynes or the Lange-Taylor Model.

It is clear that democracy and the free market tend to reinforce each other. In fact, the possibility of dissent in the Western democracies has nearly become the "inevitability of a challenge to legitimacy." To put it simply, it is hard to love capitalism. When we discussed Schumpeter earlier, we spoke a bit about the hostility of the intellectuals. There are very few "dirty words" or "expletives to be deleted" left in the popular culture of America today. The "silver screen" has decided that anything goes, night-club comics have been totally free for years, and family newspapers and even economics textbooks use asterisks to spell out gross obscenities. The only really dirty words which might actually cause embarrassed snickering among college sophomores and progressive intellectuals today are: the "profit motive," the "free enterprise system," and the "free market." At a somewhat more substantive level, we might think a bit about the "cultural contradictions of capitalism," to borrow Bell's alliterative title.

Daniel Bell has suggested that contemporary society in the market-type economies or industrial democracies of the West can be thought of consisting of three different realms. The first of these is the "techno-economic order," which is concerned with the production and allocation of goods and services — in a word, the capitalistic economy. In this realm, there is a great emphasis on "functional rationality," and, in Bell's words, "the regulative mode is *economizing.*" The basic goal of most activities is to maximize utility, which is generally measured in monetary terms. Although the profit maximization story in its mathematical form (firms producing where marginal revenue equals marginal cost) is a bit of a bed-time fairy tale we dutifully repeat for generations of beginning economic students, managers do pay attention to profitability. Indeed, the "bottom line" does matter in business and the stock market — and alternative courses of action are evaluated in monetary terms. Business firms and other organizations are governed by hierarchical bureaucracies; a person's place in the scheme of decision-making is entered on an organizational chart, and his personal worth is calibrated quite precisely by his salary. As Bell says:

> "...Authority inheres in the position, not in the individual, and social exchange (in the tasks that have to be dovetailed) is a relation between roles. A person becomes an object or a 'thing,' not because the enterprise is inhumane, but because the performance of a task is subordinated to the organization's ends. Since the tasks are functional and instrumental, the management of enterprise is primarily technocratic in character."[1]

However, in sharp contrast to the hierarchy of the organization chart of the business enterprise, democratic politics emphasizes egalitarianism. While the techno-economic realm responds to the "dollar votes" of its participants as owners of productive resources and consumers, the democratic polity is ruled by the "one man, one vote" idea. To be sure, all of the voters in America (in particular) do not exercise their right to vote — but it would be hard to argue that political decisions these days are strongly influenced by considerations of rationality and efficiency. The last several Presidential campaigns have been a very good example of the laws governing our contemporary American polity. Most candidates avoided discussing issues as much as possible, emphasizing instead a favorable "image" to appeal to the voters.

In 1992, Mr. Clinton was very careful to stress "Mainstream Moderate from the Midwest" as his main signature, and won by avoiding the issues as much as possible. Bell views the past half-century of American history as a struggle between traditionalism and modernity. The traditionalists have emphasized the "Protestant Ethic" of hard work, thrift, an abstemious morality, and religion itself. The last clear-cut victory for the traditionalists was the Prohibition, though the election of Ronald Reagan and George Bush in 1988 and the Republican sweep in 1994, shows that such sentiments are still quite powerful. To continue Bell's line of argument:

> "...The forces of modernity, which took the lead against the traditionalists on these social and cultural issues, were a melange of intellectuals, professors, and welfare-and-reform-minded individuals..., joined, for political reasons, by labor leaders and ethnic politicians, who represented urban forces. The dominant philosophy was liberalism, which included a critique of the inequalities and social costs generated by capitalism. The fact that the corporate economy had no unified value system of its own, or still mouthed a flaccid version of Protestant virtues, meant that liberalism could go ideologically unchallenged."[2]

Did Clinton's second victory mean retrenchment for the traditionalists? Probably. Why only two cheers for capitalism? While capitalism has created economic abundance

---

[1] Daniel Bell, *The Cultural Contradictions of Capitalism* (Basic Books, 1976), p. 11.
[2] *Ibid.*, pp. 78–79.

and contributed to the preservation of political freedoms, it has no ideology as such. There is no overriding organizing principle — capitalism claims its superiority only pragmatically and not theologically. A hundred years ago, most intellectuals probably accepted the Protestant Ethic and "laissez faire" economics as providing a moral philosophical framework. In a sense, the legitimacy of the free market economy was rooted in the feudal past, a point well recognized by Schumpeter, who spoke about certain "habits of super- and subordination," but also the eventual "destruction of the protective strata." Today, these ideological justifications and institutional constraints have been challenged and loosened by the forces of liberalism and modernity, so much so that these ideas have become quite dated — a point recognized by Schumpeter as well as Fred Hirsch in his *Social Limits to Growth*. A good summary of this are provided by Krishan Kumar:

> "*...Capitalism, by itself, is essentially amoral and anomic. Individual outcomes are the result simply of the 'free play' of the market. But no social system can work without a morality. Capitalism lives on borrowed time off a borrowed morality. For a long time capitalism has lived off 'the accumulated capital of traditional religion and traditional moral philosophy...', elements which are extraneous to the market. Even the secular philosophies of liberalism and utilitarianism were able to offer a sustaining set of values to capitalism only because...they were buttressed by the shadowy frame of a Christian ideological inheritance...Their own logic and that of the capitalist system they served gradually undermined that inheritance, finally yielding a reductive and mechanical egoism which was as potentially threatening to liberal values of tolerance and democracy as it had once seemed benevolent to them. In a sense therefore we might say that the Protestant ethic was not simply the origin but the persisting condition of capitalism. It restrained the wants and appetites which, in the pure utilitarian felicific calculus, are unlimited and insatiable.*"[3]

Thus, according to this argument, we are left maddeningly, frighteningly *free* to choose our own purpose in life. As I've told my children and my students: "The meaning of life is to search for meaning, but not too hard, and not all of the time." Indeed, some will choose the approach of pure hedonism — I think that there is a bumper sticker which reads, rather simply, "he who dies with the most toys, wins." Others will search for the meaning of life by maximizing the value of the estate that they leave behind, the number of citations in journal articles, or perhaps the number of children and grandchildren. Still others will function productively as the members of some larger community, be it a religious congregation, an ethnic group, a political organization, or a "counter-culture commune." In a number of Asian countries discussed in the previous

---

[3] Krishan Kumar, "Pre-capitalist and Non-capitalist Factors in the Development of Capitalism: Fred Hirsch and Joseph Schumpeter," in Adrian Ellis and Krishan Kumar (eds.), *Dilemmas of Liberal Democracies* (Tavistock Publications, 1983), p. 156. That volume is devoted to a discussion of the ideas in Fred Hirsch, *Social Limits to Growth*, (Routledge and Kegan Paul, 1977).

chapter, as well as in Japan, that larger community is the entire nation, the country as a whole, perhaps as embodied in the firm where one works. While most American probably do not regard their "9-to-5" activities with such patriotic zeal, most people are reasonably proud of their place of employment, and derive considerable satisfaction from doing their job well. Still, most of us treasure our independence as consumers somewhat more than our contributions as producers, in the final analysis. Thus, it is certainly true that capitalism does not deserve a third cheer — profit-maximizing behavior seemingly has lost its "heroic purpose," if it ever really had it. Its ideals are varied and flexible, which is simultaneously both a strength and a weakness.

Professor Kristol notes that capitalism did lay a strong claim to being a just and virtuous social order for about the first century of its existence. Indeed, along with the ideas embodied in the Protestant Ethic, the elaboration of economic theory by the classical school provided the theology for capitalism. The economic system was then viewed as a self-equilibrating mechanism, and most critics of the burgeois society that was beginning to emerge could be dismissed as people who "did not understand modern economics." Since most countries were much poorer in those days as well, politicians and reformers simply could not afford to tinker with economic rationality very much. Today, the situation has changed a great deal. As Kristol points out:

> "...an amiable philistinism was inherent in bourgeois society, and this was bound to place its artists and intellectuals in an antagonistic position toward it. The antagonism was irrespressible — the bourgeois world could not suppress it without violating its own liberal creed; the artists could not refrain from expressing their hostility without denying their authentic selves. But the conflict could, and was, contained so long as capitalist civilization delivered on its three basic promises. It was only when the third promise, of a virtuous life and a just society, was subverted by the dynamics of capitalism itself, as it strove to fulfill the other two — affluence and liberty — that the bourgeois order came, in the minds of the young especially, to possess a questionable legitimacy."[4]

Most of us do not understand fully the pluralistic nature of democratic capitalism, and pressure groups are forming continually to exploit that. Most such groups readily grasp the pre-eminence of politics over economics, especially those on the left. As pointed out by Michael Novak:

> "...There are many on the democratic left in the United States who interpret their own experience, judge the system in which they live, and try to direct its development, according to the ideals of socialism. Democratic capitalism, which is exceedingly flexible and experimental, has learned much from their efforts. Yet in the end, it is surely better for them and for the American system to be clear about each other. Insofar as socialism is a unitary system, dominated in all its parts by a state apparatus, socialism is not an improvement upon democratic capitalism but a relapse into the tyrannical unities from which the latter has emerged. A

---

[4] Irving Kristol, *Two Cheers for Capitalism* (Basic Books, Inc., 1978), p. 258.

unitary, dominant, central state authority has been tried before. The enforcement of high moral ideals by coercion of law has been tried before."

As Schumpeter clearly foresaw, in the long run, the greatest danger to the continued functioning of democratic capitalism lies in inflation. The monetary system, along with financial markets and institutions, epitomizes private property and links the present to the future. This has been expressed, most reverently and beautifully, by George Gilder in his *The Spirit of Enterprise.* To paraphrase his argument, people produce things, work hard, and innovate in order to earn money. Money is the promise of a positive future, the symbol of a stable and a secure politico-economic system, and a store of value. The entrepreneur has to believe that his money will be convertible into an equivalent value of goods and services, or into other currencies, at about its present purchasing power. As Gilder puts it:

> *"...Entrepreneurs seek money chiefly for positive reasons: to perform their central role in economic growth. Just as a sociologist needs free time and access to libraries and research aides, and a scientist needs a laboratory and assistants, and a doctor needs power to prescribe medicine and perform surgery — just as intellectuals need freedom to write and publish — capitalists need economic freedom and access to capital and financing enterprise. Entrepreneurs must be allowed to retain the wealth they create because only they, collectively, can possibly know how to invest it productively among the millions of existing businesses and the innumerable visions of new enterprise in the world economy.*
>
> *...Entrepreneurs provide a continuing challenge both to men who refuse a practical engagement in the world, on the grounds that it is too dangerous or corrupt, and to men who demand power over others in the name of ideology or expertise without first giving or risking their wealth. Capitalism offers nothing but frustrations and rebuffs to those who wish — because of claimed superiority of intelligence, birth, credentials, or ideals — to get without giving, to take without risking, to profit without sacrifice, to be exalted without humbling themselves to understand others and meet their needs."* [6]

As I have said elsewhere, currency standards based on paper may be incompatible with pressure-group politics in the long run. If I had started writing this chapter about fifteen years ago, I would probably have predicted a continuation of the trends of the 1970s, with a rapidly expanding public sector and a growing money supply leading to ever-greater inflationary pressure in the U.S. and most of Western Europe. The final result of a couple of years of inflation in the twenty-percent-plus range for the industrial democracies would have been a system of comprehensive wage and price controls, with which the United States toyed briefly, even under Nixon surprisingly. The failure of

---

[5] Michael Novak, *The Spirit of Democratic Capitalism* (Simon & Schuster, for the American Enterprise Institute, 1982), p. 334.

[6] George Gilder, *The Spirit of Enterprise* (Simon and Schuster, 1984), pp. 254–55.

government "guide-posts" was easy to predict, but one would have expected them to be replaced by a much tougher mandatory regime — eventually leading to a total transformation of competitive, capitalistic free markets and eventually a system of government-directed allocation. This would probably first take the form of interest ceilings and government guidance in credit allocation in banks and other financial institutions, but the stock and bond markets would provide such a gigantic "loophole" against such efforts that they would just have to be closed. Initially, there would probably be a ban on new issues, but the chances of "obscene" and "windall" stock market profits in the early stages of such a hyper-inflation would no doubt lead to demands to suspend trading at first ("trading suspended on Big Board") — and to ban it altogether a bit later. Outright nationalization of industries, and especially agriculture, would probably not be countenanced in the United States, but the incomes of shareholders and farmers would certainly have to be regulated by the government.

Now I'm not so sure about this pessimistic scenario. The industrial democracies started down this road, but they have pulled back. To be sure, the current economic situation in the market-type economies is not really wonderful either, except in comparison with much of the rest of the world. In the European Economic Community, there is a lot of concern about the environmental problems of further industrial expansion (e.g., "acid rain" and "Waldstarben," literally "forest death," especially in Germany) and technological unemployment. Considerable discussion has also taken place about the causes of a significant slowdown in economic growth in Western Europe, coupled with significant rises in unemployment, sometimes called "Eurosclerosis." The author of the term, German economist Herbert Giersch, argues:

> "...that the welfare state inhibits economic adjustment in a variety of ways. Generous unemployment compensation removes the incentive for discharged workers to seek new employment and removes pressure on still employed workers to moderate their demands. Restrictions on hiring and firing prevent adjustment and...reduce employment. Industrial change is blocked by protection and industrial policy. Heavy charges for social insurance raise employment costs relative to take-home pay. Legal restrictions on wage competition reinforce the market power forces from working and thus lead to the European problems of low employment and slow growth." [7]

Moreover, over time, high unemployment rates have tended to raise the so-called NAIRU rate (the "non-accelerating inflation rate of unemployment"). One possible explanation is that governments have become particularly fearful of inflation, and are reluctant to stimulate aggregate demand. The other version of this phenomenon, often termed "hysteresis," argue that high actual unemployment raises the NAIRU rate

---

[7] Further discussion of these issues can be found in Paul R. Krugman, "Slow Growth in Europe: Conceptual Issues," in Robert Z. Lawrence and Charles L. Schultze (eds.), *Barriers to European Growth: A Transatlantic View* (The Brookings Institution, 1987), especially pp. 69–71.

either by discouraging capital formation during recessions or, perhaps even more importantly, by "writing off" workers with substantial periods of unemployment on their records.

While it is beyond our scope here to discuss in further detail the future prospects of Western Europe, which should probably become more favorable after greater economic integration in this decade, it is important to note the inflation rate in the industrial market economies as a group was brought down from an average annual rate of 9.5 percent in the 1970-80 period to a significantly smaller 4.3 percent in the 1980-93 span. This is in sharp contrast to the experience of much of the rest of the world, where inflation accelerated significantly during the 1980-93 period — rising from 22 percent in 1970-80 to a whopping composite average of 90.1 percent for the so-called "middle-income economies" (using the World Bank's classification scheme) in 1980-93. This recent "disinflation" purge has certainly been a central feature of the Reagan and Thatcher administrations in the U.S. and Great Britain — and the Republican takeover of Congress in 1994 promises a future with somewhat less government. Coupled with Germany and Japan, which have traditionally been very wary about inflationary pressures, along with a few other such countries (Switzerland and Taiwan come to mind), this group of nations has certainly provided a positive "demonstration effect." The essence of this demonstration effect has been that it is possible to "just say no" to inflation and an ever-growing role of the government, even if it took a double-digit unemployment rate and inordinately high interest rates to do so the last time around. Thus, the pessimistic scenario outlined by Hayek, Schumpeter, and some others, appears to have been avoided for a while longer — the "Serfdom" of higher taxes, inflation, and eventually comprehensive controls no longer seems as inevitable.

For the longer term, however, the search for better institutional arrangements must continue. For the vast majority of Americans, the existing system works exceedingly well in providing both material abundance and personal freedom. The "American Dream" was fulfilled for millions of refugees from Eastern Europe, such as myself, who arrived here shortly after World War II. It was dreamed successfully by most of the Cubans, who fled Castro's "workers' paradise" a bit later, and it is being dreamed today by many of Indo-China's boat-people still making their way to these shores. But, we are not doing a very good job these days of recognizing these facts — as Herb Stein has pointed out:

> "...Some of the weakness of the U.S. model as an attraction for others is undoubt-
> edly due to our own attitudes. We have lost much of the confidence and pride in
> our system that we had thirty years ago, and consequently we project a much
> less clear image of a society that is to be admired and emulated by others. Per-
> haps because the blessings and achievements of our own society have been taken
> for granted, discussion has focused on the deficiencies. An outside observer of
> American talk and writing about ourselves would conclude that we are an op-
> pressed society, but he would not be sure whether the white males of the corpo-
> rate establishment are oppressing the black, female, and poor, or the bureaucrats
> of government are oppressing the industrious yeomen and workers. He would con-
> clude that we produce an overwhelming amount of valueless material but also

that our productivity is withering. He would find that we are polluting the earth's atmosphere and consuming its resources, and giving nothing back in return. He would see that we are either the aggressive, militaristic arm of multinational corporations, or a helpless, pitiful giant, terrorized by a handful of Iranian students. He would find us ditheringly incapable of managing inflation, the dollar, and the balance of payment." [8]

In that same book, Herb Stein coins a "bon mot" well worth repeating — for a progressive intellectual to forecast the demise of capitalism is quite similar to Typhoid Mary saying that there might be an epidemic. While in recent years it has almost become fashionable to be a bit conservative in the U.S. and Great Britain, recently I overheard a young woman saying to her companion: "You're going to vote Republican?" in tones reserved for the most unspeakable of all imaginable actions. In the media and the groves of academia, to be liberal is chic, it is with it, it is "cool" or "rad" (as a radical, you dig?) — and those defending patriotism or the free market economy are viewed either as sentimental old fools or red-neck Know-Nothings. Still, there is some hope — some of my best students in recent years have been questioning the "knee-jerk" reactions of their peers, and the political system has rejected collectivistic solutions in most industrial democracies to date.

A possible major modification of the market economy is to move toward the "share economy," as discussed by Martin L. Weitzman. While its details are beyond our scope here, the basic thrust seems quite appealing. Quite possibly one of the strongest explanations for the phenomenon of so-called "Eurosclerosis" is the existence of strong and militant labor unions, who view themselves as defending the workers' share of a constant, perhaps even a shrinking, pie of total output. In comparison to the United States, European workers generally rely more on government pensions rather than on private retirement plans, and do not see themselves as being "better off" as their firm grows and prospers. Further, in a comparison with Japan, few assembly-line workers in Europe participate in the profits made by their company. In Japan, however, even blue-collar employees receive a significant fraction of their pay in the form of a twice-yearly profit-sharing bonus. The bonuses can be quite large, sometimes worth up to five months or more of salary in a good year for the company. On average, over a fourth of a Japanese industrial worker's total renumeration consists of bonus payments. Bonus income is a significant component of national income. Japanese corporations pay out more in bonuses than they end up making in after-bonuses profits. [9]

In the United States, as well, according to Weitzman, there are "profit-sharing" plans and "employee stock ownership plans" (ESOPs), which cover about 15 percent of all firms, but these are mostly tied up with retirement options rather than immediate cash

---

[8] Herbert Stein, *Washington Bedtime Stories: The Politics of Money and Jobs* (The Free Press, 1986), pp. 284–285.

[9] Martin L. Weitzman, *The Share Economy: Conquering Stagflation* (Harvard University Press, 1984), pp. 74-75.

disbursement. Giving American workers a greater stake in their company's year-to-year performance is probably one important institutional change to be investigated — shared rather than fixed wage payments would probably have positive results on inflation, employment, and productivity. ■

SUGGESTED READINGS

Bell, Daniel, *The Cultural Contradictions of Capitalism* (Basic Books, Inc., 1976).

Berger, Peter L. (ed.), *Capitalism and Equality in America* (Hamilton Press, Institute for Educational Affairs, 1987).

Berger, Peter, and Richard J. Neuhaus, *To Empower People*, 1996 Edition by Michael Novak (ed.), (The American Enterprise Institute Press, 1996).

Berger, Peter L. (ed.), *Capitalism and Equality in the Third World* (Hamilton Press, Institute for Educational Affairs, 1987).

Ellis, Agrian, and Krishan Kumar (eds.), *Dilemmas of Liberal Democracies* (Tavistock Publications, 1983).

Gilder, George, *Recapturing the Spirit of Enterprise* (ICS Press, 1992).

Halburn, Suzanne W., and David F. Bramhall (eds.), *Marx, Schumpeter, and Keynes: A Centenary Celebration of Dissent* (M.E. Sharpe, Inc., 1986).

Hibbs, Douglas A., Jr., *The American Political Economy: Macroeconomics and Electoral Politics* (Harvard University Press, 1987).

Hibbs, Douglas A., Jr., *The Political Economy of Industrial Democracies* (Harvard University Press, 1987).

Hirsch, Fred, *Social Limits to Growth* (Routledge and Kegan Paul, 1977).

Jay, Peter, *The Crisis for Western Political Economy and Other Essays* (Barnes & Noble Books, 1984).

Kristol, Irving, *Two Cheers for Capitalism* (Basic Books, Inc., 1978).

Krugman, Paul, *The Age of Diminished Expectations* (The MIT Press, 1994).

Kumar, Krishan, *From Post-Industrial to Post-Modern Society* (Blackwell, 1995).

Novak, Michael, *The Spirit of Democratic Capitalism* (Simon & Schuster, for the American Enterprise Institute, 1982).